FAMILIES IN JEOPARDY

~ *Regulating the Social Body in France, 1750–1910*

FAMILIES IN JEOPARDY

~~~

*Regulating the Social Body
in France, 1750–1910*

RODDEY REID

STANFORD UNIVERSITY PRESS
STANFORD, CALIFORNIA 1993

Stanford University Press, Stanford, California
© 1993 by the Board of Trustees of the
Leland Stanford Junior University
Printed in the United States of America
CIP data appear at the end of the book

For L. B.

Acknowledgments

THIS BOOK HAS benefited from research and travel grants awarded by several institutions. The president and fellows of Middlebury College and the Academic Senate of the University of California, San Diego, extended generous funding for excursions to major libraries in the United States and France; their support is hereby gratefully acknowledged. I also want to thank the Camargo Foundation, and its director, Michael Pretina, for providing an environment early on that allowed this book to take its present form. Conducting a genealogy of familial discourse in France has required much time in libraries with important historical collections; this book owes much to the expert help provided by the staffs of the Bibliothèque Nationale, Paris; the Yale Medical School Library; the Sterling Memorial Library of Yale University; and the Library of the School of Medicine, University of California, San Francisco.

Portions of earlier drafts of Chapters 5 and 8 were published in, respectively, *Modern Language Notes* ("Realism Revisited: Familial Discourse and Narrative in Balzac's *Les Paysans*," vol. 103, no. 4 [Sept. 1988]) and *Studies in Twentieth-Century Literature* ("Modernist Aesthetics and Familial Textuality: Gide's *La Porte étroite*," vol. 13, no. 2 [1989]). I thank the editors of these journals for permission to reprint these essays.

I have translated texts from the French throughout, and unless otherwise noted, all English translations are mine. For those passages referred to but not quoted, English page references will be given only when a current edition is available (as for *Paul et Virginie* and *La Porte étroite*).

The researching and writing of *Families in Jeopardy* has enjoyed support from many quarters. Special thanks go out to Nancy Armstrong and Len Tennenhouse for their searching questions; they made me rethink literary and cultural studies and sustained this project at a crucial time. I wish to thank Fred Jameson for his unflagging interest and encouragement over the years. Joan W. Scott taught me the dangers and opportunities that confront scholars trained in literary theory when they make forays into historiography. Colleagues at the University of California, San Diego have devoted precious time to reading and commenting on various drafts of the manuscript; I want to thank them for their warm support: George Mariscal, Lisa Lowe, George Lipsitz, Winnie Woodhull, Judith Halberstam, Vince Rafael, and Val Hartouni. Exchanges with students in the course of graduate seminars have been helpful to the realization of my book; their ideas, especially those of Irene Wei and Mark Salfi, have left their mark on these pages. I also want to thank Ross Chambers, Brian Massumi, Sandy Stone, Dick Terdiman, and Barbara Cruikshank, who came through with thoughtful suggestions; Lucy Reid for her curiosity about what academics do with their time; and my parents, Roddey Reid, Jr., and Caroline Reid, who helped from afar the lengthy writing of the manuscript. My editors Helen Tartar, Ellen Smith, and Ann Klefstad gave swift, expert advice. Finally, Steve Shaviro and Lisa Bloom, who each read and commented on the full manuscript and pushed me toward more radical styles of thinking and writing about power and the body, provided me with their friendship, intellectual and otherwise, whose value they can only begin to guess.

R. R.

Contents

Introduction: Family Productions 1

PART I: FAMILIAL DISCOURSE, PRINT CULTURE, AND THE SOCIAL BODY

1. Constructing a Discourse 23
2. Museum of Social Horrors 63

PART II: LACK OF FAMILY AS FICTIONAL STRATEGY IN FRANCE

3. *Paul et Virginie*: "Family" and the Politics of the Sentimental Body in Prerevolutionary France 101
4. Inside Out: Domesticating the Social in Eugène Sue's *Les Mystères de Paris* 137
5. No Future: Disembodied Domesticity in Balzac's *Les Paysans* 186
6. Midwiving Subjectivities and Female Knowledges: Sand's *La Petite Fadette* 213
7. Perverse Commerce: Familial Pathology and National Decline in *La Curée* 240

8. Straight Is the Gait: Modernism as Celibate Writing in Gide's *La Porte étroite*   278

Epilogue: A History of the Present   303

Notes   319

Works Cited   335

Index   351

FAMILIES IN JEOPARDY

~ *Regulating the Social Body
in France, 1750–1910*

Introduction:
Family Productions

A case presentation is always a
biographical narrative, a little novel.
—Jean Borie, *Mythologies de l'hérédité*

IN 1801, PHILIPPE PINEL, chief physician of La Salpêtrière, considered today as one of the founders of French positivism, published his *Traité médico-philosophique sur l'aliénation mentale* [Medical-philosophical treatise on mental illness]. Pinel concluded his discussion of the new, nonviolent cure he devised for the mentally ill with the following depiction of his patients' return to health:

> I can generally testify to the pure virtues and severe principles often manifested by the cure. Nowhere, *except in novels*, have I seen spouses more worthy of being cherished, parents more tender, lovers [e.g., fiancés] more passionate or persons more attached to their duties than the majority of the insane fortunately brought to the period of convalescence.[1]

What Pinel constructs here for our consumption is a sentimental melodrama of desire, knowledge, and power, in which the attending physician orchestrates an emotional recognition scene that generates at once a community of intense feeling between participants and observers and a hierarchy of spectatorship and knowledge (the privileged perspective of the physician-choreographer and readers). In this passage the return to reason signifies the restoration of the patient to his or her family, or better yet, to his or her familial role as best defined and sanctioned by contemporary prose fiction. Here, reason is at once familial and novelistic. As if to confirm this, Pinel's writing waxes Rousseauist in this passage and reproduces the very vocabulary of Rousseau's familial utopia *La Nouvelle Héloïse*: "pure virtues," "severe principles," "attached to their duties," and so on. The positivist Pinel's appeal to contemporary novels as a way to legitimate new methods for treating the mentally ill may startle us today. We live in a culture that continues to police the boundary between the sciences and literature (C. P. Snow's notorious "two cultures") opposing the former to the latter as the real to the imaginary and the objective to the subjective; in today's scientific writing, literary quotations and references serve at best as belletristic embellishments of articles whose rhetorical authority lies in other scientific references or in the well-established reputation of the authors.[2] In invoking novels not as dangerous imaginary discourses but as purveyors of an ideal of "family" that authorizes his own psychiatric reforms, the French clinician indicates a different relationship between novels and medical and human sciences. This is a relationship that the epigraph by Jean Borie on medical case histories and fiction foregrounds nicely: that both kinds of practices may construct and enact common cultural narratives. Pinel and Borie, each in his own way, do not oppose science to fiction as true to false but rather forgo such distinctions in favor of considering both practices in light of a common mode of discourse. Thus from the standpoint of this epistemology, novels, in their mobilization of imaginary characters and plots, are just as real *in their effects* as the cures physicians effect within the confines of asylums; prose fiction can articulate emotional and physical responses, inscribe bodies with normative narratives and desires, and align subjectivities and social practices. In this way novels and alienist practices can be seen as technologies of subjectivity. They are both particular discursive practices associated with specific institutions, and in their respective domains they engage in assembling stories and tales that we enact, and by means of which we narrate and make sense of ourselves and others.

Familial Discourse and Print Culture

This simple observation leads to the heart of the present study. I will argue that from the late eighteenth to the early twentieth century many forms of writing—especially novels—and institutional practices were engaged in organizing little narratives such as Pinel's for the consumption of ever-widening groups of people, from the cultural elite, artisans, laboring classes, and housewives to rentiers, mental patients, prisoners, bureaucrats, and professionals. In so doing they produced in France, under the controlling aegis of a discourse of "family," new forms of desire and a way of understanding self and other in terms of novel concepts of gender, household, social class, and public space.

Prose fiction had a particularly powerful role to play as a social actor in constructing a discourse that rewrote the social body and cast social relations of postrevolutionary France into a language of family and sexuality. Moreover, I argue that this was the language that was to serve as the foundation for what Benedict Anderson has termed modern, discursively based "imagined communities" of national identity.[3] Once this social discourse achieved currency among literate groups in the nineteenth century, it became the tool through which they inscribed and located individual and collective identities in relation to social "others" (for example, the working poor, prostitutes, homosexuals, and the colonized). What Pinel understood to be the peculiar province of the novel (as in the phrase "nowhere except in novels") will, in the course of the nineteenth century, eventually be everywhere embodied in the productions of a new "democratic" print culture and in the daily practices of those groups who like to think of themselves as "middle class." As such, familialism[4] can be understood as an example of what Ernesto Laclau and Chantal Mouffe call a "discursive structure," that is to say, "an articulatory practice which constitutes and organizes social relations," and, it must be added, maps the social body.[5] In this way I see familial discourse as partaking of the larger transformation described by Laclau and Mouffe in which a new social body was mapped and the relative fixity of Old Regime social, caste, and corporate identities gave way to the "nonsutured" openness of post-absolutist society and its flow of discursive differences.⁶

Now, several things have spurred me on in my investigations of familial discourse. First of all, in the United States, where I live and work, the hegemonic force of familialism is such today that it enjoys a long afterlife, even as daily family household practices break away from its grip: the statistic that only 14 percent of American households embody the ideal of male breadwinner and female homemaker never ceases to surprise my social acquaintances and colleagues at work.⁷ Clearly, as one feminist critic recently put it, "the most powerful household is the one we carry around in our heads."⁸ And if readers have doubts as to the material force of family rhetoric and discourse in our lives today, they have only to pick up any of the "safer-sex" literature issued by the Surgeon-General's office; there, the normative family operates murderously on the social body by fostering the idea that true "safer sex" is heterosexual and monogamous.* Moreover, new reproductive technologies, although they have marginalized and reduced the traditional figure of women as mothers to containers of fetuses (now promoted to the rank of "person"), have nonetheless occasioned yet new paeans to middle-class domesticity.⁹ Meanwhile, in France, Jean-Marie Le Pen and the National Front have successfully appropriated the rhetoric of national decline put forth by French demographers worried by falling birthrates; the extreme right now blames contemporary "decadence" (the AIDS pandemic, unemployment, and crime) on resident North Africans, whom they paint as powerful threats to the well-being of (white) French families. Finally, twenty years of observation of family households in France have impressed me with the role of the narratives family households have told each other and themselves in the course of radical changes in French private life. These stories introduce and suture new relations within the seemingly continuous fabric

---

* Thus no consideration is given to the real possibility that it now may be necessary to know the intimate details of one's partner's sex life for the last ten or fifteen years in order for monogamous relationships to be considered "safe" from the threat of HIV infection. On the role of the domestic family in AIDS discourse see Watney, *Policing Desire*.

of a discourse of "family," and they have opened my eyes to the workings of "family" in a way that my daily life in the United States would never have.

Family Woes: Tales of Loss and Lack as Discursive Tactics

Just why familial ideology can continue to persist in flagrant contradiction to social practice is a real issue. Obviously, its continuance has been favored by the flood of liberal and conservative commentary in the press and by the crumbling of state-sponsored social solidarity and services upon which citizens depend, but I also think it is linked, among other things, to a rhetoric of danger, lack, and loss. This rhetoric has presided over familial discourse in Britain and the United States since the mid-nineteenth century, and in France since its very inception in the eighteenth century. Hence the ironical title of the book: *Families in Jeopardy*. By means of their plots, reports, and treatises, novelists, physicians, jurists, and social workers penned narratives of family life deferred, disrupted, or destroyed by all manner of agents, internal and external: the cash nexus, criminals, disease, nonnormative sexuality, and hereditary disorders, to name a few. I argue that it was primarily through tales of endangered or lost family life that in France familial discourse negatively constructed and disseminated new, positive norms of household living, the body, subjectivity, and social relations. Consequently, for my purposes, Pinel's melodrama can be turned around: it was as much through the *perception of transgression or lack* as through idealized scenes of restored family life that cultural narratives produced the desire for the normative conjugal family household.

Thus serious consideration should be given to the following idea: from a genealogical perspective, "lack" is better understood not as the fundamental truth of subjectivity but (more pragmatically) as simply a particular mechanism deployed by familial discourse onto individual and collective practices. This constitutes a break with the Freudian and Lacanian orthodoxy that weighs so heavily in cultural and historical studies today and whose political liabilities are becoming more apparent. Radical feminists' objection to the psychoanalytic ideology of lack (the doctrine of penis envy in particular) has long been the object of scorn by Lacanian feminists and Althusserian Marxists, who have never tired of ridiculing them for their literal-mindedness (mistaking the penis for the Phallus). However, the transformation of specific images of lack into a linguistic structure by Lacanian psychoanalysis does little to change matters, because, as Gilles Deleuze and Félix Guattari have pointed out, this only serves to reintroduce a linguistic transcendentalism whose politics of gender and desire remain oppressively humanist to the core:

> Consequently, everything is played out from the start; everywhere we encounter the analytic process that consists in extrapolating a transcendent and common something, but that is a common-universal for the sole purpose of introducing lack into desire, in situating and specifying persons and an ego under one aspect or another of its absence, and imposing an exclusive direction on the disjunction of the sexes. . . .
> This common, transcendent, absent something will be called phallus or law, in order to designate "the" signifier that distributes the effects of meaning throughout the chain and introduces exclusions there (whence the Oedipalizing interpretations of Lacanianism).[10]

Psychoanalysis, no less than psychiatry, social philanthropy, and prose fiction, is a technology of subjectivity and the social,* and I think it is time to experiment with and affirm other modes of understanding the practices of bodies that do not return us to the same litany of transhistorical "truths": one ambition of this book is to conduct a study of how these "facts" were elaborated in the first place and inscribed in the heart of individual and collective life such

---

* See Linda Williams's remarks on psychoanalysis and the cinematic apparatus as mechanisms of power/knowledge (p. 46): "psychoanalysis should not be regarded as the key to understanding the cinematic apparatus; instead, like the cinema itself, it should be seen simply as another late nineteenth-century discourse of sexuality, another apparatus for aligning socially produced sexual desires with oedipal and familial norms. . . . Freud's theory of the fetish develops out of a particular way of seeing women as 'lacking' that cinema participates in as well. Neither institution actually reflects the confessional truths they purport to record; rather, they *produce* these truths in their new forms of power and pleasure."

that today we intellectuals, journalists, professors, and artists can range across historical periods and cultures and enjoy the reassuring spectacle of rediscovering ourselves through "familialized" others. The subsumption of multiple discursive and nondiscursive practices under the aegis of one signifier or law furthers this process of power, and indeed is just one more moment of familial discourse. Relations of power, knowledge, and desire operate in present-day liberal societies in ways more obvious, flexible, fluid, and changing than any static metaphysics of lack allows us to understand.

Thus, a genealogy of lack as a tactic of familial discourse will allow me to explore one of the major paradoxes of liberal societies, as laid out by Michel Foucault in his *History of Sexuality*—namely, how, by the end of the nineteenth century, a regime of norms and pathologies that worked through productive inducements, pleasures, and empowerment came into its own in the guise of the older regime of law that operated on the basis of negative prohibitions and deprivations.[11] It is not simply that a bio-politics of the normal and the pathological helped set into place the conditions for violent repression (as in the colonies or during the Commune) but also that the play between licit and illicit often *produced* the very "laws" that gave the impression of operating in a negative, prohibitive manner while instead they functioned differentially and fluidly. (This will be especially the subject of Chapter 7, which is devoted to Zola.)

Now, once "lack" is considered as a discursive technology for inscribing "family" in the social body, in turn, it becomes difficult to conceive the domestic family household in any straightforward empirical or realist sense. Reformulated from a plurality of social practices, adjusted and reiterated, "family" is no prediscursive sociological given but rather a highly productive articulation of discursive and nondiscursive relations, which has been realigning bodies, spaces, and subjectivities since the late eighteenth century. I want to argue that we must entertain the very real possibility that "family," too, has always been a moment in strategies of governance (generating its secrets, truths, and desires); and that it has existed only to the very extent that it was constructed by discourses and institutional practices that were invested by a political and social imaginary,

Introduction

which, in a circular fashion, these same discourses and institutional practices helped construct in the first place.

Moreover, insofar as the so-called modern domestic family has largely been constructed through narratives of absence and figures of pathological deficiency, in daily practices it has seemed never to "work" either; it has been always already dysfunctional, in crisis, *en miettes*, porous, and open to the outside. However, the mobilization of desires for "family" has been no less powerful because of its discursive basis. The rhetoric of absence and loss seems to have been peculiarly powerful in the context of the political upheavals that racked France during the period under study, for narratives of lack of "family" helped render the new norms impervious to either the vagaries of individual and collective experience or to "empirical" refutation. Catastrophic private or social events tended not so much to discredit "family" as to renew calls for its protection and revival. Thus, for example, in the aftermath of the Revolution of 1848, François Guizot, Louis-Philippe's deposed prime minister, and in the aftermath of the Paris Commune, Maxime Du Camp, the photographer and journalist, each issued urgent appeals and called for the restoration of "family" life as a means for combating revolutionary movements.[12]

Family Games in Cultural and Social Theory

This manner of viewing the workings of familial discourse has been confirmed in an unexpected way by contemporary writing on the subject, for one place where familial discourse continues to operate today is in cultural and social theory, notably in the recently translated early work by Jürgen Habermas, *The Structural Transformation of the Public Sphere*, and in Jacques Donzelot's *The Policing of Families*. Other examples would include Christopher Lasch's *Haven in a Heartless World* and Richard Sennett's *The Fall of Public Man*,[13] but I will focus on Habermas and Donzelot because the former includes the role of novel-reading in his account of the domestic and public spheres and the latter's deconstructive approach to the rise of the social is closer to my own. That contemporary theory reproduces the rhetorical tactics and figures of familial discourse comes as no surprise to feminist theorists; Michèle Barrett and Rayna Rapp have even suggested that "family" as unstated norm has so permeated scholarly writing on the subject by sociologists and historians that, from the perspective of feminist theory, ideally we should drop the concept of "family" altogether and speak of household forms and their attendant familial ideologies.[14] For my purposes here, I will frequently use the phrase "family household" to keep before readers' eyes those changing arrangements between kin, servants, boarders, and work and living space often erased today by the word "family," and I will employ "family" in quotes to refer to the domestic family household in its social and discursive construction.

What the four books I have mentioned do is this: their theories and analyses of what they term the social (understood as the site of welfare practices) are based on a conceptualization of family household history in its relations with the state that produces a powerful mobilizing nostalgia for the "lost" patriarchal family household variously located in the Old Regime or in the nineteenth century. Again, feminists, alert to the ideological implications of such stories (who and what are empowered or constituted as historical actors, victors, victims, or objects of fear or desire) have been quick to point this out.[15] Narratives recounting the decline of male authority in public and private life have been the staple of many writings by men on the "family" ever since the 1840s and represent an attempt to stimulate a desire in readers to see the domestic household reinstated under male aegis. In the case of each of these four authors the stories of the "death" of "family" (at the hands of the state, welfare workers, the marketplace, housewives, what have you) serves as the basis for the scripting of a retrospective cultural and political history that takes its origin in an empirical event (the "family") that perhaps never took place at all in terms of straightforward realist epistemologies that would situate *real* history outside of discursive practices. To put it the other way around, the modern domestic "family" has existed only insofar as it has been lamented in discourse as loss or absence and thus desired: first in the eighteenth century as absent among the nobility and thus also among those bourgeois households aspiring to join its ranks, then, in the nineteenth century, lacking among the laboring classes, the enslaved, and the colonized, and finally (as our authors now try to persuade us) lost today for the white working and middle classes and thus for society as a whole. To repeat, this idea of "family" continues to inform our desires, social imaginary, and cultural studies precisely so long as it is believed to be no longer there.

Take, for example, Donzelot's account of the organization and establishment of welfare practices that constituted an institutional and discursive domain, the "social," in which households and public and private agencies interacted so as to blur any distinction between the two. Despite the deconstructive force of his analysis of nineteenth-century middle- and working-class households—as not so much independent institutions that reproduce society as mechanisms for furthering social control—he fails to extend it to what preceded them; in an oft-quoted phrase, "the transition from a government of families to a government through the family,"[16] Donzelot simply assumes the prior existence of an autonomous, male-dominated household free from intervention by public or private organizations. What has "vanished" remains throughout the book largely unanalyzed, removed from history and the vagaries of institutional and discursive practices Donzelot otherwise documents so well for the other family household arrangements.[17]

Much the same can be said for Habermas's conception of the private domestic sphere on which his study of the European bourgeois public sphere so heavily depends. In Habermas's account, the bourgeois public sphere is that domain of new spaces and networks of communication and rational-critical debate that came into its own over the course of the eighteenth century, evolving out of private correspondence into novels, newspapers, journals, coffeehouses, and salons; they rivaled the absolute monarchy's political theater of representation. For Habermas, this new sphere was a direct extension in speech and print of the "conjugal family's intimate domain," which he credits as "the source of privateness in the modern sense of a saturated and free interiority."[18] In this way did the bourgeois domestic family and its peculiar sensibility control and dominate the literary and political public sphere. Habermas devotes a great deal of energy to recounting how, in the nineteenth century, the commodification of culture and the growth of welfare policies transformed the critical public sphere into a "manipulative" one that invaded and dissolved the intimate sphere that fostered rational-critical intercourse.[19] He writes:

> The model of the bourgeois public sphere presupposed strict separation of the public [e.g., the state] from the private realm in such a way that the public sphere, made up of private people gathered together as a public and articulating needs of society with the state, was itself considered part of the private realm. To the extent that the public and the private became intermeshed realms [in the nineteenth century], this model became inapplicable.[20]

Just how the "conjugal family's intimate domain"—from which the classical bourgeois public sphere emanated—came about remains a mystery. Its static character can be read in Habermas's definition of the public sphere, a definition that returns as a refrain throughout the book: "the coming together of private individuals in public."[21] In this narrative, *first* you have private individuals, *then* they meet in the public sphere. The public sphere has a history but private individuals and the conjugal family household seemingly do not.

What drops out of Habermas's account is any sense of the immense discursive and semiotic labor that went into the fabrication and construction of the domestic family and private individuals in the first place. I propose that what is needed is not just more supposedly empirical facts about the rise of these new household arrangements and forms of subjectivity, but a different narrative, a story of print culture and proliferating discourses that did much to invent and establish the domestic sphere and its attendant categories (what was to be understood by the words "male" and "female," "home," "middle class," "self," and so forth). In other words, discursive and institutional practices presided over the constitution of the private and public spheres as meaningful categories and domains of activity. Habermas comes close to this other kind of history in his analysis of novel-reading, family life, and bourgeois subjectivity in their relation to the public sphere:

> The sphere of the public arose in the broader strata of the bourgeoisie as an *expansion* and at the same time *completion* of the intimate sphere of the conjugal family. Living room and salon were under the same roof; and just as privacy of the one was oriented toward the public nature of the other, and as the subjectivity of the privatized individual was related from the very start to publicity, so both were conjoined in literature that had become "fiction." On the one hand, the empathetic reader repeated within himself the private relationships displayed before him in literature; from his experience of real familiarity (*Intimität*), he gave life to the fictional one, and in the latter he prepared himself for the former. On the other hand, from the outset the familiarity (*Intimität*) whose vehicle was the written word, the subjectivity that had become fit to print, had in fact become the literature appealing to a wide public of readers. The privatized individuals coming together to form a public also reflected critically and in public on what they had read, thus contributing to the process of enlightenment which they together promoted.[22]

Habermas's dialectic draws up short: novels' relation to the private sphere is demoted to one of supplementarity, as the words "expansion" and "completion" suggest in this passage and as "clarity" suggests in the following one, which closes Habermas's development. Speaking of the creation of subscription libraries and novels, Habermas concludes: "They formed the public sphere of a rational-critical debate in the world of letters within which the subjectivity originating in the interiority of the conjugal family, by communication with itself, attained clarity about itself."[23] Once again, the familiar chronology interposes itself: *first* there was the interiority of the "family," *then* came the world of letters and critical discourse. In the end, discourse and fiction amount to being the expressive appendages of a previously constituted private subjectivity, and in his study what little analysis of the constitution of the conjugal family there is will ultimately revert to an unconvincing classical-economist argument.[24] I will argue that Habermas's discursive dialectic began long before he imagines. In his theory, "family" just *is*; as in much familial discourse, it enjoys an ontological state of grace and stands all-determining (the "pillar of society," people said in the nineteenth century) before "falling" into the social and a strange state of passivity. This is the consequence of Habermas's strategy of trying to theorize a rational-critical communicative sphere that would somehow stand outside of mechanisms of power. The ideality of "family" and of the public sphere mirror one another and are essential to the functioning of Habermas's dialectical narrative.

Good Jargon: Production, Inscription, and Strategy

To the degree Habermas regards writing and fiction as either the auxiliaries of subjectivity or as the playthings of commodity relations, not only does "family" escape analysis as a powerful force but, as Joan Landes has demonstrated, so do some of the fundamental organizing categories of the public sphere such as gender (to take one salient example).[25] Thus Habermas's narrative must be seen as not only a nostalgic one but patriarchal as well. The point of my remarks is to alert readers to the stakes involved in *not* considering written discourses and novels as historico-semiotic actors but as primarily "expressions" of something else. This is why I have used such terms as "produce," "production," "inscribe," "inscription," and "strategy," which emphasize discourse and writing as narrative apparatuses and as social agents. These terms have been around for a while now, circulating through the channels of academic theory. "Production" stems from Marxist criticism, particularly that associated with the theories of Althusser,[26] and remains useful on several accounts: it reminds us that discourses and novels (and their effects) are artifactual and not given; neither are they static objects or "representations" (as in current definitions of ideology) but rather constitute in themselves semiotic material forces and processes that involve transformative labor, such that a plot, a description, or a discourse is never identical with the narrative, formal, or discursive materials that preceded it and went into its making. Thus, for example, I am interested in how new forms of knowledge and social desire are constituted and transmitted to readers, how different forms of authority undergo transformations, how new kinds of speech receive validation. Despite its masculinist connotations (insofar as it discounts "reproduction"—childbearing, education, modes of socialization—as a secondary, "female" activity),[27] "production," when applied to novels and familial discourse, has rhetorical value precisely because it assigns political and social agency to those "feminine" domains considered weak or having little or no power when viewed from the grand perspective of traditional social and political narratives: writing, letters, culture, subjectivity, and "private life." Similarly, while military metaphors commonly employed in Foucauldian analysis of discourse (formation, strategies, tactics, deployment, operation, and so forth) are not as disruptive as they once were in certain fields,[28] nonetheless in this study I believe they retain analytic force by situating the normative family and its discourses in a field of power and struggle. "Inscription" and "inscribe" are more recent coinages; they allude to the fundamental emphasis I give to semiotic processes, especially to the mechanics of writing and the various surfaces writing affects and transforms (paper, bodies, spaces). I am particularly attached to this spatial metaphor of *surface*, which helps me switch the focus away from a desire to look for hidden depths of meaning or "truth" (say, in the psychology of an author or character, the description of a household interior, the inflection of a voice, or a program for regulating prostitution) to the question of how those semantic "depths" and the desire to plumb them are constituted and elicited in the first place through rhetorical and narrative strategies.

This stress on discourse as a material force, and on the construction of the interpretive categories we apply to ourselves, others, and cultural artifacts, necessarily represents a departure from some of the richest investigations of ideology, literature, gender, and class in nineteenth-century France whose critical methods are drawn in varying degrees from Freudian and Lacanian psychoanalysis or from Althusserian theory of ideology.[29] From this perspective prose fiction, poetry, and treatises are read as so many expressions of an authorial or even "political" unconscious structured by fundamental repressions and drives; in contrast, I am concerned with following the performative aspect of discourses in the process of their production of these very repressions, desires, and complexes. Thus I view "incestuous desire," "sexual difference," and so forth as being as much constructed, elicited, and authorized by discursive practices as they are expressed through them. Like "family," bodies, gender, and desire are *made*, not simply given.

"Production," "inscription," "strategy," and "discourse" prove helpful in keeping our attention fixed upon a central problem: many of the categories and oppositions with which we live our social and gender relations, read novels, and write books have a genealogy that is worth tracing. I was reminded of this by several colleagues—historians—who read a draft of Chapter 4 on Eugène Sue's *Les Mystères de Paris*. This is a study of the semiotic politics of a nineteenth-century serial novel whose narrative simultaneously destabilizes and constructs readers' desires and sense of social class in terms of a paranoid discourse of "family" and urban pathology. "Very good," I was told by one of them, "now all that remains for you to do is to *politicize* your analysis by linking it to the state and political events." The old cultural reflex had returned: *real politics* and *real history*, that which grounds and lends meaning to the rest, reside outside discourse, novels, subjectivity, and the domestic sphere. That is where the action is, that is the zone of the real. Such a view comes all too close to replicating the cultural split, handed down to us by discourses of the nineteenth century, between public and private spheres, male and female, class and gender, the political and the personal, work and home. I had thought, apparently erroneously, that detailing the discursive strategies and effects of a major serial novel that managed to garner the enthusiastic following of a vast public around these very same categories constituted "political analysis." Here Joan Scott's comments on the categories and monocausal theories that govern historiographic practices and that have been naturalized by cultural narratives prove helpful:

> Directing inquiry at discourse permits a more powerful account of human activity than one that insists on opposing material reality and interpretation. The notion that there is a primary causality for economic relationships, for example, is a self-evident fact neither for workers nor for historians; rather it is a way of perceiving or theorizing social

organization. . . . General belief in monocausal interpretations makes them no less partial and selective. Rather, such interpretations must be understood as part of the apparatus of cultural production of subjects.[30]

The question, then, is what the politics of these various cultural categories are, what they authorize and ratify as legitimate activities, narratives, knowledges, and desires, and what, on the contrary, they stigmatize, displace, and otherwise shunt aside. My sense is that *in their very binary opposition* (masculine/feminine, work/home, politics/culture), they give the impression of accounting for all that matters in collective and individual life. We find it impossible to think one term of an opposition without mental or affective reference to the other; they mutually constitute and reinforce each other in cultural narratives that tell tales of one disrupting, disabling, or impairing the other in a dynamic in which the desire to restore a proper balance or hierarchy between the terms (say, between home and work) remains constantly solicited but rarely satisfied. So we enact new familial narratives in discourse and in our daily lives, including academic discussions. Telling the rather different tale of how these tropes of familial discourse deploy themselves in dominant modes of thought, perception, and feeling then perhaps becomes worthwhile. As Nancy Armstrong put it with her customary succinctness, any history of political events, women, the "family," or the novel that fails to take this into account "remains, by definition, locked into the categories replicating the semiotic behavior that empowered the middle class in the first place."[31]

The present study is divided into two parts. Part I outlines some of the principal figures and rhetorical strategies of familial discourse in France from 1750 to 1910 deployed in writings by novelists, philosophes, educators, experts in legal medicine and public health, philanthropists, journalists, and politicians. Through their diagnoses, briefs, articles, and practical advice they tied issues of domesticity, sexuality, and gender to questions of personal worth, public hygiene and order, and military and economic strength. They elaborated a discourse of lack and loss that often took the form of descriptions of familial and sexual deviance or pathology and that especially targeted bodies and the desires they were thought to enclose. Particular bodies were constructed as favoring or preventing particular household arrangements and vice versa. Disruptive individual and social practices were named and policed in terms of an endangered or defunct "family" and its master tropes of gender and sexuality. By the end of Part I readers should have a sense of how familial discourse provided for years to come the terms whereby a new subjectivity and social imaginary—a new "common sense"— both confronted gender and social alterity and constituted those shifting, ill-defined social groups of the middling sort as "middle class." A new set of universal categories, dispersed across different writing and institutional practices, at once unified the social—Anderson's "imagined community"—and engaged in gender and social distinctions.

Building on the web of intertextual and rhetorical relations sketched out in Part I, Part II analyzes how French novels constructed and transmitted familial discourse through narratives of the endangerment or loss of "family" from the Enlightenment to literary modernism, the latter a movement whose aesthetic and ideological practices tended to oppose the dominant discourse of domesticity. I examine six novels, each representative of a major fictional genre: Bernardin de Saint-Pierre's *Paul et Virginie* (pastoral); Eugène Sue's *Les Mystères de Paris* (serial), Honoré de Balzac's *Les Paysans* (realist), George Sand's *La Petite Fadette* (pastoral), Emile Zola's *La Curée* (naturalist), and André Gide's *La Porte étroite* (modernist).

From Literary Masterpieces to Socio-Semiotic Forces

The literary chapters of Part II tend to fall into two groups: those analyzing decisive shifts in writings on "family"—Bernardin de Saint-Pierre's *Paul et Virginie*, Sue's *Les Mystères de Paris*, and Zola's *La Curée*—and those studying semiotic struggles within a particular paradigm—Sand's *La Petite Fadette* and Balzac's *Les Paysans*, which constitute polemical responses to the *question sociale* initiated most notoriously by Sue in print culture; and Gide's *La Porte étroite*, which attempts to exit from the heavily policed culture, exemplified by naturalist fiction and medical writing, of gender and class of the late nineteenth century.

Now, the unexpected focus in Part II on less-"great" novels by Bernardin de Saint-Pierre, Sue, Sand, and Zola constitutes a reversal of aesthetic choices made by many Marxist critics over the last hundred years, from Marx to Adorno, Lukàcs, Williams, Macherey, Prendergast, and Jameson, who have tended, across their differences, to agree on dismissing sentimental novels, melodramatic narratives, and naturalist fiction as either incorrigibly conservative or superficial, or simply marginal and beside the point in favor of masterworks of realism and modernism.[32] I will show that, on the contrary, these texts were social forces to be reckoned with, highly productive of new relations, knowledges, topographies, and bodies—in short, that they stand as major inscriptions of fundamental terms and categories that articulate French social, cultural, and economic life. Thus, for example, I will argue that the discursive crossover between lachrymose, kitsch narratives such as *Paul et Virginie* and revolutionary thought and new economic practices is greater than most cultural critics and historians would allow. As I have said before, all too often the practices of cultural narratives in general, whether works of fiction or of, say, social philanthropy, are reduced to the status of superstructural symptoms of some prior economic or political "truth." I think genealogical analysis makes such intellectual and political complacencies difficult, and imposes more serious consideration of material semiotic practices as social forces in their own right. This has lead me to a new way of reading that stresses the performative character of semiotic practice: discursive practices elicit bodily sensations (tears, fear, guilt, paranoia, voyeuristic mania for fetishistic detail, etc.), help construct norms and truths of individual and collective life, map social and private depths and secrets to be explored (thus inciting the desire to know the labyrinths of subjects' interiority, closed households, closeted sexualities, forbidden slums, and colonized lands), and introduce "timeless laws" of gendered desire.[33]

Analysis of single novels is warranted in my view for the simple reason that the material operations and effects of rhetoric cannot be easily passed over in favor of, say, a sweeping, continuous "history" of the novel; at the same time much of the force and power of familial discourse lay in the attempt to train readers in the hermeneutics and small pleasures of deciphering the detail of texts, words, characters, clothing, bodies, and households to find the dispersed minutiae of wayward desire and lack of "family." Understanding how that training transpires in reading novels is crucial to grasping how deeply ingrained familial discourse remains in the ways we have come to read novels, ourselves, and others.

PART I

Familial Discourse, Print Culture, and the Social Body

Aristocratic nights are traversed by lights . . .
bourgeois nights are peopled with demons.

—Aron and Kempf, *Le Pénis ou
la démoralisation de l'Occident*

~ CHAPTER I

Constructing a Discourse

> Within every society one finds *the family*: it is the primary foundation of the social edifice. Considered from the point of view of the perpetuation of the species, it is the first link in the chain of humanity. Finally, the family is related to political institutions whose form it determines.
>
> —Larousse, *Grand dictionnaire universel du XIXe siècle* (1866)

> Retention is the primary function of the family: it is a matter of learning what elements of desiring-production the family is going to reject, what it is going to retain, what it is going to direct along the dead-end roads leading to its own undifferentiated (the miasma), and what on contrary it is going to lead down the paths of a contagious and a reproduceable differentiation. For the family creates at the same time its disgraces and its honors, the nondifferentiation of its neurosis and the differentiation of its ideal, which are distinguishable only in appearance.
>
> —Deleuze and Guattari, *Anti-Oedipus*

Familial Discourse

The two epigraphs that preface this chapter precisely situate the role that the domestic family household would play in the discursive battles to come: moved to the center of a new print and political culture, "family" worked to reformulate and distribute social practices, subjectivities, and forms of authority around a normative pole that divided them into various degrees of the normal and the deviant, the licit and the illicit. This inscription of the domestic family as ideal was, as Deleuze and Guattari remind us, actually part and parcel of a dialectic of self and other whereby "family" and its "deviant" outside are *produced* by discourse as mutually authorizing concepts. In other words, "ideal" and "neurosis" work in tandem to inscribe "family" as the sole grid of intelligibility of human desire and social relations and, as such, share a fundamental discursive complicity, if not identity. How this production operates and what are its mechanisms and tactics are the subjects of this chapter and the next.

In the sections that follow I will foreground some of the major rhetorical figures and discursive strategies of French familialism from the mid–eighteenth century through the nineteenth century, especially those that refigure Old Regime notions of the social body, self, household, and sexuality. It is not a comprehensive overview; rather, it draws attention to the elaboration and functioning of key figures that dominated familial discourse at particular times. I will thus move among different sites and objects of discourses: for example, from the female aristocratic body in Enlightenment and revolutionary writing, to manuals of domesticity and their emphasis on the inner qualities of the self, to the colonization of the Old Regime aristocracies by the new familialism, to (finally) the parade of psychosexual "monsters" who name the normative family by virtue of their departure from it.

The main focus is on writings dealing with bodily and household practices. In discourses of the day, particular household arrangements implied particular bodies and vice versa. Those readers who know the new work in the fields of gender and social history will find much that is familiar, but this overview attempts to stimulate new thinking by shifting emphases. In particular, concepts such as "family," "body," "sex," and "gender" are defamiliarized, and become more fluid than is often the case in those studies that have focused on Rousseau's writings, the documents of republican patriarchy, or the Napoleonic Code.[1] Thus, for example, the opposition between "male" and "female," "masculine" and "feminine," is less clear and determinate than some might think: for familial discourse not only recast these terms in radical opposition to each other but also claimed that men and women of the middling groups were capable of sharing a common sensibility, common sense of selfhood, and common inner qualities. These qualities were precisely those that allowed men and women to come together in the first place, marry compatibly, have sex, and set up homes.[2] Thus the "body" was the site not only of a new sex/gender system[3] (with its distinctions, hierarchies, and divisions of labor) but also of liberal subjectivity and interiority. The paradoxical play of gender difference and common liberal sensibility is also crucial in accounting for the discursive constructions of "middle class" around "family" and "gender" in the nineteenth century and for the powerful appeal they exerted for a wide segment of French society. Conversely, the role of gender (as opposed to sex and sexuality) in the scripting of liberal subjectivity has been overlooked by most writers whose main concern has been with sexual practices and social regulation.[4] In this way I view gendered, liberal subjectivity as part and parcel of the construction of the imagined community of French "democratic" culture: it writes men and women as a unity (they are just all alike— at least, they *can* be equal and alike if they wish) but nonetheless inscribes upon the social body differences and hierarchies in which they find their places.[5] "Family" is one of those mechanisms for writing the postrevolutionary French social body (replacing blood, birth, proximity to the king's body) and, to no one's surprise today, "family" was thought to be embodied best by the "middle class." A discourse that purportedly embraced and included everyone (all can enjoy the satisfactions of "family," can they not?) actually policed an inside in opposition to an outside "other."

Toward the latter half of the eighteenth century in France, a new tone of urgency crept into lay discourses on the family and related issues, of which the following quotation provides a good example:

> If there were a country where women were sterile; if an inhuman luxury or a barbaric jealousy castrated either or both sexes; if perverse tastes, caprices, the preservation of some charms, a misunderstood voluptuousness, weariness of conceiving and giving birth put women off from commerce with men; if children, brought up without the precaution and care required by their feeble state, perished before reaching maturity; certainly that nation could not long maintain itself and would soon vanish from the face of the earth.[6]

26   Familial Discourse

This passage is drawn from *Recherches et considérations sur la population de la France* [Research and considerations on the population of France], published in 1778 by Moheau, France's first demographer. The book was one in a series of population studies that proclaimed the poor condition of the French population and the disastrous consequences this would have for the nation's economy and the state. Moheau's prose constructs a populationist nightmare that turns on vivid images of castration (of *both* genders, no less) and the withdrawal of women from heterosexual relations.

In my view, it would be a mistake to dismiss Moheau's rhetoric as simply the bizarre expression of some personal anxieties projected onto the social. To do so, I think, would miss the point and power of such writing; for it is rather a question of discursive tactics meant to mobilize readers and public opinion in terms of some radical and catastrophic *insufficiency* in marital and sexual relations. That is to say, Moheau's prose articulates at once a way of seeing things and a social-political agenda. On the one hand, in this passage the preoccupations of familial ideologues in the eighteenth century are writ large: libertinage, conjugal sexuality (duties and pleasures), the beginnings of contraception, the risks of childbirth, childcare, and education, and, not least, power relations between genders. His denunciation of what he erroneously perceived to be France's population decline had immense implications. From Moheau's depiction of familial lack it followed that only through the redefinition of marriage and of women's and men's roles in terms of an affectionate valorization of maternity and childhood could society achieve the biopolitical imperatives of social (re)production neglected, so it was claimed, by current custom. A new household arrangement in opposition to other household practices was called for, namely, that of the conjugal family household and its ideology of domesticity. This entailed new notions of self, body, gender, and sexuality.

A generation earlier, Rousseau had already sketched out the broad contours of the new household's structure and mission:

> If women would only deign to nurse their children, morals would reform of themselves, sentiments of nature would awaken in every heart, the

State would become populated again; this first point, this point alone resumes all the others. The attraction of domestic life is the best antidote to bad morals. Thus, the mere correction of these excesses would result in a general reformation; soon nature would reassert its rights. Once women become mothers again, men will soon become again fathers and husbands.[7]

The new family household, organized around intimacy and the bringing up of children, eventually became a privileged discursive object for the social elites. Both a model and a desired actuality, its history intersects with that of other discourses—medical, economic, political, philosophical. It intersects as well with the history of social practices that have as their nexus the family household, with its issues of marriage, childbirth, breast-feeding, child education, the "woman issue," sexuality in its various aspects (gender identity, reproductive and nonreproductive sexuality, homosexuality, celibacy, and bachelorhood), the gender division of labor, and population control. These discourses constitute a configuration that can be called *familial* discourses; they draw on and displace a tradition of church and lay literature that had previously treated most of these issues solely with reference to the old corporate hierarchy and to the moral concerns of the Christian perspective on redemption and salvation. In most of this literature, with the exception of manuals of domesticity and child care, writers rarely designated the domestic family household as such but rather, by means of narratives of familial and sexual disorder, constituted it as their oblique point of reference and norm.

Around 1750 there was a sudden acceleration in the publication of purely lay discourses, which were an integral part of high Enlightenment culture and coincided with the beginnings of the modern medical and human sciences (demography, sociology, political science, history, psychology, and anthropology).[8] The authors promulgating the new familialism were high functionaries and administrative officers (*receveurs de finances, intendants, lieutenants généraux de police*, etc.), jurists, physicians in large numbers, philosophes, educators, and, of course, novelists, drawn mostly from the middling groups and *noblesse de robe*. Their writing belongs to an expanding print culture that began to dismantle the absolutist sphere of political representation and to forge new, discursive social and gender identities; these identities structured alternative stories of national community (the nation, the *patrie*) centered around what came to be designated as "middle class." That the emergence of a new print culture and regime of social discursivity should coincide with the production and circulation of familial discourse and the construction of a discursively based middle-class identity should surprise no one. Not only did many of the middling groups publish the new literature and elaborate new institutional practices that turned on new household norms, but their very social identity rested in part on the mental labor of manipulating written words and concepts, and, as Benedict Anderson has aptly suggested, on their consumption of written discourse to a degree that distinguished them from the feudal aristocracies. Anderson describes this fundamental social difference succinctly:

> The pre-bourgeois ruling classes generated their cohesion in some sense outside language, or at least outside print-language. . . . Solidarities were the products of kinship, clientship, and personal loyalties. . . . The relatively small size of traditional aristocracies, their fixed political bases, and the personalization of political relations implied by sexual intercourse and inheritance, meant that their cohesions as classes were as much concrete as imagined. An illiterate nobility could still act as a nobility. But the bourgeoisie? Here was a class which, figuratively speaking, came into being as a class only in so many replications. Factory-owner in Lille was connected to factory-owner in Lyon only by reverberation. They had no necessary reason to know of one another's existence; they did not typically marry each other's daughter or inherit each other's property. But they did come to visualize in a general way the existence of thousands and thousands like themselves through print-language. For an illiterate bourgeoisie is scarcely imaginable. Thus in world-historical terms bourgeoisies were the first classes to achieve solidarities on an essentially imagined basis.[9]

The discourse of "family" assigned a new affective value to intimacy and childhood that was an integral feature of the aggressive sentimentality characteristic of lay writings on marriage in prerevolutionary France and gave it an overtly political twist.[10] *Sensiblerie* and its shameless displays of emotion were detached from aristocratic culture and made an integral part of a discourse of "family" that demanded radical reform of Old Regime laws and customs governing marriage and sexuality. For example, in the name of companionate marriage and conjugal bliss de Cervol, another demographer, proposed the progressive measure of legalizing divorce, which would have the happy consequence of encouraging more marriages, and thus more children and population growth. Here, early on, companionate marriage is considered an affair of state one hundred years before welfare practices began to "invade" the household. The context here is that of eighteenth-century political economy, for which, as Foucault insisted, population—particularly the laboring population—was the source of wealth. Cervol writes:

> The object of marriage is to have children; however, to constrain people who hate one another not only to live together but moreover to love each other because at one time they were compatible is to require of an athlete that he recommence his career over and over again. If you ask the multitude of bachelors that live among us why they have not made any conjugal commitments, they answer that these engagements are unbreakable and that this indissolubility, which deprives us of many unions, influences in no small way those which have already been formed. . . . Let us not search elsewhere than in the indissolubility of marriages the cause of depopulation. All other causes derive from this one or are imperceptible in their effects. This cause has given birth to celibacy, and, by natural filiation, to the corruption of morals.[11]

Familial discourses' promotion of new family household arrangements constituted an attempt to reorganize and regulate a plurality of practices thriving in various regions, social castes, and classes in the eighteenth and nineteenth centuries. And (as I shall show in Chapter 2) new familial customs and habits were in turn to serve as a reterritorialization of psychic and social energies that writers felt were no longer framed by the collapsing corporate structures in capitalist civil society. The "policing of families" instituted at once a restructuring of the social field and an inscription of new politico-familial subjects: housewives and mothers, husbands and fathers, children, workers, patients, detainees, marginals, and, not least, readers.

Familial Discourse on the Offensive: 1750 to 1789

Family, class, nation, the body, gender, and sexuality received a powerful articulation that was to dominate discourse for years to come. It was in the name of the state, the nation, and the universal good that familial discourse proceeded to attack Old Regime customs as the period of absolute monarchy came to a close. Charges focused on the corporate world whose regulations required celibacy on the part of large numbers of men and women: the clergy and the younger sons of aristocratic families, of course, but also soldiers, servants, and journeymen. In writers' eyes society overflowed with members lost to the task of biological reproduction due to the scandalously arbitrary and inefficient alliance system; this system, practiced primarily among the social elites, tended to separate sexual and psychological satisfaction of individuals from the imperatives of political marriage, continuance of the line, and the preservation of patrimony. The new writing was to bind biological reproduction and conservation of fortunes to personal "happiness" (now understood less as public power and personal pleasure than as the inner joys of intimacy and family life) through the miracle of domesticity.

Enlightenment writers pressed hard their attack on practices associated with the sumptuary lifestyles of the aristocracy. Here is a list of charges from the pen of Messance, a tax collector and author of *Nouvelles recherches sur la population de la France avec quelques remarques sur divers objets d'administration* [New research on the population of France with some remarks on various objects of administration] (1788). The accusations come under the chapter heading, "Effets de la dépravation des moeurs sur la population" [Effects of the depravity of morals on the population]:

> The calculation that leads men to celibacy (... we are not speaking here at all of that celibacy that has as its motive and goal a greater purity).
> The calculation that leads men to want only one or two children.
> The false grandeur that leads men to have a great number of servants, a great number of guests at their table (instead of seeing themselves surrounded by children); and the greatest depravity—that crowns them all—to destroy in the very act of sowing.

In true physiocratic fashion the author deploys the metaphors of natural and agricultural catastrophe to arouse the indignation of his readers:

> All these errors of the human mind are to the spirit and population what frost, great rains, severe drought, fog, hail, wind, and storms are to physical existence and the productions of the earth.[12]

In the first two paragraphs material self-interest that leads to celibacy or contraceptive practices receives the requisite condemnation. The heaviest rhetorical charge, however, is reserved for ostentatious aristocratic sexual practices and sociability that shunned family life; for they were both economically unproductive (neither masters nor servants were engaged in productive work but rather in leisure activities or service) and sexually unreproductive (servants were by corporate custom unmarried, and libertines were notorious practitioners of birth control).[13] For Moheau, the aristocratic life of leisurely dissipation had destroyed the primary requirement of the nobility as the warrior class: the male fighting body. It was now found only among the people:

> If one compares the force of the old French knights to that of those who inherited their name; if one weighs the armor they wore in combat which their descendants can scarcely lift, one is tempted to believe that the human species has degenerated in France, at least among the nobility; and this assumption will not be completely unwarranted if one considers that successive generations of men softened by leisure must result in men less strong than their forebears. Happily, there are no such signs of degradation in force among men of the people.[14]

In one stroke, Moheau transformed aristocratic (sumptuary) excess into an abyss of lack.

Much of the same line of reasoning structures the article "Célibat" of the *Encyclopédie*. Ironically, the philosophes' resolutely populationist stance drove them to align their position with church policy concerning nonreproductive sexuality. Both parties were hostile to wasteful sexual activities such as contraception, libertinage, and masturbation. With greater rigor, the philosophes included among these practices celibacy as well.[15]

Male primogeniture also came under attack. In France, unlike in Great Britain, it was restricted to several regions (Normandy and the southernmost provinces), and elsewhere to the French nobility, which was the only class to adopt male primogeniture systematically; this custom stood at the heart of an alliance politics whose goal was the preservation of the line and its network of clienteles constituting the traditional foundation of aristocratic privilege, honor, and power. Noble primogeniture offended the new familial sensibility, which coincided with liberal theory's reformulation of individuals' formal rights in support of democratic inheritance practices. Moheau wrote:

> With respect to the rights and prerogatives of masculinity and primogeniture, for the good of humanity, morals, and the nation, and for the interest of the population, one can not bemoan the preferred vocation which in families only recognizes a single individual, shunts aside daughters and younger offspring, corrupts one man with wealth and reduces others to indigence, to dependency, to the everlasting feelings of regret which are excited by unequal treatment, and prevents reasonable parents from giving life to those unhappy children who would complain of having been brought into the world.[16]

Clearly, what these texts called for was a new politics of the body now defined in its productive and reproductive capacities. And what these same writings do is institute a transfer of authority from the male and female aristocratic body to a "democratic" one more readily defined in terms of its biology, "health," and gender. In this context the male fighting body is transformed from one of prowess and skill, animated by the noble qualities of courage and audaciousness, into a body whose fundamental qualities are physical fitness and strength.

The aristocratic body wasn't simply the male fighting body; it was also, for both genders, the body of alluring surfaces and theatrical self-presentation molded to fit the prescriptions of a life of intense sociality and pleasure in Old Regime society. This body of pleasure and spectacle became the object of extremely violent attacks; in the process it received a gender: female. One figure dominated the writings of familial ideologues and condensed all their preoccupations: the worldly, aristocratic mother who forsook the duties of maternity and domesticity for the pleasures of urban salon society and extramarital liaisons. Jean Charles Des Essartz, author of *De l'éducation corporelle des enfants en bas âge* [Of the physical education of very young children] (1760), was peremptory on the matter: "Nothing contributes more to population decline than the irregular life [*irrégularité*] adopted by the fair sex which indulges in all its pleasures. With such conduct it is impossible for young ladies to enjoy good health and to bring healthy children into the world."[17] With the figure of the noblewoman a long semiotic struggle over the female body began. The stakes were high, for women's bodies were to be the site of a new politics of gender that rewrote the aristocratic body in terms of reproductive finalities, promoted revamped concepts of gender as master tropes of the social body, and elaborated a new, liberal subjectivity rooted in "family."

Des Essartz was seconded by Moheau, who, as usual, had something to say about everything: even faithful wives of society did not escape the general indictment and are taken to task for their foolish worldliness, which obliges them to cede their maternal duties to wet nurses:

> Even among virtuous women, there are a great number who, indulging their frivolous tastes, neglect the cares involved in the marital state; they feel justified by example and custom. They are mistaken; they betray their duties as citizen, wife, and mother. To hand over a child to an unknown woman is a cruel and denatured act, which, if it were unique, would be considered an atrocity. The multitude of sins does not diminsh their perversity.

The worst punishments await them: "Fooled Nature wreaks vengeance and exacts punishment; and the milk which should have been the nourishment of children becomes for those mothers who deprived them of it a cause of illness and death."[18] Two of the most commonly recurring figures of familial discourse raise their ugly heads in these texts: the aristocratic *mère dénaturée* (unnatural mother) and the mercenary peasant wet nurse. They, together with libertines, bachelors, and unmarried women, peopled familial discourses of the period. They stood accused of endangering family life. Moreover, they were the foils of what Jacques Donzelot has called a positive economy of body flows and social flows; this combined physiocracy's economic theories with eighteenth-century medicine's theory of fluids. The political economy of two fluids was foremost in writers' minds: male sperm (wasted in libertinage and masturbation—more about which later) and mothers' milk.[19] The shrill tone in these passages is symptomatic of a campaign of intimidation launched against noblewomen and their would-be bourgeois emulators. With medical treatises in the lead, a substantial body of literature on maternity, breastfeeding, and child care flourished up through the nineteenth century.[20] The virulence of these texts is fueled in part by the ambition of surgeons and physicians to discredit and remove women (particularly midwives) from a field of knowledge and practice that was an exclusively female domain up to the eighteenth century: obstetrics. Already the claims of the male medical corps had won legal recognition in 1755 with the passage of a law forbidding women to practice surgery or dentistry independently of male medical authority. The exclusion of women from the medical field was completed under Napoleon at the very moment of the rise of the university, which contributed so much to the decline of the power of the salons and of the women who ran them: in 1806 Napoleon named Baudelocque, renowned for his conservatism, to a newly created chair in obstetrics, the first French chair ever in a specialized field of medicine.[21] Opposing their "knowledge" to female "ignorance," physicians and other men coerced and cajoled women into assuming the duties of motherhood and child education.

Some of the treatises' titles are worth mentioning for their suggestiveness: Chamousset, *Mémoire politique sur les enfants* [Political report on children] (published in 1756, it went through many printings); Raulin (a physician), *Instructions sur les sages-femmes* [Instructions concerning midwives] (1770); Pierre Roussel (a physician), *Le Système moral et physique de la femme* [The mental and physical system of woman] (1775, a huge literary success); Alphonse Leroy, *Médecine maternelle; ou, l'Art d'élever et de conserver les enfants* [Maternal medicine, or, the art of raising and preserving children] (1803); and Verdier-Heurtin, *Discours sur l'allaitement et l'éducation physique des enfants* [Discourse concerning the breastfeeding and physical education of children] (1804). In these writings, responsibility for the broken household is laid squarely at women's feet. Maternal duties have as their corollary the reterritorialization of women's sexuality onto reproduction. Verdier-Heurtin wrote in 1804: "Women, do not expect me to encourage your criminal behavior . . . I do not blame your pleasures when you are free . . . but once you have become wives and mothers, leave behind the vain finery, flee deceptive pleasures: you are guilty if you do not do so."[22]

However, it would be mistaken to view the rewriting of the female body and female knowledge in terms of domesticity as strictly the enterprise of men. On the contrary, as I will show, many women writers published widely read household manuals that substituted a rhetoric of empowerment and emulation for one of coercion and enjoined women to the duties and pleasures of new family life. Still, in both styles of writing the body of alluring surfaces, sociality, and sexual pleasure was exchanged for the highly gendered body of biology on the one hand and sentiment and interiority on the other. Indeed, by the end of the eighteenth century, what Thomas Laqueur has called a "biology of incommensurability" prevailed in European medical theories of human reproduction: absolute biological difference founded the distinction between genders, replacing one based on degrees of difference relative to a unitary (male) model.[23] This model of absolute difference was to play off a second, contradictory one positing a common liberal subjectivity—inner psychological qualities fostered by domesticity—available to men and women alike. The tension between the two proved to be actually a productive one: it set in motion endless cultural narratives whereby women, by virtue of their difference, would embody the new subjectivity and make it desirable to men. This will be the fundamental narrative of Bernardin de Saint-Pierre's *Paul et Virginie*.

By the early nineteenth century the Old Regime body had lost so much ground in medical discourse that the earlier theories that had actually made female orgasm a precondition of fertilization were dropped and the opposite theory gained favor. Female pleasure as such was finally considered suspect by the *Dictionnaire des sciences médicales* (1812–22): "A woman is not modest whose heart has been corrupted by lustful desires, even should she be pure of body. However, she who has experienced the approaches of a man without her heart's participation in lust remains chaste."[24]

In this context the family households replete with servants, retainers, and kin characteristic of aristocratic families (and even those of the old urban bourgeoisie) would no longer do. Now, its replacement, the simple conjugal family organized around intimacy and children, had as its novelty the collapsing of sexuality and the family household into one and the same entity. Up till the mid-eighteenth century the two had been separate, giving rise to three institutions whose goal was to take care of those who were victims of traditional marital strategies: convents for single women, foundling hospitals for illegitimate children, and brothels (*maisons closes*) for single men.[25] Such was the high cost of Old Regime practices, which critics claimed valued men and women (particularly women) less for "themselves" (that is, for their individual qualities and sentiments, their vocation as mothers and fathers) than in terms of political alliance, continuance of the line, preservation of landed property, and physical pleasure.[26] The new discourses related sexual practices back to the imperatives of reproduction, which were realized most completely in the intimacy of companionate marriage. From this perspective nothing was more utilitarian for the general population than the legitimate love-match; nothing more sentimental than the imperative to bear children. Feeling became the mainstay of reproductive sex, and pleasure less so. We shall see that, as a consequence, the vagaries of desire and inner life fell under new scrutiny by domestic discipline; from then on nonreproductive practices were cast as pathological and devoid of sentiment.

The French Revolution: Questions of Gender and Class

Familial discourses, like family household history, were implicated in and overdetermined by (among other things) political history. No single event in the period 1750 to 1910 better crystallized familial discourses than the French Revolution. To begin with, the taking of the Bastille (where prisoners, ordered detained at their relatives' request by the infamous *lettres de cachet*, were held) was as much a revolt against state power in the service of arbitrary alliance authority as against despotic royal power; and, significantly, the paternal image of royal power was replaced by the female images, on the one hand, of the revolutionary *nation, patrie,* and *liberté* bearing the Phrygian bonnet of the enfranchised slave and, on the other, of the *République* (often portrayed as a nursing mother).[27] More generally the familial paradigm in its broadest implications furnished the discursive and ideological terrain upon which—ironically enough—*both* revolutionaries and counterrevolutionaries vindicated their respective positions during those turbulent years. Of 36 revolutionary festivals which Robespierre decreed on May 17, 1794, 8 fall within the confines of familial discourse. They were devoted to "*l'Amour,*" "*la Foi conjugale,*" "*l'Amour paternel,*" "*la Tendresse maternelle,*" "*la Piété filiale,*" "*l'Enfance,*" "*nos Aïeux,*" and "*la Pudeur.*"[28] A profoundly moralized political discourse was operative at this time, and it was in no small part due to the familial idiom already widespread in political and intellectual circles. Saint-Just's speeches overflow with Rousseauist visions of postrevolutionary society, which, in its combination of small agrarian property with austere family life safely removed from the old corrupting sociality, reproduces the utopia of physiocratic familialism:

> We offered you the happiness of virtue, of comfortable and modest living; we offered you the happiness born of the enjoyment of basic necessities without superfluity; we offered you as happiness hatred of tyranny, the pleasure of a cabin and of a fertile field cultivated by your hands. We offered the people the happiness of a life of freedom and tranquillity and of peaceful enjoyment of the fruits and customs [*moeurs*] of the Revolution; the happiness of returning to the nation, to morality, and of founding a Republic. It is the people that makes the Republic by the simplicity of its morals. . . . The happiness that we offered you does not belong to corrupted peoples . . . a plow, a hut safe from taxation, and a family safe from the highwayman's lust—that is happiness.[29]

Here, the new domesticity has found its way into a renewed peasant society of independent small producers.

Now, while "family" may have served as a common idiom for revolutionaries and counterrevolutionaries alike, what the two camps meant by the term was at first vastly different. Indeed, like the female body itself, the family household was the object of intense semantic struggle at this time and validated opposing political ideologies. Thus it is worth remembering that the French Revolution introduced important reforms in legislation governing families and sexuality. In the name of companionate marriage, democratic inheritance practices, and better management of the population, male primogeniture was abolished, divorce established (even allowing for the dissolution of marriages on grounds of incompatibility), paternity suits instituted, and celibacy for clergy no longer required. Moreover, a gendered bourgeois public sphere was in the making, which enfranchised men as political actors whose families were to be overseen by women in their now strictly private roles as mothers and wives. These new gendered arrangements constituted a break from Old Regime practices, some of which were less patriarchal than commonly believed. For example, revolutionary electoral law dictated that only *male* heads of households should vote, which was contrary to peasant custom in many regions. In fact, many widows defied the new ordinances and continued joining electoral bodies and, in the Basque region, eldest daughters, in accordance with local custom, still ruled over their husbands and younger siblings and voted for their families on election day.[30] The republicans' and revolutionaries' emphasis on domesticity, autonomous household life, and the private, gendered body conflicted with the Old Regime sense of vertical networks of hierarchical relations, dependencies, and clienteleships. When reactionary writers chose their discursive arms they naturally refurbished the old patriarchal metaphors of the still vigorous corporate idiom. Louis XVI's decapitation was likened to a parricide, the worst conceivable crime for the social imagination of the period.[31] This cliché was to be standard fare in ultra discourse during the Restoration and the July Monarchy. One of Balzac's aristocratic characters states, "In cutting off Louis XVI's head, the Revolution cut off the head of all family fathers. . . . Every country that does not take paternal authority as its basis is without an assured existence."[32] As might be expected, counterrevolutionary ideologues imagined the (violated) social order in terms of a pyramid of homologous relations. For example, the family-state analogy was a central tenet of Abbé du Voisin's *Défense de l'ordre social contre les principes de la Révolution française* [Defense of the social order against the principles of the French Revolution] (published in 1798): "Nature herself submits woman to man, children to parents, the imprudence of youth to the experience of elders. All men are born in a state of dependence. Obedience is the necessity more than the duty of the early years. Families, like political societies, essentially presuppose authority and submission."[33] The legitimist Bonald followed suit during the Restoration. In the eyes of this prolific writer the state and the family were mirror images of each other. The state "sees and must see man only within the family, just as it sees the family only within the state; in its eyes there is no other individual than the family."[34]

The discursive struggle over "family" continued long past the revolutionary period. Indeed, it would be fair to say that the French Revolution was refought repeatedly in familial discourse throughout the nineteenth century in all sorts of publications from political treatises to novels. However, after 1830 or thereabouts the lines between liberal and conservative writings began to blur: the liberal call for social order and stability adopted the vocabulary of feudal nostalgia (the domestic family as a social cell of "natural" relations of dependency); meanwhile, the legitimists' own literature on the family was colonized by the imperatives of companionate marriage, intimacy, and child care, and accordingly discarded the aristocratic body completely. Where did that body go? In a sense, as we shall see, in the nineteenth century the Old Regime noble body was gradually transferred down to the lower classes in the gendered form of the body of the working woman or *ouvrière*, the demi-mondaine, and the prostitute, whose bodies signified scandalous sociality and pleasure.[35]

The retirement of women from public politics was forced upon them by the Revolutionary Government in 1793. The action brutally put a halt to women's revolutionary activities that had attracted attention, from the March on Versailles (October 5, 1789) to the publication of The Declaration of the Rights of Woman in 1791 to the founding in February 1793 of the Society of Revolutionary Republican Women by Pauline Léon and Claire Lacombe. Often, women authorized their claim to political subjecthood by virtue of their identities as housewives and mothers but, as Joan Landes has aptly remarked, republican domesticity associated public women with the discredited absolutist public sphere to such a degree as to undermine any feminist demands for political representation.[36]

The Jacobin crackdown came on October 30, 1793. At the time when Robespierre and the Montagnards proclaimed the Revolutionary Government, women's political clubs were dissolved. In November, as part of the continuing repression of the Girondins, Olympe de Gouges and Madame Roland were executed. The grounds for which these two women were sent to the guillotine were not public, political ones (say, Girondin sympathies) but private and domestic. The recoding of Madame Roland's politics in familialist terms is particularly ironic, for she was a well-known apologist of the new domesticity and applied her ideas to her daughter's education. Although while in prison she devoted her time to writing *Mémoires pour ma fille* [Memoirs for my daughter], in the eyes of her judges she was a *mauvaise mère*. The *Moniteur Universel* of November 19, 1793, commented:

> The Roland woman, a great, ambitious wit . . . was a monster in every way. Her disdainful demeanor towards the people and its chosen judges, her proud, headstrong replies, her ironic gaiety and the assurance she paraded about on the way from the courthouse to Revolution Square prove that no painful memory preoccupied her thoughts. However, she was a mother, yet she had sacrificed nature in wanting to rise above herself; her desire to be learned induced her to forget the virtues of her sex, and this forgetfulness—always a dangerous one—in the end lead to her death on the scaffold.[37]

Clearly, *as a woman*, Madame Roland could not be condemned for Girondin sympathies; *that* would have transformed her into a man, an entitled political actor; but she could be sentenced to death on account of her political allegiances for having ventured into what was thenceforth constructed as the exclusively male province of advanced learning and public discourse. This was made clear by the *Feuille du Salut Public*, which issued an appeal to French womanhood:

> Women! Do you want to be Republicans? Love, follow, and teach the laws that recall your spouses and children to the exercise of their rights ... be plain in your attire, industrious in your household; never follow popular gatherings with the desire to speak there but with your presence encourage your children; then the motherland will bless you because you will have performed for her what she has the right to expect from you.[38]

Events, however, reserved an ironical twist for Robespierre and his followers. For it was under the very aegis of the celebration of familial virtues and the new domesticity that the Thermidoran reaction overthrew them in July 1794. The "Déclaration des Devoirs annexée à la Constitution de l'an III" [Declaration of duties, annexed to the Constitution of the Year III] proclaimed: "No one is a good citizen if he is not a good son, good father, good brother, good husband."[39] Citizenship was not to be for women under the new regime. In fact, the following May 23, 1795, the exclusion of women from the public arena was completed when the government prohibited them from attending political gatherings. The National Convention decreed

> that all women will retire to their respective homes until new orders are given. Those who are found on the street one hour after the posting of this decree in gatherings of greater than five people will be dispersed by armed force and placed under arrest until public calm has been restored in Paris.[40]

The New Dispensation

In the opening pages of her widely read *L'Education progressive ou étude du cours de la vie* [Progressive education or study of life's course] (1834) Albertine Necker de Sassure, a Swiss aristocrat, proclaimed the goal of her book:

> Above all it is the history of the soul that I propose to outline, a history that is not so different in divers individuals as the history of their fate considered externally, but more important for each one of them. *Revolutions that take place within us are for us the true events.* Not only does our inner contentment depend on the state of our hearts but also the sequel of deeds that our need to satisfy our penchants may bring about.[41]

The history that counts is less the exterior one of the world of politics and public life than those events that constitute the "history of the soul." This requires nothing less than a rewriting by women themselves of the aristocratic body in terms of a different body, one that, much like the "family" itself, is now the haven of a powerful new interiority, free of "an impure alloy of personality,"[42] that is, of the theatrical play of rank and name in absolutist representation.

Necker de Sassure's treatise displays the extent to which familial discourse had colonized the French-speaking aristocracies in the fifty years that followed the French Revolution. While recalcitrant elements of the high nobility successfully held at bay the discursive onslaughts of domesticity during the period 1789 to 1815, the trials many noblewomen underwent (many while in exile were forced to work for a living and take care of their children) disrupted the ritual affirmations of aristocratic selfhood; later on during the Restoration these women finally rejected their former social and sexual independence—which they held responsible for the downfall of the Old Regime—and embraced the bourgeois familial ideal.[43] More profound than the fashionable infatuation with breast-feeding that swept through upper-class households under the influence of Rousseau, this was something of a conversion, and fit well into a general discursive strategy of a class under political pressure. Margaret Darrow claims that in some cases it was a conscious, well-timed political act:

> The aristocracy appropriated domesticity as a class ideal in an effort to answer middle-class criticism of the nobility and, consequently, to forestall the political triumph of the bourgeoisie during the Restoration. Domesticity, along with royalism and clericalism, was fundamental to the aristocracy's program for class preservation and political survival.[44]

While the political maneuver failed, the adoption of domesticity was to have lasting effects. It coincided with, on the one hand, a large number of religious conversions by many of the most worldly noblewomen of the old court, some of whom went on to publicize their example in books and memoirs, and, on the other, the decline of the power of salon society. With the July Revolution and the subsequent exile of the great families to the provinces further restriction of high noblewomen's power ensued. Indicative of the inroads made by the new familial culture among the high nobility by the end of the Restoration is the fact that its *men* in the high chamber refused in 1827 to restore the law of male primogeniture for noble families, much to Prime Minister Villèle's disappointment.

After the French Revolution, noble and bourgeois women returned to the field of discourse not as political actors or as brokers of networks of influence and sociality but as mothers; this role authorized their production of a deluge of education manuals and treatises. Therein, they elaborated what was to become the figure of the *mère-éducatrice* or *mère-institutrice* (mother-educator or governess), whose new responsibilities for the education of children of both sexes struck something of a compromise between her former public power in the political and intellectual world and her present confinement to the household and its chores.[45] This entailed in turn a reorganization of the private rooms belonging to the mistress of the household: the boudoirs had to go to make room for a small office to be used for overseeing daily activities and chores:

> You should have, if possible, near your bedroom and in the same [southern] exposure, a private study that is plain and commodious. *Boudoirs*, whose mere name indicates their ridiculousness and which are only objects of luxury and frivolity, can be of no use to the woman who, like you, wishes to devote herself to governing her house for the happiness of her husband and children. It is upon their happiness that her own depends. Set up your government in a place where you will not be disturbed. This small cubbyhole should be cleaned and made ready also for when you get up.[46]

The new literature reproduced in its essentials eighteenth-century familial discourse of demographers, educators, physicians, political economists, and philosophes—but with a difference. The manuals were punctuated with backward glances at the Old Regime and the Revolution and had a wider readership consisting of many newly arrived bourgeois households. For example, Natalie de Lajolais wrote in her *Education pratique des femmes. Manuel à l'usage des mères de famille et des institutrices* [Practical education of women: Manual for the use of mothers of families and governesses] (1841), which received a prize from the French Academy, "One will notice, for example, that what women have lost in the way of social influence since the reign of seduction, intrigue, and frivolity has vanished, they are called on to acquire in private life through the influence of real merit."[47] Women's power no longer resides, as before, in the spectacular Old Regime female body of surfaces bearing a name in the network of caste, kin, and clienteles, but rather in the moral, psychological, and rational qualities of the retired *femme d'intérieur* (housewife). Moreover, in education and home economics manuals of the day household practices founded upon feminine interiority virtually supplant male primogeniture and political marriages as the means to preserve the patrimony. If the newlywed "neglects or disdains to fulfill her domestic responsibilities," contends Lajolais, "this money will dissipate into thin air and will be for the children only a cruel disappointment."[48] Imagine the potential appeal this model of the housewife might have to a broad readership: through practice and education seemingly *any* woman could acquire the habits of mind and practical expertise necessary for organizing and maintaining a proper "middle-class" household.

In this context what is the fate of the woman of leisure? Here we follow the same logic but in reverse order. By virtue of her lifestyle she violates the ends of the conjugal family household, and her selfish pursuit of pleasure can mean only one thing: it is the sign of a body devoid of any redeeming interiority or inner qualities. She lives the sentient life of an animal. That, at least, is the opinion of Mme de Flesselles, who published *La Jeune mère institutrice* [The young mother-governess] (1830): "The woman of leisure seems, on the contrary, to lead the life of an animal—drinking, eating, sleeping are the three parts into which her life is divided—and when death comes to put an end to her uselessness, she, considered to be a hopeless being by society, is not entitled to be mourned by those for whom she never made a sacrifice."[49] In the end, domestic manuals are quite explicit in proposing a deal to their new readership, an exchange: domestic power for public power. Louis Aimé-Martin, an educator as well as Bernardin de Saint-Pierre's biographer, editor, and successor (he married Bernardin's widow), wrote a highly successful treatise (another recipient of the French Academy's prize) entitled *De l'éducation des mères de famille ou de la civilisation du genre humain par les femmes* [Of the education of mothers of families or of the civilization of humankind by women]. The title could not have been more to the point. He exhorted his readers with a stirring vista: "Oh women! If only you could catch sight of some of the marvels promised by maternal influence, with what noble pride you would enter that career which nature has opened to you for so many centuries! This lies in the power of no one, of no nation, but all you must do is desire it for it to happen."[50]

The widespread publication and consumption of manuals of domesticity were an integral part of the new print culture that benefited from radical changes in the technologies of printing and systems of distribution, which made available at low cost books and daily newspapers to a rapidly expanding reading public.[51] In these manuals the construction of a wide, social readership intersected with and was authorized by the figure of the domestic housewife and mother who, by virtue of not having any professional occupation outside of the family household, was actually thought to embody a new universal positionality, that of humanity itself and of "nature." Speaking of women, Necker de Sassure declared: "Domestic relations play a greater role in their lives and they are thus subject to the influence of natural events. Since they do not take up any particular occupation, since they are neither merchants, soldiers, nor magistrates, in them the human vocation makes its presence felt."[52]

The stability, coherence, and scope of the new print culture can be measured by the fact that Gacon-Dufour's immensely popular *Manuel complet de la maîtresse de maison* [Complete manual for the mistress of the house], first published in 1826, went through successive printings and new editions at the hands of Mme Pariset and Mme Celnart right up through 1913![53] This stability lay in the ability of manuals to construct a readership that cut across class lines by proposing a common domestic model that allowed for significant differences in income and lifestyles.[54] This approach characterizes that rhetoric from very early on. Take, for example, a lengthy treatise published in 1789 by Achille Le Bègue de Prasle and the Abbé C. F. A. Lalauze, *L'Economie rurale et civile, ou moyens les plus économiques d'administrer et de faire valoir ses biens de campagne et de ville* [Country and town economics, or the most economic ways to administer and exploit one's rural and city capital]. They proposed the revolutionary idea of a common set of household practices—"home economics" and its utilitarian calculus of expenditure and savings—for all classes; but it did demand careful negotiation of old discursive obstacles. Thus the authors are at pains to excuse the extended attention given to the vulgar details of household management, which may violate the acceptable registers and conventions of polite, literate discourse familiar to Old Regime elites: "One should expect to find in this work things that are common or, as perhaps some will say, trivial; but that will not at all be a reason for condemning them; they are not generally known."[55]

In their call for readers of all classes (but especially the rich) to abandon Old Regime customs of excessive prodigality the authors take equal care to distinguish the new concept of *thrift* from the traditionally despised practice of *avarice*:

> To prefer what is useful to that which is agreeable, the more useful to that which is less so, is to use carefully and to save without avarice. This economics—synonymous with or equivalent to household and savings—is equally necessary to the poor in order to help them escape from poverty and to the well-off or wealthy in order to conserve their fortunes. *Economics is the source of independence and liberality*; however, one senses that differences in stations [*états*] will make a great difference in the extent to which this economizing must be carried out.[56]

The broad social appeal cannot mask, however, other major discursive shifts. While Le Bègue and Lalauze continue to address the husband as household head in accordance with Old Regime patriarchy, the bulk of their remarks are destined for the wife on whose acts now the success of household management depends (see part I, chapter 2, "Necessité d'une maîtresse de maison pour l'économie domestique" [Necessity of a mistress of the house for domestic economy]); moreover, the manual stresses that the new methods will ensure domestic harmony. Finally, and most important, the text introduces a new notion of honor and reputation that quietly supplants the aristocratic one:

> We will show that domestic economics is not only useful but that it will still do credit to him who through service, good actions, and through expenditures of a decent luxury, deserves the reputation of good husband, good spouse, good citizen almost always awarded him who, besides making his necessary expenditures, makes others out of philanthropy or friendship.[57]

A "decent luxury" sounds like a call for a more moderate practice of noble sumptuary display, but by the end of the sentence the modest theatricality turns into a solidly bourgeois sense of reputation based on family and favorable community opinion. Here the aristocratic body of blood, honor, pleasure, and privilege gives way to the virtuous body nurtured by regulated family life and democratic social obligations, the basis of an entirely new imagined community. And from behind the good husband, father, and citizen will emerge the figure of the housewife upon whom everything will depend.

Interiors: Bodies and Households

The reorganized household outlined in these manuals presupposed long periods of intimacy between mothers and children of both sexes in which the quality of care was differently conceived from that which had been practiced before.[58] Mothers were urged to anticipate the child's minutest needs through constant observation and close supervision. Such care was psychologically demanding of both mothers and children. Instilled with a sense of self-discipline and duty, children were punished not for the consequences of their acts but for their supposed motives. This opened up an infinite field of observation and interpretation, and the power to read it lay in the mother's hands.[59] Here, familial discourse worked to introduce lack of normative behaviors in the heart of the most intimate relationship of family life. There, too, "family" was endangered. Detailed, intense surveillance was called for, particularly regarding threats to the children's development, such as servants. The *Bibliothèque des propriétaires ou Journal d'Economie rurale et domestique* [Library of property owners or journal of rural and domestic economics], in its July 1803 issue, enjoined mothers to constant vigilance, however burdensome:

> This obligation will doubtless seem to more than one mother to be an irritating constraint. However, one really deserves the title of mother only when one religiously fulfills one's duties; and although one's duties are great, numerous, and tedious, how much more important is the success of a good education? Can one pay too high a price for it? The active surveillance, indefatigable perseverance, the renunciation of oneself that the cares of raising children [*éducation*] require of a mother will not prevent her at all from overseeing the servants and from inspiring in her children benevolent feelings towards them.[60]

Pariset and Celnart repeated the same litany fifty years later in their new edition of Gacon-Dufour's *Manuel complet*: "We ask you above all to know how to listen and look. . . . Be concerned by what lies close by you and even far away." The practices of literacy—especially reading—and private thinking are part and parcel of the new surveillance: "Reading, observing, and thinking will thus figure among your most cherished preoccupations."[61] Finally, disciplinary practices were linked to an increasingly grim, Malthusian vision of what awaited children outside the family in the public sphere:

> What children want least to understand is restraint. They imagine that they are put in this world only to amuse and enjoy themselves freely. Now, since life is in perpetual contrast with this assumption, which is tinged with ignorance and naïveté, it is very important to render youth early on subservient to discipline and to keep it obedient and morally speaking on tenterhooks.[62]

What preoccupied commentators during the Restoration and the July Monarchy was no longer demographers' fear of a population decline; by then it was clear the French population was expanding at a steady pace. Rather, the idea gained favor that quality child care together with the necessity of amassing and conserving family fortunes required fewer offspring. Jean-Baptiste Say in his *Cours d'économie politique* [Course on political economy] (1828) expressed well the new reigning Malthusianism: "The institutions most favorable to the happiness of humanity are those that tend to multiply capital. It is thus advisable to encourage men to save money rather than to have children."[63] Domestic order was the byword. Lajolais exclaimed: "Order in its full development is a moral virtue upon which family well-being is based. It contributes to building a fortune and preserving it. On the contrary, disorder is like an inner canker that brings on every sickness. If one offers the guarantee of peace and happiness, the other leads to shame and degradation."[64] This entailed the now-familiar modern preoccupation with incessant cleaning. For Gacon-Dufour a woman's work was never done: "It is not enough to clean house every day, that is to say, to sweep everywhere, to dust and polish various pieces of furniture; every week, every month, every year must have its particular cleaning."[65] And like household, like body: as with daily dusting, the mother's personal hygiene and attire was a matter of *conservation* and *preservation*. Quoting Pariset, Gacon-Dufour stated:

> "It is with habits as with everything else," says Madame Pariset in her *Lettres sur l'Economie domestique* [Letters on domestic economics], "it is order [*arrangement*] and tidiness [*propreté*] that preserve everthing." . . . The mistress of the house must always be meticulously tidy and clean with respect to herself [*d'une propreté minutieuse sur elle-même*]. In the morning when she is busy with household duties, over which she must always keep a close watch, she will be plainly but always appropriately and neatly [*proprement*] attired.[66]

According to Erna Olafson Hellerstein, within the parameters of this paradigm, "women were healthiest in response, in the shadow of domestic duties, affections, and interests. The contained and regulated female body served ultimately as a symbol of the healthy social order."[67]

Familial discourse accelerated the reorganization of household architecture among the elites that began in the seventeenth century. An evolution started away from the general-purpose room toward a new functional space: corridors, dining rooms, reception rooms, and bedrooms developed.[68] The new literature of family encouraged the withdrawal of families from Old Regime sociability, which did not observe sharp distinctions between public and private space or between family members on the one hand and servants, friends, and corporate colleagues on the other. Indeed, strictly speaking, the intelligibility of the "family" dates from the large-scale adoption of the normative family household in the nineteenth century. Until then, family households were dominated by the imperatives of kinship and clientele networks among the nobility, the constraints of professional milieus among the middle classes and artisans, and the exigencies of village and kinship organizations among the peasants.

Familial discourse heavily promoted the reorganization of the private sphere, but its effects were not immediately felt in the early nineteenth century, even among the established bourgeoisie. Bonnie Smith has recounted how wives of industrialists and merchants continued to work in productive activity (as bookkeepers, store managers, or even overseers in spinning mills) and showed little interest in either the Catholic religion (this was often the case in the presumably Catholic department of the Nord) or those activities that later were the only ones allowed women in the public sphere: charity and social philanthropy. Responding to pressure of all kinds, by the 1840s women had dropped their roles in productive work and assumed positions as mothers and educators in a transformed household. It was at that time they began to see themselves as "middle class." Some went very far in the execution of their duties: they ended up transforming domestic space into a veritable cult of reproductive feminine sexuality, replete with rituals, furniture, clothes, and numerous children that signified over and over both women's power as mothers and the very fragility of the restricted private sphere over which they reigned.[69] Bonnie Smith comments:

> The quality of the reproductive experience was described metaphorically by these women. For one thing, it gave them power and domestic

symbolism highlighted the power of women. Full skirts, bodices, huge sleeves gave substance to female claims of importance by increasing their physical size to at least double that of men. Women wearing hoop skirts, crinolines, bustles, or trains filled the social space and made people aware of their presence. Women were so powerful that sometimes doors could not let them pass; they overflowed the small chairs, cushions, and footstools of mid-century. . . .

Yet objects so thoroughly reflected women that they had to tell of weakness as well as strength. Pictures of the Northern bourgeoise show her dressed in voluminous clothing, but her dress at mid-century had embroidery and tiny tucks in the bodice that give a delicate air to the bulk . . . this emphasis on fragility terminated in the hobble skirt, but throughout the century layers of clothing reduced the importance of the body itself while simultaneously creating mass.[70]

The play of the images of power and vulnerability both authorized the new familial arrangements and required the continual reenactment of "family" in order to safeguard the latter's survival. "Family" became a nonstop performance.

Through the daily practices of family household life, the theater of domesticity endlessly reinscribed the mother's and children's bodies with the signifiers of sentiment, intimacy, and order. Yet it would be mistaken to assume that the skills and inner qualities cultivated in household life stood opposed to those mental and psychological aptitudes required in economic and political activity. There is reason to believe that the links with the outside were never severed, for the "angel of the house" was of necessity trained by her mother, teachers, and domestic economy manuals in the very rationalist principles of organization, work, and time-discipline practiced in the new ateliers in the public sphere. Necker de Sassure was clear about this with respect to children's education:

> In a century where the spirit of commerce and association predominates, exactitude in making appointments and being on time [*l'exactitude à observer les conventions à l'égard des heures*] is a necessity of social life and already is to a child's advantage. The habit of punctuality alone can provide him with a tranquil conscience during his recreation time and can help him move along in his studies with self-assurance.[71]

Domesticity and what ultimately became Taylorism were not strangers in the nineteenth-century bourgeois family household.[72]

Familial Teratology

Literature of various kinds—from manuals of domestic economy, educational treatises, books on household medicine and hygiene to monographs on sexuality, novels, and private diaries—elaborated a new gaze that took as its object the physical and psychological minutiae of daily life in domestic interiors. What predominates in these voluminous writings (with perhaps the exception of manuals of domesticity) are the foils of familialism, or rather, figures who fall outside of authorized familial practices yet remain within their discursive parameters. Here, the process of constructing self and other through discourse takes place *within* the household through the proliferation of "monsters," figures of domestic pathology (social monsters will be dealt with in Chapter 2). Now, Peter Stallybrass and Allon White contend that capitalist society locates "its most powerful symbolic repertoires at the borders, margins, and edges, rather than at the accepted center of the social body."[73] In this view the familial "other," in a necessary return of the repressed, resurfaces at the heart of discourse. I want to argue, on the contrary, that the repeated occurrence of orphans, hysterics, masturbators, and other familial outcasts in familial discourse operates not so much as the return of the repressed in dominant discourse as the promotion of a sociopolitical agenda through the relentless tactic of inventing and defining sexual-social deviance, or, put another way, through the introduction into the social body of *a mobilizing perception of the lack* of normative familial and sexual relations. Hence the title of this section: "familial teratology," or the taxonomic science of domestic monsters. Philippe Fritsch has astutely assessed this process of familial discipline:

> Disciplines . . . are legible not so much in the wording [*énoncés*] of codes and rules as in statements [*énonciation*] of pathology or anomy. They are disciplinary exigencies that are figured negatively [*en creux*], in the stunned or scandalized fate of anomalies, illnesses, disorders that pre-

suppose an order and norms in the manner in which vice pays tribute to virtue.⁷⁴

The effect is presumably to create a social demand to institute *positively* familial fictions. Indeed, the novel's role in propagating this negative interpretive schema is not negligible: the *familles en miettes* (broken families), suborned from within and without, populate narratives and transmit to readers a familial real that both is and is not. The familial lack creates a goal to be met, posits a necessary operation of supplementarity by state, private, and individual intervention.

These family monsters are so many deformed bodies and desires. The focus of familial discourse on constructing a new gendered, virtuous social body—heterosexual, reproductive, and healthy—entailed a sexualization of both the body and family household relationships. At a time when the domestic family becomes the "truth," the criteria of a new social class (at least in the minds of those who wish to see themselves as "middle class"), so does sexuality, or rather *familialized* sexuality, that is to say, a sexuality framed by the imperatives of the sex/gender system of domesticity. The policing of gendered sexual practices produced a long list of suspect bodies, acts, and desires, beginning with the old bugaboos of the eighteenth-century aristocratic household: unmarried servants and single men and women. The *mise-en-scène* of the fecund bourgeois mother surrounded by unmarried, sexually restrained servants was predicated on the very figures of wanton, unreproductive sexuality presumably relegated to the street, to the public sphere. From Rousseau to Freud, the irresponsible peasant wet nurses of the eighteenth century and the governesses of Belle Epoque Europe were to keep families and physicians in a state of watchfulness for 150 years.⁷⁵ More threatening still was the figure of the black wet nurse who, in the colonies, passed on to white Creole babies the "depravities" of race and class:

> This education that is close to nature leaves [the young children] in natural ignorance; however, the vices of Negresses which they ingest along with their milk and the personal whims they tyrannically impose upon the poor slaves introduce therein the whole depravity of society.⁷⁶

Worse, servants' and bachelors' supposedly wasteful sexual practices (concubinage, libertinage, the frequenting of prostitutes) cropped up in other figures in the writings of physicians and educators: the sexualized, masturbating (male) child and young adult. The dissolute bourgeois adolescent prefigured the juvenile delinquent that would dominate juridical-medical literature in the twentieth century. Already in 1760 Doctor Tissot, in his *L'Onanisme, dissertation sur les maladies produites par la masturbation* [Onanism, report on illnesses produced by masturbation], furnished the following portrait. He put together a set of symptoms, an interpretive grid (that reads more like a prognosis) that could be applied to any young male body by parents, guardians, or physicians. The masturbator was racked by

> the weakening of all bodily senses and of all faculties of the soul; the loss of imagination and memory; imbecility; the disdain, shame, disgrace that follow in onanism's wake; all the bodily functions [are] troubled, suspended, painful; long, unfortunate, bizarre, disgusting illnesses; wrenching, forever recurring aches and pains; all the sicknesses of old age in the prime of life; an unfitness for those occupations for which man is born; the humiliating role of being useless to fellow men on earth.[77]

From the utilitarian perspective of political economy, the male bachelor and the masturbator are one and the same. A poor politics of male body flows (to use Donzelot's term) amounts (exactly as in the case of the non-nursing mother) to a poor management of social flows and energies. It is by no means a mere coincidence that the term *onanisme* in its eighteenth-century meaning was applied indifferently to those who refused sexual intercourse (as in the biblical story) or practiced contraception, to masturbators, and to unmarried men.[78] According to numerous writings on the subject, once the hydraulic homeostasis of sperm is disrupted, paleness, loss of appetite, apathy, melancholy, consumption, madness, even death (often through suicide) may ensue. This effeminate, "oriental" dissipation threatened to lay family and society to waste. M. Lallemand, in his treatise *Des pertes séminales involontaires* [Of involuntary losses of semen] (1830), claims, "Masturbation undermines the social body like the establishment of taxes [*tabescens*], for it ravages, with full force, man in the most important period of his life; it prevents, loosens, or destroys conjugal bonds and attacks thereby the family, the essential foundation of society."[79]

The stakes invested in the disciplining and repression of masturbation enjoined adults to an even closer, more anxious observation of children's bodily and verbal behavior. No detail was devoid of meaning or inconsequential. The minutest element in the child's environment could elicit the desire to masturbate, even in the body of a small baby alone in the cradle:

> The most attentive and enlightened parents feel exempt from having to keep watch over the actions of their children concerning their genital organs until they notice signs which announce a new evolution; there are few physicians who are inclined to suspect bad habits before this period. This is an error one must guard against: a host of causes may give birth much sooner to abuses which are all the more dangerous that one suspects them least. The cradle of a nursling is not even free from such dangers.[80]

Translated into practice, it is not difficult to imagine how the loving gaze of parent or guardian could initiate exchanges with the child in which the play of watchful concern and resisting response becomes a serious game of solicitation and repression, whereby the child's body would be written with the script of the prospective finality of reproduction that would restrict the play of bodily pleasure, desire, and sanction to the genitals alone.

Constructing the Homosexual Threat

Closely related in the discourse of sexuality to the figure of the masturbating child or adolescent stood that of the homosexual, particularly that of the male "sodomite," "invert," or "pederast" (the term "homosexual" did not enter the French language until 1907, whereas the term "lesbian" in its modern sense was found as early as 1867). Along with female and male hysterics, their bodies constituted privileged targets of the new sciences of psychiatry and hereditary biology. This was all the more the case since homosexual acts were *not* considered crimes by French law (until the Vichy regime in 1940) unless violence or a minor were involved.[81] Much like prostitutes, homosexual men and women were "studied" by those disciplinary sciences forming part of the informal configuration of knowledges attached to public hygiene and legal medicine. The literature on homosexuality grew toward the end of the July Monarchy, and especially after Louis Napoleon's coup d'état in 1851. The social threat posed by criminals and the "dangerous classes" was "homosexualized" in legal and medical treatises such as Lauvergne's *Les Forçats* [On convicts] (1841) and Tardieu's *Etude médico-légale sur les attentats aux moeurs* [Legal-medical study of offenses against public morals] (1857) and in novels such as Balzac's *Splendeurs et misères des courtisanes* [Splendors and miseries of courtesans] (1847).

The discursive link between masturbation and homosexuality was a pervasive and simple one: the former led to the latter in both sexes. The same surveillance of children was in order, especially in "nervous" families. In the chapter entitled "Education et hygiène sexuelles" of his book *L'Instinct sexuel. Evolution et dissolution* [The sexual urge: How it grows and wanes], Charles Féré wrote:

> If surveillance of the arousal of the sexual urge is indispensable in normal subjects, it is even more urgent in subjects who belong to nervous families, especially if there has already been a manifestation of psychosexual anomalies. One must not take lightly homosexual tendencies concerning games and clothing nor other strange behavior that can be tied to sexual anomaly. One must oppose as early as possible the development of these tendencies in order to resist the birth of the anomaly which is the more serious for being precocious. The elective sympathies must be watched with the greatest care. The circle of family and friends must be the object of careful selection: *often a single word or contact suffices in order to arouse an idea that will become fixed or obsessive.* Onanism is particularly dangerous in children; it is associated with representations concerning abnormal tendencies and can only fortify them.[82]

Like masturbators, homosexuals hide their secret vices on their person; beneath a proper, tidy exterior lies inevitably a filthy, fetid body. Yet they can no more escape the all-knowing medical gaze than onanists because they display the same unmistakable symptoms. Lauvergne reassures his readers:

> The doubtful sexes give themselves away to the trained gaze of a physician who complains of lapses in conduct that they hide through their silence and forgetfulness. You will scarcely be wrong, when, at first glance, you perceive in a hospital bed a languishing, soft, feminine face (however discourteous it may be) with moist eyes and a peach-fuzz beard [*une figure étiolé, adoucie, féminine, avec l'oeil humide et une barbe en duvet*]. The man's voice is weak, approaches that of a castrato. His gaze is extinguished and without civility. You question him as would a physician and you will not find any great distress but much laziness.[83]

Familial discourse in the nineteenth century framed homophobia in the same terms that underwrote the alarmist literature on contraception, mercenary wet-nursing, and masturbation. Emile Zola concluded a preface he penned for a medical treatise titled *Tares et poisons: Perversion et perversité sexuelles* [Defects and poisons: sexual perversion and perversities], by Dr. Laupts, on a familiar note: "All that concerns sex concerns society. An inverted man or woman is a disrupter of the family, nature, humanity. Man and woman are on earth only to make children, and they kill life the day they no longer do what is necessary to create it."[84] From this perspective cunnilingus and fellatio between men and women were likened, by virtue of their consequences, to homosexual lovemaking.[85] Other presumed causes of homosexual practices that writers advanced, especially toward the end of the century, were degenerative biology, cultural decadence, and, in middle-class women, female education and professional ambition, that is to say, women's emancipation. The physician Julien Chevalier warned:

> This point does not require stressing: through professional autonomy and talent, women have come to manage by themselves; they have emancipated themselves from the tutelage and protection of men; they have freed themselves from all subjection; they have won [the possibility] of disposing of themselves freely. That is not all; after social emancipation they desire equality before the law and claim political rights, civil personhood, the right to vote, to hold office, and to be civil servants,

etc. . . . Let us put it down this way: women do more than emancipate themselves, they are becoming masculinized. . . . In foregoing the protection of men and managing by themselves, they will soon forego the love of men.[86]

Chevalier's allusion to a change in gender brings us back to a master trope of familial discourse and the corresponding concepts of sexuality and subjectivity: you *are* your desire and sexual orientation; they are derived from your gender and your gender stems from your biological "sex." Indeed, Krafft-Ebing, a fervent admirer of Zola's, wrote:

> After the attainment of complete sexual development, among the most constant elements of self-consciousness in the individual are the knowledge of representing *a definite sexual personality and the consciousness of desire*, during the period of physiological activity of the reproductive organs (production of semen and ova), *to perform sexual acts corresponding with that sexual personality,—acts which, consciously or unconsciously, have a procreative purpose.* . . .
> If sexual development is normal and undisturbed, *a definite character, corresponding with the sex, is developed*. Certain well-defined inclinations and reactions in intercourse with persons of the opposite sex arise; and it is psychologically worthy of note with what relative rapidity each individual psychical type corresponding with the sex is evolved.[87]

And Chevalier argued that complications regarding gender identity can be anticipated at birth by those guardians of the gendered body, obstetricians, who should take greater care in identifying the sex of the newborn; he proposed even a third category—the *sexe douteux*—that would be the object of early intervention and care.[88] Thus the only true homosexuals for Laupts and Krafft-Ebing are those "born that way," with effeminate or masculine bodies that match their desire for the same sex. Ultimately, in this scheme of things, there are only two sexes and only opposites can attract. As a consequence, a true male homosexual has a woman's body and loves a virile man, who in turn is fundamentally heterosexual and for whom the love affair is merely a passing fancy with yet another woman.[89] Such is the functioning of what Judith Butler terms the "heterosexual matrix."⁹⁰ This is what the burgeoning literature of sexology and psychiatry in the nineteenth century inscribes again and again in the social body by virtue of case studies of "deviant" behavior. On the one hand, behind all sexual pathology lie homosexual desire and transsexual bodies (witness the title to Krafft-Ebing's book, *Psychopathia Sexualis: With Especial Reference to the Antipathic* [read homosexual] *Instinct*); on the other, homosexual desire and practices are rewritten in terms of a fundamental *heterosexual* drive.

Hysteria and the Discursivity of Gender

The proliferation of the discourse of "deviance" on homosexuality in the middle to late nineteenth century that recast the Old Regime body as gendered, reproductive, and healthy was part of what Henry Abelove calls the invention of the discourse of heterosexuality.⁹¹ Moreover, in these verbal practices the referral of desire back to gender identity and the imperatives of biological reproduction marked the rhetorical moment where the discourses of *interiority* and *utility* were once again joined. The story told by biology was to map the field of desire. However, as with the figures of homosexual men and lesbian women, this junction of desires and bodies remains problematic and uncertain in the hysterical body, be it female or male. In both cases the play of lack of normative identities and behaviors becomes extremely fluid and shifting, threatening to erupt in the smallest details of the body and desire. This is one consequence of the putting into discourse of gender as endangered: a "true" heterosexual man or woman will be hard to find. And just as the cultural construction of homosexuality in the sex/gender system produces "sex" and "heterosexuality" as "nature," so too does the figure of hysterical desire discursively inscribe the heterosexual, gendered body as the "natural" norm.⁹²

What is striking is how gender operates in medical treatises on hysteria in the nineteenth century. Up until midcentury, common medical wisdom associated hysteria with women almost exclusively and repeatedly located its seat in female reproductive biology, in the "disorders" of the uterus.⁹³ Now in 1859, P. Briquet in his *Traité clinique et thérapeutique de l'hystérie* [Clinical and therapeutic treatise on hysteria] took a liberal view of the issue. Following Philippe Pinel, who long before had claimed that neuroses were less cases of physical afflictions than of mental ("moral") alienation,[94] Briquet detached hysteria from the uterus because (among other things) he asserted that the disorder could affect men as well. Statistically, however, "hysteria is something of the privilege [*l'appanage*] of the female sex."[95] He tied it to a peculiarly feminine sensibility defined by *feeling*:

> I recognized that hysteria is not that shameful illness whose name alone calls to mind for those outside of the medical profession and for many physicians the verse of our great tragic poet [Racine]: "It is Venus entire jealously guarding her prey"; but that, on the contrary, hysteria was due to the existence in women of sentiments more noble and more worthy of admiration, sentiments that they alone can have.[96]

He continues, on women's calling as mother, nurse, and housewife: "The education of children, the consolation of adult men, and thus the care of the old are the responsibility of wives. In order to fulfill this role, which lasts a lifetime, in women force is sacrificed to feeling." Hysteria, then, remains fundamentally a question of sexual difference: "What does such a difference between the sexes signify if not the effect of their providential destiny? Women are meant to feel, and to feel is almost to be hysterical; men, on the contrary, are meant to act and to them belong the drawbacks and consequences of action."[97] And this sexual difference Briquet ultimately founds on the gendered body, not in the reproductive apparatus per se but in what Janet Beizer calls the "metaphorization" of the uterus, the generalization of biological difference to the whole body, to women's oversensitivity to physical sensations in general, unlocated in any set of organs.[98]

I want to argue that it would be mistaken to view Briquet's theory as simply a disguised return to biological difference. The power of his theory is that it redistributes the question of hysteria, biology, and gender in such a fashion as to render gender difference more subtle and flexible (it resides in the discursively amorphous notions of excessive "sensation" and "sensibility") and therefore urgent, for even men can be "hysterical." Something shifted here in the dynamic tension between a medical model of gender underwritten by a "biology of incommensurability" and a model of liberal subjectivity that encompassed men, though it was embodied by women as mothers. It is as if the long work of replacing the body of pleasure and representation by one of sentiment and interiority had gone so far as to make the biological body (to paraphrase Foucault) the prisoner of the hysterical "soul." Here, hypersubjectivity—in the form of hysteria—threatens to undo the distinctions and imperatives of biological difference. In other words, no longer the literal province of women but still "naturally" a female malady, hysteria renders the border between male and female permeable, less secure, and thus in great need of constant policing and inspection. The weaker the discursive differences between men and women, the stronger the solicitation to define, detect, and perhaps control them.

Briquet's theory was adopted and cited by psychiatrists and clinicians from Charcot to Tourette and Féré. This "putting into discourse" of gender through the figure of hysteria (and the figures of "perversion") stands as an instance of the discursivity of gender, the fact that in the nineteenth century gender becomes virtually the dominant trope of difference, and also that "gender" as a founding identity increasingly partook of the fluid and shifting nature of discursivity itself.[99] Indeed, the power of gender was due to its ability *as discourse* to change, evolve, and expand so as to encompass ever more finely gendered subjectivity, readable less on the surface of the body than under the skin and beneath words and gestures, those proliferating signs of sentiment and desire. It is in the field of bodies and signs, in their aches and pains, their fits of apathy and dizziness and bouts of consumption and madness that women (and eventually men) found an authorized avenue for either affirming or challenging the increasingly polarized constructions of gender after midcentury.[100] This struggle was often undertaken in tandem under the solicitous gaze of the psychiatrist or the family physician.[101] Eventually, it seems that hysteria in men, understood as a transgression of their gender identity, became a structuring component of the construction of female hysteria: female hysterics were understood as denying their femininity, refusing to relinquish masculine ambition and desire, rejecting their attraction to men—in short, as being under the sway of homosexual impulses. In this manner the concepts of hysteria and homosexuality cross and merge in a relation of mutual implication in medical literature.

The tension between the biological, gendered body on the one hand and desire and sexual practices on the other proved immensely productive of endless numbers of personal and cultural narratives of "deviance," even of "monstrosity." It is as much through the negative figures of familial teratology (servants, unmarried relatives, masturbating children, homosexuals and lesbians, hysterics) as through the figure of the domestic housewife and well-cared-for children that familial discourse continued to rewrite the social body throughout the nineteenth century. These monsters signified over and over a dangerous lack of "family" and, by implication, called for saving the family and warding off its enemies. As the nineteenth century wore on, however, these threats were increasingly located not only in the infinite recesses of bodies of family members but also outside in the morbid biology of the urban "dangerous classes" and the colonized peoples of the French empire.

~ CHAPTER 2

Museum of Social Horrors

> When it is a question of governing men, it is good to know and use their weaknesses in order to lead them.
>
> —Parent-Duchâtelet, *De la prostitution dans la ville de Paris* (1836)
>
> Virtues abound in the family and good feelings in hearts. We have the wherewithal to fight against the evil which is devouring us.
>
> —François Guizot, *De la démocratie* (1849)

The City and the Colonies

Throughout the nineteenth century, the construction of self and other in familial discourse continued apace, but now targeted spaces, household arrangements, and sexual practices other than just those associated with either the Old Regime nobility or the middle and upper ranks of postrevolutionary France. The new objects of knowledge, fear, and policy were the urban laboring classes and the colonized people of color. They stood as so many spaces to be conquered and managed and bodies to be tamed that otherwise might invade and suborn the new family life that had just been established in France. A social threat was simultaneously "discovered" and recoded as a familial one. In the process, on the one hand "family" and the social order it guaranteed underwent a rearticulation through discourses on the city and the colonies, and on the other, familial discourses scripted those same narratives and stories of otherness in turn. I think it would be fair to say that in the nineteenth century the discourses of domesticity, urban pathology, and colonial disorder operated in a manner that fully implicated them in a reciprocally authorizing relationship. Rhetorically, they ratified and sanctioned each other's constructions and figurations. This is borne out by the intertextual circulation of metaphors and by institutional activities and individual histories. For example, French experts in urban public hygiene and social philanthropists were very eager to play a part in the conquest and domestication of colonial lands and peoples; and nonnormative sexual-familial practices were thought to thrive in the far-flung reaches of the empire.

The discursive links between the city and the colonies can also be read in the solutions devised for the "urban crisis": working from the perspective of a militant pastoralism, some proposed that the plight of the biologically "unfit" urban poor could be resolved by shipping them overseas to set up families in fortified hamlets on "empty lands"; thus, in one stroke, one could transform the objects of social discipline and philanthropy from social enemies into the very agents of colonial settlement and the new domesticity. As this "solution" suggests, the introduction of the *question sociale* (as the social crisis was termed) and colonialism in familial discourse not only involved constructing the laboring classes as dangerous and the colonized as familial barbarians but also entailed a shift in the definition of "family" and the national imagined community based upon it. For familial discourse was at once to situate the urban laboring poor on the margins of the French national community, to extend to them the possibility of gaining entry into it by virtue of their "moralization" (the adoption of new norms of domesticity), and to exclude the colonized who had been forcibly brought under France's imperial control. In this way the model of normative family life was reinscribed with and rebuilt around negative figures of social alterity and sexual-familial pathologies. So, for example, the prostitute and the colonized woman of color entered the home as threat and defining foil of the (white) domestic woman. In discourse and eventually in the political unconscious of the middle and upper classes the latter figure conjured up the former and vice versa. This incorporation of sociopathological others in familial discourse was to prove a shock to the stalwart defenders of the older domesticity, as was the idea that urban workers too could share the same familial values and practices as the middle class and the well-to-do. Finally, I want to suggest that this new turn in the various writings on the "family" rendered the normative family more fragile (placed in jeopardy by the urban and colonized masses) but also more permeable (the poor could adopt its way of life) and thus *more powerful.* Here the will to discourse, knowledge, and power has as its precondition vulnerability and weakness. This dynamic is very much like the one I described in the last chapter for gender: the more tenuous and fragile an identity or norm, the greater the need to police and affirm it and thus the greater the power of that same identity or norm to authorize renewed discursive and institutional action. Here the lack of "family" will reach a new pitch, and then stands as the very enabling condition of familial discourse's power to expand and articulate social relations at home and in the colonies. By the late nineteenth century, the discursive machine for moral panics and social paranoia is in place.

The Pathologies of the City

Once the Revolution and the Empire were past, a new set of concerns arose from below. The common perception was that urban disorder and the growth of workshops compounded the need for social control; this dated from the French Revolution and the Le Chapelier law of 1791 that abolished guilds and work organizations. In this view, the demise of the Old Regime released the laboring classes from the old forms of social constraint and the lines of authority grounded in the paternalist idiom and its attendant analogies (king/people, husband/wife, father/children, master/servant, and master artisan/apprentice). Formerly each corporate block (cities, towns, estates, commercial corporations, guilds, clans, and family households) was held legally responsible to the Crown for its members. Once they were dissolved, anxieties regarding the laboring poor previously excluded from the official structures of the corporate world doubled. Commentators wrote that the "dangerous classes" persisted in wasteful, irregular work and living habits inimical to public order and to the requirements of larger workshops and, later on, factories.[1] The baron Joseph de Gérando, member of the Institute and of the governing board of the Hospices de Paris, claimed in his six-volume philanthropic study, *De la bienfaisance publique* [Of public charity] (1839), "It is incumbent upon modern states to establish good poor laws, as an obligatory consequence of the abolition of slavery, servitude, and guild and town privileges and because of the growth of population, industry, wealth, and luxury."[2] To material and social disorder resulting from the dismantling of Old Regime structures commentators added the specter of mental alienation, of sick minds and desires. H. Girard, in an article published in *Annales médico-psychologiques* in 1846, painted the following tableau of postrevolutionary France in the throes of capitalist competition:

> The movement of ideas and political institutions having unsettled occupations which were immobile and stable, there has been as a result, in addition to a great benefit, the excesses of unrestricted competition and a forgetting of what was good about the old institutions in theory and practice. Lacking any regulator, the present generation, which finds itself in a period of genuine transition and organization, has launched itself in a new career it has created for itself and has encountered new causes of misfortune and destruction. Many minds, overexcited by unbridled ambition, have worn themselves down and perverted themselves in a struggle that exceeds their strength and leads to madness, and they have found in the forgetting of virtue or in insufficient education the cause of their trouble [*accident*]. Other minds, in the grip of necessity, deprived of the protective support of the old guilds, have felt too weak to resist, and discouragement and poverty have induced them to lose their sanity.[3]

Social order was to become more than a question of an economy of material and bodily practices (household budgets and organization, health, wet-nursing, and procreation); it also became, fundamentally, one of interiority and desire. Upon this social psychiatry founded and authorized its practices.[4]

What is striking is that these quotations already contain the fundamental narrative underwriting orthodox modernization theory: political, economic, and social events "occurred" and the state, philanthropists, psychiatrists, what have you, "responded" and rushed to "cure" the modern city of its social pathologies. Social stories like this, recounting the beginnings of welfare policies, are charming by virtue of their simplicity and clarity, and function as powerful narratives of self-justification: first you have the "facts" or "events," then you have the heroic intervention of science and philanthropy— either social or medical—as diagnostician and surgeon. Modernization theory, with its positivist narratives of progress (or in a later disenchanted version, of decline), is just the latest avatar of such thinking. Now, this theory has of late come in for sharp criticism. Let us consider Louis Chevalier's classic *Classes laborieuses, classes dangereuses à Paris pendant la première moitié du dix-neuvième siècle* [Laboring classes and dangerous classes in Paris during the first half of the nineteenth century], a lengthy study of nineteenth-century Paris and its social observers (demographers, public health officers, and novelists). Charles Tilly has pointed out in a notorious review essay how Chevalier replicates the biological metaphor of the diseased social body current in writings on the city at that time and unwittingly reproduces a discourse that stigmatizes collective (especially revolutionary) violence as disorderly, irrational, and deviant in order to distinguish it radically from "orderly political life."[5] That distinction both authorizes the new social sciences (for they now have an object of study, "deviance") and their projects of social control, and delegitimizes popular movements of revolt as issuing from "dangerous," biologically sick classes living on the periphery of the social body. On the contrary, Tilly argues that, upon close inspection, "The violent masses turn out to be those integrated into the setting rather than those at the margins of society."[6]

This raises the question of the extent to which the crisis of postrevolutionary society has been discursively constructed. I think such a hypothesis demands serious consideration. Alain Corbin has published a suggestive study, *The Foul and the Fragrant*, that shows how a vast literature on the "smells" of the city's dwellings and public places transformed these odors into the repellent "stench" of the "crowd" and then finally into something "unhealthy" associated with the poor long before France's urban centers underwent significant demographic and economic expansion in the nineteenth century. What had changed was less the actuality than its perception.[7] François Furet and Joan Scott (echoing Marx) have cautioned historians against adopting any period's historical accounts and categories of self-understanding (such as "people," "nobility," etc.) as the conceptual frames of their own analysis. So too should we analyze the effects of the discourse of social pathologies and its rhetoric of crisis and dissolution.[8]

Take, for example, the inaugural text of *Annales d'hygiène publique et médecine légale* published in 1829 and edited by those men destined to become the most prominent authorities in social pathology: Villermé, Parent-Duchâtelet, and Esquirol, among others.

> Medicine not only has as its object the study and cure of illness, it also has close ties with social organization; sometimes it aids the legislator in the making of laws, often it enlightens the magistrate in their application, and always, along with the state, it looks after the maintenance of public health. Applied in this way to the needs of society, this part of our knowledge constitutes *public hygiene* and *legal medicine*.[9]

What designated objects fell under hygienists' scrutiny? Climate, foodstuffs, sanitary regulations, hospitals, insane asylums, prisons, and cemeteries.[10] Not content with this familiar list of institutions, spaces, and practices, the authors adroitly maneuver this new social science from the marginal location of its initial objects of study to the commanding position of a utilitarian moral discourse that oversees a vast project of social knowledge and engineering:

> However, medicine has before it another future in the moral order. From its investigation of habits, occupations, and the nuances in social position it deduces reflections and counsel which are not inconsequential for the strength and wealth of states. Through its association with philosophy and legislation, it can exert great influence over the march of the human spirit. . . . Misdeeds and crimes are illnesses of society that one must strive to cure, or at least to diminish; and never will the means of cure be more powerful than when they draw their method from revelations concerning physical and intellectual man and when physiology and hygiene lend their illumination to the science of government.[11]

As we shall see, an identical rhetoric will power the extension overseas of the hygienist movement to the far-flung reaches of the colonial empire.[12]

Such a well-formulated project was poised to capitalize on the ruin of older theories and practices of public health discredited by the 1832 cholera epidemic, which claimed 18,000 lives in Paris alone.[13] Later on, the Revolution of 1848 lent further credibility to the hygienists' biological theories of social pathology, for the political upheavals were followed by a new outbreak of cholera in 1849, proof positive in commentators' eyes of the necessary link between social disorder and disease. Indeed, these events led to the passing of the Law Melun of 1850 which granted public health officers legal access to dwellings for the first time.[14] My point is that events such as rural migration to cities, devastating epidemics, or social revolution are not purely external occurrences to which experts simply react but rather constitute occasions that on the one hand are always already framed by discourse, and on the other, may destroy one set of discourses and practices in favor of others.

Domestic Discipline and the "Dangerous Classes"

What looms large in the numerous treatises of legal medicine, social philanthropy, and public hygiene is the burgeoning urban population, the growing number of indigent, poor, homeless, and ill. Single men and women without conventionally conceived families and "floaters" (those without housing) constitute the bulk of the presumably deterritorialized urban masses. The presumed general social crisis was perceived as a crisis of those institutions whose goal was to contain the disruptive forces of the popular classes: these social organizations were simply swamped by the number of cases and inmates. Such institutions were prisons, dispensaries, and the infamous asylums and general hospitals, such as Bicêtre and La Salpêtrière, whose functions largely overlapped to the point that the mad, petty criminals, prostitutes, vagabonds, and unruly minors were indifferently incarcerated in them. Practices of incarceration follow a logic of general equivalence between those outside or on the margins of the familial paradigm (minors and prostitutes) and social outcasts (the insane, criminals, and vagabonds).

The modern city had to put its house in order, as it were. Indeed, the reorganization of urban space was in many ways discursively identical to that of the household. In the chapter of her book titled "De l'ordre et de l'économie" Natalie de Lajolais lauds domestic tidiness in the following fashion: "Moving on from the observation of nature to that of cities, one is struck by the sight of regular streets and well-ordered and properly constructed squares, well-kept yards, a pretty flowerbed, a tidy bedroom, as compared to the sight of these same objects poorly arrranged [*irréguliers*] and in disorder." A tight domestic discipline engenders a new contemplative subject and an austere aesthetics of private and public space: "One who has felt only the impression that order and arrangement afford, were he to be transported in the midst of a jumbled confusion of objects, would feel a real malaise. (That is what happens in the case of filth.)"[15]

What was ordained in household domestic manuals was also enacted in the streets in Paris. At this time in Paris, the spread of arcades and tree-lined public gathering places constituted a new kind of enclosure movement that recuperated squares, passageways, and promenades for the bourgeoisie, in a sense privatizing them.[16] Similarly, *réglementariste* initiatives attempted to clear the streets of prostitutes and, failing that, to restrict street activity as much as possible to the controlled and policed interiors of the officially sanctioned brothels [*maisons de tolérance*].[17] This reorganization of public activities and space in a struggle against the morbid infirmities presumably introduced into the social body by the laboring poor amounted to nothing less than a rearticulation of the imagined national community elaborated at the turn of the century and thereafter. The distinction between public and private (and male and female) became part and parcel of a new process of social mapping whereby the middle groups now constituted themselves through discourses and the practices of the new social sciences and philanthropy as middle class over against the urban laboring classes. The focus on the pathologies of the city once again inscribed Paris, the metropolitan capital, as that imagined location for the forging and articulation of a new national identity along the lines of a modified discourse of domesticity. As Lajolais's words suggest, orderly domesticity began to be conceptualized in tandem with militant ideas about other spaces and practices that lay outside its immediate horizon. But it would be mistaken, I think, to see this semiotic work as the simple colonization of the public sphere and of laboring classes' households by a prior familial discourse dating from the Empire and the Restoration. Indeed, as I stated in the opening pages of the present chapter, I want to argue that the prospect of domesticating the social created a new sense not only of (urban) public space and social class but also of domesticity and the private sphere. By colonizing the "outside," familial discourse itself underwent an internal change of its own in which the most private recesses of "family" were deeply marked in discourse by references to its spatial and social other. In a sense, the price of an expanding, conquering familialism will be a greater vulnerability to the "outside." I will explore the paradoxical mechanisms of this discursive dynamic most fully in Chapter 4, which focuses on Eugene Sue's *Les Mystères de Paris* (1841–42), the most important serial novel of nineteenth-century France.

In these mechanisms lie the discursive workings of the "social" itself, or the sphere of the modern welfare state understood as that curious domain, first outlined by Jürgen Habermas and Jacques Donzelot, which stands between the "state" and "civil society," between the public and private spheres. It is the terrain where the family and its "outside" intersect and overlap to such a degree that to speak of the autonomy of either term becomes meaningless.[18] However, I differ from Donzelot's account of the social insofar as, in my view, the rise of the social is not the death of the family or its dissolution, for in my terms "family" never did exist independently or prior to its "outside" (be that the state, the street, the world of commerce and politics, the court, and so on). Only now, in the new literature of the social sciences and philanthropy, familial discourse turns on both the *distinction between* and the *proximity of* the new normative family and the social pathologies that surround it. Less a "fall" of the family into the social (though that was felt to be very much the case by earlier proponents of familial discourse), the new discursive configuration operates as a powerful articulation of "family" in the field of social relations. That is to say, domesticity and urban pathology became mutually determining concepts and tropes. The domestication of the "dangerous classes" was an ambitious goal that entailed many and varied strategies. An integral part of this campaign were the Catholic charities and liberal philanthropic societies, whose numbers expanded greatly. They sought to promote Christian marriage and morals (the Société Saint François Régis, the Société des Amis de l'Enfance, and the Société Saint Vincent de Paul), child care, better private hygiene in order to privatize scandalously public poverty; more especially they tried to break laboring classes' sociality and solidarity (that flourished in cabarets, clubs, and the street) by tying household members to their private lodgings and instilling habits of economic discipline (a morality of savings). New low-income housing (with differentiated interiors that virtually eliminated any social, non-familial space for visitors) were designed (though rarely built before the end of the century), and frequent visits by *dames patronnesses* and other private citizens who dispensed both financial support and advice to households were the order of the day.[19] This watchful observation took on a medico-hygienic coloring and created the means for public and private authorities to intervene in these households in the name of "objective" norms. Meanwhile, if school served to spread middle-class norms of health and education, it also was reorganized into a specular image of the family as teachers reproduced the intense care and attention that education manuals had advised parents to practice at home.[20]

One of the chief weapons favored by commentators was the dissemination of literacy and reading among the working poor. For them written discourse was extremely important. De Gérando contended that manuals of domesticity were among the best presents that one could make to the poor: "A good manual of popular domestic economy would be one of the most precious gifts that could be made to the laboring class. The working man [*l'homme de travail*], when he lives from day to day without plans, rules, and calculation, almost without fail prepares his own distress. To have no care but for the present moment is the way to lose the future."[21] Moreover, in his view, the encouragement of reading would contribute mightily to the endless task of breaking old, corrupting lines of solidarity and social relations among workers. Periods of leisure in isolation with a good book would exert a positive moral influence over individuals and would have the beneficial effect of returning them to the workplace refreshed and ready to submit to the rigors and discipline of labor:

> Properly selected reading, far from diverting [the worker] from the painful labors which fill up the course of his day, would serve to refresh him agreeably and would dispose him to return to them with renewed ardor. Experience has proven this: sequestered by various obstacles from social commerce and deprived of relations apt to enlighten his mind and to purify his tastes while elevating his soul, he would find in a good book a companion and friend which would replace to his advantage relations of little profit.[22]

Family sentiment cultivated through reading was meant to serve as the basis of healthy mores among workers.[23] In a very concrete manner, de Gérando is proposing the insertion of the laboring classes into the new imagined community of print culture in which isolated individuals' sense of selfhood and collective existence is mediated by new *written texts and narratives* embodying the biopolitical norms of domesticity.[24] The moralization of the poor involved the highest political stakes. Not surprisingly, François Guizot, Louis-Philippe's prime minister, whose Law Guizot of 1833 had instituted the first public primary schools in France,[25] interpreted the 1848 Revolution that deposed him and his king through the familialist lens. While living in exile he published a treatise in January of 1849 in which he claimed that only the domestic family and the feelings it nourishes stood as the last defense against the political instability and anarchy stemming from pathological urban life:

> Our great cities, their hustle and bustle of business and pleasure, and the temptations and disturbances that they spread ceaselessly, would soon throw society in its entirety into a state of ferment and deplorable laxity if domestic life everywhere present throughout the territory, its calm activity, its permanent interests, and its immutable ties did not oppose this peril with solid barriers. . . . It is infinitely important to

society that these dispositions—I would willingly say these affectionate passions of men's hearts—have their assured sphere in which they may freely deploy themselves and whence sometimes through several beautiful examples they may make their presence felt in that political sphere where they so rarely appear. It is in the midst of domestic life and through family affections that this social goal is met.[26]

Throughout the nineteenth century lack of "family" (i.e., "broken" or "disorderly" homes) was considered constitutive of the urban poor and as rendering them "dangerous" to the social order. Maxime Du Camp was to give this trope its strongest formulation in the following passage, which discusses the "moral" cause of urban poverty:

> The other cause is purely a moral one and derives from the very nature of man, which is improvident, above all in Paris. He lives from hand to mouth with no care for tomorrow; sometimes he spends in a single evening a week's earnings; most of the time, he does not know how to save anything, neither for his clothing, nor for his rent, nor for a possible illness, nor for unforeseen unemployment, nor for his children. The tavern lures him and retains him. His wife, more bent on saving, keeps an eye on him and wants to bring him back but to no avail.[27]

Constituted in discourse as lacking "family" and self-discipline, male workers were relegated to the margins of the family-based French national community. Such an interpretation suggests itself in the remarks made by Villeneuve-Bargemont, prefect of Lille and author of *Economie politique chrétienne* [Christian political economy] (1834). According to him, workers who were recipients of charity automatically lost all claims to paternal authority and to rights of citizenship:

> Indigent workers who solicit or receive charitable help . . . tacitly declare to society that they cannot provide for themselves.
> They ask in reality that others work for them. They place themselves in a veritable state of minority, for these rights exist only when duties are accomplished, and, when they are not or cannot be carried out, these rights cease or the exercise of them is suspended. Many of the poor resemble children by their ignorance, lack of foresight, and irresponsibility. They require the protection of a guardian [*tutelle*]. It is up to government and charity to exercise it.[28]

This echoes the proclamation of the Thermidoran government forty years earlier: "No one is a good citizen if he is not a good son, a good father, a good husband."[29] Workers' deficient family life and their poverty meant deficient citizenship and thus positioned them as minors in need of tutelage. As such, workers joined the ranks of other sociopolitical marginals: women, children, unmarried adults, the mad, drifters, and prostitutes. In the discourses of the day, all these groups were considered minors and in many cases that was precisely the legal status conferred upon them by the Napoleonic Code. It is by rhetorical operations of this kind that writers prepared the way for assertion of new forms of private and state authority over workers' lives. Finally, women workers were especially targeted by discourses of the day. In the texts of political economy and philanthropy their bodies were sexualized, becoming sites where social disorder and poverty were rewritten as female sexual disorder.[30]

Many social inquests, while they did much to call public attention to the poverty of the new class of urban workers, deployed a *misérabilisme* which was familialist to a fault. Villermé, one of the cofounders of the public health movement, closed a description of the living conditions of Lille factory spinners on the following note:

> I do not wish to add anything to this detailed account of the hideous things that reveal at first glance the deep misery of these unhappy dwellers; however, I must say that in several of the beds of which I just spoke I saw lying together individuals of both sexes, most without nightshirts and repulsively filthy. Father, mother, children, and adults are piled together. I stop . . . the reader will complete the picture but I warn him that if he wishes to have an accurate one, his imagination must not draw back before any of the disgusting mysteries that are performed in these impure beds in the midst of obscurity and drunkenness.[31]

Villermé's text achieves a sensational effect through a mixture of protosociological voyeurism and moral horror worthy of high melodrama. This is a common staple of sociological investigations of working-class life in the 1840s. A perfect example of a rhetoric of sexuality in Foucault's sense—a "repulsive" secret that must be divulged, a repressive silence that authorizes a torrent of garrulity—Villermé's text constructs a social hermeneutic that recodes utmost misery in terms of carnal incest, the "truth" of the laboring classes.

Producing Social Expertise

This rhetorical play between normative family relations and the spectacle of urban destitution encodes not only the laboring classes targeted by social inquests but the philanthropists and public health officers as well. I want to suggest that these ritual investigations of the urban poor, in which writing played an immediate and continuous role from the note-taking of casework to written reports and statistical surveys, amounted to an ethnographic enterprise that involved the simultaneous discursive production of the objects of social pathology and welfare (the workers) and the knowing, liberal subjects who studied and aided them.[32]

Let us consider, for example, a passage from de Gérando's book on philanthropy. This author is very serviceable for my purposes, for not only did he pen treatises on social welfare, as we have seen, but early on in his career he wrote one of the first theoretical essays on the principles and methods of modern ethnography as a guide for a Napoleonic expedition to the South Seas.[33] (I will return to this essay in the section on colonialism that closes this chapter.) In both texts the encounter between self and other entails the inscription at once of subject and object. Indeed, in *De la bienfaisance publique* de Gérando's focus falls as much on the author's and readers' putative reactions to scenes of human misery as upon the suffering poor:

> Reader! Have you at times visited the home of the poor? Have you entered that narrow alley, have you set foot in that run-down house, climbed the dark, steep stairway in order to reach a remote cubbyhole, almost inaccessible and which resembles some other lair rather than a human habitation? What a spectacle meets you! Will this picture ever be effaced from your memory?[34]

Contact with the poor can be moving and its immediate effects are the moral improvement, not of the poor, but rather of those who witness their misfortunes:

> There is not one of us who, in visiting institutions created through charity and collecting a host of useful observations in the midst of deep pity and intense emotion, has not felt compelled to serious reflection and has not been at times elevated to an order of views which have contributed to his own improvement; who has not felt the need to serve according to his ability, what am I saying, the need to devote himself entirely to the holy cause of humanity; who has not learned faced with a heartrending and gloomy scene that there exists, even on this earth, a sublime happiness—the devotion to misfortune.[35]

Happily, this precious experience can be extended by print to a wide reading public. "Virtual witnessing"[36] by absent readers and observers through written accounts can have the felicitous effect of encouraging philanthropic impulses already stirring in "beautiful souls":

> While thus our research has been limited to obtaining and presenting a description of so many monuments for the most part unknown, how fertile in results it has been! . . .
> If similar works could be properly carried out, they would have eminently practical as well as salutary consequences. They would by themselves become a service to humanity.[37]

In the end, the publication and distribution of the results of social inquests should lead to the betterment of all: the agents of philanthropy (presumably *dames patronnesses* and other private citizens recruited from those who have read these reports) as well as those "experts" who analyze the accounts and the poor: "Not one of their least fruits would be to contribute to the improvement of morals: everyone would become better—those who would carry [the studies] out, those who would study them, and those to whom [these studies] would apply."[38]

Threatening Proximities

I have been arguing that familial discourse underwent a rearticulation that turned on figures of social pathology and in which the domestic family household was recast in close relation to a threatening social other, the "dangerous" classes. A rhetoric of melodrama came into play to narrate the discovery and naming of lower-class "disorder" in terms of the transgression of normative familial and sexual behavior. Now, Tilly has pointed out that the rhetoric of social pathology sought to discredit artisans' and laborers' political action by drawing a sharp distinction between them and orderly political life, between biologically ill classes and healthy ones. Yet it seems to me that for such a discourse to work effectively, frontiers between self and other must be left porous, thus in constant need of policing; otherwise the discourse will mobilize very few readers and very few government officials. Hence the role and power of the rhetoric of melodrama, in which otherness is iterated in the very moment it is brought within threatening proximity. I think it is much more helpful to envision the play of pathological figures as involving both a destabilization and a reformulation of boundaries and distinctions than to see it as conserving stable identities and the status quo. This will be the peculiar force and power of widely published novels as opposed to the rather tame and predictable narratives by philanthropists, in which the melodramatics of proximity and otherness are less poignant, and which were read by a smaller public.[39]

This play of boundary and transgression helps explain the massive presence of one figure, who was depicted as circulating freely between private space and the street, confusing those distinct spheres and blurring the strict boundaries that manuals of domesticity and treatises on public health drew and redrew: prostitutes and courtesans. Intriguingly absent from that extremely meticulous piece of bourgeois legislation that was the Code Civil (whose ambition was to replace the patchwork of Old Regime legal statutes and privileges that imperfectly covered society), prostitutes, much like homosexuals, were a legal anomaly. This left them exposed to the arbitrary measures of the general police and hospital administrators throughout the nineteenth century. Up until around 1870, prostitutes were the object of utilitarian *réglementariste* policy. According to Alain Corbin, prostitution was not considered a crime because it had a social function; in the words of Parent-Duchâtelet, cofounder of the public health movement and of legal medicine, prostitution was consonant "with the principles of civilization, the interest of mores and families, the life of society and the fears of mothers." Prostitutes "are as inevitable, in a dense population of men, as sewers, road maintenance, and garbage dumps."[40] Over 30,000 strong in Paris, prostitutes were understood to service largely the petty bourgeoisie and lower classes, especially the single rural immigrants who poured into Paris by the thousands. Both a channel of social flows and an instrument of the sexual regulation of bachelors and men in general, prostitution only posed a threat when it became "disorderly" (escaped the watchful control of the police and became too visible). To guard against this eventuality, public health officers pursued a policy that forced prostitutes to register with the police and restricted their movements to designated neighborhoods and the *maisons de tolérance* to which they were assigned. There, they were subject to close surveillance by public health officials working with the police, often with the madam acting as an informal agent of the state apparatus. In this manner, one can say that the *filles soumises* were both created and repressed at one stroke by legal medicine.

Precisely because prostitution was integrated into a bio-politics as a safety valve for the supposedly disruptive effects of male sexuality on the tranquillity of home life, so that prostitutes were strategically located within the horizon of family household life while standing on the outside, these women became the social melodramatic figures par excellence. By their proximity they both threatened and reinscribed (by contrast) domestic values. Prostitutes were endowed with all the features of familial marginals. Alphonse Esquiros in his book *Les Vierges folles* [The mad virgins] (1840) claimed paternalistically that they constituted "a class of women who perpetuate among us the childhood of the human race . . . who have remained in the primitive state of nondevelopment."[41] Written into the social body as monsters of concupiscence, they were discursively refigured as reproducing the faults of worldly, aristocratic women of the Old Regime: they were irrational, impulsive, improvident, spendthrift—in short, *dénaturées*, and displayed a cynical capacity for manipulation through artifice and appearances. Yet at the same time, often in writings of public health officers, these women did not stray irreparably outside feminine nature as redefined by the ideology of domesticity. According to Parent-Duchâtelet, beneath the alluring surface sensuality of these "aristocratic" bodies often lay hidden a feminine interiority, rich in maternal sentiments of generosity and love worthy of the attention of bourgeois mothers.[42] Here, the prostitutes' ambiguous figuration recapitulates the play of otherness and proximity upon which the mobilizing discourse of "family" and urban pathology depended: as *other* they traded sex for gold; as *proximate* they, too, were capable of the most elevated of democratic, middle-class sentiments: motherhood.

Urban prostitution was a highly efficient figure that had tremendous polysemous value: it condensed both private obsessions (female eroticism and female independence) and public ones (syphilis, street sanitation, sewage, urban crowding, working-class political threat). Parent-Duchâtelet, who wrote extensively on sewage treatment and public sanitation, in his texts obsessively associated prostitutes—and especially the sanitary conditions of their bodies and of the houses where they worked—with other closed spaces such as slaughterhouses, dissection rooms, morgues, and underground sewers. These revolting, foul spaces amounted to the dystopic tropes of bourgeois privatized space. Parent-Duchâtelet asserted that they could be found in the same parts of town.[43] Here the analogy of Paris/whore returns in the trappings of medical science and confirms Peter Stallybrass and Allon White's thesis that social discourse in the nineteenth century was governed by the analogy city/body.[44] To map one involved mapping the other.

The Decline of the West

The literature and discourse of social pathology underwent a general intensification in the aftermath of, first, the Revolution of 1848 and then the Paris Commune, which followed the French defeat in 1870. Writers projected an image of incipient decline against the background of social disease. In his *Essai sur l'inégalité des races humaines* [Essay on the inequality of the human races] (1855) Joseph Arthur de Gobineau claimed for the modern West the privileged consciousness of its own mortality: "It is that we moderns are the first to know that every agglomeration of men—and the mode of intellectual culture that results from it—must perish."[45] And Maxime Du Camp in his study of Paris (*Paris: ses organes, ses fonctions, sa vie de la seconde moitié du XIXe siècle* [Paris: its organs, its functions, its life in the second half of the nineteenth century], (1875) graphically compared the Commune to a festering sore on the social body: "These furious uprisings, which seem to us to be isolated events, are the result of a general state of morbidity, just as an abscess is the sign of a vice-ridden or polluted [*vicieuse ou viciée*] constitution."[46] At the same time older figures dating from the French Revolution were trotted out, fitted in new garb. The sinister knitting women [*tricoteuses*] of yesteryear exchanged their knitting for firebombs and became hysterical *pétroleuses*, inciting workers to riot, making demands for women's rights, and fraternizing with the army regulars and guardsmen. Moreover, the appearance of an armed working class with a socialist ideology, and its bloody repression by the National Guard, identified with the middle class, discredited those who had envisioned a new national community capable of embracing disparate sectors of society. Faced with a new social enemy, writers and commentators dropped their expansive belief in social progress for a defensive pessimism characteristic of disenchanted Republicanism and liberalism. Michelet's vision in *Le Peuple*, published two years before the Revolution of 1848, was, according to Jean Borie, the last tableau of the middle classes and working classes marching together toward a radiant future.[47]

The new sciences of evolutionary biology, heredity, eugenics, and psychology furnished familial discourse with a determinist component that sounded the imminent collapse of "decadent" French civilization before the onslaught of the barbarians of the working class and of the newly colonized peoples. If the discursive inscription and emplotment of self and other through writing involved a policing of the sexual-familial other both within oneself and within the family household (masturbators, hysterics, homosexuals, servants) and without (the streets and the laboring classes), it also entailed the simultaneous inscription of the colonized—their geography, customs, and bodies. Indeed, these different figures of alterity tended to merge in contemporary discourses. The presumably orderly competition of the liberal marketplace was rewritten in terms of an interclass, interracial war, a Darwinian natural selection.

According to the new literature, the crowd—the public, violent presence of the working class—imposed a regression to irrational primitivism. Gustave Le Bon in *Psychologie des foules* (1895) delivers a vivid picture of the "backward" colonized peoples irrupting in the midst of late nineteenth-century France:

> By virtue of the fact that he belongs to a crowd, man descends thus several degrees on the scale of civilization. Isolated, perhaps he is a cultivated individual, in a crowd he is a creature of instinct, thus a barbarian. He has the spontaneity, violence, ferocity, and also the fits of enthusiasm and the heroism, of primitive beings. He is nearer to them still, by virtue of his fascination with allowing himself to be impressionable to words and images and to be led to commit acts detrimental to his clearest interests. The individual in a crowd is a grain of sand that the wind blows about at will.[48]

The thematics of the involutionary movement of civilization achieved its most unremitting construction in hereditary biology. Physicians and public health officers wrote grim assessments of the biological state of the working poor. There among the "dangerous classes" they discovered morbid examples of hereditary disorders unmitigated by the restraining influence of moral sentiment and disciplined interiority. B. A. Morel's *Traité des dégénérescences physiques, intellectuelles et morales de l'espèce humaine, et des causes qui produisent ces variétés maladives* [Treatise on the physical, intellectual, and moral degeneracy of the human race, and on the causes that produce these sickly varieties] (1857) made the following assessment with regret:

> It is sad to say for the honor of the human species that the degenerative causes act with all the greater intensity in classes demoralized by poverty because the complete lack of moral and religious education in their circle of family and friends and the disdain of those social conventions (often fictive if truth be told but salutary under certain circumstances) do not establish a counterbalance to the excesses of the worst passions . . .

But, *science oblige*, Morel's gaze was pitiless:

In the heart of such a civilized society there exist authentic varieties [of people] who do not possess either an understanding of duty or a moral awareness of their actions and whose minds are not able to be enlightened or even consoled by any idea of a religious kind. Several of these varieties have been rightly designated as dangerous classes.[49]

In the eyes of many writers recent revolutions constituted incontrovertible proof of the link between criminality, madness, and degeneracy. Dr. Charles Féré, a physician at Bicêtre, published in 1894 a treatise entitled *La Famille névropathique. Théorie tératologique de l'hérédité et de la prédisposition morbides et de la dégénérescence* [The neuropathic family: Teratological theory of morbid heredity and predisposition and of degeneracy], in which he wrote:

In providing an opportunity for criminal urges and a stimulus for mad [*vésaniques*] predispositions, great social upheavals can bring to light hereditary physical monstrosities and show, experimentally so to speak, the kinship of crime and madness. Messieurs Belhomme, Laborde, Lunier, and Mundy have cited, among those who took part in the insurrections of 1848 and 1871, several subjects who have been treated as mentally ill [*aliénés*] and who had mentally ill persons in their family.[50]

Hereditary biology marked laboring-class bodies as virtually irredeemable, and its determinist component seemed to spell the doom of the project of moralization and stood as the measure of the degree to which the discourse of the day excluded the working poor from any potential national community based on normative behavior. Their deviant customs and lack of "family" were profound and unalterable.

If manuals of domesticity, treatises of education, and medical monographs aggravated familialist paranoia by inciting parents, physicians, teachers, philanthropists, and other experts to eternal vigilance over private and public space (from the bodies of individuals to the conduits of sewage systems), Borie's study demonstrates how the recent literature on degeneration and eugenics introduced a disturbing new element: temporal depth. The growing middling and professional groups who once saw themselves as the wave of the future—the "progressive bourgeoisie"—now riveted their attention to the murky past of their low origin. Their recent past was rewritten in terms of shameful familial practices whose hereditary effects in the present were as unpredictable as they were unavoidable. In this sense the social enemy without (revolutionary workers) turned out to be also within (the tainted blood of mad, perverse, or criminal ancestors). Moreau de Tours in his *La Psychologie morbide dans ses rapports avec la philosophie de l'histoire, ou de l'influence des névropathes sur le dynamisme intellectuel* [Morbid psychology in its relations with the philosophy of history, or the influence of neuropaths on intellectual dynamics] (1859) was brutally frank about the matter:

> You may be certain that, every time you encounter in a family those corrupt [*gangrenés*] members, those fundamentally vice-ridden natures, and, finally, those creatures who, from their first years, are the despair and, all too often, the shame of their unhappy parents, whose worthiness and exemplary morals would appear to preserve them surely from these calamities; we repeat, you may be certain you will find some neuropathic defect concealed in some portion of the genealogical tree. You will find one of those nervous ailments which have been discussed in the present work: madness, hysteria, every form of convulsive illness, either serious or mild; lesions of the nervous centers, of the spinal cord, etc.[51]

I have shown how, in displacing the aristocratic ethos of blood at the end of the eighteenth century and its narrative of the name of the race [*nom de la race*], the new writing disseminated an ontology of individual sentiment and the concomitant utilitarian concept of the body. Later, after 1848, a voluminous literature disseminated a social pessimism and uncertainty that can be read in the anxiety-producing images that recoded the middling groups' modest origins in terms of sick sentiments and nervous disorders destructive of the body's positive functions in the life of the family household and civil society. In a sense, an ethics of sin and its vision of historical entropy resurfaced wearing the physician's white frock. The family household, still the source of social stability and cultural values, now also harbors the springs of its own dissolution. A different kind of family portraiture began to be practiced, particularly by the psychiatrists of sexual deviance. One can read Krafft-Ebing's study as a kind of negative family album that friends and neighbors never get to see. Here is one very condensed example:

> X. came of a neurotic family. His paternal grandfather died by suicide while insane. His father was a weak, peculiar man. One brother masturbated at the age of two. A cousin was sexually perverse, and practiced perverse acts, similar to those of X., while a youth; he became weak-minded, and died of spinal disease. A paternal great-uncle was a hermaphrodite. His mother's sister was insane. His mother was said to have been healthy. X.'s brother is nervous and irascible.[52]

The Paris Commune, denigrated by Du Camp as "that monster of March 18, which, after two months of alcoholism, collapsed in the burning of Paris,"[53] brought up once again the figure of the prostitute and spelled the end of *réglementariste* policies. The utilitarianism of the early *réglementaristes* gave way to a purely moralistic discourse for which prostitution condensed all the sociofamilial paranoia. Du Camp appeals to his readers thus: "Will we allow unregulated prostitution [*la prostitution insoumise*] to invade us and engulf our morals?"[54] Prostitutes in the number of 120,000 are ready to take the bourgeoisie by assault, he claims, four times the number Parent-Duchâtelet had compiled in his census! They fill up the streets, cafés and restaurants, bearing with them "demoralization, sickness, and ruin."[55] "*Minotaures femelles*," they devour the French youth and depredate family wealth:

> One would think that they had been charged with some important and secret social mission. One wonders whether they are not the distributors of capital, whether the extraordinary mobility they lend to money is not their excuse if not their reason for living, and whether in the democratization [vulgarisation] of fortunes they do not play the role which in agriculture is reserved for the draining off of fields.[56]

In Du Camp's nightmare, the Commune broke the established channels of sociosexual energies and diverted flows of capital to other social classes. The bio-politics of Malthusian self-control and savings on the one hand and *réglementarisme* on the other seemed to Du Camp on the verge of collapse.

Du Camp's urgent tone may have something to do with the fact that prostitution had undergone a significant evolution at that time. The old *maisons de tolérance*, which had serviced the lower orders of society and were confined to specific quarters, had declined and luxury bordellos for the men of the aristocracy and the bourgeoisie had sprung up in well-to-do neighborhoods. The marginal but "necessary" sex industry had moved from across town to next door. In this change Corbin discerns a "crisis" in bourgeois marriage also signaled by the cultural obsession with female adultery. This may well have been the case, but what I find striking is the fact that the new prostitution, when it started to cater to an upper-class clientele, began to imitate the style, tone, and comforts of domesticity in response to clients' desires.[57] This example reminds us that often or even especially when in "crisis" or under pressure, domesticity displays remarkable powers of resilience, cooptation, and expansion.

Framing the obsession with prostitution was the Great Fear that dominated public opinion between 1890 and 1910: syphilis. Corbin gives a good account of this, providing examples of the extraordinary rhetorical turns familial discourse took. The context was the wave of natalism (the latest avatar of eighteenth-century populationist thought) that swept through France on the aftermath of the defeat in the Franco-Prussian War in 1870. Directed mainly at the working classes, it dropped the Malthusian acceptance of contraception and railed against birth control practices that left France dangerously behind in the population race to field large armies. Dr. Le Pileur in 1889 claimed that out of "100 babies conceived in Paris, 13 perished because of maternal syphilis." Once the long-awaited Great War was under way, one writer lamented, "with 10 kilos of rubber, William II could prevent the births each year of thousands of soldiers."[58] Dr. Le Noir solemnly warned that 12 to 15 percent of the male population of Paris was infected. The future of the *patrie* was in danger.[59] It was an unmistakable sign of the degeneracy of the French nation. Huysmans had already written in *À rebours* [Against the grain] (1884):

> "All is syphilis and syphilis alone," mused des Esseintes.... And he had the sudden vision of a humanity tormented by the virus of former ages.

Since the beginning of the world, from father to son, all creatures have transmitted the inexhaustible heritage, the everlasting illness that has ravaged man's ancestors and has burrowed right down to the bones of old fossils which have now been dug up![60]

The solution? The repression of prostitution and, as a corollary, the suppression of pre- and extramarital sexuality. Alain Fournier, founder in 1901 of the Société de Prophylaxie sanitaire et morale [The Society for Sanitary and Moral Prophylaxis] assured readers that "if humanity returned to innocence and to the golden age, the days of syphilis would be numbered." Also, experts recommended the introduction of sexual education in order better to discourage adolescents from erotic contact: "In reality," Queyrat concluded, "what we must obtain is that people marry one another while virgin."[61] In the name of the battle against prostitution and the spread of syphilis, then, writers called for a renewed familialization of sexuality. This applied particularly to female sexuality, which the spread of adultery and the feminist movement, it was claimed, was attempting to liberate, to the detriment of families. Dr. L. Reuss compared the sexually active woman to a prostitute in his *La Prostitution au point de vue de l'hygiene et de l'administration en France et à l'étranger* [Prostitution from the point of view of administration in France and abroad] (1889): "Generally, all debauched women are prostitutes: a great lady who has lovers is in this respect on par with the unregulated streetwalker [*fille insoumise*] who solicits customers on boulevards."[62]

The question of female sexuality finds its full discursive resonance in the context of what Sartre termed the post-1848 ideology of *distinction*. A reformulation of early nineteenth-century Malthusian notions of discipline and self-control, the ideology of distinction designated a bourgeois way of life that tirelessly marked itself off from the lower classes through a new theater of the body. A politics of underconsumption (austere, nonostentatious clothing and eating habits, restrained sexuality), such bodily control was the example that those sectors of the bourgeoisie, traumatized by social revolution and the political disenfranchisement of Louis Napoleon's coup d'état, gave to the undisciplined masses and the imperial court. Distinction signified a victory over nature, now defined as wild, demonic, and morbid.[63] Distinction involved a latent asceticism and an attendant investment in *anti-physis* (antinature, artifice) that took the familialist rewriting of female sexuality one step further: in this new construct, an ethereal, civilized "passion" designated upper-class sexuality, while unbridled "instincts" and "animality," and wanton, illegitimate reproduction ran rampant among the laboring classes. Fathomless bourgeois interiority, infinitely interpretable, opposed the vulgar sexual pulsions easily read on the surface of the working-class body. In its literary enterprise at this time, "the bourgeoisie," Sartre remarked cryptically, "escaped into interiority" [*se sauva en profondeur*].[64]

After midcentury familial discourses began to make some headway among the laboring classes, though progress was slow. Tellingly, one new working-class housing unit [*cité ouvrière*] in Paris, which had redesigned low-income housing, complete with small vegetable gardens to occupy the men's leisure hours, did not join the protest against the coup d'état of December 2, 1851.[65] But *cités ouvrières* were small in number and very few were built before the end of the century.[66] Male and female workers' associations adopted positions that, while they recognized women's distinct role in domesticity, didn't always oppose women's work outside the family household.[67] They did lend support to women's groups demanding certain reforms that indeed were realized by the return of Republicans to power in 1878–79. The Republicans reinstated liberal measures introduced by the French Revolution and suppressed by the Restoration— divorce (1884, but still without grounds of incompatibility), *recherche légale de la paternité* (1884)—and passed a new law on *la déchéance paternelle* (paternal dereliction, 1889), which authorized the intervention of private and public agencies in order to protect and aid family members.

Familial Discourse at "Home" Abroad

In a section of his book on the education of women titled "De l'influence des femmes. Que la civilisation n'existe que dans le mariage," Louis Aimé-Martin concluded a development on conjugal love this way: "To this picture of the European family you may place opposite the oriental family: the first is based upon love and equality; the second upon polygamy and slavery, which leaves love its brutal fury but which removes its sweet proprieties and its divine illusions."[68] Aimé-Martin's invitation to familial spectatorship is a depoliticized lesson in colonial geography. Outside of metropolitan France and Europe, the colonies become the ideal surface of inscription of a host of negative familial features. Invoked in 1834 to impress readers and public opinion, these familial features sketched out the lineaments of nascent colonial policy. The same rhetoric crops up in Necker de Sassure's manual of education. Women's role is essential to civilization; oppress them in marriage and all of society suffers. Witness, she says, the East:

> The oppressor also frees himself from the yoke of duty; he is without charity or justice, a mad pride swells his heart. Soon, however, the entire race is punished by the violation of the most holy of rights: humanity's development and progress are arrested; the mind of man is deprived of its necessary complement, and the mind of woman is little by little extinguished; the king of the universe falls into a moronic state [*abrutissement*] of stupid sensuality; finally, he himself loses the liberty that was his glory and the chains that he forged for woman fall upon him. Such is how he appears to us in the East.[69]

The discursive elaboration and circulation of the domestic household and its sexual-familial norms involved the simultaneous construction of the city and the colonies as spaces of human and social pathology. Neither modern domesticity and those classes that adopted it, nor the laboring classes, nor the colonized were conceptualized in familial discourse without reference to each other. No one term stood alone, least of all the normative conjugal couple. The new, family-based imagined community of postabsolutist France required the differential inscription of the spaces and bodies of the "dangerous classes" and of people of color.

The close, continuous links between the discursive mapping of the city, on the one hand, and of the colonies, on the other, can be read in the career of the baron de Gérando, who, before initiating his influential studies of urban poverty and modern philanthropy, performed early work as a colonial ethnographer. Member of the Ideologues's short-lived Société des Observateurs de l'Homme [Society of Observers of Man], he wrote in 1800 a document entitled, *Considérations sur les méthodes à suivre dans l'observation des Peuples Sauvages*. It was meant to serve as a guide to a major naturalist expedition to the South Seas.[70] In a preface to the English translation, published in 1969, E. E. Evans-Pritchard praised de Gérando's treatise as an adumbration of techniques now employed in anthropological fieldwork declaring, "The paper reads as though it might have been written yesterday."[71] Buoyed by a philosophical and anthropological optimism inherited from the Enlightenment, de Gérando frames the contact between Europeans and "natives" in terms of a philanthropic relation (to the benefit of both parties) identical to the one he would later apply to social workers and their poor urban clients:

> And even should we not see in savage peoples a useful object of instruction for ourselves, would there not be enough high feelings of philanthropy to make us give a high importance to the contact that we make with them? What more moving plan than that of reestablishing in such a way the august ties of a universal society, of finding once more those former kinsmen separated by long exile from the rest of the common family, of offering a hand to raise them to a happier state! You who, led by a generous devotion on the far shores, will soon come near their lonely huts, go before them as the representatives of all humanity! Give them in that name the vow of brotherly alliance![72]

Eugène Buret, fellow writer on political economy and philanthropy (*De la misère des classes laborieuses en Angleterre et en France* [On the poverty of the laboring classes in England and France] (1841), was less sanguine and charitable. He advocated a policy of aggressive colonization of Algeria: "In this moment, the great civilized nations are battling against barbarism; one would say that a huge crusade has organized on its own in order to wrench the most beautiful part of the ancient world from the undisciplined races and to conquer new lands for civilization."[73] The hygienist rhetoric that suffuses his prose suggests that one occupies and "saves" foreign lands as one does a city convulsed by social crisis and illness: "We are pursuing a legitimate conquest in Africa, a conquest that demands more devotion than ambition. It is not about enslaving a people but about occupying, farming, and saving from insalubrity, solitude, and barbarism a portion of the old world!"[74] Finally, like moralization of the urban poor, colonization is above all an affair of "families":

> African colonies cannot resemble colonies of the Ancients; I would say [that they resemble] those in North America if the differences (which I will discuss below) did not forbid comparing them. [African colonies] should be made up not of enterprising speculators who will pass through but of families who will come there seeking land ownership, productive work, and a new fatherland [*patrie*].[75]

Such militant colonial "philanthropy" may help explain the "razzias" conducted in rural Algeria by the French colonial army, which razed entire villages in its campaign to "pacify" the countryside;[76] it may also explain the ferocious brutality with which French soldiers put down the June 1848 insurrection and the Paris Commune in 1871. The "barbarians" within perhaps deserve the same treatment as those without. And we must not forget that many survivors of those bloody repressions were deported to . . . the colonies.

Familial discourse provided to colonial ideology some of the key features of its idiom and in return the colonized furnished the domestic family household yet another foil, much as had the servants, prostitutes, masturbators, and homosexuals. Indeed, many examples we have encountered of sexual and familial dissolution bore latent signifiers of colonial discourse: black slave women's "corrupting" milk, masturbators' "oriental" dissipation, prostitutes' and crowds' "primitive" psychology. Furthermore—and this is amply demonstrated in Part II of this study—the empire and its subjugated inhabitants were fundamental to the production of familial discourse by novels: from the construction of the ideal community in *Paul et Virginie* on the colony of Ile de France (Mauritius) and the promises extended to the poor in *Les Mystères de Paris* of land and family life in Algeria, to the hothouse full of exotic plants that serves as the site of incest in *La Curée* [The kill], to the presence of the sensual Creole aunt in *La Porte étroite* [Strait is the gate], who disrupts the Vautier household. As Edward Said has stated again and again, the classical European novel cannot be properly understood without taking into account how the colonies constitute its discursive horizon and one of its conditions of possibility.[77]

Predictably, colonized lands, like households of the poor, served as a vast repertoire of familial alterity, particularly of sexual promiscuity, male and female prostitution, and homosexual practices. The Italian writer Lombroso, whose book on prostitutes was widely read in France, actually claimed that "primitive" women were always prostitutes.[78] Louyer-Villermay claimed in his entry on *nymphomanie* for Pankoucke's *Dictionnaire des sciences médicales* that climate was a determining factor in sexual conduct between men and women:

> Must not we attribute to the dominant influence of the reproductive organs—the result of high temperatures—certain customs established in warm climes—polygamy, harems, the despotism of men, and the slavery of women which, in depriving the latter of any chance of giving themselves up to tastes which their entire education would ward off, forestalls in many cases the development of nymphomania?[79]

Later in the century, the Larousse *Grand dictionnaire universel du XIXe siècle* [The great universal dictionary of the nineteenth century] (1866) repeated the same motif but this time in relation to homosexuality. It assigned *pédérastie* (homosexual acts between men) a geographic and meteorological etiology that it implicitly held to be as valid for the nineteenth century as it was for the Ancients:

> One of the causes [of pederasty] has to be the temperature of the warm regions, for in all climes scorched by the fieriness of the sun one observes violent passions and yet the women have fewer opportunities of meeting men. In the cold regions, on the contrary, the men are less fervent, the

women are freer, and desires more moderate and for that very reason even easily satisfied.[80]

Adopting the same logic, Ambroise Tardieu, author of *Etude médico-légale sur l'attentat aux moeurs* [Legal-medical study of offenses to public morals] (1857), located such practices in the warm climes of Italy and French North Africa and warned that they were on the verge of invading metropolitan France.[81] Finally, the psychiatrist Julien Chevalier, in his study *L'Inversion sexuelle, une maladie de la personalité* [Sexual inversion, a personality illness], termed male prostitution "the Eastern Sickness" [*le Mal d'Orient*], a disorder that extended in his view from Morocco and Algeria to sub-Saharan Africa and throughout Asia.[82]

In a similar manner, Lallemand, whose description of the consequences of masturbation I quoted in Chapter 1, exorcizes the nightmare of onanism by transposing his diagnosis to a colonial setting and imparting to it a hallucinatory refinement that perhaps his medical profession's legal impunity from censorship afforded him:

> On the one hand, [you have] polygamy, harems, and seraglios, hence sexual excesses, barbaric mutilation, revolting acts of sodomy, and a thin, inactive, lethargic population condemned to ignorance and thus to poverty and to all kinds of despotisms. On the other hand, you have monogamy, Christian austerity, a more equal distribution of domestic happiness, growing expansion of liberty, equality, and well-being, and a rapidly multiplying population that is dense, active, hard-working, enterprising, bold, and invasive by impulse and by necessity.[83]

These words were penned in the early 1830s, shortly after France invaded Algeria and resumed its colonial expansion in Africa and Asia. In this sexual-social geography, certain household arrangements imply particular sexual practices which require specific bodies, subjects, and economic and social structures. Clearly familialism, economics, and colonial expansion were of a piece in nineteenth-century liberal thought. The passage's logic works this way: burgeoning families produce disciplined, acquisitive individuals who collectively would stimulate and invigorate the economy; in turn, this necessitates a search for colonial outlets for surplus population and goods. Fortunately, there exist "empty," unproductive lands outside of Europe. In their economic and sexual perversion—unfinalized, wasteful activity—these countries await their redemption and admission to the world community through colonialism's miracle of economic development and medico-hygienic clean-up. Here again, as elsewhere, where familialism introduces a perception of lack of "family," it promotes a political agenda. In the third volume of his study, Lallemand returns to his imperialist vision of Western society founded on normative family life but now confirmed by the successful colonization of Algeria; the author is flushed with satisfaction at the turn of events:

> After having shown the influence of monogamy and increasingly strict morals on the growth of European populations, on their restless and adventurous courage, on their ceaseless activity, and on their insatiable ambition, and their continuous need for conquests in science, the arts, industry, etc., I said that the future of the world lay in the hands of the Caucasian race of the West. The most significant events, sooner than I thought, have confirmed and developed these predictions; the explosion of the *Eastern question* has been only one of the applications of the general law discovered through observation.[84]

Indeed, some fifty years later, after the triumph on the Continent of the hygienist movement in alliance with Pasteurian biology,[85] when European powers were completing their colonization of sub-Saharan Africa, the tasks of consolidation of European empires constituted, like the city earlier in the century, an unusual opportunity for hygienists to work their scientific miracles for the "common good." The primary sciences of the social in Europe—hygiene and legal medicine—made equal claims in the colonies. Dr. Alphonse Poskin is refreshingly straightforward in his assessment of both the origins and the risks of the colonization of Africa. In the introduction to his *Afrique Equitoriale. Climatologie, nosologie, hygiène* [Equitorial Africa: Climatology, nosology, hygiene] (1897), he argues that Europe needs Africa, for the Aryan race is by nature expansionist:

> [The reason is that] equatorial Africa is the only part of the globe that has remained to this day closed to colonial enterprises because nations

have found other more hospitable fields to work; it is because the needs of the Aryan race have grown to a tremendous degree and because, in order to satisfy them, new outlets and new markets are needed in which European products may be exchanged for products of the African soil.[86]

However, only hygienists can protect the new settlers from the health hazards of the inhospitable climate:

> First, one will have to consult with physicians and hygienists; they will dictate a regime for living, impose hygienic rules for public and private use; it is they who inform us of illnesses that lie in wait for us at every turn in the road; it is they who will provide us with prophylaxis and will indicate proper treatment; it is they who, in discovering the cause of morbid manifestations, will give us the means either to make them disappear or to avoid them; finally, it is they who, if they are not met with disbelief or indifference, will prevent colonial expansion from being only one long series of disasters and painful sacrifices of men and money.[87]

As Georges Canguilhem said, norms are expansionist by nature or they do not exist at all.[88]

Finally, the inscription of colonial lands and peoples in a discourse of self and other was sometimes performed by Westerners who, in the wake of Romanticism's fascination with the Orient, sought the obverse side of familialist practices in the very world that was an anathema to Lallemand.[89] Such was the case of those cultural-sexual explorers, Gustave Flaubert and Maxime Du Camp. One with his pen, the other with his camera, they set out in 1849 to discover the Middle East and its countless exoticisms, not the least of which were the pleasures their status as *colons* afforded them daily: the erotic satisfactions obtained by frequenting luxurious brothels and Egyptian boys.

Richard Terdiman has analyzed with finesse the cultural paradoxes that beset and undid the entire enterprise. He has characterized Flaubert's project in particular as the common desire of Western travelers for the simultaneous dispossession and absorption by the uncontaminated culture of the colonized, a project that was irreparably compromised by the actuality of European cultural penetration and appropriation. Disillusionment became Flaubert's fundamental experience of the "East." In his notebook on his visit to Constantinople and its environs, Flaubert made the following entry:

> The streets of Galata are deep with customs and color. Dirty streets, windows opening out upon back courtyards from where emanates the strident sound of a mandolin or a violin; here and there, at a window or on a doorstep, the dirty faces of whores dressed in European fashion and their hair done up in the Greek style; the invasion of licentious engravings of Heloisa and Abelard. Will the emancipation of Oriental women make its entry through the Faublas fad?—The importance of ballet.—In a hundred years they will abolish harems in the East; the example of European women is contagious; one of these days they will begin to read novels. Farewell Turkish tranquility! Everything everywhere is crumbling of decrepitude.[90]

It would be difficult to find a better example of the intersection between writings on the city and on the colonies. Flaubert's short description narrativizes the metaphor of the whore/city so dominant in publications of the day. Narratively, the passage moves from the streets to women's bodies. However, the prose enacts an important reversal. Less a titillating story of the dangers and fascinations presented by the contaminating but also possibly redemptive contact with the urban other, Flaubert's notations present the obverse scenario, one of outrage and repugnance at the corruption of the fantasized other by the self and by the Western culture to which one belongs—more especially by the popular middle-class culture signified by the novel. As the passage shifts from diagnosis to prognosis, from analysis to a projected future, it expands on this "corruption" of prostitutes' and courtesans' bodies by Western domestic and serial novels. Seemingly, the consumption of novels by women will lead straight to revolution in male-dominated private space constructed around a fantasized harem; that is to say, through novels women's bodies will be transformed from sites of male domination and physical desire to sites of female interiority and power. Thus, in Flaubert's eyes, the exotic stands on the verge of becoming the familiar: the "ugly," vulgar culture of nineteenth-century France. For Flaubert, novels have already succeeded all too well in Europe. They are the sign of bourgeois hegemony that has "feminized" civil society and empowered women through domesticity to a dangerous degree. In this way, the coming of age of middle-class culture threatens France with ideological closure, ossification, and a social revolution whose primary markers are popular fiction and upstart women. Hence the paradoxical application of the adjective *vétuste* (decrepit) to the *evolution* of Constantinople society: as a "traditional" society Westernizes under the pressure of colonialism it becomes old. Evolution is involution and decadence. Here, Flaubert transposes French cultural pessimism and visions of historical entropy to a major capital of the Middle East.

Clearly, the colonial setting serves for Flaubert as a sexual-social repository of prebourgeois relations in a society whose public and private spheres have not been reorganized by the new domesticity; their organization approaches that of the *maison close*. That is precisely the risk and allure of both the metropolitan city and urban colonial space. In both places, sentiment and liberal interiority are felt to be absent and the very physicality of social and gender relations is played out under the aegis of an older, imagined patriarchal order. Unfortunately for Flaubert, Middle Eastern cities provide only a fleeting glimpse of this desired state of things; in his mind the "other" (the Orient) will soon revert to the "same" (the West). There is no cultural escape from France. The discursive dead-end of his colonial experience will set the stage for the author's return to France, and his return to the task of writing novels against the dominant modes of fiction as one of the first authors of protomodernist "bachelor" or celibate literature.[91]

Familial discourse was a formidable machine instrumental in transforming postrevolutionary France into a capitalist society endowed with a liberal state apparatus, a system of assistance, and a new social hermeneutic elaborated by the emergent social sciences from sociology to legal medicine and psychiatry. Part and parcel of this process was the reorganization of the social field and the subjecthood of individuals. Sexual differences were refigured and assigned the valences of familial discourse. In turn, these differences were used to organize and distribute social ones. Accordingly, subjecthood and class identities were often defined in terms of sexual-familial differences. Two parallel sets of figures faced each other and were paired off as the occasion warranted: on the one hand, family members of all sorts—hysterics, masturbators, homosexuals, lesbians, bachelors, prostitutes, adulterers, *mères dénaturées*, spinsters, libertines, orphans; on the other, noblewomen, laboring-class women, the lower classes *en bloc*, colonized peoples, anarchists, and revolutionaries. The semantic slippage from one figure to another provided familial discourse with great elasticity and suppleness. These signifying figures constituted an interpretive language and grid for hegemonic social classes and individual subjects alike. Physicians, social workers, and novelists, in their voluminous reports and works of prose fiction, recast the forces and conflicts of liberal, capitalist society in the discourse of familialist preoccupations and in so doing helped bring that society to realization. Individuals in the privacy of their diaries, educators in their treatises and classrooms, mothers at home, and psychiatrists in their clinics and offices would perform similar discursive operations—would construct a new subjectivity replete with desires, drives, stages, concepts of the body, and a set of terms whereby the singular individual could understand him- or herself. The novel's exceptional capacity in this regard would be to construct *both* the social and subjective real, an imagined community in which readers could find their place or from which they could discover their painful exclusion.

PART II

Lack of Family as Fictional Strategy in France

> Where the family is lacking, [Tuke] substitutes for it a ficticious family decor of signs and attitudes.
> —Michel Foucault

CHAPTER 3

Paul et Virginie: "Family" and the Politics of the Sentimental Body in Prerevolutionary France

> Rather than an extra-historical residue, invariant, and mute, [the] body is as ready for coding and decoding, as intelligible both in its presence and absence, as any of the more frequently recognized historical objects. The site of an operation of power, of an exercise of meaning.
>
> —Francis Barker, *The Tremulous Private Body*

> All the idyllic representations that reach the level of art attract the greatest favor because the life-styles natural to man, those which return eternally, and which delight us, are treated therein with the simplicity of truth: relations between mother, father, and children (especially boys), the toddlers' games and joys over candy, the care devoted to bringing them up, the adults' seriousness and worries, all these things mingle together their reflections in a very charming manner.
>
> —Goethe, as quoted by Mantion

A Community of Tears

In the year of its publication, 1788, and for over a half-century thereafter, Bernardin de Saint-Pierre's short novel *Paul et Virginie* repeatedly set France and Europe weeping. The tragic tale of Virginie's death and the subsequent dissolution of her ideal community on the island of Mauritius enjoyed such affective power over the novel's early readers that even the young Napoleon Bonaparte was moved to confide to the author his emotions: "*Paul et Virginie* cost me many tears and doubtless Paul did not shed more tears when he was separated from his sister." At the end of the century, the tears of the Physiocrat destined to found the largest American munitions company matched those of the future general. Dupont de Nemours wrote: "I have just burst into tears in rereading *Paul et Virginie*. In terms of simplicity of design, excellent sentiments, and sheer beauty of execution, I know nothing more perfect." The novel's popularity even cut across lines of caste and gender; Racine Garde, a poor seamstress from Aix-en-Provence, presumably declared that it was a popular book "which touches the heart in everyone." In the nineteenth century, *Paul et Virginie* exerted a formative influence over the major novelists. Chateaubriand knew the narrative practically by heart, the novel enjoys a massive intertextual presence in the novels of George Sand, and *Paul et Virginie* figured prominently in the ad hoc canon that Balzac claimed as his literary inheritance in the 1842 preface to *La Comédie humaine*. The critic Sainte-Beuve also placed Bernardin among his favorite authors and added his voice to the tearful chorus in terming the novel "an immortal work that cannot be read without weeping."[1]

The preceding remarks strongly suggest that the novel's appeal was a universal one that reached beyond class, gender, and ideological differences during a long period of political upheaval in France stretching from the eve of the French Revolution through the July Monarchy. Indeed, *Paul et Virginie* was an exceptional best-seller: Bernardin's work was the most reprinted novel of the eighteenth century. By 1914 it had gone through 207 editions, outstripping Rousseau's *Julie, ou la Nouvelle Héloïse* [Julie or the new Heloisa] (74 editions) and Voltaire's *Candide* (174 editions).[2]

In this chapter I will demonstrate that the pastoral novel's twin features of shameless sentimentality and commercial success signified its participation in new discursive practices that were transforming print culture and social relations in France in multiple ways. First of all, the novel must be seen as an inscription device that, by virtue of its production of tears both within the frame of the narrative and in readers, was part of an ongoing project to replace the aristocratic body of the Old Regime with the sentimental and "feminine" one of the liberal subject.[3] This semiotic work entails the double transformation of Virginie's own body, on the one hand, and that of the novel's readers, on the other. Second, the sentimental body—the flow of tears that was constitutive of *Paul et Virginie*'s readership—helped produce and circulate in turn a new discourse of "family" that worked to dismantle the absolutist sphere of political representation and to inscribe a new sense of national community structured by the norms and sensibility of domesticity. This "imagined community"[4] did much to redraw the social map of France at that time in terms of new reading habits and publics, family household structures, concepts of gender, and a middle-class theory of social class.[5] Third, *Paul et Virginie*'s peculiar verbal practice—its lachrymose pastoral narrative—partook of a new discursive economy, which not only broke with Old Regime social and cultural practices and reworked them into new structures but also transformed what used to be largely fixed, nondiscursive social identities into shifting, discursive ones.[6]

Bernardin's own career confirms the novel's widespread acclaim, which set it beyond accepted class and ideological differences during a long period of political upheaval. The novel's popularity among different publics, together with some adroit political maneuvering on Bernardin's part, allowed him not only to survive but even to benefit from successive political regimes. A pensioner of the king before 1789, Bernardin was later named by the Convention in July 1792 the *intendant* (overseer) of the Jardin des Plantes; in 1794 Robespierre's Revolutionary Government gave him the title of Professeur de la Morale Républicaine at the newly created Ecole Normale Supérieure. The Thermidoran reaction brought Bernardin membership in the Institut de France in 1795, and finally, Napoleon made him one of the forty "immortals" of the Académie Française in 1807. The ascending trajectory of Bernardin's career qualifies him as one of those "new men" whom Balzac never tired of writing about, and whose fortunes were made during this period. In the present case, Bernardin's success was as much discursive as pecuniary, and attests to the fact discussed earlier, in Chapter 1: that political and ideological differences from 1780 to 1815 were often fought out on the familial terrain that Bernardin comfortably occupied.

However, the flow of tears constitutive of *Paul et Virginie*'s readership was not to outlast the mid-nineteenth century—at least among the intellectual elite, where it soon dried up. Flaubert ranked it among the causes of Emma Bovary's literary "alienation" and cynically rewrote the text—though not without a modicum of sympathy—in his short story *Un coeur simple*.[7] Since then, *Paul et Virginie* has never regained favor among the elite public. Bernardin's novel finally passes away, among the cultivated public, in the twentieth century. The last shovels of dirt were thrown on the grave by Camus who termed it "a properly pathetic work" and the critic Etiemble provided its epitaph: "one of most mediocre and read books of French literature."[8] From the late eighteenth century down to our day, the unusual career of *Paul et Virginie* closely parallels the history of the production of familial discourse in the official canon of French prose fiction. *Paul et Virginie*'s literary success marks out the shifting fortunes of familialism in France, particularly among intellectuals; its wide reception by different reading publics afforded it a strategic position in the emerging familial politics of the French novel. Bernardin's text was instrumental in generating an economy of feeling and sentiment that reconceived social relations and reformulated individual subjectivity before, during, and after the French Revolution.

One Discourse, a Multitude of Publics

Paul et Virginie's role in the new "discursivity of the social" must be read in the particular ways that the book became a best-seller. It occupies an exceptional place in the history of French literature if only by virtue of its numerous authorized editions. Moreover, clandestine printers published over 300 pirated editions, according to Louis Aimé-Martin, Bernardin's literary executor, biographer, and editor.[9] The novel's wide diffusion resulted in part from innovations in production techniques (new presses, new energy sources), new distribution outlets (rental libraries and railway libraries), and a growing, diverse reading public. Also, in the nineteenth century the expanding publishing industry incorporated *Paul et Virginie* in collections targeting a wide range of readers: deluxe editions for the elite, dime novels for the "popular classes," anthologies of literature for children, and grade-school readers. Tellingly, Louis Aimé-Martin's first edition of Bernardin de Saint-Pierre's complete works (1818) was meant for young readers. *Paul et Virginie* became a central text in literacy and acculturation campaigns and in the new public elementary school system founded by Guizot in 1833, which required all communes to establish primary schools.[10] In 1837 appeared the first school edition, the following year the first expurgated children's version. Ten years later, the novel was incorporated in the series *Librairie populaire des villes et des campagnes* [Popular bookshop of town and country] and in 1849 it was included in the collection *Librairie de l'enfance et de la jeunesse* [Bookshop for children and young people]. *Paul et Virginie* began to lose the adherence of writers after 1848, but that was surely a sign of their alienation from hegemonic culture and their rejection of the commodified popular literature that made its massive entry in the literary market around midcentury. The disaffection of intellectuals notwithstanding, *Paul et Virginie* continued to enjoy popularity well into the twentieth century, repackaged as the market warranted it in publishers' eyes. Its last avatars have been a *roman-photo*, a comic book, and a film.[11]

Indeed, *Paul et Virginie* not only transmitted to Bernardin's contemporaries and successive generations a new sensibility and political agenda but also the *very desire* to write popular fiction destined to reach beyond the small numbers of an elite audience. For example, *Paul et Virginie* offered the young Balzac a compelling example of the mechanics and techniques required for composing a best-seller. The earliest reference made to it by the fledgling novelist in his collected correspondence is a letter to Louis Mame, a leading publisher, dated September 1832:

For a long time I have been struck by and desirous of the popular fame that comes with selling countless thousands of copies of a small-format [*in-18*] volume such as *Atala, Paul et Virginie, Le Vicaire de Wakefield, Manon Lescaut,* Perrault, etc.[12]

Four years later Balzac was to achieve literary fame with *Le Père Goriot* and *La Vieille fille,* the first serial novel published in France. Clearly, *Paul et Virginie* can serve as the herald of a new, popular novel, "democratic" in diffusion, "familial" in ideology.

From Treatise to Novel: Bernardin's New Politics

Political reform for Bernardin is mediated through the family and more especially—in true Rousseauist fashion—through wives and mothers. The gendering of the agents of social and political renewal draws on a new militant humanism that lays down the basis of a new reading public and recasts the very foundations of the monarchy's political authority. This is most strikingly articulated in his *Discours sur l'éducation des femmes* [Discourse on the education of women] (1777), written in competition for the prize for eloquence offered by the Academy of Besançon.

Although his treatise was meant for a small group of readers— the academy's membership—Bernardin's rhetorical ambition was to reach a much wider public. The *Discours* opens with a defense of the general appeal of his subject: to speak of women is to speak to everyone:

> To speak to men of art, science, fame, fortune, even liberty is to interest only a small number of them; but to speak to them of the sex who shares with them the burden of life's wants, and bears the burden of their childhood; of the sex whom they would call "industrious," "consoling," and "nurturing" had they not given it the name of "fair"; and of the sex who, born in equal numbers everywhere on earth, appears to be the only possession that nature has divided equally among them individually, is to address all of humankind.[13]

Bernardin's new reading public is nothing less than humanity itself. The text of *Le Discours* is for men (the Academy's members) but since it is about women it interests all, from Court to plebe. The treatise's topic transforms a rather limited reading public into the humanist subject par excellence. Collectively addressed by Bernardin's essay in terms of the new domesticity and its definitions of gender, men and women—as *new men* and *new women*—will be enjoined to jettison Old Regime social and familial practices in favor of moralized public and private relations.

In turn, the text addresses royal authority from the position of the new familial humanism and thereby reworks the very political basis of the monarchy. Bernardin appeals to Louis XVI by assigning the young king the imaginary role of grateful spouse whose queen has sponsored the reform work expected of all wives and mothers. The *Discours* ends with a tableau of national unity and felicity suffused with a sense of moral renewal. Bernardin has the king address Marie Antoinette with the following words:

> "At the sight of the happy countrysides that you embellish, foreigners forget their homelands and their resentment. Crime and poverty disappear in those places where you live. In order to make men good one must make them happy. . . . You are my happiness, the joy of your household, the good of nations, and the most beautiful gift that heaven has made to earth. Dear spouse, enjoy the only possession worthy of you, the supreme happiness of being loved."
>
> Thus he spoke and he clasped her against his heart; her children, moved to tears, surrounded her and squeezed her with their little arms . . .[14]

The text replaces the sumptuary values attached to royal power and aristocratic distinction with sentimental display of marital affection and familial love. This new spectacle, worthy of a Diderotian *drame bourgeois*, marks also the construction of a new type of political authority and community based on the new domesticity. The treatise addresses the political subject and figure par excellence, Louis XVI, whose legitimacy as man and king is now mediated by Marie Antoinette. *Her* authority, however, is no longer one based on blood, lineage, or name but solely on her role as wife and mother. Her new qualities as a domestic woman effect those political and moral reforms advocated by proponents of familialism, and are capable of lending the monarchy a new legitimacy, universal in scope. The *Discours'* readership that Bernardin invokes in the opening paragraph—humanity itself—has found its collective identity and validation in the closing lines: domesticity in the guise of royal authority.

At the close of Bernardin's text, royal power emerges renewed in the depoliticized form of companionate, bourgeois marriage, which, at a time in which the monarchy's political prerogatives were increasingly contested, might have been a convenient political expedient. However, it was to take years of discursive warfare and several revolutions before a "bourgeois" king would take the throne. In 1830 Louis-Philippe finally answered Bernardin's call.

When *Paul et Virginie* reached booksellers in 1788, eleven years after he penned the *Discours sur l'éducation des femmes*, it constituted a more fundamental address to the reading public. It dispensed with the corporate appeal to royal authority and relied rather on the lachrymose economy of pathos to unite its readers in a more radical rejection of Old Regime lifestyles and customs. The new sociopolitical subject and its imagined community—the novel's readers—was less authorized by Old Regime institutions than by the novel and the sentimental narration process itself. This stands as nothing less than the transference of political authority to the "people" (who turn out to be middle-class) in which sovereignty translates as access to the joys and duties of "family."

The Politics of Pastoral

Paul et Virginie's familial politics entailed a reworking of Enlightenment genres fashionable in prerevolutionary France: exotic or Creole literature and *la pastorale*.[15] With respect to the *pastorale*, Bernardin de Saint-Pierre transforms the elements inherited from the eclogue and the idyll—vignettes of rural life of rustic simplicity, simple but refined sentiments, social and spiritual peace—imparting to them a social content and tragic dimension otherwise absent in the genre. Bernardin dispenses with shepherds and shepherdesses and substitutes for them contemporary eighteenth-century characters. He stages the action in the French colony of Ile de France (present-day Mauritius), a small island off Madagascar, whose geography, flora, and fauna are laid out for readers in minute detail. Finally, he destroys the idyllic peace through the tragic death of Virginie and the consequent dissolution of the *petite société*. In a sense, Bernardin has revived and claimed for bourgeois prose fiction the seventeenth-century aristocratic pastoral romance that evoked a bygone noble lifestyle abandoned for the new life at court under absolute monarchy.[16] But here the nostalgia has been transformed into a forward-looking, energizing discourse, almost revolutionary in tone.

Moreover, the novel's narrational machinery subtly alters the mode of distanciation common to pastoral. *Paul et Virginie* deploys the structure of the framed tale that introduces a locus classicus of pastoral: the melancholic meditation on a natural landscape whose beauty is heightened by reminders of human mortality.[17] An extradiegetical narrator, engaged in the contemplation of an exotic landscape marked by the ruins of two rustic huts, encounters the timeworn figure of an old man, who is obviously the survivor of earlier, simpler times in Mauritius's colonial history. Their chance meeting motivates the narrative that follows, recounted by the old inhabitant, the novel's intradiegetic narrator. The old man's tale explains how the ruins came to be: it is of broken families and their eventual demise. Their story is the untold history of the aesthetic construction of both the landscape and the observer's position with respect to it. However, the tale's telling will generate a pathos that violates the aesthetic distance afforded by contemplation, and transports *Paul et Virginie* beyond the confines of melancholic pastoral. The tears break with aristocratic decorum and make a bid for a wider public by shifting to a "democratic" aesthetics of shameless sentimentality. This move imparts a political thrust to the novel that the pastoral mode might otherwise blunt altogether.

Familial Lack and the Sentimental Body

Paul et Virginie deploys what is arguably one of the most powerful strategies of familial discourse: the inscription of the social body with familial lack through reading. This sounds paradoxical but a consideration of the quote from Foucault that prefaces Part II will be helpful: "Where the family is lacking, [Tuke] substitutes for it a fictitious family decor of signs and attitudes." Foucault is referring to the familially constructed notion of psychiatric cure adopted by Tuke in England and Pinel in France, which I briefly discussed in the Introduction to this volume. The cure posits the social-psychiatric subject as lacking both reason and family; the means of attaining cure lies in the patient's recognition of this *lack*; for this process engenders the desire for sanity and familial reinsertion, which, of course, the asylum provides by means of the hospital's internal organization, or better still, through institutional fictions. According to Foucault, the asylum constructs two things: a lack and a desire (defined as lack) that turn on a new notion of reason and a redefined concept of the family. Thus, before confinement, it was entirely possible that the absent family and the disruptive behavior were not at all perceived and interpreted as a fundamental ontological and social deficiency. Pinel's interpretive procedures and cure will ensure the production of a new desiring patient.

Similarly, I will argue that *Paul et Virginie* inscribes familial lack in readers, but the tactic employed is more complex: the "family" as such will be a victim of lack and the resulting pathos will set in motion a lachrymose process of reading whereby the model family to which the lack obsessively refers will reorganize readers' sense of self and others around the imperatives of the new domesticity. The narrative process's forward movement is marked by critical moments in which family household life is threatened and in which, later on, moments of loss (the absence of fathers or mothers, for example) are commemorated or even compensated for through the constant bonding between family members or the projection of a future marriage. The recurring effect and signifier of these rites of familial loss and remembrance is the shedding of tears. In *Paul et Virginie* this narrative process takes a radical form, for the inscription of the lack or absence of "family" culminates, not in the restoration of household life, but in its destruction, in the death of Virginie, Paul, and their two family households—the *petite société*. Lack and loss preside over the opening and closing episodes of the narrative. It is by virtue of this narrative movement that the novel constructs the sentimental body. These narrative constructions are related to what Jay Caplan terms pathetic discourse in Diderot's works, particularly in *La Religieuse*. However, although our approaches deal with similar issues, I part company with Caplan insofar as his analysis is based analogically on the Lacanian model of desire and its concept of castration, for my intent is to explore how *Paul et Virginie* introduces a perception of lack where there wasn't one there to begin with. I wish to steer clear of psychoanalytic categories (lack as fundamental, the castration complex, the Name of the Father) which owe so much to familial discourse in the first place.[18]

Repeatedly, throughout the novel, tears flow: first, when Marguerite and Mme de la Tour recount their victimization at the hands of dominant sexual and alliance practices (such as aristocratic libertinage and taboos of *mésalliance*); later as they dote over their children's future union in marriage; when the children return home after losing their way on a day trip (the famous runaway slave episode); again upon Virginie's forced departure for France at the insistence of a great-aunt who wishes to leave her fortune to her niece; still later at Virginie's funeral; and finally when, in the frame of the tale, the old narrator finishes telling his story to his listener.

Narratives of victimization and the subsequent tears they produce constitute the *petite société* in its beginnings and construct what was to become a romantic trope par excellence: the reclamation of familial innocence—that of children and women—against hegemonic social practices and institutions, be they customary in prerevolutionary France or in the liberal, capitalist nineteenth century. In the latter case there is often a deep feudal nostalgia, but one that is (ironically) thoroughly rewritten in terms of the dominant discourse of the day: middle-class familialism. (We shall examine in Chapters 4 and 5 just such cases of nostalgia in Sue's *Les Mystères de Paris* and Balzac's *Les Paysans*).

Bonaparte closed his letter to Bernardin with the question readers, editors, and publishers all asked authors at that time: "What is true? What is false? [*Quel est le vrai? Quel est le faux?*]"[19] I want to suggest that with the novel's production of tears in readers, Bonaparte's question was rendered irrelevant; or it would be more accurate to say that the tears in one stroke prompted the question and set it aside. That is to say, that the performative aspect of reading—the tears—moved readers such as Bonaparte beyond the true/false distinction of a realist epistemology (hence Bonaparte's "confusion") onto a new ground; for what mattered was what *happened* to readers; what counted was the inscription of bodily sensation—pain and tears. This was the somatic constitution of a signifying process based on the sentimental body. Meaning and sensation are constructed here as indissolubly intertwined in one performative moment. And, as I will make clear, that pain, that loss—the death of Virginie, what D. A. Miller terms the *fantasmatics of sensation*—signify not only a new body but also a new familial ideal inscribed as an absence.[20]

The *petite société* constructs not only a new concept of "family" but also—literally—a "community of tears" that ultimately extends beyond the households to the entire island of Mauritius and outward to readers back in France. Whether you adhere or not to the new models of gender, household arrangements, and the body, whether you cry or do not cry over this kind of narrative, whether, finally, you embody more or less these new notions of self—your response situates you either at the center or on the margins of the new imagined community of revolutionary and postrevolutionary France. Thus this new desire is a profoundly social one and is part and parcel of a new reading process for both novels and human relations or, better still, a way of reading the social as one reads novels, in terms of the presence or absence of "family."

The New Discursivity: Inventing the "Family"

The novel's lachrymose economy involves a negotiation between two types of family households: the older, male-dominated one associated with the Old Regime nobility and the newer one that embodied domesticity and over which wives and mothers were called to preside. The narrative begins with two broken families, which are the direct product of Old Regime social practices and are constituted by them. Marguerite, a peasant woman, is a victim of aristocratic libertinage and Mme de la Tour is a woman of noble origins who, dowryless, married a commoner out of love and was disowned by her kin and milieu. Both women fled to Mauritius, and there Mme de la Tour subsequently lost her husband to tropical disease. The two outcasts gave birth to the two main protagonists—Paul, Marguerite's son, and Virginie, Mme de la Tour's daughter. The novel's line of flight from dominant Old Regime social relations has as its textual figuration the absence or death of the fathers. The paternal absence inscribes and enacts a crisis in the old corporate world with its networks and alliances of households, kin, and clienteles, which was unabashedly patriarchal in idiom (king/people, father/children, husband/wife, etc.).[21]

Yet the restoration of "complete" family households would not mark a return to the old male-dominated, patriarchal family. To make clear what I mean, I adduce a remark from a French philosopher writing 140 years later in a period in which middle-class civil society had finally become what familial discourse had long preached. In an essay published in 1927, Alain declared his agreement with Hegel and Comte that "the society that the mother and child form is first in importance"; "here is now the true couple."[22] Indeed, Marguerite's and Mme de la Tour's households both signify the emergence of a new child-centered family household overseen by women that stands in opposition to what is now marked as the male-dominated public sphere. The narrative work performed by *Paul et Virginie* entails replacing one form of lack—the husbandless and fatherless patriarchal household of the Old Regime elites— with another—the dissolution and loss of Marguerite's and Mme de la Tour's new model families. This process thus transforms the signification of absent fathers. The absence of adult men no longer signifies a "broken" household but rather introduces a new perception of the family household and what lies outside of it.

The fatherless *petite société* does not signify the regretted "loss" of patriarchal structures but rather the need for a new type of father and husband, whom I shall call the "New Man." Represented by

Paul, the future spouse of Virginie, the "New Woman," the New Man would be both companionate and dutiful, faithful to domesticity's norms and capable of mediating between the public and private spheres. From this perspective Old Regime customs are disowned not only because they are authoritarian and capricious but also because they are patriarchal and intrusive, unwilling to observe and respect the new distinctions between public and private, male and female worlds.

The two women and their children form a *petite société* on a stretch of land at a remove from both Port Louis and Pamplemousses, the local village. Their social contract is sealed by an exchange of life stories and tears upon their first meeting:

> Marguerite was moved to pity by her narrative, and desiring to win the confidence rather than the esteem of her new acquaintance, she confessed to her, concealing nothing, the indiscretion of which she was guilty. "My fate was deserved," she added, "but you, Madame, have been honest and unfortunate." And, shedding tears, she offered her both shelter and friendship. Touched by so affectionate a welcome, Madame de la Tour embraced her, saying: "Ah! God must want to put an end to my affliction, for He inspires you, to whom I am a stranger, with more goodness to me than ever I found in my own kin."[23]

Tears constitute the very grammar and syntax of the novel and designate at once a loss or absence, and often the compensation for that pain through the experience of community and solidarity they afford; community can take place within the *petite société* (88/46, 109/68), between the Old Man and his listener (175/136–37), or between Bernardin and his readers. All are recipients of a new set of bonds, a new social contract defined by the new domesticity and its attendant sensibility.*

---

* It is noteworthy that, elsewhere in Bernardin de Saint-Pierre's works, Blacks are relegated to a place outside the economy of tears. Commenting on a slave he once owned, Bernardin claimed: "I can only protest my experience and claim that I know of no more depraved a race [*point de nation plus vicieuse*]. I had a young seventeen-year-old slave who lied with the greatest effrontery, stole out of no need [*nécessité*]. He was equally indifferent to rewards and punishments, and what was most singular was that after having been severely punished and having uttered the most piercing cries we were stunned to see him dry-eyed

The nature of the text's semiotic labor requires us to pause. Here, the social body is clearly a sentimental one. But how is it related to the so-called discursivity of the social? What *Paul et Virginie* does is join disparate elements of Old Regime society—a widowed aristocrat and her daughter, a peasant single mother and her son, and their slaves Domingue and Marie—in a unitary, fatherless double household that is situated on two abutting stretches of land that belong to Marguerite and Mme de la Tour respectively. Now, what *are* this "family" and this "society"? Absolutely unidentifiable in terms of the relatively fixed corporate practices and relations of the Old Regime, the *petite société* works to pry loose these traditional identities from their Old Regime framework and to reinscribe them in a new field of social meaning organized by familial discourse. Thus, in this narrative, the dispersed and marginalized fragments of Old Regime society come together in a new "imagined" articulation: the *petite société*, a model "family" that is a profoundly discursive invention destined to enjoy a wide circulation among men and women of different social classes for the next half century.[24]

Inventing the Middle Class

The community of small landowners is something of a reformist dream-wish: the two women's victimization by Old Regime social relations has brought together in harmonious, familial union the two extremes of society: the peasantry and the nobility. The characters reproduce figures of social harmony thrice: Marguerite and Mme de la Tour, Paul and Virginie each within themselves (by virtue of their mixed origins), and Paul and Virginie as a couple.

Like most utopias, the self-enclosed economy of the families is based on a minimal exchange with the outside, figured in Pamplemousses and Port-Louis; the lack of exchange in turn is predicated

---

with stern countenance and steady voice" (Bernardin de Saint-Pierre, *Voyage*, p. 17). Incapable of registering pain as loss or guilt, Blacks are constructed here as devoid of interiority and thus beyond the humanist embrace—and social discipline—of paternalist control. They escape the circuits of utility, need (*nécessité*), and sentimentality in which physical and psychological pain are the purveyors of truth.

on a break with Old Regime sociality and the attendant sumptuary display of the body:

> The two friends spun cotton from morning to evening, maintaining themselves and their families by their work. Otherwise, so unfurnished were they with goods of civilization that they went barefoot about the settlements, putting on shoes only on Sunday to go to early-morning mass in the church at Pamplemousses, which you can see over there in the distance. This church is much further away than Port Louis, but they seldom went to the town, afraid of being scorned because they dressed in the coarse Bengal cloth usually worn by slaves. But what is public consideration compared to domestic happiness? If these two ladies had to endure some slights abroad, their pleasure was the greater on returning home. (87/45)

> Each day was a day of peace and happiness for the two families. Neither envy nor ambition tormented them. They had no desire to have in the world outside the kind of empty reputation that is got by intrigue and lost by slander; they were content to be their own witnesses and their own judges. (99/58)

A different order, maternal and familial, awaited them at home:

> At home they found cleanliness and freedom, possessions that they owed to no labor but their own, and eager and affectionate servants. Between themselves there was a bond of common need; the injuries they had suffered were nearly of the same kind. With one another they used the tender names of friend, companion, and sister; they had but one will, one interest, one table. Everything was shared between them. (87/45)

At this point we arrive at a major paradox: their social identity, their *distinction*, lay not only in uniting the extremes of Old Regime society in a harmonious *petite société* of domesticity but also in their exemplary private lives, which set them off from both the *grands* and the plebeians, from both of whom they kept their distance:

> But they always declined these offers with civility and respect; for they were persuaded that the powerful look only for indulgence and compliance in the weak and that one can only be compliant to others by flattering their passions, whether good or bad. On the other hand, they were no less careful to avoid familiarity with the poorer class of settlers, who were commonly jealous, rude, and backbiting. (107/66, translation modified)

The new family can have it both ways: as a universal principle it can also engage in social distinctions. The families are the fulcrum of liberal subjectivity, which is discursively identified with a new social class. They occupy the political-social middle ground that the middle class eventually claimed for itself in the nineteenth century, that of social mediation *and* distinction, the principle of a new dispensation: "At first one group supposed them diffident and the other proud; but their conduct, though reserved, was accompanied by such obliging marks of politeness, especially towards those in need, that, by imperceptible degrees, they gained the respect of the rich and the confidence of the poor" (107/66). This is an excellent example of what Jean Borie termed the middle-class "cult of the family, the irrefutable alibi of its imperialism."[25] So what we have here is a model of social reform—a project that would reconcile the peasants and the nobility of the Old Regime—that ends up discrediting both groups in favor of an invented yet unnamed social class whose existence is defined and authorized by new familial and gender practices. The reformist dream-wish underwrites what is truly a revolutionary project.

Lachrymose Bodies, Incest, and Family

A common worship of their children holds the two families together under the aegis of "natural" duties and obligations: "The duties laid upon them by Nature were a source of additional happiness of their society. Their mutual affection redoubled at the sight of their children, each of whom was the fruit of an unfortunate love" (87/45, translation modified). The two women take "child-cult" very far: "They delighted to bathe them together and to put them to sleep in the same cradle; often one would give her milk to the other's child. 'Dear friend,' Madame de la Tour would say, 'each of us will have two children and each of our children will have two mothers'" (87/45–46).

The flow of milk—the biological bonds of the new familialism—follows closely upon the sentimental and psychological exchange and flow of tears. However, the notion of milk, bound up as it is with domesticity's emphasis on moral qualities, sentiment, and interiority—in short, liberal subjectivity—operates quite differently from the aristocratic concept of the body and the metaphysics of blood. The question of milk unites in an identical thematic family, the body, health, and social (re)production, or, put another way, "bourgeois" sentimentality and utilitarianism. This authorizes what is for our still Freudian period the text's shocking combination of a naive moralism with a straightforward promotion of incest as "natural."

> As two buds left on two trees of the same kind, when all their branches have been broken by the storm, will bring forth sweeter fruit if each is taken from the maternal trunk and grafted upon its neighbor, so these two infants, deprived of all other relations, were filled with sentiments more tender than those of son and daughter, brother and sister, when they were exchanged at the breast by the two friends who gave them life. (87–88/46)

The pastoral novel proposes a model of desire:

> Indeed, nothing could compare to the attachment they already displayed. ... I never came here without finding them both naked, as is the custom in this country, scarcely able to walk and supporting each other by the hands and under the arms, like a picture of the twins in the constellation of the Gemini. Even the night could not part them; they would often be found lying in the same cradle, cheeks and breasts pressed together, their hands round each other's neck, embracing as they slept. (88/46)

Today, many academic readers of this passage probably exchange not tears as did Bernardin's contemporaries but rather knowing glances and condescending laughter. Indeed the text is rife with maudlin reworking of Old Regime sexuality, what Angela Carter calls in another context "the sentimental transformation [of] the denial of lust into a kitsch admiration of the 'cute.'"[76] Yet I would suggest that as readers, our "knowledge" and "glances" and "laughter" are not what we take them to be and that perhaps the joke may be on us. The reason is as follows: *Paul et Virginie* constitutes a key genealogical moment of the very knowledge and gaze that we readers habitually bring to the text. Bernardin and his contemporaries are not *naïve*; rather it is *we* who are unaware as to the historically constructed nature of our Freudian reading activity. Novels such as *Paul et Virginie* did much to set up and construct the discourse of our knowledge (what we see in texts, ourselves, and the social field). The text's deployment of the thematics of incest requires *no interpretation*. It is all there on the surface for all to see, remember, and cry over. What we have here is the unabashed, unapologetic familialization of sexuality and of desire. The operation is shameless and that is perhaps what makes us Freudians smile. But where is the guilty secret? Right there in full view. The circuits of desire have taken the Oedipal route denounced by Deleuze and Guattari as the "familialist reduction."[27] And our smiles, while they may be ironic and mocking of the text, do not question these parameters of desire and subjecthood; they thus confirm us as thoroughly familialized reading subjects. Unknown to ourselves, we qualify as worthy readers of *Paul et Virginie* and unwitting guardians of the familial faith. What we "discover" as textual "truth" *Paul et Virginie* and familial discourse constructed and taught the public long ago.

The very incestuous character of this new family household arrangement will ensure the reproduction of privatized, familial desire, as the *petite société* purposefully demonstrates. The successful outcome of this process requires a strict sexual division of labor that is one with a rigid gendering process:[28]

> When they were able to speak, the first words they learned to exchange were "brother" and "sister"; and childhood, if it knows tenderer caresses, knows no sweeter names. *Their upbringing only strengthened their attachment by fostering a sense of reciprocal need.* All that belonged to the management and good order [*l'économie, la propreté*] of the household and the preparation of their rustic fare soon became Virginie's province, and her efforts were always rewarded with compliments and kisses from her brother. On his side there was restless activity: he would dig the garden with Domingue or, a little axe in hand, follow him into the woods; and if on these outings he spied a pretty flower, a tempting fruit, or a bird's nest, even at the very top of a tree, he would climb up and bring them to his sister. (88–89/46–47, emphasis mine, translation modified)

Conversely, the *petite société*'s enclosure, its sequestration from the outside ensures that desire will not stray from the path of incest and that the gendered division of labor will inscribe heterosexual desire in terms of the mutual dependency of the couple. Bernardin de Saint-Pierre indeed insists upon companionate marriage that is self-consciously incestuous to the core:

> Already, over their cradles, their mothers were talking of the day when they would marry; and, assuaging their own grief with this prospect of conjugal felicity, they were very often brought to tears, one remembering that her injuries were the result of having neglected the laws of marriage, the other of having submitted to them; one had suffered for having reached above her condition, the other for having married beneath hers. But they comforted themselves with the thought that their children, luckier than they, would one day enjoy the pleasures of love and the happiness of equality far from the cruel prejudices of Europe. (88/46)

Paul et Virginie reworks desire and household organization and in one stroke lays down the basis of liberal social reform. The "cruel prejudices of Europe" must be done away with if such a family—and social class—are to see the light of day. Indeed, *Paul et Virginie* proclaims the radical newness of its familial-political project; the heroes' childhood idyll is predicated on a blissful ignorance of the past:

> They had no other studies but helping and pleasing each other; they were as ignorant as Creoles and could neither read nor write. What had taken place long ago and in the far-away countries troubles them not at all; their curiosity did not reach beyond the limits of the mountain.... Their affection for each other and for their mothers entirely occupied their hearts. Never had useless learning made them shed tears; never had the teachings of a gloomy morality filled them with worry. (89/47, translation modified)

There is no need for written discourse here; their education is that provided by the internal organization and activities of the "natural" child-centered family, much in the manner that Bicêtre and La Salpêtrière, reorganized under Pinel, "reeducated" the mentally ill.

The Female Body as Laboratory

At this stage, the novel has completed its transformation of the two family households. Old Regime practices first constituted them as incomplete and wanting: a process of victimization of Marguerite and Mme de la Tour—abandonment, exile, and death—had left the two households without fathers and husbands. The text then converts the *lack* into a *positivity*, the very lineaments and features of a new, militant family household, organized around motherhood and domesticity, that unites opposing social castes and estates in a state of pastoral harmony. This is what I called the reformist's ideal whose implications are nonetheless revolutionary. The text will now raise the ante in the second half of the novel. There, the Old Regime social logic makes a second disruptive return and destroys the two families, so that their loss authorizes a more radical indictment of the institutions and practices of absolutist France.

It should not then come as a surprise that the novel casts, as the agents of the idyll's destruction, Old World social relations in the guise of discredited familial and caste practices on the one hand and the sexually mature female body on the other. Indeed, they mutually signify each other. Virginie's approaching puberty leaves the *petite société* vulnerable to a social logic that had victimized Marguerite and Mme de la Tour and now risks transforming Virginie into the figural opposite of the domestic housewife: the sexually active aristocratic woman. Virginie's puberty raises the question of the new domesticity's economic basis that is unanswered by the discredited use of slave labor, and actually forces her mother to consider marital strategies of a very material sort: "However, as she watched her daughter develop with so many charms Madame de la Tour felt her anxiety increase with her fondness. She would say to me sometimes: 'What would become of Virginie if I were to die and leave her without fortune?'" (90/49, translation modified). The novel dramatizes a cultural and semantic struggle over Virginie's body, in which the body of the Old Regime, as figured by the aristocratic woman, will be discarded in favor of a new one, that of the liberal subject represented by the domestic woman. The answer will be as simple as it is audacious: female modesty. As I will make clear, a transformed female body will not just "symbolize" new social relations but will positively transform the old ones and require the new. The text's semiotic gall is altogether admirable. Female modesty is literally the cultural and semiotic precondition of a new political economy. Virginie's body restates the issues at stake in the mothers' stories and serves as a kind of laboratory whose task is to finish the experiment begun with the earlier generation.[29]

The onset of Virginie's puberty takes place in the celebrated bath episode, which is worth quoting here:

> During one of these burning nights, Virginie felt all the symptoms of her malady return with redoubled force. Several times she got up, sat down, then returned to bed, but in none of these positions could she find sleep or rest. By the light of the moon she turns her steps towards her fountain; she can see the stream which, despite the drought, continues to trickle in silver threads over the brown sides of the rock. She plunges into her pool. The first shock of cool water revives her spirits and a thousand pleasant memories come to her mind. She remembers that her mother and Marguerite enjoyed bathing her with Paul in this very place when they were children. . . . She can make out in the dim water, on her bare arms and on her breast, the reflection of the two palm-trees that were planted at her brother's birth and at her own, intertwining their green branches and their young coconuts above her head. She thinks of Paul's affection [*amitié*], softer than the scent of blossom, purer than spring water, stronger than palm-trees joined together; and she sighs. Her thoughts turn to the night and to solitude, and suddenly she is possessed with a consuming fire. Filled with fear by these dangerous shadows and by these waters that burn hotter than the sun in the torrid zone, she leaves the pool and hurries to her mother's side to seek support in this struggle with herself. (114–15/73–74)

At which point, a violent tropical storm strikes, devastating everything in its path: "Foaming torrents rushed down the sides of the mountain; the floor of the valley became a sea, the plateau where the cabins stood a little island, and the entrance to the valley a sluice through which earth, trees, and rocks were carried pell-mell by the roaring waters" (115/74).

The critic Etiemble, unmoved by the "pathetic fallacy" operative in the bath scene, accused Bernardin of indulging in "the stale obscenities of an old peeping Tom" [*les fades obscénités de vieux voyeur*].³⁰ What is a case of poor taste for Etiemble harbors for later critics, Freudians to a fault, a fascinating thematics of incest. Yet what is disruptive here is not so much incest in itself; as we have seen, that is affirmed by the novel as the very nature of the two protagonists' love for each other, upon which the reproduction of the two families depends. What perturbs the *petite société* is not incest in our Freudian sense of "incestuous desire" but rather the possible irruption of physical love as an aristocratic practice and a signifier of Old Regime culture.

We have remarked how for the metaphysics of blood *Paul et Virginie* substitutes the symbolism of milk as the fundamental body fluid. In the present episode menstruation is where the blood line discursively crosses with milk and motherhood. Two outcomes are possible here: an aristocratic body or a (bourgeois) domestic one. These are the high semiotic stakes for which *Paul et Virginie* plays. Virginie's menstrual flows set in motion flows of money and exchanges of women and signifiers of social distinction through the traditional noble circuits of remote kinship and arranged marriage. That is the significance of the great-aunt's letter. An aristocratic relative living in France, she writes Mme de la Tour and offers to educate Virginie and leave the young Creole woman her vast fortune: "She summoned her niece to return to France; or if her health would not permit her to make such a long voyage, she enjoined her to send Virginie in her place. She would see to it that her daughter received a good education and a place at court, and she would settle her entire estate upon her. The renewal of her favors, she added, was conditional upon her orders being obeyed" (118/77).

The nature of the aunt's intervention is not lost on Paul: it is nothing less than the reinsertion of the *petite société* and Virginie back into Old Regime caste and clientele networks and its consequent submission to the customary *droit de retrait lignagier* (the legal right of even far-flung kin to interfere in household life).³¹ Astonished, he queries Virginie: "'But,' returned Paul, 'you are leaving us for a distant relation whom you have never seen. . . . Where will you be able to bring together fonder companions than those who love you? How will you exist without your mother's caresses, to which you are so accustomed?'" (125/85). In the end, Mme de la Tour gives in to the entreaties and threats of representatives of Old Regime patriarchal authority—the island's governor and priest who intervene on the aunt's behalf—and her daughter's departure causes all to shed tears once again.

At this point it is necessary to lay out the manner in which constructions of gender and liberal subjectivity are articulated in *Paul et Virginie*. Now, men and women within and outside the narrative's frame cry alike and thus are positioned as "feminine" in their opposition to the Old Regime structures, but they do so as New Men and New Women. I mean that, while the novel feminizes victims and discredits traditional arrangements as oppressively patriarchal, it also promotes a different social order under the banner of the domestic family household whose daily activities are presided over by women. This is the position of oppositional, liberal subjectivity open to all characters and readers; and within that common "feminized" oppositional culture and discourse, gender is redefined and the distinction between women and men ("feminized," "nonpatriarchal" males and "domestic" females) emerges as a fundamental trope. Paradoxically, New Men and New Women embody a common new sensibility and subjectivity, are able to speak to each other, hold hands, and eventually have children so long as they agree to the novel idea that ultimately men and women are fundamentally distinct because of their reproductive systems.

It is important to grasp how only within this field of liberal (feminine) subjectivity are the positionalities of the New Woman and New Man articulated and even radically opposed. This is done by attaching Virginie's gender—her new "femininity" and, later on, her "modesty"—to her sex, e.g., her biological existence, her body understood as reproductive organism. In a sense, the text anchors an otherwise potentially shifting system of gender differences—in which there is, based on the new sensibility, something of a sliding continuum from "men" to "women"—in a putatively absolute biological difference (what Thomas Laqueur calls a "biology of incommensurability")* that turns on distinct reproductive systems and the gender roles and divisions of labor implied thereby. Since the "feminized" *petite société* is a new *discursive* construct—a social identity devised and promoted in a semantic field organized in print language—gender differences, distinctions between masculine and feminine gender of a new sort, require the rhetorical figure of immutable biology to stabilize discursively a field of possible overlapping identities. Hence the importance of the bath scene, in which Virginie accedes to biological femininity while bathing nude beneath a presumably masculine gaze.

Clearly, the privileged discursive figure is the woman Virginie, from which an entire social logic is to be derived. The pornographic structure of the short bath scene stabilizes, in terms of their desires, Virginie as biological "woman" and men as biological "men" (and, I would add, women as biological "women"); meanwhile it initiates a sequence that will ultimately address readers in terms of a familialized masculinity and femininity that has little to do either with the patriarchal positionality of the priest and the governor who force Virginie to go to France, or with the Old Regime identities of Mme de la Tour and Marguerite. Old political and social identities are jettisoned in favor of purely gendered ones. Thus, for example, readers are appealed to as New Women and New Men insofar as they transfer their sympathies from the corporate positionality of the mothers (presented both as members of different Old Regime castes or estates and as mothers) to Virginie, who exists strictly in terms of her classless, "depoliticized" gender, as a domestic female and her "modest" body, rejected by traditional French society.

In this light, it would be mistaken to view the feminization of the *petite société*, the narrator, and readers (all of whom are presumed

---

* Laqueur, p. 24. However, Laqueur's thesis must be read in conjunction with Armstrong's (the modern, liberal subject was first and foremost a [middle-class] female) in order to grasp how the discourse of biological difference works off and against the logic of liberal subjectivity, which, according to Armstrong, was not gender-neutral as Laqueur claims, but figuratively coded as feminine in its differential opposition to Old Regime elites and, later on, to the great masses of "unwashed" invading the public sphere in the nineteenth century. See Laqueur, pp. 18–19, and Armstrong, pp. 3–27.

to cry and weep) as a case of social "castration" whereby they are confined to a pitiful passivity. Such a psychoanalytic interpretation, while powerful, is phallocentric and relies too heavily on fixed, gendered positions of subjectivity. My contention is that the novel, on the contrary, modifies old positionalities and formulates new ones in which new familial and gender identities replace customary ones.

This is where I disagree with both Jay Caplan and Joan Landes on how the battle between Old Regime practices and Enlightenment critiques is staged in terms of gender on the eve of the French Revolution. What I stress, and what Caplan and Landes undervalue, is the extent to which notions of sentimentality, sensibility, rationality, and self-discipline are ascribed differentially to *both* men and women in opposition to Old Regime practices and customs. In their analyses of this moment of transition and transformation of gender distinctions, Landes and Caplan at times tend to essentialize masculine and feminine positionalities rather than favoring an approach that considers their modification and reformulation in the late eighteenth century.[32]

In response to Old Regime patriarchal practices symbolized by the noble system of alliances, *Paul et Virginie* deploys a radically *productive* strategy of familial and gender discourse that sets aside the old corporate system in favor of something new. Moreover, just as the *petite société* does not simply remain a fatherless or husbandless Old Regime household but constitutes a new affirmative concept of "family" linked to a novel sense of social class, so too "femininity" is not formulated as simply an absence of "masculinity" (patriarchal authority and agency) but rather as a strange new positivity, that of the "feminine" liberal subject, but—and this is essential—a subject who, like the "family" that nurtures it, is never fully *there* in its (gendered) particularity (as a New Woman or New Man) but must always be desired and sought after, forever remaining to be realized: throughout the novel the *petite société* and the liberal subjectivity it fosters enjoy at best a precarious existence amid signs of weakness, lack, or absence.

The Experiment Continues

The experiment on Virginie's body does not end with her forced departure for France but is pursued up to her disastrous return to Mauritius. The dynamic of familial absence and loss reaches its climax in the spectacle of Virginie's drowning during the shipwreck of the *Saint Geran* in the midst of a storm off the coast of Mauritius. Her melodramatic death in full view of the islanders pushes the logic of loss as a means of social bonding to the limit, and constitutes the final metamorphosis of Virginie's body.

Virginie's tragic end is the direct consequence of her failure to adopt Old Regime notions of aristocratic femininity. In France her great-aunt placed her in a convent, where she received the intellectual education expected of young noblewomen destined for life at court (music, letters, and the sciences); for in the contemptuous words of her benefactor the skills of the new domesticity she had acquired constituted "the upbringing of a servant-girl" (132/92, translation modified). An aristocratic mind requires an aristocratic body and the accessories necessary for its *mise en scène*, as well as an aristocratic name and title: "She gives me new dresses for each season and has provided me with two chambermaids who are as finely attired as great ladies. She has made me take the title of countess and give up the name of La Tour. . . . She has replaced it with your family name, which is also dear to me, however, because it was your maiden name" (132/92). The aunt's efforts are in vain, and fail to convert Virginie to values other than those practiced by the domestic family household; furious, she disinherits her niece and sends her back to Mauritius during the height of the hurricane season; that is, she sends Virginie off to die. The second storm, which sends her ship to the bottom, marks a second transformation of her body: no longer the potential site of Old Regime systems of alliances and sexual practices, Virginie displays the virtues of female modesty and self-possession that render her impervious to the old ways. In the first storm, "nature" as sexual pleasure and meteorological calamity threatened the *petite société* from within and without, and acted as an ally of Old Regime society, which sought to draw the two families within its destructive embrace. Logically, if Virginie's body undergoes a transvaluation as disruptive, so must "nature" with which it was identified. Now, however, the threat is purely external; to the hurricane's violence Virginie stands in opposition as the bearer of the power of a radically new interiority in the guise of female "modesty." Thus the text splits off familialized desire—sentiment or passion and their immediate consequences (marriage and children)—from carnal love. *Paul et Virginie* takes the first step toward the nineteenth century's distinction between "passion," an aestheticized, ethereal sentiment assigned to the upper classes, and "animality," at first attributed to aristocratic libertinage and later to the unwashed.[33]

The novel stages Virginie's modesty in the climax to the shipwreck scene. A sailor attempts to rescue Virginie from her sinking ship, but she refuses to strip in order to swim to safety. Finally an onrushing wave puts the sailor to flight: "At this dreadful sight the sailor sprang alone into the sea; while Virginie, seeing that death was inevitable, kept one hand on her clothes, placed the other on her heart, and raising upwards eyes shining with serenity, seemed an angel taking flight to heaven" (159/120–21, translation modified). The following day, the islanders discover Virginie's body, which death has reified into a veritable icon of bourgeois female *pudeur*:

> She was half-covered with sand, her head and limbs in the position in which we had seen her perish. Her features were not visibly altered. Her eyes were closed and her face was still serene; but on her cheeks the pale violets of death mingled with the roses of modesty. *One of her hands was on her clothes; the other, pressed against her heart, was tightly closed and stiffened.* (160/121, my emphasis)

What the novel constructs here is not the martyrdom of an aristocratic woman. Rather, it is the display of a new (female) body in public space. Within the confines of the new family household, Virginie and Paul could romp *nude* with impunity. The private, familial gaze constituted them in their incestuous innocence. Virginie's puberty signaled the imminent entry of her body into the public sphere, here coded as intrusive Old Regime society with its practices and sociality, its peculiar *gaze*. Aristocratic bodies displayed themselves with a different impunity, publicly engaging in bodily functions involving nudity, from defecating to fornication. Unless caste or clan honor were at stake, noblemen or women could have stripped themselves bare and swum to safety. Virginie's unwillingness to do so initiates the spectacle of a new *public* social body: the clothes signify not the spectacle of sumptuary aristocratic display but a closing up of the body from public view (Virginie tightly grips her clothing even in death) and the affirmation of a new interiority, an inner life (her hand on her heart) that Old Regime practices disallowed and refused to recognize.[34]

In a sense, Virginie is a female version of Norbert Elias's *homo clausus*. She thus contradicts Dorinda Outram's thesis that in late eighteenth-century France the latest avatar of the *homo clausus* was the strictly male stoic or Republican body of the Revolutionary public sphere, which she understands as being in opposition to the feminine-coded *sensibilité* of the old aristocratic salon culture. However, I would argue that, on the contrary, a militant familial discourse appropriated *sensibilité* and reworked it for the purposes of discrediting the Old Regime. As a consequence, *sensibilité*—the emotive, tearful body—was not so much displaced by the public, stoic body as it became that which defined the private sphere of family life for men and women alike, and therefore worked in tandem with the new style of public self-presentation (the *homo clausus*). Virginie embodies precisely *both* complementary modes of behavior. But I will agree with Outram by saying that after the French Revolution women entered the public sphere strictly as mothers and wives and (unlike their male counterparts) not as political actors.[35]

The text weaves a veil that is then thrown over the physical act of love in the new family household, where incest discursively reigns in disembodied form on the level of metaphor and desire. Carnality would constitute a fall into the physical world of bygone social and sexual practices.[36] Henceforth, children will be born in cabbage patches and what were to become middle-class men and women could thereafter distinguish themselves *as a class* in terms not only of the new domesticity and its emphasis on gender differences but also of a familialized sexuality according to which *somehow* well-scrubbed, clean children were born in their households without the messy, sweaty business of fornication, an activity identified with the old aristocracy and peasant laborers.

A sense of personal worth, an inner self that, much like the new family household, presumably requires no confirming public gaze in order to constitute it socially or morally, empowers the individual in his or her singularity either to organize a household and to discipline children or to seek out the challenges of the marketplace with the detachment and critical eye needed for the new calculus of economic rationality.

The text works to grant Virginie and her body that sentimental recognition and demands it of us as readers. We are witnesses to a spectacle of collective lamentation:

> Such were the arrangements made by the administration to render homage to Virginie's virtue. But when her body reached the foot of this mountain, in view of the cabins whose inhabitants she had made happy for so long and whom her death now filled with despair, the whole population fell into confusion: the hymns and chanting ceased; only sobbing and sighs of grief rose from the plain. Troops of girls from the neighboring settlements ran up to touch Virginie's coffin with handkerchiefs, rosaries, and crowns of flowers, invoking her as a saint. Mothers asked God for a daughter like her, young men for lovers as constant as she, the poor for a friend as tender-hearted, slaves for so kind a mistress. (162/123)

It took the French Revolution in order for the new female body to receive the recognition that was its due. At least that was Bernardin's retrospective assessment in his preface to the 1803 edition of his novel. He addressed French "womanhood" thus:

> Women of France! It is for you that Indian women create fine cotton fabrics and brighten your lives! It was for you that the daughters of Athens devised those commodious and charming dresses so favorable to modesty and beauty that wise Fénélon himself found them preferable to those cumbersome and proud costumes of our Old Regime. *The Revolution clothed you with them and they have added to your natural grace.* Mothers and nurses of your childhood, what power do your charms not add to your virtues? (70–71, emphasis mine)

The death of the virginal heroine precipitates the deaths of the remaining members of the two families: Paul, Mme de la Tour, Marguerite, Domingue, and Marie. The link between the thematics of virginity, self-destruction, and politics in another novelist, Richardson, elicited the following remarks by Raymond Williams:

> The specialization of virginity, and the paradoxical isolation and even destruction of the individual as a means of survival, are connected with that specialization of pity and charity, and the retreat from society into a nature which teaches humanity, which we shall later trace as responses to the continuing crisis of a basically ruthless social order, to which there was not, as yet, any available and adequate social response.[37]

Earlier I wrote of the text's semiotic audacity in proposing "modest" Virginie as an answer to the economic question raised by the *petite société*. I want to argue against Williams that, rather than simply symbolizing a political stalemate, *Paul et Virginie* is actually a powerful discursive strategy. The figural solution to a "real" infrastructural problem is not so much false, or a substitute for real political and economic struggle, as Williams claimed; instead, domesticity and female modesty on the one hand and a radical transformation of the public world on the other are of a piece. The former is not the reaction to the latter (as is often argued for the later period of industrial upheaval); rather, it is the necessary precondition of the latter's full development (notions of absolute property, individuals' formal rights [over against the claims of clan or guild], free circulation of labor and goods, the desire to work outside the household, etc.). What must be done is to regulate domestic flows and thus social ones. What is exchanged, what circulates, is identical: blood, milk, sperm, desire, feeling, women, men, capital, labor power, some more intensely in the private sphere, others in greater volume and intensity in the public domain. The pity and tears inscribe a very political desire.

This returns us to the question of slave labor. Readers will remember that the autonomy of the new domesticity from the public sphere and intruding Old Regime patriarchal authority is predicated on the work of slaves. Slave labor was the only imaginable way to put *male* labor power at the households' disposal within the framework of a strict division of labor without the encumbrance of male power; it also preserved the new family's reorganization of the household in terms of female dominance and the fundamental couple of mother and child from the threat of adult, white males whose authority derived from traditional power or, later on, from their "productive" work. The two family households had temporarily resolved the issue of the relation between the public and private domains by constituting a society unto themselves. There is a double division of labor, between men and women on the one hand, and between masters and slaves on the other. However, slave labor radically compromises the utopian qualities of the *petite société* and postpones the question of the economic survival and continuance of the two families that the mothers' and children's labor only partly assures.

The aristocratic inheritance proffered by Virginie's great-aunt has the attractive advantage of placing wealth in the hands of Virginie herself. Yet her offer is a poor solution, for it is at the cost of folding the new family back into the patriarchal idiom of Old Regime relations dominated by clan, the state, and the church. Capital from such a dissolute, discredited source cannot enter the circuits of the new family without disrupting it, any more than a desiring female body can. The circuits based on sentiment and a cult of intense feeling are too tenuous and fragile; or rather (which is the same thing) the new definitions of gender and subjecthood do not allow it. Moreover, *that* would associate the new household with the disowned practices of other social classes.

So Virginie's newly found and displayed modesty constitutes an implicit answer to the question concerning the new domesticity's economic relation to the public sphere. The practice of modesty, its asociality and distance from the public sphere, is the modus operandi of the New Woman and the New Family in the outside world. And what the New Woman requires is a New Man, content to wield and practice his authority and power in the public sphere and, as companionate husband and father, respectful of the imperatives of domesticity. As Auguste Comte was to write many years later of the husband's role in the household: "By marriage he enters into a voluntary engagement of subordination to Woman for the rest of his life. Thus he completes his moral education. Destined himself for action, he finds his highest happiness in honorable submission to the ennobling influence of one in whom the dominant principle is affection."[38] And that, in turn, implies a radical transformation of social structures and institutions, whereby wealth is indeed produced by men and located outside the household, either in the shop, factory, or office; there would male authority lie, and less so in the home.

Desire "modest" Virginie and, ineluctably, you will desire a new set of social and economic relations. New "private" mental and affective categories and desires require new public ones. Virginie's dead body is a political and politicizing marker. Her sexual maturity and the question of the *economic* reproduction of the *petite société* are identical events. Liberal, readerly subjects are called upon to enter and transform the absolutist sphere of political representation dominated by patriarchal Old Regime structures. Thus Virginie's kitschy "sainthood" is hardly a fall-back, makeshift position; it creates radical semiotic power: the familial politics of the sentimental body.

The Power of Discourse and the Politics of Powerlessness

The thematics of powerlessness, played out in terms of Virginie's virgin body, may perhaps be seen, as Williams claimed, as the symptom of a political impasse. But it occurs at, paradoxically, the cultural moment when domesticity and novel production were about to enjoy unprecedented discursive sway over French life, particularly that of the middling groups. The lack of family and lack of power are an overdetermined homology produced by the text and signified by tears. This is not only true of the novel's *histoire* but also on the level of the *récit*, the narrational machine and frame to which I shall now return.

Between the destructive patriarchal figures of the governor and the priest on the one hand and the new domestic man to come (Paul) on the other, stands the figure of the intradiegetic narrator, the Old

Man. He occupies a peripheral position with respect to the two families and hovers on the edge of the lives of Paul and Virginie. As Vivienne Mylne observed long ago, he is an unusual example of the emergent nineteenth-century omniscient third-person narrator. The Old Man recounts scenes and characters' thoughts of which he could not possibly have had any detailed knowledge.[39] Nascent nineteenth-century narration is constituted, as it were, under a new paternal aegis that produces at a transcendental distance or *in its apparent absence* tales about family households embodying new notions of domesticity, femininity, and so forth. The seeming price the emerging omniscient narrator—the Old Man—has to pay for his privileged spectatorship is a pitiful passivity. The helpless bystander to familial tragedy, he shares in this sense the position of his listener, or of Bernardin's readers. As dispenser of information, advice, and new values, he and his discourse are helpless before the intrusion of royal and church power. Indeed, he occupies a rather "feminine" positionality akin to that of the two families as a whole, which makes perfectly good sense: his authority, after all, is mediated by the example of Virginie and her *petite société*.

I want to argue that the thematics of powerlessness in *Paul et Virginie* is highly disingenuous; not only does it elicit strong investment in a familial ideal and perhaps social reform but it also smuggles in a new type of discursive power in the guise of weakness. D. A. Miller has caught this play of novelistic self-authorization off of traditional modes of force and repression perfectly: "Yet by now the gesture of disowning power should seem to define the basic move of a familiar power play, in which the name of power is given over to one agency in order that the function of power may be less visibly returned by another."[40]

Tellingly, the other price the Old Man pays for his privileged spectatorship is his celibacy. Discursive impotence is identical to a familial one: he is without family. However, the familial lack inscribed in his life is by virtue of his fidelity to the new models of marriage and private life: "There I pass my days alone, without wife, children, or slaves. If we except the rare good fortune of finding a partner who is well suited to us, surely the least unhappy state of life is to live alone" (136/96). The choice is laid out before the reader in intolerably polarized but galvanizing terms: either companionate marriage or a life of solitude. Emblematic of the workings of the narrative of familial lack is the fact that, be the "family" present or absent, the new family values prevail.

The transmitter of a narrative of families without fathers is a father without a family: he never met with a love-match. The "family" exists neither in the life of the agent of familial discourse nor for very long in the narration he produces. The inscription of lack and powerlessness structures the tale's frame as well as the tale itself and closes the novel. The narrator calls out one last time to the dead families: "'As for myself, since I looked upon you for the last time I have been like a friend bereft of friends, like a father who has lost his children, like a traveller left to wander over the earth alone.' As he spoke these words the good old man went away shedding tears, and my own had fallen more than once in the course of his melancholy narration" (175/136–37).

An agent of power in the "depoliticized" form of sentiment and femininity, Bernardin de Saint-Pierre's pastoral novel produces sentimental bodies that discredit customary social practices, authorize in their stead a new model of "family," and construct and order readers' desires. Once the rather straightforward political goals of dismantling Old Regime structures had been met, the novel was perhaps susceptible to a different political reading, a more conservative one; more subtly, yet perhaps just as obviously, the novel continued to exert a political effect in the guise of imparting a new familial sensibility, new notions of social and individual identity, by means of its sensational tears, whereby readers in postrevolutionary France, particularly those who were the targets of literacy campaigns, would come to understand that life's lasting satisfactions were to be found in the privacy of the home and not outside it.

Many years would pass before familial discourse could claim hegemony over the newly formed middle class. Indeed, familialism was part and parcel of the formation and definition of that loose constellation of social groups. By the 1840s, Bonnie Smith reminds us, middle-class women began to come around and answer the new domesticity's call.[41] Doubtlessly, too, it was at that time that they first saw themselves *as middle class* and that households we group today under that rubric became aware of themselves as such. This discursive process of class formation and social consciousness was pursued in conjunction with the investigation of the new "laboring classes," and there, too, familialism intervened decisively in novelistic form. It is time we turned to Eugene Sue's *Les Mystères de Paris*: familial discourse dons a protosocialist mask by means of the century's most influential *roman-feuilleton* or serial novel.

~ CHAPTER 4

Inside Out:
Domesticating the Social
in Eugène Sue's
Les Mystères de Paris

What does it matter that a book is within reach of the
pecuniary resources of the poor if it is not for their use?
Do you believe that these everlasting descriptions of heinous
crimes that fill the pages of most of the daily papers are for
their use and particularly that they can produce a salutary
impression upon them? Do you not know the extent to which
such images can trouble the mind, lead the imagination of
unenlightened readers astray? One always overcharges the
poor for what is of no use to them, and even more for what
may harm them in perturbing their minds and perverting
their ideas.
—de Gérando, *De la bienfaisance publique* (1839)

I have not seen M. Sue. His book is all the rage here every
evening. My nieces read of Sue what we allow them and
dream only of him. What is a philosopher, a politician,
a poet next to this Richardson of the people [*du Richardson
populaire*] who can make his readers live and love all that
in the form of drama?
—Alphonse de Lamartine, as quoted by Bory

THE PRODUCTION OF familial discourse by *Paul et Virginie*—the invention of new social space, family household structure, forms of desire, and concepts of gender—corresponds well to Ernesto Laclau and Chantel Mouffe's "discursive structure," an "articulatory practice which constitutes and organizes social relations."[1] Indeed, this is what I meant when I concluded that in its day *Paul et Virginie* wielded a semiotic style that signified the emergence of a new form of politics: a politics of discourse itself. Furthermore, Bernardin's novel lay at the heart of the process of transformation described by Laclau and Mouffe in which the relative fixity of Old Regime social, caste, and corporate identities gave way to the "non-sutured" openness of postabsolutist society and its field of discursive differences.[2]

That is to say, not only did *Paul et Virginie*'s economy of sentiment break with Old Regime cultural and social practices and rework them into new ones; the novel also labored to insert social structures and identities into the modern field of social discursivity, and, in so doing, imparted to the social as such a fluid, indeterminate nature that it didn't have before. And it is this discursive field of social differences that discursive structures such as "family" and domesticity will work on, redistributing and fixing them in a process of social mapping. The *petite société*'s fatherless family household dissolves Old Regime identities and causes them to float and drift only to fuse (or to use Laclau and Mouffe's Lacanian terminology, "suture") them into a radically new entity, the female-dominated domestic household. This "family" entailed nothing less than the invention of a new "imagined community" and a regulated social body, a new notion of femininity and female authority, and the creation of a new social class of the middle ranks. It is precisely this double work of dispersion on the one hand and articulation on the other—which is what novels perform—that produces and renews familial discourse throughout the nineteenth century.

The question then arises of what happens to familial discourse as an articulatory practice in a postrevolutionary, emergent capitalist era, when, moreover, new readers from the urban laboring classes enjoy access to the new written culture of daily newspapers and their serial novels. And what changes does familialism's imagined community undergo? The answer can be found in the pages of Eugène Sue's *Les Mystères de Paris* (published in *Le Journal des débats*, 1842–43), the nineteenth century's most renowned *roman-feuilleton*, or serial novel. Indeed, *Les Mystères* will provide us with an opportunity to observe how familial discourse adjusted its tactics and rhetoric as it expanded the scope and ambition of semiotic work to construct and encode yet another new social class, the urban laborers.³

Print Culture Old and New

I want to argue that the following five events must be held simultaneously before the mind's eye: the serial publication of *Les Mystères de Paris*; the rapid extension of national print culture by the large-circulation dailies and their serial novels to urban workers; the introduction of the laboring classes and a new urban topography under the rubric of *la question sociale* among the field of discursive objects; a new expansion of social discursivity to yet other collective and social identities; and a reworking of what it meant to be "middle class." The first four events involved a subtle dialectic of recognition in which many readers and journalists of the laboring classes excitedly praised Sue for being the first writer of national prominence to give voice and representation to their conditions and miseries and in which Sue, in turn, modified his narrative in response to the requests of these readers.⁴ The last event was a new process of class definition whereby the middle class was constructed in terms of nostalgia for the Old Regime nobility on the one hand and anxiety with respect to urban workers on the other. The admittance of urban workers as both objects and readers into an expanded national print culture was very much felt as a violation, not just of taste but of social boundaries, by many readers in the cultivated public. Benedict Anderson's notion of the "imagined community" helps us understand how this might have been the case. He argues that the novelistic presentation of objects (for example, Parisian streets and quarters, buildings, and landmarks) introduces within the frame of "homogeneous, empty time" of calendar and clock at least a tacit sense of "community in anonymity" among readers.⁵ Thus the reading of best-sellers and the daily consumption of newspapers by the middle class and workers alike amounted to identical rituals of "imagining" a national community, however internally differentiated or divided it may be. Anderson observes that the newspaper is merely an "extreme form" of the book, a book sold on a colossal scale, but of ephemeral popularity. Might we say: one-day best-sellers? The obsolescence of the newspaper on the morrow of its printing—curious that one of the earlier mass-produced commodities should also prefigure the obsolescence of modern durables—nonetheless, for just this reason, creates this extraordinary mass ceremony: the almost precisely simultaneous consumption ("imagining") of newspaper as fiction. . . . Furthermore, this ceremony is incessantly repeated at daily intervals throughout the calendar. What more vivid figure for the secular, historically-clocked, imagined community can be envisioned? . . . As with *Noli Me Tangere* [a novel by Filipino nationalist José Rizal], fiction seeps quietly and continuously into reality creating that remarkable sense of community in anonymity which is the hallmark of modern nations.[6]

This identity between best-seller and newspaper received its most powerful form, of course, in serial novels such as Sue's. No wonder that the new "imagined community" of *Les Mystères* (the redrawn social topography and modification of the "real" by familial discourse) met with stiff resistance from conservative critics and readers. To write and publish serial novels about urban workers inadmissibly conferred upon the latter something of an aura of cultural legitimacy; the new public sphere produced by the commercial print media granted the laboring classes a *droit de cité* that they had not enjoyed before (except briefly, perhaps, during the First Republic). At the same time, the figural and narrative work in Sue's novel circumscribed and, up to a certain point, contained the process of legitimation of the lower orders of society within the framework of familialism's new social logic.

Familial Discourse and the Field of Discursivity

Critics from Karl Marx to Umberto Eco and Peter Brooks have never tired of pointing this out: characters such as Fleur-de-Marie and Le Chourineur are indoctrinated by social and religious paternalism;[7] the text respects bourgeois morality in having Fleur-de-Marie, the fallen woman of aristocratic origins, die, and thereby enforces conventional social hierarchies and distinctions whereby the upper and lower ranks of society remain in their separate spheres.[8] But these critics are at pains to reconcile both the transgressive and conservative aspects of Sue's text in particular and of serial novels of the city in general. Eco's essay on *Les Mystères* ends with an embarrassed note in which he is forced to account for the novel's immense popularity among urban workers, and how it may have contributed to their long-term mobilization prior to the Revolution of 1848, by invoking the unfathomable hazards of literary reception:

> the message which has been evolved by an educated elite (in a cultural group or a kind of communication headquarters, which takes its lead from the political or economic group in power) is expressed at the outset in terms of a fixed code, but is caught by diverse groups of receivers and deciphered on the basis of other codes. The sense of the message often undergoes a kind of filtration or distortion in the process, which completely alters its "pragmatic function."[9]

Two things are worth observing here. First, like most semioticians, Eco thinks in terms of contained sealed codes that may or may not reach their receiver by virtue of his or her own codes. But that "synchronic closure" of codes dispenses with the very process of textual production of codes themselves. This is the semiotic work of a text that may implement provisional effects of rhetorical and semantic "closure"; but the emphasis should more properly fall on the work process, which then leaves us with that sense of indeterminate discursivity that Laclau and Mouffe claim is the distinguishing feature of social practices in a postfeudal age. By that I wish to suggest that *Les Mystères* does not begin with a fixed code, and that it deploys its code narratively only to bind it and fix it once again at the end of the text. Rather, it seems to me that what is at work is a capitalizing by the novel on the very porousness of the discursive objects, their openness to the outside, to the play of radical semantic difference in the field of social identities, in order to construct a new discourse that is not the same as that which "preceded" the novel's labor. Rather than affirming an ideology that existed prior to *Les Mystères*, Sue (but he was scarcely alone in this) produced a new social discourse that left the social with a different configuration and outline. This will become clear as we move through the novel.

Second, clearly the problems of reception theory constitute the vanishing point of Eco's approach. They also dog other attempts to analyze the intersection of middle-class or culture-industry commercial literature and their working-class consumers.[10] Again, the replacing of a traditional notion of the semiotic by that of the discursive will lead us out of the dead end of a false problem. Foucault, and after him Laclau and Mouffe, remind us that the field of social discursivity is never totally articulated by any one discursive structure or code, and that both hegemonic practices and, conversely, those of resistance provide points of fixation and drift where the flows of power are brought into play. The effects of hegemonic discourse are unpredictable, and not only because any one discourse can be "interpreted" differently, "stolen," or "reappropriated." They are unforeseeable by nature simply because the construction of, for example, the "laboring poor" along the lines of a modified familial discourse, and their subsequent insertion in the play of social maps, boundaries, meaning, and identities, also may politicize the "laboring poor" by clearing a space for those who are classified under that rubric to affirm themselves collectively in *discourse* even though the field of meanings and concepts is limited by the new hegemonic print culture, its imagined community, and familial ideology. Thus it is entirely possible for those urban workers who responded to *Les Mystères* to set forth social demands within the public sphere of print culture and politics, then to refuse to leave it once they were summoned to do so in February and June 1848, and finally later in the century to implement trade union agendas based on the needs of the working-class family defined in terms of the new domesticity.[11]

To summarize: the very entry of urban workers as objects and readers in the expanded domain of national print culture enjoyed political effects of the same order as did the articulation of that culture by familial discourse. This is the finer implication of Foucault's point that both hegemony and resistance are situated on the shifting terrain of discursive practices.

"L'Homme invisible": The Serial Novel, Print Culture, and Domesticity

The identification of the older print culture with the early discourse of domesticity in the eyes of the literate elite can be read in their simultaneous transgression heralded by the publication of *Les Mystères de Paris*. One of the earliest critical studies of serial novels, Alfred Nettement's *Etudes critiques sur le feuilleton roman*,[12] denounced their publication. It is worth observing that Nettement addressed his remarks in epistolary form to an imaginary male aristocratic reader; this confirms for us that on the one hand he was attached to an older print culture that had its roots in the Enlightenment, and that on the other he also assumed the nobility now shared the new norms of domesticity. For him the consumption of serial novels by the general public and by mothers and wives in particular amounted to nothing less than a violation of the sanctity of the home:

> Eden is still in our day that sweet and chaste life of the domestic hearth [*de foyer domestique*], that pure and charming private life [*intimité*] in which no outside noise resounds, that harmony of sentiments and ideas which makes heaven on earth. If the serial novel enters your interior, all that disappears. Woe betide you! The enemy is in your homes [*foyers*]. It has penetrated inside with its train of disappointing illusions, misleading ideas, spineless and dangerous emotions, corrupting dreams, incendiary images.[13]

The serial novel's power of disruption *as discourse* is a matter of utmost seriousness to Nettement; he goes so far as to claim that the serial novel has insidiously replaced the priest, the wife's confessor, who had enjoyed until recently invisible and secret authority and influence in the household:

> But tell me, you who speak of an invisible man seated in the home [*foyer*] between husband and wife, do you not dread anything of that counselor, that interlocutor of a new kind, who during two months, three months, sometimes a year, returns every morning with the newspaper, who seizes hold of the feelings, thoughts of a young woman, who will create for her a new ideal, who will reign over her hours of solitude, who will stir

up her imagination, and who, instead of being dominated like the priest by an unvarying rule from which he cannot depart, makes himself his own rule, or rather has no other rule than his own whim and fancy?[14]

These passages are drawn from a long section entitled "Influence du roman-feuilleton sur la famille" (The influence of the serial novel on the family). If we follow Nettement's line of reasoning, to read a serial novel was literally to introduce the street ("the outside noise," "the enemy") and the authority of another discourse (the male stranger, "the counselor") into the privacy of the household.

Conversely, the extension of national print culture to the popular classes as both subject matter and readership meant detaching it from its moorings in the old domesticity. Nettement makes this point with reference to earlier novelistic embodiments of the new family norms—Richardson's Pamela and Bernardin de Saint-Pierre's Virginie—that he opposes to Sue's young prostitute Fleur-de-Marie; she is inadmissible as a heroine: "Is that the portrait of another Pamela or of a new Virginie, minus the inimitable color of great painters who have made their canvases shine with those elevated types of moral beauty enhanced by physical beauty? . . . No, this woman is the prostitute whose type I tried to outline."[15] Nettement was surely right in that Fleur-de-Marie was not Virginie in terms of the older discourse; but she did occupy a similar position in the context of a new print culture, wider reading public, and transformed discourse of class and domesticity. That is what Nettement failed to grasp or could not accept.

The idea that reading serial novels was a family affair was a commonly held assumption during their heyday in the 1840s. Louis Reybaud, a contemporary novelist, commented with no small amusement:

> Savored by mother and father, the serial goes straight to the children who lend it to the servants from where it descends to the doorman (if the latter has not already read it first). Do you understand the kind of roots a serial novel consumed in this manner has in a household [*intérieur*] and what kind of situation that it immediately secures for a newspaper? From now on this newspaper is an integral part of the family. If in order to save money one drops it, the mother pouts, the

children complain, the entire household [*maison*] is up in arms [*en révolution*]. It becomes necessary to take it again, to resubscribe in order to reestablish domestic harmony and conjugal bliss. That, Môsseur, is how the serial plays from now on a social role, and takes its dominant place next to the stewpot and kitchen utensils.[16]

I think we can safely assume that what also upset Nettement was not only the entry of the Parisian laboring classes into the domestic household but also the association of middle- and upper-class families with more modest ones in their common membership in the imagined community of readers of large-circulation dailies. Put rather crudely, in the eyes of the older domesticity working-class households can no more be called true "families" than can Fleur-de-Marie be Virginie. I want to argue that the elaboration of a new discourse of family and social space worked precisely on establishing these unsettling "monstrous proximities" between socially opposite households to a double effect: on the one hand that of rooting middle- and upper-class identity in a domestic sphere under constant threat of disruption from the urban environment, and on the other hand that of promising to the newly literate that they, too, may enjoy the satisfactions of domesticity and of perhaps a higher social station. In turn, these hopes remain as vulnerable (if not more so), as the established households of their social betters to the pressures that the city and its pathologies exert on them.

Monstrous Proximities

In a sense, *Les Mystères de Paris* achieved the same effects as *Paul et Virginie*: the invention of a national community based on new norms of "family" that potentially includes in its embrace all social groups while in actuality maintaining social distinctions and differences. Only now, fifty years later, when the fixed identities of blood, caste, corporation, and title had come unstuck before the fluid nature of postrevolutionary society, domesticity held sway over the upper echelons of society and, consequently, the perceived threat was no longer from above (the First and Second Estates) but from below (the urban laboring classes). With the appearance of the urban unwashed, familialism's *modus operandi* of simultaneous inclusion within and exclusion from the broad middle-class fold shifted to an endless and supple dynamics in which the inclusion of its targets (aristocrats, prostitutes, criminals, working-class men and women) would never be definitive nor their exclusion ever final. In novels the characters are always strong enough to stand and free to fall. There was already an example of this dynamic in *Paul et Virginie* when Mme de La Tour weakly acquiesced to the old social logic that underlay the governor's forceful pleas to allow Virginie to depart for France so that she may claim her inheritance. In Sue's novel, much of the melodrama turns on the intensification of these moral uncertainties.

The general plot of *Les Mystères* runs as follows: Rodolphe, German prince of Gerolstein, lives incognito in Paris where he performs clandestine acts of charity to the deserving poor in penance for having raised his hand against his father, who forbade his love marriage to Sarah, an ambitious and scheming British aristocrat. With the help of Polidori, Rodolphe's Italian tutor, she managed to trick Rodolphe into marrying her illegally, which plot he later discovered. During one of his forays into the Parisian underworld, Rodolphe saves Fleur-de-Marie, a very young prostitute otherwise known as La Goualeuse (The Songstress), from a brutal beating by Le Chourineur (The Ripper or The Slasher) whom Rodolphe will eventually befriend. As the plot evolves, Fleur-de-Marie turns out to be his long-lost daughter, whom Sarah had abandoned after their marriage was declared null and void. Meanwhile, Rodolphe's actions pit him against a sinister cast of characters: Le Maître d'école (The Schoolmaster), a master criminal, and his companion La Chouette (The Screech-Owl), who was Fleur-de-Marie's procuress; Ferrand, a corrupt notary and moneylender; Polidori, now a dangerous assassin and back-street abortion practitioner; and a band of petty criminals including La Martial (The Fighter) and her daughters and son, Bras Rouge (Red Arm) and his son Tortillard (Hoppy), and Le Squelette (The Skeleton). Conversely, Rodolphe's acts of charity will lead him to befriend Rigolette (Miss Dimpleton), a hardworking seamstress, her lover Germain (also Le Maître d'école's son), La Louve (The She-

Wolf, Fleur-de-Marie's rival, later her friend), Martial (son of La Martial and La Louve's companion), Morel, a poor gem cutter, and his family, and Mme d'Harville, an unhappily married woman. By the novel's end (some 2,500 pages later in the 1844 edition), Le Maître d'école has been put away in an insane asylum, Le Chourineur and La Chouette are dead; so are Sarah, Ferrand, Polidori, La Martial, and her daughter Calebasse (Calabash). Rodolphe and Mme d'Harville have married, as have Germain and Rigolette and La Louve and Martial. Morel's family is saved from ruin at the hands of Ferrand but Fleur-de-Marie, although she has been restored to family life and her high social station with Rodolphe, dies of guilt for her past life, leaving Rodolphe and his wife bereaved.

Originally, Sue intended to subtitle *Les Mystères de Paris* "Le Convertisseur."[17] And indeed, something of a schema of narrative conversions is operating in the novel's multiple plots. Characters discover or are won over to the norms of the new domesticity and thus marry and establish bustling model households by the novel's end. Hence the many companionate marriages that conclude the narrative. Conversely, we can speak of other stories of nonconversion (Sarah, Le Maître d'école, La Chouette, La Martial, et al.) in which characters refuse to change their ways and "return" to family life; thus they die. These plots, then, seemingly turn on the clear-cut presence or absence of "family." However, as in *Paul et Virginie*, the general narrative both begins and ends with a lack of "family." More important, just how the lack of realization of "family" is distributed across the social spectrum is never assured before the last page. Indeed, the dynamics of familial lack at work in *Paul et Virginie* undergoes a transformation whereby it is generalized to all characters. No one group or class fully realizes the new model family, nor are the vilest characters such as Le Maître d'école or Sarah totally exempt of moments of familial desire. The conversions do not meet with either complete success or failure. Thus the "family" is neither altogether present nor fully absent. Similarly, the shifting proximities of characters and their households in relation to each other with respect to the norms of family life does not convert readers to the new models of desire and gender relations so much as it contaminates them with a constant anxiety, if not paranoia, concerning the eternal fragility and possible renewal of familial practices and values in the new social landscapes of the urban metropolis. One's spouse may marry one out of ambition (Sarah) or selfishness (M. d'Harville) or go mad (Mme Morel), one's daughter may end up pregnant (Louise Morel), perhaps even a prostitute (Fleur-de-Marie), one's father may actually be a criminal (Le Maître d'école); or, conversely, the son of an unnatural mother may give up a life of lawlessness (Martial), an orphaned criminal may become a farmer (Le Chourineur), a morally loose seamstress will settle down and start a family (Rigolette). The inscribed instability of the familial map is identical with a social one, and maintains sociopolitical identities in a state of flux that matches the potential porousness of post–Old Regime relations. The force and point of Sue's serial novel is its peculiar reformulation of a familial social imaginary by means of shifting and floating social distinctions. The obsessive hand-wringing over social differences in novels like Sue's and in contemporary writing did not *reflect* the instability of urban life in France's transition to capitalism; rather, the recurrent blurring and transgression of fundamental boundaries between classes, genders, and public and private spheres by these novels did much to promote the porousness of social relations. And this recalls the new discursiveness of the social itself. In serial novels uncertainties around class derived in part from uncertainties about "family" and marked the eternal return of the familial, which by virtue of its lack or absence both fixed and unfixed the social, produced subjecthood and collectivities (families and classes for one thing) within a field of differences that ultimately cannot be mastered.

Fixing the Social, I: A New Urban Topography

A good example of "monstrous proximity" can be found in the opening lines of *Les Mystères*:

> On the cold and rainy evening of December 13, 1838, a man of athletic build, wearing workman's clothing, crossed the Pont-au-Change, and dived into the City [*la Cité*], a maze of dark, narrow, crooked streets, which spreads from the Palace of Justice to Notre Dame Cathedral.

The Palace of Justice quarter, though very delimited and closely watched, serves as the asylum and gathering-place of malefactors in Paris. Is it not strange, or rather fatal, that an irresistible pull makes criminals gravitate towards this formidable tribunal which condemns them to prison, to the penal colony, to the scaffold!

On this night, the wind, we say, fiercely swept through the cheerless quarter's alleys. The wan and flickering light of the street-lamps, swinging in the breeze, danced by reflection in the black water of the stream that ran midway in the muddy paving stones.

The mud-colored houses were broken by a few worm-eaten window-frames with hardly a pane. Dark and filthy alleys led to flights of steps even darker and more filthy, while being so steep it was hard to climb up them even by help of a rope iron-cramped to the sweating walls.

Some of the ground floors were shops of coal-dealers, tripe butchers, or those who resold bad meat [*revendeurs de mauvaises viandes*]. Notwithstanding the paltry value of the foodstuffs, the fronts of the windows were nearly all iron-barred, so much did the shopkeepers dread the audaciousness of the quarter's thieves.

The man we noticed slackened his pace on reaching the Rue aux Fèves, situated in the heart of the City, feeling that he was "on his own ground."

It was very dark, and the strong gusts of rain lashed the walls.

Far off ten o'clock rang from the Palace of Justice clock.

Women, lying in wait under porchways as in deep, vaulted, ill-lit caves, hummed refrains of popular songs.[18]

D. A. Miller has pointed out that the second paragraph encapsulates in several revealing lines the relationship studied by Foucault whereby in the nineteenth century the criminal justice system, by virtue of its methods of policing, investigation, classification, and incarceration, created a criminal milieu that in turn resembles in its practices and organization the operations of the police themselves.[19] This may indeed be the case. But the copresence of the Palais de Justice and loitering criminals is not simply symptomatic of some relation of power; more interestingly, this textual construction actually performs an anxiety-provoking act on readers whose sensibilities are perhaps worked up by this taunting and mysterious proximity of criminals to the main courthouse. Or better still, this compromising *rapprochement* may elicit the very new perception that a social boundary has been compromised and thus the desire to see its integrity restored.

But let's explore this map and these nascent readerly desires in more detail.

Readers are walked through a quarter of town where presumably they've never set foot, or if they have, *they should never have visited*. The layout of the streets, the street lighting, even the architecture of the buildings obstruct the readers' gaze while at the same time soliciting it. The cramped, irregular space (the winding, narrow streets; the windowless, closed-up houses and shops) encodes the city anachronistically as a medieval château replete with hidden dangers—concealed entrances, traps, and dungeons—that in turn stage the drama of physical dissolution in which the repulsive confusion of worm-eaten structures, rotten meat, and prostitutes' fallen bodies is matched by the equally unsettling identity of the street and the sewer. Parent-Duchâtelet could have authored this passage, for the *mystery* of the Cité is predicated on social differences that are medico-hygienic to the core. (Sue will acknowledge the importance of *De la prostitution dans la ville de Paris* later in the novel [1:65].) The text brings into play several desires here. First, the transgression of the imagined community by the presentation of unfamiliar social space teases readers to want to know more; this new desire will in turn permit the novel to continue the semiotic work it has already begun. Moreover, the mechanics and power of social voyeurism position the readers as middle or upper class, imaginatively exploring the shady parts of town from the safety of their private homes. Here is Nettement's outraged assessment of readerly slumming:

> That urge [*instinct*] of unhealthy curiosity, which thirsts after new, harrowing thrills [*émotions*], was the first element of public favor bestowed upon the work by the *Journal des débats* novelist. *Les Mystères de Paris* could be compared to a public execution that everyone can witness at home [*chez soi*], or to a visit made to a penal colony by the reader without leaving his study. The ease with which one can take pleasure in this spectacle together with the horrible novelty of the emotions it affords had a great deal to do with the book's success.[20]

Second, the "knowledge" the novel constructs—the "other" Paris as deeply pathological—inscribes in the landscape the need for the intervention of public health officers, philanthropists, and the police, and inscribes in readers the wish to see it done. Finally, the social pathology negatively designates the new familial norms that solicit readers' approval; for *if only* the quarter could be redesigned, proper sewage lines and street-lighting introduced, and new housing built, *then* perhaps we would witness the propagation of bustling households overseen by virtuous mothers who prepare healthy meals for their families. As in *Paul et Virginie*, familial discourse and desire power an entire social agenda.

Of course, nothing better illustrates the flow of social desire in *Les Mystères* than the figure of the prostitute. She is the end point of the entire excursion through the Cité. Readers are guided metonymically down its shadowy, twisting streets, past flickering streetlamps, darkened houses, and pestilential "second-hand" meat shops that line the polluted thoroughfares to the women selling sex for subsistence. Their bodies are condensed figures for the play of transgression and desire that organizes the whole passage, indeed much of the novel itself. In their flesh thrives a "monstrous proximity" of two opposites—women and the street—a blurring of social boundaries that reaches its fullest expression in Fleur-de-Marie herself. Le Chourineur's progress through the Cité will fatefully end in bringing together Fleur-de-Marie and Rodolphe, her father. Here, the familialist nightmare of evanescent distinctions and corrupted identities is literally a family one: Rodolphe's lack of "family" (he has lost his daughter, as we later learn) is mirrored in and compounded by Fleur-de-Marie's lack of virtue. His daughter is doubly "lost," for she is a teenage prostitute. The power of this shocking narrative of the violation of normative family life was such that Nettement claimed that for mothers and housewives even to read it amounted to reproducing a scandalous *rapprochement* between these virtuous *mères de famille* and the streets from which they are sheltered:

> You conduct the young mother to the dreadful Lapin Blanc [White Rabbit] cabaret, you put her in contact with *mère* Ponisse's boarders, you initiate her in La Louve's and La Goualeuse's [Fleur-de-Marie's] morals, and, after placing a bookmarker on that page and scarcely

having exited from that hell, you will then send her to make her accustomed visit to her children, who must find heaven on her lips, in her eyes, in her words, in her heart![21]

Upper- and middle-class women readers of Sue's novel risk henceforth being no more "at home" in their households than common prostitutes in a family setting, and conversely, like public women, all too "at home" in the streets of *Les Mystères*. That is the fear that grips critics such as Nettement. But again, what he does not grasp is that this new tactic deployed by serial novelists promotes the boundaries of domesticity in a new form, by means of the perception of their transgression as giving rise to "monstrous proximities."

Sue turns the play of transgressions in the plot and in the reading process to his favor. Quite lucidly, he associates his exploration of urban disorder with a general strategy of moralization of the urban laboring classes that involved the descent of high society housewives—the first welfare caseworkers—into workers' households, workhouses, prisons, and asylums. These are the *dames patronnesses*, whose task was a disciplinary one of gathering knowledge, dispensing advice, and, in general, policing the down-and-out:

> These ladies . . . come every week to pass long hours with the miserable prisoners of Saint-Lazare [a prison for prostitutes]; espying in these degraded beings the least aspiration after virtue, the least regret for a past crime, they encourage the better tendencies and sow repentance; and, by the powerful magic of the words "duty," "honor," "virtue," sometimes they rescue from the depths of degradation one abandoned, despised, ruined being. (2: 301/374, translation modified)

> By turns indulgent and firm, patient and strict, always just and impartial, these ladies, in constant contact with the detainees, end up acquiring after long years of service such a science of the physiognomy of these unhappy women that they almost always judge correctly after one look and instantly classify them according to their degree of immorality. (2: 303, my translation)

Sue, as if in anticipation of Nettement's attacks, reverses the trope of mothers of families [*mères de famille*] in order to authorize his own verbal practice:

> Accustomed to the refinements of the best society, these courageous women leave their age-old town houses, pressing their lips to the virginal cheeks of their daughters, pure as the angels of heaven, and go to the gloomy prisons to brave the gross indifference, or the criminal conversation, of thieves and prostitutes.
> Faithful to their mission of high morality, they valiantly descend into the pestilential gutter, place the hand on all those ulcerated hearts, and if some feeble pulsation of honor reveals to them the slightest hope of saving them, they contend and tear from an almost irrevocable perdition the wretch of whom they do not despair.
> The scrupulous reader to whom we address ourselves, will calm, then, his sensibility, in thinking that he will only hear and see, after all, what these venerated women see and hear every day. (2: 301/374–75, translation modified)

"Family" empowers the new social philanthropy, *Les Mystères*, and their common field of knowledge. Clémence d'Harville, the *dame patronnesse* of *Les Mystères*, spells it out for readers: "Poor women! It seems that I take a greater interest in them when I think of my daughters" (2: 277, my translation). Conversely, philanthropy and *Les Mystères* consecrate "family": helping or reading about destitute women seemingly returns us all the more "home" to our loved ones:

> this prison house [Saint-Lazare] holds really guilty creatures. If I were not a mother, I would have doubtless judged them with still greater severity. Whereas I feel a pity full of pain for them in thinking that perhaps they would not have been led astray had they not been left abandoned and in poverty since childhood. *I do not know why but after these thoughts I seem to love my daughter even more.* (2: 279–80, emphasis mine, my translation)

Thus familial discourse marks here a new shift: the utopian marginality and isolation of *Paul et Virginie*'s *petite société* gives way before domesticity's new public militancy, which seeks to impose itself on the world outside in the most straightforward manner. This comes, however, at the cost of destabilizing the new model family itself, for its internal identity and cohesion are now inexorably linked to the public sphere that it still rejects but now wishes to colonize actively. And like all missionary enterprises, Sue's militant familialism constructs a disturbing, paranoid landscape in which the novel's characters and readers must circulate.

Fear and Loathing in Paris

The streets, buildings, and bodies of the Cité are the first strokes in Sue's tableau of Paris. However, his novel does not cover the capital in a detailed fashion. Few other quarters receive the extensive treatment that the Cité does. Rather, the plot takes readers through a rather sparse symbolic landscape which other novelists such as Balzac, and the manifold "panoramas" of Paris, had already begun to dot with the landmarks of social pathology. First, there are the filthy, ill-lit taverns and cabarets such as mère Ponisse's Lapin Blanc [White Rabbit] (1: 20) and the fencer Bras Rouge's Coeur-Saignant [Bleeding Heart], where criminals congregate pell-mell (1: 113–22). Bras Rouge's dive incarnates the now familiar confusion of interior space, the sewer, and the street; the cabaret barely rises above street level:

> A flight of steps, cut in the deep and greasy ground, led to the bottom of a sort of deep ditch, at the end of which, cut perpendicularly, stood a low, mean, dilapidated hovel. Its roof, covered with mossy tiles, scarcely rose above the step on which Rodolphe was standing; two or three huts, built of worm-eaten planks, serving as a cellar, wood-house, and rabbit-hutches, formed fitting appurtenances to this wretched den. (1: 113/71)

Indeed, when Rodolphe "descends" into the Coeur-Saignant he barely avoids being drowned by treacherous Bras Rouge in a cellar filled with water from the largest sewer of all—the Seine.

Second, there are the shabby, tawdry furnished rooms—the famous *garnis*—like the one on Rue du Temple, overseen by the Pipelets and where Rodolphe, Rigolette, Polidori, Bras Rouge, and the Morel family all have lodgings. It combines the closed, watery depths of sewers with the features of a garbage dump:

> Situated in a dense trading neighborhood the house in question externally possessed nothing very remarkable; it was composed of a ground floor, occupied by a man keeping a low drinking shop, and of four stories, surmounted by garrets.

A dark and narrow alley led to a small courtyard, or rather to a sort of square dry well, five or six feet wide, completely excluded from air and light, and serving as a filthy receptacle for all the refuse thrown down by the several occupants of the respective chambers; for apertures lacking windowpanes on each landing opened upon this pit. (1: 185/ 116, translation modified)

The association between sewers, social marginality, and criminality is virtually systematic in Sue's text and logically leads straight to the Martial family, who inhabit a house located on an island in the middle of the Seine. A pathological household of criminals, the family was founded by the grandfather, later guillotined for his crimes, whose livelihood was literally living off the sewage and refuse dumped daily in the river (3: 48–54).

Third, the novel conducts tours through those institutions meant to contain and cure the diseased social body: Saint-Lazare, Bicêtre, La Force, and a civilian hospital for tubercular women. They are characterized as much by their inmates as by their architecture. Here, too, metaphors of the sewer and street structure readers' perceptions. For example, Saint-Lazare is populated by the "filthy slime" [*boue infecte*] of prostitutes (2: 301); La Force and other prisons like it are so many "great centers where tides of corruption surge and ebb [*affluent et . . . refluent*] without cease, invading little by little the capital, and leave bloody flotsam" (3: 94, my translation). Most disturbing of all, however, is the fact that anyone—even if honest or of exalted station—can end up in the sewer by misfortune: Fleur-de-Marie and Louise Morel turn up at Saint-Lazare, the impoverished Mme de Fremont and her daughter wind up at the clinic for tubercular women, Germain is locked up in La Force, and Morel himself is committed to Bicêtre.

Miasma and the sewer are particularly effective constructs of social dissolution. They suggest mephitic depths, unmonitored social energies that violate at random those differences dear to ideologues of domesticity. The power of the image of the sewer is doubtless due as well to the fact that it condenses both public and private space in one dystopic figure of indistinction: it is both endless (God knows where it may lead) and compressed and claustrophobic (it is suffocating). Fundamentally, the miasma and the sewer are meant to connote, of course, the crowds of urban unwashed. The crowd, like the sewer, refuses to stay put; it "wells up," "overflows," and "swallows up" people and things indiscriminately, and it imposes an intolerable physical closeness of intense sociality and unchanneled social desire.

Interestingly, the most developed crowd scene occurs almost at the end of Sue's novel; it closes the last Parisian episode and thus the body of the narrative (the chapters that follow form the novel's epilogue, which situates the action in the court of Gerolstein). What mobilizes the riffraff [*la racaille*] are vestigial Old Regime practices that postrevolutionary authorities sought to stamp out or at least get off the streets, for they constituted the privileged occasions for the venting of popular sentiment publicly: the Shrovetide carnival and the public execution—here of La Martial and her daughter Calebasse. The naked execution of repressive justice in the context of carnivalesque inversion of social differences and hierarchies could only portend *political* disorder. The description of the crowd begins with the sewer and the transgression of perhaps the primary distinction erected by familial discourse, that of gender:

> Although it was broad daylight, yet still could be heard at a distance the resounding music of the orchestras of the drinking-dens, where, above all, could be distinguished the sonorous vibrations of the cornets-à-piston.
> It needs the pencil of a Callot, or Rembrandt, or of Goya, to portray the bizarre, hideous, almost fantastic appearance of this multitude. Almost all, men, women, children, were dressed in masquerading costumes; those who had not been able to obtain this luxury had fastened on their clothes old rags, of flaunting colors: *some men were attired in women's apparel*, torn and soiled with mud: all these faces, haggard from debauch and vice, bloated by intoxication, sparkled with savage joy, in thinking that, after a night of drunken orgies, they were going to see the two women put to death, for whom the scaffold was raised.
> The miry and fetid scum of the population of Paris, an immense mob, was composed of bandits and abandoned women, who demanded each day from crime their daily bread, and who each night returned well filled to their dens. (4: 246/751, my translation, emphasis mine)

Let the reader imagine all that is lowest, most shameless, and most monstrous in this idle, reckless, rapacious, sanguinary debauch, which shows itself more and more hostile to social order, and to which we have wished to call the attention of reflecting persons on terminating this narrative.
May this last horrible scene symbolize the imminent peril which continually menaces society! (4: 248/752)

To drive the political point home, Sue sets up a confrontation between Rodolphe and the crowd egged on by the criminals Le Squelette, Nicolas, and Le Tortillard (Bras Rouge's son), who shouts "Vive la Charte!" ("Long live the Charter!"), the old cry of the 1830 Revolution (4: 250). The face-off is a violent one, based in class and politics and will cost Le Chourineur (at Rodolphe's side) his life:

"Frantz, order the postillons to turn and go to Charenton by another road, whatever it may be," said Rodolphe. "It is too late, your highness! We are in the crowd. They have stopped the horses. Some ill-looking people . . ." The footman could not say another word. The crowd, exasperated by the sanguinary shouts of Le Squelette and Nicolas, suddenly surrounded the carriage. In spite of the efforts and threats of the postillons, the horses were stopped, and Rodolphe saw himself surrounded on all sides by horrible, threatening, furious faces: preeminent among all, from his great height, was Le Squelette, who advanced to the carriage door. . . .
"What do you want? Why do you stop my carriage?"
"Because it pleases us," said Le Squelette, placing his bony hands on the door. "Everyone in his turn: yesterday you trampled on the poor man; today the poor man will trample on you, if you make a move." (4: 251/755, translation modified)

Thanks to Le Chourineur's intervention the newly reconstituted family (Rodolphe and Fleur-de-Marie) will narrowly escape being engulfed by the violence and the anarchy of the street. Here things have come full circle. Both the opening and closing episodes of the body of the novel unite Rodolphe, Fleur-de-Marie, and Le Chourineur against a hostile urban background. The political character of Sue's paranoid landscapes, which was latent in *Les Mystères*' opening descriptions of the Cité erupts in the final crowd scene. Revolutionary upheaval is overtly rewritten as criminal pathology that threatens family life with extinction.

Fixing the Social, II: Tales of Familial Woe and Social Class

The diseased features of Sue's modern Paris construct an anxiety-inducing social hermeneutic based on the discourse of family and its attendant themes of public and private, gender, public hygiene, and social deviance. This grid for interpreting and knowing the social is successively elaborated through a series of crime narratives and family dramas. The conspicuous absence of middle-class norms of space and codes of behavior in the urban environment is articulated in a complex web of interlocking tales that take place for the most part behind closed doors. This general drift toward the private and the concealed is the very movement of a will-to-know in which the "answer" to the *question sociale* will be placed in the sphere of family life or what *should* be family life. By virtue of this process, *Les Mystères* completes the work of transforming the social and political into the familial and of encoding the "laboring classes" as the "dangerous classes."[22]

The characters' lives tell the same tale as the rotting urban environment, stories of absent families and family grief. Seated around a table in *mère* Ponisse's tavern, Rodolphe, Le Chourineur, and Fleur-de-Marie recount their life stories. At one point, La Goualeuse [Fleur-de-Marie] interrupts Rodolphe's short tale:

"And your family?" said La Goualeuse.
"The cholera ate them," replied Rodolphe.

Then it is her turn:

"Let's begin at the beginning," said Le Chourineur.
"Yes, with your parents," added Rodolphe.
"I never knew them," said Fleur-de-Marie.
"Ha, ha!" said Le Chourineur.
"Never saw nor knew them: I was born in a cabbage patch as they tell children."
"Hey, that's funny, La Goualeuse! You and I come from the same family."

"What, you too, Le Chourineur, alone?"
"Yes: an orphan of the streets of Paris, the same as you were, my girl." (1: 28/13, translation modified)

Finally Le Chourineur must divulge his family origins like his two companions:

"And your parents, your family?"
"My parents? Oh, lodged at the same address as those of La Goualeuse. My birthplace? Why, the first corner of any old street either on the right or left-hand side of the way, going up or coming down the stream."
"So you cursed your mother and father for having deserted you?"
"That would have done me a lot of good! But I don't care, they played me a dirty trick in bringing me into the world." (1: 41/22, translation modified)

These lines mark the beginning of a new narrative deployment of familial lack. The verbal exchanges in which the characters identify themselves to each other generate a rudimentary social taxonomy whereby low social standing and marginality are translated into the figure of the orphan, or even the illegitimate orphan. Unlike in *Paul et Virginie* where the fatherless households served as a preliminary step toward elaborating a new model of "family," here the lack of "family" is the identifying label of an entire social class. It seemingly signals a frozen social category, a sociological dead end. Being an orphan irreparably classifies Le Chourineur, Fleur-de-Marie, and Rodolphe as occupants of the bottom of the social scale.[23] The reason for this is simple. Sue's novel can simply assume the existence of the domestic family as normative to the newly formed middle class, just as it can count the middle class among its potential readership. Thus by the 1840s "family" can be used to construct and categorize diverse social groups.

A glance at other characters will confirm the operations of this taxonomy. The seamstress Rigolette recounts to her neighbor Rodolphe how she wound up in prison as a young girl:

"After the cholera, I found myself alone in the world. I was at that time, I believe, ten years old."

"But until then, who took care of you?"

"Oh! Some very good people! But they died of cholera! (here, Rigolette's large black eyes became moist). What little they possessed was sold in order to pay off some small debts, and I was left without anyone to take me in. Not knowing what to do, I went to a soldier who was across the street from our house, and I said to him, 'Mr. Soldier, my parents are dead, I don't know where to go: what must I do?' Thereupon the officer came and had me conducted to the commissioner who had me put in prison as a vagrant, and I got out when I was sixteen."

"But your parents?"

"I don't know who my father was. When I lost my mother I was six years old; she had withdrawn me from the foster home where she had been forced to place me at first. (2: 159/288, translation modified)

La Louve, a prostitute whom Fleur-de-Marie befriends at Saint-Lazare, grew up in a broken home that was rife with illicit sexuality:

"And your parents, La Louve, where are they?"
"How do I know!"
"Has it been a long time since you saw them?"
"I don't even know whether they are dead or alive."
"Were they mean towards you?"
"Neither good or bad: I was eleven years old, I'm pretty sure, when my mother went off with a soldier. My father, who was a day laborer, brought home to our attic a mistress who had two boys, one six years old, the other my own age. She sold potatoes out of a cart. It wasn't too bad in the beginning, but then while she was off with her cartload of potatoes, my father cheated on her with an oyster seller and the other found out. From then on, there were fights almost every evening so furious that me and the two boys I slept with were frightened to death (because we only had one room and there was only one bed for the three of us . . . in the same bedroom with my father and his mistress). . . . But in the end my father had enough; he left her what little furniture there was, and he never came back." (2: 324/389, translation modified)

In this decidedly nondomestic setting, the physical closeness of the children could only lead, not to the incestuous desire that constituted Paul and Virginie as an innocently companionate couple destined for marriage but rather to a carnal liaison between La Louve and one of the boys. That is, she became a fallen woman, a "whore," whereupon her father's former mistress took her down to the police station and literally enrolled her—the notorious *réglementariste mise en carte*—as a prostitute (2: 325).[24] These examples suggest that familial destitution was constitutive of the lower orders of society.

Unfixing the Social, I: Social Mobility, Absence of Family, and Melodrama

The new social topography and the stigmatization of the laboring classes as orphaned or without "family" unfixes the social only to freeze it again in a determinate way. The elaboration of new social geographies and groups along the anxious lines of familial discourse by virtue of the new norms' absence or transgression, while disturbing and disruptive (particularly to an older generation of readers), does not produce the discursive fluidity and instability that are required to establish a melodramatic social dialectic of inclusion and exclusion capable of accounting for the immense appeal of *Les Mystères* to a broad spectrum of readers. The middle and upper classes would occupy one extreme of the social geography and the criminalized "dangerous classes" the other. The urban landscape and its tales of familial woe would rigidly fix social relations in a manner that would interest perhaps only a readership that sought to see itself as middle class with perhaps upper-class aspirations. And if we accept the fact of the very discursive and therefore *relatively fragile* character of middle-class identity, it would be difficult to imagine how a static taxonomy of social classes would exert any fascination for those readers. A polarized landscape with its familyless class of lumpen characters is too immobile to excite middle-class readers, and readers of more modest origins, to the point of constituting a new popular reading public. Again, what is needed are porous, dynamic social relations both within the novel's frame and between it and the readers. This requires an economy of reading that sets in motion readers' social desire and, as a consequence, renders their social identities more fluid and precarious.

Hence the importance of Sue's tactic of generalizing lack of "family" to all characters and classes. Crucially, Sue ties this play of lack to upward and downward mobility which turns on the ability or inability of characters to register and recognize their lack of family in the form of sentiment and interiority. These are so many narratives of successful or failed "conversions" which make available to a wide readership the new model of household relations and social desire. Thus Sue's social topography acquires a truly dynamic and paranoid character, for lack of family may turn up *anywhere* and the melodramatic shock can collapse social distinctions or cause them to slip. The *mysteries* of Paris are, more often than not, the secret dramas of family life and the unsuspected links of close kinship that relate a story of social advancement or degradation.[25]

The meeting between the bereaved aristocrat Rodolphe and Fleur-de-Marie, his daughter-prostitute, is emblematic of this generalized crisis in family household relations. *Les Mystères* as a whole is precisely an elucidation of how things could have come to such a pass, but the method is tautological: one case of lack of "family" leads to and is explained by yet another. Rodolphe's descent into the Cité had as its immediate motive the search for Germain, the missing son of Madame Georges, who oversees Rodolphe's model farm at Bouqueval (1: 95–96). He will not discover Germain's whereabouts right off, but his foray into the underworld brings him face to face with Fleur-de-Marie and with the primary motivation of his expedition and his private charity work: his mourning over the loss of his daughter. This in turn conceals still other narratives of familial disorder: Rodolphe's stormy relations with his authoritarian father over his clandestine marriage to Sarah; and the plot organized by Sarah (herself the victim of the bad influence of her wet nurse [1: 216]) to trick Rodolphe into what turns out to be a bogus marriage. Lack of family proliferates everywhere, at every turn, and stands out as the general organizing principle of this serial novel.

Fear of Falling

From the perspective of a dynamic of upward and downward social mobility, the position of the criminalized "dangerous classes" at the bottom of the scale of deficient family life is just one position among others that Sue's characters may occupy. But it is the most reprehensible and feared fate that awaits them and leads straight to those forbidding institutions erected to survey and contain the familyless lumpenproletariat: Saint-Lazare, La Force, Bicêtre, and the tuberculosis ward. The "dangerous classes" are the very figures of social *déclassement* that haunt the pages of *Les Mystères* and all social classes, from Rodolphe and Fleur-de-Marie of the aristocracy to the artisan Morel and his family. It is the threat of social and familial exile to one of the remotest regions of the novel's imagined community. La Louve's "fall" out of the working class into prostitution began when her mother abandoned her family and her father, a day laborer, brought home a mistress (2: 324); under pressure from Jacques Ferrand, the corrupt notary, Morel's family disintegrates into so many cases of lumpen pathology that mark the decline of the household's fortunes: his wife is ill and he must do the housework (1: 208); his daughter Louise is made pregnant by Ferrand and later arrested for infanticide after burying her miscarried fetus (2: 194–98); the grandmother is afflicted with idiocy (2: 119–20); the youngest daughter Adèle dies of tuberculosis (2: 137); and Morel, not surprisingly, goes mad (2: 218–24).

Appropriately, as if Sue followed to the letter Philippe Pinel's definitions of mental disorder, the onset of Morel's madness signifies not only the breakdown of rationality but also the melodramatic death of the *familial* subject; there is literally nothing left to be interpellated:

> Then, attempting one last effort in order to bring Morel back to his senses, Louise cried out once again: "My father, farewell! They are taking me off to prison. I won't see you again! It's Louise saying farewell. My father! My father! My father!"
> To these heartrending cries there was no response.
> There was no echo in this poor wreck of a soul.
> The paternal chords, always the last to snap, vibrated no longer. (2: 220)

Their dreadful destiny is decipherable in the disorderly state of their apartment's interior: "The ground, of a nameless color, filthy and sticky, was strewn with rotted wisps of straw, squalid rags, and large bones which the poor purchase from the lowest of resellers of rotten meat in order to gnaw on the remaining cartilage." The unsettling practices of the streets of the Cité have invaded the privacy of the Morel household. The text instructs readers how to interpret the scene: "Such a dreadful negligence is always a sign either of loose behavior or of honest poverty but so crushing, so hopeless that the ruined and degraded man no longer feels either the will, the force, or the necessity of escaping the mire [*fange*]: he squats in his misery like a beast in its mire [*fange*]" (2: 118). Only once Rodolphe has intervened and undone Ferrand's machinations is Louise released, the family fortunes saved, and Morel restored to reason. And as in Tuke and Pinel's conception of cure, to recover one's mind is to recover familial sentiment:

> "My father, do you recognize me, I'm Louise, your daughter," she cried, bursting into tears and throwing herself in the lapidary's arms, just as Morel's wife, Rigolette, Madame Georges, Germain, and the Pipelets were entering.
> "Oh my God!" said Morel as Louise showered him with kisses, "Where am I? What do they want from me? What happened? I can't believe . . ."
> Then, after a moment of silence he suddenly took Louise's head in his hands, stared at her, and cried out as his feelings built up:
> "Louise!"
> "He's saved!" said the Doctor.
> "My husband, my poor Morel!" exclaimed the lapidary's wife who joined Louise.
> "My wife!" answered Morel, "My wife and my daughter!" (4: 225–26/738, translation modified)

Similarly, upper-class households threatened with *déclassement* undergo the destruction of family life. There is the story of the Baroness de Fremont and her daughter Claire, who, ruined by Ferrand, sink into the depths of misery. Confined to a filthy garret, they eke out an existence performing menial work. Exhausted by their ordeal, the daughter falls victim to a fever (3: 102–16) and is transported to the tuberculosis clinic while her mother collapses and expires, with the name of her daughter on her lips, before help can arrive (4: 164–77).

The most spectacular case of *déclassement* in the novel besides

Fleur-de-Marie's is of course Le Maître d'école's. Less a victim than a willful instigator of his own social descent, Le Maître d'école is an agent of antifamily practices. Of the *noblesse de robe* family Duresnel, he manipulated the old system of arranged marriages to his advantage and married the noblewoman Mme Georges (*née* Mlle de Lagny) shortly after the fall of Napoleon; in short order he dissipated both of their fortunes, and then turned to crime to underwrite his vices (1: 174). He went so far as to kidnap their son Germain in order to extort money from his wife. As Le Maître d'école explained it to her from behind prison bars: "I kidnapped your child because you love him, and because it's a way to force you to send me money (which he may or may not benefit from—that's my business). That he lives or dies is no concern of mine; but if he lives he will be in good hands; you will drink the shame of the son as you did that of the father" (1: 96/60, translation modified). He later planned to have Germain work for a bank that he and his cohorts were conspiring to rob. His exploitation of family relationships for criminal gain and his attempt to murder Murph, Rodolphe's old servant, designated him as a privileged subject for Rodolphe's experiment in social punishment and discipline.

Unfixing the Social, II: A Counterdialectic of Communities and Conversions

The pathologies of lumpen life threaten both the upper and lower orders of society with irrevocable ruin and humiliation, yet the menace is countered by another dialectic, that of sentiment and interiority. For if all the characters' situations are either explained by or presented in terms of failed or absent family life, their social degradation can be palliated, perhaps even reversed, psychologically. This involves the recognition of themselves in terms of "family" by naming that failure or absence and realizing that lack. Whereupon they acquire a new body, not of simple material misery and infirmity, but one that reveals a depth, psychological in character, in the form of some inner feeling or emotion. This is what individuates them, sets them apart from others (and their social class), and impels them to seek out new social bonds based on the norms and practices of the new domesticity.

Rodolphe's story is one of the many conversion narratives that organize the novel. It bears all the markings of the struggle, commonly staged in eighteenth- and early nineteenth-century novels, between camps representing two kinds of family and marriage. On the one hand, there's Rodolphe's father, the German archduke of Gerolstein, a firm believer in the aristocratic system of alliances and arranged marriages, and Sarah, a British aristocrat who schemes to become the future archduchess of Gerolstein, bartering her body and sentiments for political power and wealth; on the other stands Rodolphe, who mistakenly desires companionate marriage with Sarah. Sarah is very much a leftover from an earlier literature and moment of ideological warfare waged by familial discourse. She's the sexually independent aristocratic woman capable of instrumentalizing even the most sacred of the new values, motherhood. Shortly after their secret marriage she becomes pregnant and she uses her new state to exact concessions from the hapless Rodolphe: "Motherhood was regarded by Sarah merely as another means of subjecting Rodolphe, but shed no softening influence on her bronze soul" (1: 230/244–45). She's the now familiar *mère dénaturée* denounced by a long tradition of family literature. Only retrospectively does Rodolphe realize the extent of her perversity:

> "I imagine that this bad mother neglected her; and that once the countess's ambitious hopes were ruined by my marriage, she in her pitiless egoism abandoned our child to mercenary hands and that my daughter may have died for lack of care. It is also my fault; I did not sense the extent of sacred duties that paternity imposes. . . . I should have foreseen that the countess would never be but an unnatural mother [*mère dénaturée*]." (3: 255/555, translation modified)

His bitterness is compounded by the fact that he was fooled into defying and even threatening his father by Sarah's profession of love. Events lead him even to lose control of his explosive temper and threaten his father with physical harm (4: 130–35). In a melodramatic confrontation with a dying Sarah, he tortures her with the thought that she's perhaps guilty of both parricide and infanticide:

"This ought to be; I have drawn the sword against my father; I am stricken in my child. Just punishment of the parricide. Listen to me, madam."

"Parricide! You! My God! Oh, fatal day! Of what are you going to inform me?"

"It is necessary that you should know, in this awful moment, all the evils caused by your implacable ambition, by your unbounded selfishness. Do you understand me? Woman without heart and without conscience? Do you hear me, unnatural mother?"

"Oh, have pity, Rodolphe!" (4: 130/679)

Rodolphe's love for Sarah may mark him as belonging to a new postrevolutionary world, but his excessive, violent anger marks him as the willful, destructive aristocrat of the old order. Thus Rodolphe's story is multiple: he must do penance for his youthful ignorance and for having transgressed the paternal law; yet the same act of retrospective recognition and conversion is performed in the name not of the values of the Old Regime but of those of the new family: sentimental familial piety that emphasizes feeling and psychological states. That is to say, Rodolphe's narrative is one of reworking the old paternal idiom in terms of the new familial dispensation. Thus, as he does, he must first put his lawless aristocratic anger in the service of righting wrongs and restoring the helpless to family life through acts of charity. How does he come to do this? Through the loss of his daughter, which introduced a dimension of lack into his life around which his social and erotic desires will henceforth turn. This is made explicit in the following remarks made by Rodolphe to Murph, his assistant, to whom he confesses his love for the widowed Clémence d'Harville:

"I can now confess to you, my old friend, I'm in love, yes, I love deeply a woman worthy of the most noble and devoted affection. And since my heart is now open once again to tender emotions, I feel even more strongly the loss of my daughter. I could have feared after a fashion that a sentimental attachment would weaken the bitterness of my sorrow. It is nothing of the sort: all my amorous faculties have grown; I feel like a better man, more charitable, and more than ever I suffer from not having a daughter that I can adore." (3: 254/555, translation modified)

Second, his violent temperament and his slumming in the Parisian underworld must give way to new love and new life with Clémence d'Harville and Fleur-de-Marie. Here are the terms in which Rodolphe proposes marriage to Clémence:

> "First let me think of the interest of my heart—of that of my cherished daughter; make us both happy, oh, very happy. Permit me, who but now *was without family*, to say, 'My wife, my daughter'; allow this poor child, *also without family*, to say, 'My father, my mother, my sister'; for you have a daughter, who will become mine." (4: 189/714, emphasis mine)

At this stage we recognize something decidedly familiar: as in *Paul et Virginie*, two households whose origins were tainted by discredited alliance practices (manifest in Sarah's schemes and the archduke's fidelity to arranged marriage, on the one hand, and Clémence's arranged marriage with her epileptic husband, on the other) and as a consequence lacking "family" (and literally so: Rodolphe rebelled against his father and Sarah is dead; Clémence's husband committed suicide) are the very preconditions for the constitution of the domestic family household. Rodolphe's narrative life skirts the social dangers represented by nonfamilial relations in the household. His daughter's catastrophic *déclassement* to the rank of a common prostitute is shared by Rodolphe himself, who metaphorically "works through" the threat of downward mobility by donning the clothes of a working man and crossing to the "other side" of Paris in his escapades in the Cité. Only then may "family"—and his life at the court of Gerolstein—be restored to him.

The trajectory that Rodolphe describes encapsulates not only an earlier moment of familial discourse—that of *Paul et Virginie*'s indictment of Old Regime alliance practices—but a radically new one in which familial discourse recasts its norms of family and conceptions of class relative to a hostile urban environment. In his example, "family" is disrupted by old aristocratic practices—his father's notion of acceptable marriage, Sarah's plots, and Rodolphe's own (aristocratic) violent character—and by the machinations of various lumpen characters of the city. Indeed, the novel draws a straight line from one to the other, situating the domestic family between two historical threats: one from above and the past, the other from below and the future. Yet at the same time the text is suffused with a backward-looking feudal nostalgia. Still, the return to the Old Regime, the desire for feudal relations, is very much a part of the history of the novel's "present," for the deployment of the Old Regime language of clan and deference is something of a metaphor for a social order whose foundations receive no other textual figuration outside of those of the new family. That is to say, through Rodolphe Sue's writing recodes aristocratic practices in the more acceptable postrevolutionary concepts of marriage, family, children, and selfhood favored by the new domesticity. Thus the novel displays a very modern admiration for the power, prestige, and wealth associated with the nobility in the form of sentimental family life centered on the joys and satisfactions of the home. Rodolphe is the Louis-Philippe of the serial novel and the modern metropolis.

Rodolphe's desire for companionate marriage and his love for his daughter set him off from most members of his class; while his sentiments individuate him in this way they also draw him into a new "imagined community." A community of pathos is established among characters and, implicitly, between readers of the novel. This we have seen operative in *Paul et Virginie*, of course, but the scope of the community and its setting are quite different. The rudiments of such a new community are already visible in the conversation between Rodolphe, Fleur-de-Marie, and Le Chourineur at the beginning of *Les Mystères*. They name themselves, their social origins, and their lack of family all at once. Moreover, they display signs of interiority that elevate them above their lumpen condition. Already alerted by the novel's presentation of Rodolphe as prone to bouts of melancholy (1: 23), readers actually witness the first signs of psychological depth in the other two characters. Fleur-de-Marie's story of repeated beatings as a child elicits this unexpected reaction from Le Chourineur, a convicted killer:

> "By thunder! That's overdoing it!" shouted the ruffian, banging the table fiercely with his fist, and knitting his brows. "Beat a kid, that was natural enough; but torture her, blood and thunder!"
> Rodolphe had listened attentively to the narrative of Fleur-de-Marie;

he now looked with astonishment at Le Chourineur, whose outburst of feeling [*éclair de sensibilité*] surprised him. (1: 30/15, translation modified)

We later learn that after his murders he was haunted by dreams of his victims, who seemed to be the brothers he never had as a child:

"But the more I hacked down [*chourinais*] the soldiers, the faster did the others present themselves; and as they died, they looked at me with an air so kind, so gentle, that I cursed myself for killing them; but I could not prevent myself from doing it. That was not all! I never had a brother! And yet it seemed as if every one of those whom I had killed was my brother, for whom I would have done anything. At last, when I could bear it no longer, I used to wake, covered with sweat, as cold as melting snow." (1: 44/25, translation modified)

The process of merely recounting one's life, lending it a temporal dimension, introduces melancholy and sadness, emotive depth, in Fleur-de-Marie; it is therefore not for nothing that Le Chourineur calls her narrative a confession:

"I understand," said Le Chourineur; "I know you as well now as if I were your father and mother, and you had never been off my knee. Well, this is a confession and a half, rather!"
"Telling the story of your life makes you sad, my child," said Rodolphe.
"The fact is that I find it upsetting to look backwards; since my childhood this is the first time I have recalled all these things to my memory and my tale is not a cheerful one. What do you say, Chourineur?" (1: 36–37/20, translation modified)

Marx astutely remarked how the priest's ministrations instilled a religious sense of guilt and remorse in Fleur-de-Marie, who otherwise had not been burdened by a bourgeois conscience.[26] Yet his observations oversimplify the process. Before her encounter with the priest (2: 19–22) Fleur-de-Marie's "innocence"—her Pre-Raphaelite angelic face and her singing that allowed her to forget her profession—was a mark of her upper-class origin and her presocial nature. What happens to her is not so much an initiation into the grim sensibility of middle-class religion as a conversion to "family" as loss or absence in the context of the metropolis. Much in the same way that domesticity and the lineaments of a middle-class private sphere are elaborated *negatively* by the novel, so must "innocence" too be worked out differentially in terms of a sensibility, a sensitivity to loss and pain. The introduction of lack is done through the narrativization of Fleur-de-Marie's life, which splits her self between past and present; "innocence" is not locatable anywhere in time but in the very action of the psyche that registers suffering. This process, then, is well under way before she meets up with the priest at the Bouqueval farm.

In their conversation with Rodolphe, Le Chourineur and Fleur-de-Marie thus make the first steps on the path to conversion: they now claim to know each other as "family." Each with some guidance and aid from Rodolphe and other agents of the new philanthropy will be on his or her way to those destinies mapped out by familial discourse. Le Chourineur will become a cattle farmer in newly colonized Algeria (1: 162–63). Upon his fateful return to Paris shortly before his final departure Le Chourineur shows signs that he is already a changed man and can no longer see himself as part of a popular collectivity; on the contrary, the carnival crowd at the end of the novel repulses him: "Although formerly he had associated with the degraded classes to which this mob [*populace*] belonged, Le Chourineur, on again finding himself among them, felt invincible disgust" (4: 247/751). As for Fleur-de-Marie, she will rejoin Rodolphe's household where she will have the privilege of being consumed by her excessive interiority, of dying out of guilt for her former life as a prostitute (4: 313–14).

To belong to this community is both to be a victim and to recognize familial lack or loss. This recognition at once lends a new sensibility to characters, *unfixes* their social identity, and allows them to rise in social rank. The outward signs of the converted or the worthy are moral outrage and melancholy or sadness. Still another sign is domestic orderliness. Rigolette, the hardworking seamstress who is Rodolphe's neighbor in the apartment house, preserves her working-class standing by maintaining a spotless home and following closely the strictures of a domestic economy that includes the morality of budgets and savings:

I am happy just as I am: I know the life I lead, I don't know what life I would lead if I were rich. You see, neighbor, when after a long day's work I retire in the evening and I turn out my light, I see by the glow of the little coals that remain in my stove my neat and clean room, my curtains, my dresser, my chairs, my birds, my watch, my table full of cloth that has been entrusted to me, and I say to myself 'at last all that belongs to me, I owe it only to myself.' That's true, neighbor; those ideas lull me tenderly, and sometimes I fall asleep full of pride and always content. Well, were I to owe my home to the money of some relative, it would not give me as much pleasure, I am sure. (2: 173–74/300, translation modified)

Are sentiment and economic autonomy the founding features of the working class? It would seem so, yet if the novel claims that the health of the working class depends on the application of the principles of domestic economy and the adoption of a new sensibility (read interiority), *Les Mystères* also holds out the possibility of social advancement. The novel produces the following paradox: what qualifies Rigolette as a "healthy" working-class woman also will procure her a marriage with "gentle" and "sad" (4: 51) François Germain, a son of the upper class. A true proletarian is a potential bourgeois in the field of familial social desire.

Another case of conversion and upward mobility is that of the prostitute La Louve. Fleur-de-Marie is the great agent of La Louve's transformation. La Louve bursts on the scene during Fleur-de-Marie's imprisonment in Saint-Lazare. True to her name, she displays a quasi-animal violence that puts her beyond behavior deemed civilized by the novel. Indeed, when she makes her first appearance, out of spite she drives a crowd of fellow inmates to attack Mont Saint Jean, a helpless pregnant woman, in order to steal the clothes she's been knitting for her baby (2: 310–11). Only angelic Fleur-de-Marie's intervention in the name of the sanctity of motherhood and the newborn saves her from physical harm (2: 314–17). Fleur-de-Marie's quiet demeanor and her evocation of maternal duties stops La Louve, leaves her dumbfounded. There then follows a long dialogue between the opposed women and before long the first glimmers of interiority makes themselves felt in La Louve; she complains: "There is another thing: until now I have always been gay or angry but never a thinker [*songeuse*]: and you have made me think [*rendue songeuse*]. Yes, there are some words you say which, in spite of me, have touched my heart, and always make me think [*songer*] all manner of sad things" (2: 321/387, translation modified).

One thing leading to another, La Louve ineluctably discloses the tale of her life to Fleur-de-Marie. The exchange of personal stories allows Fleur-de-Marie to attempt to convert La Louve to the new ideals of marriage and family by painting an imaginary picture of domestic bliss, hard work, household chores, and companionship with her lover Martial (2: 327). At first the hardened prostitute's skepticism is unshakable: "Why have you come to make me desire what I can't have?" (2: 332, my translation). Yet the process of conversion continues apace. Between the two women bonds are sealed by Fleur-de-Marie, who promises material help should La Louve desire to reform herself. Fleur-de-Marie's influence works its proven effects, for soon thereafter La Louve is seen crying (3: 165) and once she's out of prison and united with Martial she shares with him her new desire: "'to go with you in the woods, where we would have a nice little house, children whom I should love; oh! how I should love them! how your Louve would love the children of her Martial; or, rather, if you wished it,' said La Louve, trembling, 'I would call you my husband; for we shall not have the place unless you consent to this,' she hastened to add, quickly" (3: 202/520). Martial is of the same disposition; so with Rodolphe's help they plan to join Le Chourineur in Algeria and start a new life and family, but under the precarious and fearsome conditions of colonial life. True domestic bliss is not something that *Les Mystères* ever grants freely; it is a never-ending process in which the borders of the "home" must be policed and the sanctity of the hearth defended, be it in the city or at a colonial outpost.

The consolidation of the new familial norms would not be complete without the extension of the values of the new community to those who would seek to overturn them. Even Sarah and Le Maître d'école, the novel's truly unnatural parents, must pay homage to the very norms by which the novel condemns them before they are dispatched to oblivion or death. The jousting between law and felon is no longer a public contest, as in the Old Regime theater of outdoor executions, but takes place behind closed doors in private apartments or state institutions.

Sarah, Fleur-de-Marie's mother, who, ignorant of her identity, tried to have her murdered by drowning, is convalescing from a nearly fatal stabbing at the hands of La Chouette when she learns from Rodolphe that she has probably killed her own daughter (4: 130–35). This revelation converts her to those sentiments she has presumably "repressed" in her desire to gain power: "the ghost of my drowned daughter—drowned by my fault—is there—always there, before me. It is not an emotion—it is incessant remorse. I am really a mother now, since I no longer have a child" (4: 197/719).

Her conversion to "family" by virtue of the horrifying murder of her own child is a mortal one and doubly so, for hereafter Sarah herself slips slowly toward death and does not recover even when Rodolphe apprises her that Fleur-de-Marie survived the attempted drowning, and decides to marry her in order to legitimize their daughter (4: 198–200). Here, too, a character's sentimental acceptance of "family" is also the precondition of upward social mobility, for, minutes before she dies, Sarah finally becomes a member of the princely house of Gerolstein. Inscribed with the soulful interiority of bourgeois motherhood, she can accede to the highest ranks of the nobility.

The most striking example of the text's politics of familial discipline and punishment is of course that of Le Maître d'école. The spectacle of his pain and conversion is, as with all the characters, a private one, and targets his body, more especially those organs that are the threshold between the physical outer world and the inner universe of the liberal subject: the eyes. Rodolphe's blinding of Le Maître d'école is a form of mutilation of the body; the effects are quite different from those arising out of the criminal's own self-mutilation designed to escape police surveillance:

> You cannot picture anything more horribly repugnant than the countenance of this crook, furrowed in all directions with deep livid cicatrices. The corrosive action of the vitriol had swelled his lips; the cartilages of his nose were split, and two misshapen holes supplied the place of

nostrils. His grey eyes were very bright, small, circular, and sparkled with ferocity; his forehead, flat as a tiger's, was half hidden beneath a fur cap, with long yellow hair, looking like that of the monster's mane. Le Maître d'école was not more than five feet two or three inches; his head, disproportionately large, was buried between shoulders broad, powerful, and fleshy, which displayed their muscle under the loose folds of his coarse cotton blouse; he had long muscular arms, hands short, thick, and hairy to the very fingers' ends; his legs were somewhat bowed, and their enormous calves betrayed his vast strength.

This man presented, in a word, the exaggeration of everything short, thick, and condensed, in the type of the Hercules Farnese.

As to the expression of ferocity which glared over his hideous mask, and the restless, wild, and fierce look, more like a wild beast's than a human being's, it is impossible to depict them. (1: 48/28 translation modified)

Le Maître d'école's body is one of physical force and power; his self-mutilation has merely bestowed upon the convict a new public persona and rendered him unrecognizable to the police. On the contrary, Rodolphe's punishment has a different goal, that of transforming the body from one of physical power and a surface, public identity into a prison house of interiority. This is the forceful discipline of imposed conversion. Blinding enjoys a double effect: it literally "privatizes" the criminal by restricting him to the "house" of his now helpless body and introduces the first stirrings of a new subjectivity, psychological in character. Rodolphe's cruel act represents a conscious break with older methods of incarceration and execution. He refuses to execute Le Maître d'école publicly on very specific grounds:

Rodolphe continued:
"If, on the other hand, you had boldly met your fate, as little would it have induced me to surrender you to death. For you, the scaffold then would have been but a bloody stage, where, like so many others, you would have made a parade of your ferocity; where, reckless of the miserable life, you would have damned your soul with a last blasphemy! Neither would that have been your due. 'Tis no example for the rabble to see the criminal cracking jokes with the guillotine's blade, mocking the executioner, and rendering back with a sneer the divine spark the Creator hath breathed into us. There is an awful sanctity enshrining the

welfare of a soul. All crime may be expiated and redeemed, says the Saviour: but from the tribunal to the scaffold, the journey is too short; you must not die in this way." (1: 140–41/88–89, translation modified)

The spectacle of a public execution runs the risk of empowering the criminal by virtue of the crowd's presence to mock and ridicule the authorities, and thus may actually weaken them in the public's eyes (4: 240).

Blinding and isolated confinement are the next steps in "privatizing" the criminal, for they sever another social bond, that between the criminal and his fellow inmates, whose uncontrolled sociality defeats any sense of remorse and shame for crimes committed. *Les Mystères* presumes that their infectious gaiety effectively overcomes any manifestations of inner life and conscious sadness that individuates a criminal by virtue of newfound interiority:

> Generally the prisoners appear less sad than the visitors; for strange as it may appear, it is proved by experience, there are few sorrows and little shame which resist three or four days of imprisonment passed in company.
>
> Those who are most alarmed at this hideous communion are soon habituated; the contagion reaches them; surrounded by degraded beings, hearing only infamous words, a kind of ferocious emulation drags them on, and either to impose upon their companions by rivalling their obduracy, or to stupefy themselves by this moral intoxication, almost always the newly arrived show as much depravity and insolent gaiety as the old hands. (3: 294/585)

In this view, prisons are not the birth but rather the *death* of the liberal subject; any mournful-looking prisoner is immediately suspected of being in potential collusion with the authorities, of being an agent or a spy: "in their savage obduracy and in senseless distrust, they look upon as a spy every man (if there should be such a one) who, sad and mournful, regretting his fault, does not partake of their audacious thoughtlessness, and shudders at their contact" (3: 295/585). Criminal sociality prevents any true individuation of the subject and constitutes a counter-discourse to that which would colonize and enjoy hegemony over the margins of middle-class society.

Rodolphe follows his Benthamite reasoning to its logical end. Executing a criminal publicly is a purely negative spectacle that does nothing either for the reproduction of official authority or the reformation of the condemned man or woman. As Rodolphe says in another episode in reply to a cruel slaveowner: "To your violence which slays I oppose a violence which saves" (1: 181/114). His justice is *productive*; it produces new subjects. At least that is his goal. He explains his method thus to Le Maître d'école:

> "Far from being barren as death, your punishment may be fruitful [*féconde*]; far from losing you forever, it may redeem you. If, to render you henceforth incapable of injuring others, I forever deprive you of all the splendors of creation—if I plunge you into impenetrable night— lonely night—with the memory of your crimes upon your soul, it is that you may unceasingly reflect upon their enormity. Yes! Shut in forever from the external world you will be driven to look inward; and then I hope that your brow, now bronzed by infamy, *will blush with shame*, and your soul, hardened by ferociousness and corroded by crime, *will soften by commiseration*. Each of your words is now a blasphemy— each of your words will be a prayer." (1: 141/89, emphasis added, translation modified)

Le Maître d'école must acquire the inner eye of moral surveillance and temporal depth. This entails a process of *feminization* of the criminal subject (be it a man or a woman), and its attendant body will henceforth display guilt and vulnerability when faced with human misery. Finally, Le Maître d'école must experience the "feminine" existential powerlessness of the liberal subject. Rodolphe grimly predicts: "You are bold and cruel because you are strong; you will be mild [*doux*] and humble because you will be weak." (1: 141/89). The final step in reformation will be his restoration to family life: "After a long life, devoted to the expiation of your crimes, your last prayer shall be a supplication to the Almighty to grant you the happiness of dying in the presence of your wife and son" (1: 141/89).

The birth of the liberal subject is a familial one. Le Maître d'école's body is literally transformed into a casing of interiority that is actually a highly policed domestic space, a house of new subjectivity that finds its fulfillment in the bonds of family.

Le Maître d'école's narrative existence takes us through the steps of conversion that Rodolphe laid out. When at a later point he finds himself locked in a fight to the death with his former accomplice La Chouette, he speaks to her of his remorse and feelings of shame. He frames his confession in terms of one of the most sacred objects of the new family, childhood; he gratefully stakes his claim thereupon to personal dignity and humanity:

> "Yet sometimes a feeble ray of hope shines in the midst of the gloom—a moment of calm follows my torments: yes, for sometimes I succeed in conjuring the specters that besiege me, by opposing to them the recollections of a past life, honest and peaceful—by carrying back my thoughts to the days of my childhood.
>
> "Happily, you see the blackest villains have had, at least, some years of peace and innocence in opposition to their long years of crime and blood. We are not born wicked.
>
> "The most perverse have had the amiable simplicity [*candeur*] of childhood—have known the sweet joys of that charming age." (3: 225–26/536, translation modified)

To have had a childhood is to have a past, and thus the critical moral negativity of temporal depth; that is one of the preconditions, besides privacy, of liberal subjectivity. Le Maître d'école is not far from completing his "familialization." The process climaxes when he meets his son in Bicêtre. He recognizes Germain but his son cannot recognize him:

> Le Maître d'école made no reply, but bowed his head. At the end of some moments, from his sightless eyes there fell a tear.
> "He weeps," said the doctor.
> "Poor man!" added Germain, with compassion. Le Maître d'école shuddered; he heard anew the voice of his son, who evinced for him a sentiment of compassion.
> "What is the matter? What sorrow afflicts you?" demanded the doctor. Le Maître d'école, without replying, buried his face in his hands . . .
> He thought, with profound despair, that he should never hear again the voices of his son and wife. Confident of the just horror with which he had inspired them, of the misfortune, the shame, the fright into which he would have plunged them by the revelation of his name, he would have endured rather a thousand deaths than have disclosed himself to

them. One single last consolation remained to him: for a moment he had inspired his son with pity. (4: 220/735, translation modified)

The bonds of "family" are felt and communicated once again in the mode of loss and psychological pain. Familial lack intervenes and its recognition completes the "birth" of a new subject. Le Maître d'école may now leave the novel's pages, which he promptly does.

Familial Lack and Social Discursivity

One critic claims that nineteenth-century melodrama began with the fragmentation of "the family" in order to take the audience through the suspense of bringing about its reunion in the dénouement. Only exceptional writers were capable of moving beyond the simple narratives of this sentimental mode.[27] I have shown that *Les Mystères* allows a different interpretation of melodrama: that the desire for "family"—the new norms of domesticity—is produced by the pathos of its absence, and that this absence, while literally productive of new households (witness the companionate marriages of Rigolette and Germain, La Louve and Martial, and Rodolphe and Clémence d'Harville) is nonetheless an abiding one. That is the ultimate significance of Fleur-de-Marie's death. Her final reunion with her father Rodolphe already requires the substitution of her unworthy biological mother Sarah by Clémence, a *dame patronnesse*. More important, the former prostitute cannot completely convert to the joys of family life; her degraded past—the very condition of her first realization of familial lack—remains steadfastly irrecuperable by the present:

> At this painful allusion to the past, Rodolphe exclaimed:
> "Unhappy child! Are my suspicions founded? In the midst of the splendor that surrounds you, would you yet sometime think of that horrible time? Alas! I had thought I had made you forget it by tenderness!"
> "Pardon, pardon, father! These words escaped me. I make you sad. . . ."
> "This is the first time you have spoken of it, yes; but, perhaps, this is not the first time that these thoughts have troubled you. I have noticed

your moments of melancholy, and sometimes I have accused the past of causing your sadness." (4: 280/775, translation modified)

Rodolphe then exhorts Fleur-de-Marie in hopes of curing his daughter of her past by virtue of the presence of her new mother Clémence who, as a *dame patronnesse*, obtained Fleur-de-Marie's release from Saint-Lazare:

"You ought, feeling yourself cherished as a daughter by the noble woman who knew and loved you in the depth of your misfortunes—you ought, I say, to regard the past as sufficiently expiated by your atrocious miseries, and be indulgent, or rather just, towards yourself: for, indeed, my wife is entitled by her rare qualities to the respect of all—is it not so? Ah, well, since you are to her a daughter, a cherished sister, ought you not to be encouraged? Is not her tender attachment a full redemption? Does it not tell that she knows, as I do, that you have been a victim—that you are not guilty—that others can, indeed, reproach you only with misfortune, that has overwhelmed you from birth? Had you even committed great faults, would they not be a thousand times expiated, redeemed, by all the good you have done, by all that is excellent and adorable that has developed in you?" (4: 280/775, translation modified)

Fleur-de-Marie persists in languishing with remorse to the point that she refuses marriage with Henry, the man she loves, out of a sense of her own unworthiness for motherhood:

"I a mother!" resumed Fleur-de-Marie with bitter despair, "I respected, I blessed by an innocent and pure child! I, formerly the object of everybody's scorn, I profane thus the sacred name of mother? Oh, never! Miserable thing that I was to allow myself to be drawn away to an unworthy hope!" (4: 298/789)

In the new discourse of "family," social class, and the city—the household and the street—the urban public and private spaces are locked in a hostile, mutually determining relationship by which discursively one term cannot be held before the mind's eye without the other. They coexist simultaneously or not at all. The "family" holds out the promise of transformation and hope to the street while the street threatens the household with sexual ruin. Once one has been contaminated by the city's "dangerous classes" one's penance is never done. The play of familial lack is not the same for all characters, however. La Louve's exile to a life of danger in Algeria engages her in a continual struggle to preserve the very physical existence of her new household life with Martial from the raids of guerrilla bands. (It also foreshadows the shift in familial discourse by which the "hordes" of the colonized replaced the "dangerous classes" at the end of the nineteenth century.) Fleur-de-Marie's life as a whore undoes any plans she may have of becoming a mother. Within the familial field of the novel's imagined community, the dynamic of social mobility clearly carries an internal differentiation that circumscribes its destabilizing effects.

Fleur-de-Marie's death has been interpreted by critics such as Eco and Brooks as the reaffirmation of bourgeois moral principles and the narrative return to normalcy after the roller-coaster melodramatics of unexpected revelations; or, in our terms, the destabilizing "monstrous proximities" are subsumed in a controlling discourse of fixed social and moral differences that reassures upper- and middle-class readers. Eco writes:

> What new ideas we have acquired fade away as a few choice principles of ethics and polite behavior are quietly reiterated and wisely corroborated. After surprising the reader by telling him what he does not yet know, the author reassures him by repeating what he knows already. The machinery of the novel demands that Fleur-de-Marie should end as in fact she does.[28]

I want to shift Eco's emphasis from what readers may "already know" to what the novel has *taught* them to know and to desire: a new sense of familial norms and the mapping of the city. Fleur-de-Marie's death, then, is not the repetition of old knowledges and old desires but their reformulation in a new moment and a new topography. Her death simultaneously generates the lack and the pathos so necessary for the dissemination of a (now modified) familial discourse to a large readership and fixes once again the porousness of the social within new limits. These new limits are curious ones, for they are not based on a simple, clear-cut sense of social class. The reason for this is as follows: social class by the novel's end has a profoundly discursive character, which we must now elucidate.

Clearly, one signification of Fleur-de-Marie's death is that the street—"prostitution"—means the death of upper- and middle-class women, unlike those who, of modest origins (La Louve and Mont Saint Jean), can reconcile motherhood and the sexual commerce of their bodies. But what are the social classes involved here? What kind of system do they form?

There is something oddly anachronistic about the character of the social classes portrayed in Les Mystères: the principal figural opposition seems to be between aristocrats on the one hand, and the criminal milieu of what we have called the lumpenproletariat on the other, in which for all intents and purposes the middle class and the laboring classes are absent. Ferrand is the only truly middle-class character in the economic or occupational sense—he is a notary and a usurer; Morel and Rigolette are the only artisans or laborers. Meanwhile, all characters and classes are related to the new norms of the familial. I want to suggest that familial discourse performs a sleight of hand, though it is scarcely a hidden or clandestine operation. I offer the following paradox: the very "middle-class" definition of the social and its various classes in terms of the new domesticity and its attendant concepts posits social class for the first time here in its modern sense of horizontal relations of exchange and reciprocity (as opposed to the vertical, corporate ones of cast or estate) while *depoliticizing* the notion of social class as such, detaching it from issues of power and wealth.

The two major new social classes in the nineteenth century—the laboring classes and the middle classes—are virtually unlocatable in the social map drawn by Sue's novel. They are difficult to identify and at best seem to fall in between the aristocracy and the criminal segment of society. So in what manner, if at all, can we claim as we do that Les Mystères is a novel absolutely "contemporary" with its period when the text is full of social anachronisms (the dominance of nobles) and significant omissions (working and middle classes)? And how can this appeal to a vast readership that in some sense belongs to those very social classes that are absent from the novel's pages?

I think it is important to recall that what makes the "social" modern is its discursiveness, which produces collective identities in a relatively "unfixed" form, that is, a form both in need of constant reaffirmation and articulation and subject to modification and reshaping. Which is to say that what is being performed by the novel is something that has less to do with representations of fixed, identifiable social objects than with the production of social desire. Perhaps this is the significance of the absence of the working and middle classes in *Les Mystères*. The novel's peculiar tactic would be to frame our reading of the social in terms of social classes that are placed at the opposite extremes of the social scale. This contributes to undoing discursively social identities; social confrontation takes place between an aristocracy that "is not" one (it is *embourgeoisée* by the novel's end) and a nonclass of social marginals. This had the distinct advantage of setting in motion readers' desires in terms of what *they are not* but perhaps either fear becoming (the lumpenproletariat) or desire to identify with (an old social elite now embodying bourgeois domesticity).

In this context the criminal milieu has two functions: it clearly articulates for those readers who wish to view themselves as middle class the social fear of those new urban workers who would challenge the new postrevolutionary society from below; this makes perfectly good sense, even in terms of the older familial discourse, which had become the core of the social identity of the middling groups, for it "distinguishes" them from the ruling elites of the Old Regime. What is not of the honest, middle strata must represent some sort of familial pathology. The new teratology is the working class as projected by the new middle classes at the time France was moving toward the mid-nineteenth century. At the same time, the lumpen characters produce the fear of social *déclassement*, especially, perhaps, among those readers who are literate workers and artisans. The novel engages in a dynamic of recognition or rather a discursive exchange: workers' and artisans' plights are recognized and duly admitted among the objects of a new national print culture but only in the form of the threat of downward social mobility into the limbo of the dangerous classes, who are in turn defined in terms of a familial pathology. Thus two readings are possible. The first is to name and identify the political and social oppression of artisans and workers in terms of a pathology of one class—the lumpens—and an ideal of another class—the bourgeoisie. We then return to the following negative paradox: *not* to fall into the dangerous classes, *not* to fall victim of one of the pathologies that afflict "family" life, one has to adopt the ways and habits of the middle classes: investment in the charms and burdens of domesticity. Which is not to be working-class at all, for in the eyes of the new domesticity, the truly laboring class is potentially, if not actually, a dangerous class. (That was both the nineteenth-century Frégier's confusion and the present-day Louis Chevalier's interpretation.) Thus, Martial, La Louve, Le Chourineur, Rigolette, and Germain, when they come around to adopting the new norms, mysteriously become property owners and managers. The fundamental "mystery" of Paris is of course Rodolphe's largesse, but its fairy-tale quality does not detract from what it promises: social dignity and possible social advancement. The novel's discursive power is an insidious one insofar as it disseminates hope and fear among readers of modest background conceptualized along the lines of a discourse that comes from middle-class experts—physicians, jurists, public health officers, educators, novelists. As a consequence, the text produces a working class almost entirely in terms of its *social desire*, both within the plot and among the readership.

The construction of the laboring classes and dangerous classes in terms of "family" is clearly an extension of new middle-class thinking to the domain of the metropolitan city. But if family is potentially everywhere—if *anyone* can join the imagined community dominated by the middle ranks and its norms of "family"—so can family be absent anywhere in anyone. The price of discursive hegemony is social paranoia—the need to inspect, examine, analyze, and ferret out the potential lack of family and police it through rituals of home life, work, and reading. So what then of "middle-class" social desire, which the novel produces? The discursive nature of its own identity and of its hegemonic aspirations accounts for its desire both to *unfix* (decode) social identities, render them more porous and changing, and *fix* them in a determinate way. This explains the role of the dangerous classes in the novel in defining the laboring classes and will account for the absence of the middle class and the presence in its stead of numerous aristocratic characters, particularly Rodolphe. The purely negative definition of what it meant now to be of the "middle ranks"—you are not working class, or rather, not of the dangerous classes—is complemented by a figure of social desire—a nobility colonized by middle-class family life—that allows you to see yourself as middle class and still dream of social mobility, of rising to a higher social rank. The presence of the aristocracy both sets in motion social desire and contains its disruptive effects. Rodolphe, Clémence, and Fleur-de-Marie are the reassuring presence of social hierarchy for middle-class readers whose desire for social mobility is matched only by their dread of social disorder.

~ CHAPTER 5

No Future: Disembodied Domesticity in Balzac's *Les Paysans*

The family is more than ever the premier
element and last bulwark of society.

—Guizot, *De la démocratie* (1849)

THE NEW DEMOCRATIC print culture and its tacit admission of the urban poor as objects of knowledge and solicitude in the discourse of "family" found a formidable foe in the author of the first French serial novel to appear in a wide-circulation daily; and he was the man whom Sainte-Beuve castigated for being a chief proponent of "industrial literature," namely, Honoré de Balzac.[1] Two years after the serial publication of *Les Mystères de Paris*, Emile de Girardin published *Les Paysans* in *La Presse*, beginning December 3, 1844. In his preface, the monarchist Balzac delivered a scathing attack on the new writing on the *question sociale* for its naive faith in philanthropy and its negligence of the largest mass of the laboring poor, the peasants: "The purpose of this study, terrifying in its truthfulness, so long as society shall choose to make of philanthropy a principle instead of taking it for an accident, is to place in relief the principal figures of a class of people neglected by so many pens in pursuit of new subjects." He too offers a new social class for readers' contemplation, but less to validate the peasants and their claims than to discredit liberal philanthropy, those writers such as the ex-royalist Sue, and socialist commentators who call for social reform or even revolution in the name of the urban laboring classes: "That neglect is nothing more than prudence, perhaps, at a time when the common people inherit all the courtiers of royalty. Poetic sentiment has been lavished upon criminals, our pity has overflowed upon executioners, we have almost deified the proletariat! The sects are in commotion, in crying with all their pens: 'Arise, workers!' as in the old days they said to the Third Estate: 'Arise!'" Like any true legitimist (a very conservative French monarchist who supports the claims of the deposed Bourbon family), Balzac's obsession with social order translates into a fixation on the peasantry, the fundamental social menace:

> It is plain that not one of these Erostratuses has had the courage to go into the heart of the country districts to study the permanent conspiracy of those whom we still call the weak, against those who deem themselves strong, of the peasant against the rich man. The important thing is to enlighten, not the legislator of today, but the legislator of tomorrow. Amid the democratic vertigo to which so many blind writers succumb, is it not high time to describe at last the peasant who makes the Code inapplicable by reducing property to the condition of something that is and that is not? . . . This antisocial element created by the Revolution will some day absorb the bourgeoisie, as the bourgeoisie has devoured the nobility.[2]

In the pages that follow Balzac will offer the tale of the destruction of a great landed estate at the hands of the local peasantry and their bourgeois allies, a "didactic lesson"[3] in the perils facing the propertied classes only four years before the 1848 Revolution.

Balzac's preface bears witness to an ideological struggle within the new print culture between left and right, over what constitutes proper objects of social knowledge, what policies and politics are authorized by the new knowledges of the social, which groups are validated as authentic social actors, and who belongs to the imagined community of the French nation. Part of this struggle involves truth claims and Balzac does not hesitate to call his novel a "study" and to ally it with the presumably superior epistemology of the new social sciences whose methods and results are those of social inquests: like any modern sociologist or ethnographer, the novelist advertises in the above passage the fact that he has traveled to *la France profonde* and done fieldwork, unlike his ideological enemies.

Now, contemporary demographers and literary theorists have never ceased to be impressed by the empirical ambition and scope of Balzac's realist enterprise. In an introduction to a paperback edition of the novel, Louis Chevalier enthusiastically endorses the protosociological spirit with which Balzac approaches his *étude*. Chevalier argues that in *Les Paysans* fictive descriptions are one with social and historical facts. As with the critic Pierre Macherey, it matters little to him whether Balzac's observations are absolutely accurate or not. Rather, it is the fact that he pays attention to the subtleties and nuance of social and historical difference that counts:

> Even the study of crises and prices (such as Simiand and Labrousse's), even the study of demographics is in its own element in this novel and finds something new to discover and use in this description of the economy, budgets, and men. . . . It is this statistical curiosity that counts, and also this mindset which one might qualify today, and rightly so, as demographic: this will to reduce social facts to that which concerns not only the economy but also the mode of population renewal through migrations, mortality, and that overabundant animal fecundity which, from the odor of certain chapters, one senses the extent to which it is active in the Aigues' forest. One senses it also in the bestiality of words: "'All the same Monsieur Michaud has a pretty wife,' said Nicolas Tonsard . . . 'She is pregnant [*pleine*],' said the old grandmother, 'but if they keep it up we will hold some baptism for the little one when she calves [*vêlera*].'" It is a question of the unfortunate wife of the guard whom they are getting ready to murder. How many other allusions there are of powerful demographic interest![14]

However, I want to argue that this passage suggests that something other than an "objective" interest in demographic or sociological detail underwrites Chevalier's comments; or rather that this scientific interest produces a figure of social desire that should be quite familiar by now, namely, the old trope of lower-class animality, present in both Chevalier's remarks and Balzac's novel. This suggests in turn that insofar as *Les Paysans* functions as a conservative reply to Sue's protosocialist *Les Mystères de Paris* and thus articulates a different sense of national community, it nonetheless participates with other novels, social inquests, and reports in the common project of mapping the social field along the lines of familial discourse.

In what follows I will show how the realist text proves to be a particularly powerful semiotic device for constructing and naming the social anxieties that beset the social elites confronted with political and economic upheaval, and which familial discourse elicited, managed, and otherwise rechanneled by recoding social strife in familiar and thus more comforting terms: the split between the public and the private spheres, the imperatives of domesticity, various sexual practices, definitions of femininity, and so forth. Fredric Jameson's reformulation of Lukács's theory of realism will prove to be very helpful in articulating realism's relationship to familial discourse. He proposes that realist novels both decode—demystify—feudal literary and social forms and recode conventions suitable to the new bourgeois world; the novel in this view is a process that transforms the reader's subjective attitude and produces a new kind of objectivity. The realist novel then simultaneously unmasks old ideologies and discourses, explores the world of emergent capitalism, and reconstitutes a new, discursively overdetermined "real."[5] Traditional cultural values are shown to be irrelevant and social relations are presumably reduced to their self-interested economic core. It is my contention that this new "real" is in actuality familialist in its recurrent impulses and structures, and to that very degree epistemological claims of realist fiction must be reevaluated and relativized. Realism does not stand outside familial discourse at any critical distance. Moreover, the question of *Les Paysans*'s realism relates to how a conservative or even reactionary serial novel textualizes the social, so as at once to expand contemporary print culture's objects of knowledge (like the urban laboring classes in *Les Mystères de Paris*, the French peasantry gain entry into the discursive universe of daily newspaper readership) and to deauthorize vast segments of the imagined community of French men and women. This work of rearticulation and realignment will involve reshaping negative figures from an older familial discourse by means of a narrative in which domesticity turns out to be radically unlocatable in any one household or social milieu. Widespread familial disorder stands as the figure of Balzac's conservative pessimism. Throughout its pages, *Les Paysans* will parade successive positive figures of social desire only to dismiss each one in turn for lack of "family." Thus, as in most familial texts, Balzac's novel engages in a semiotic battle over the figural status of female bodies and households, but no one body or household arrangement successfully embodies the new norms. Hence the title of the present chapter. Rather than producing energizing, forward-looking desire for "family" by figuration of its absence in the social body, as in *Paul et Virginie* or *Les Mystères de Paris*, *Les Paysans*'s realist narratives inculcate a desire for the normative family, but so far outside of any present or future social class or formation as to form a disembodied social desire.

Literary Realism and Familial Discourse

To the degree that realism stands as just one moment in the production of familial discourse and those categories whereby individual and collective identities are constructed and affirmed, literary realism loses its exemplary epistemological status. Thus, Lukács's classic reading of *Les Paysans* must be modified. As Lukàcs claims, the tale of General Montcornet's losing struggle to defend the woods and pastures of his great estate Les Aigues against both devastation by the peasantry and the machinations of the local bourgeoisie does in some sense require a demystification of Balzac's Tory vision of a society dominated by great landowners as sterile nostalgia; and it is equally true that the novel also constructs, in the shadow of the narrative of the demise of great landed property, a second tragedy, that of small peasant landholders in the steel grip of money capital. Yet this *negative*, critical activity is vehicled by another narrative project that is busy creating specific, positive discursive effects by means of narrative figuration of deficient or deviant familial and gender relations. In *Les Paysans* the social narrative is enclosed in a familial one; the realism of Balzac's novel is predicated on a familialist subtext: familial discourse encodes the Tory social vision—legitimism—as bypassed by the tides of capitalist development; it inscribes both Toryism and its critique with its own language of "family" and sexuality. For *Les Paysans* is a story of households and interiors and of the public space that both separates and connects them. It is also one of female power and property. There is even a third narrative of different sexualities practiced within and outside households of different social milieus. These narratives are structured by a triple set of binary oppositions between private and public space, male and female dominance, and upper-class "passion" and lower-class "instinct." The second term of each binary constructs the social threat. As it turns out, the slow, ineluctable demise of the great estate Les Aigues under Montcornet's ownership before the onslaught of the peasants and money capitalists is one with a crisis in male authority and "family." The novel will rewrite the social menace (*la question sociale*), the economic power struggle in the public sphere, in terms of the end of male power in the household.

The question of rewriting social narrative in line with the preoccupations of familial discourse and a defensive masculine posture first surfaces in the novel at the end of the first chapter. It involves a struggle between different forms of writing to control the terms by which social and subjective relations are to be articulated. The chapter comprises one long letter from Blondet, the legitimist journalist, who is both family friend of the Montcornets and the countess's lover. Writing from the Montcornet's estate to his Parisian friend Nathan, the Tory journalist develops at length an erotic-political reverie encompassing the countess and Les Aigues, her château. However, in contrast to his tableau in epistolary form of Les Aigues and the waning feudal civilization to which it belongs stands the remainder of the novel, which recounts in third-person narration the growing alliance of social forces poised to destroy the great estate, of which Blondet is only dimly aware. The journalist's gaze, however, which slowly moves from the idyllic, peaceful countryside to the sixteenth-century château, finally resting upon the white, oneiric figure of the countess, will never leave the restricted confines of Les Aigues. For all intents and purposes the Tory poetic reverie—both political and erotic—stops there at the estate's gates, never to return outward to the public sphere. Blondet's Tory vision and the epistolary form in which it is transmitted emerge discredited by the narrative as a valid mode of seeing, experiencing, and writing. For in the remaining pages of *Les Paysans* a different gaze, that of the omniscient narrator, will roam, vehicling realism's vision of things through another literary form, that of the *roman feuilleton*. Now, what is fascinating to me is that the novel reformulates this opposition between literary forms as one between domestic bourgeois melodramas on the one hand and Balzac's own narrative on the other. Commenting on Blondet's letter, the narrating voice underscores the difference between what Blondet's letter may have led the reader to expect and what will actually follow in the novel's remaining pages:

> Many people expect, doubtless, to see the cuirass of the former colonel of the imperial Guard illumined by a flash of light, to see his wrath kindled and falling like a deluge upon the little woman, in such a way as to bring about toward the end of this narrative what we find at the end of so many modern dramas, a bed-chamber tragedy. Could such a tragedy be enacted in that pretty salon with paintings on blue cameo above the door, where the amorous scenes of mythology told their artless tales? . . . No: the drama here is not restricted to private life, it extends higher or lower. Do not expect passion, the truth will be only too dramatic. (64–65/31–32, translation modified)

As critics have remarked, Balzac makes claims for an urgently new social and public content of his novel that mark it off from the private melodramas characteristic of other modern fiction.[6] Like Toryism and outmoded epistolary fiction, the latter will no longer do. *Real* drama, worthy of the attention of novelists, is political, economic, and social, and takes place in the presumably masculine public sphere. These are *Les Paysans*'s true subjects, the text seems to suggest. Such pronouncements may enthrall theorists of Balzacian realism, but what they often overlook is that, paradoxically, as in the cited passage, Balzac invokes some of the categories of familial discourse in his dismissal of contemporary bourgeois fiction: male and female power, public and private space. Moreover, the theatrical metaphors that suffuse the passage ("drama" repeated twice, "dramatic," "either higher or lower") affirm a discursive continuity between both types of novels. These figures reveal an underlying aesthetic that is profoundly melodramatic and thus familial to the core.[7]

The omniscient narrator's barely concealed disdain for the narrowly "feminine" and private concerns of domestic melodrama indicates that what will ultimately be at issue is precisely domesticity and male household authority. Balzac's new "study," with its gaze fixed on the social field, will give figuration to the passing of landed property in terms of the loss of male authority: Montcornet never expulses his wife's lover but does lose his estate to emerging social forces. Moreover, the realist social narrative will reach its greatest pitch in the novel's climax, which is nothing if not melodramatic: the destruction of great landed property is consummated by the murder of Michaud and the death of his pregnant wife. The pathos of social tragedy is recoded in this instance as a familial one.

In other words, the sociological "truth" is never far from melodrama's familialist impulse ("the dramatic"). It could even be argued that one of the great tensions constitutive of realist fiction is that between the protocols of nascent positivist science (massively present in Balzac's 1842 preface to *La Comédie humaine*) and the discursive and aesthetic imperatives of familial discourse as manifested in bourgeois melodrama. All this suggests that the public and the private, the realist and the melodramatic, and the objective and the subjective are not so much opposed as mutually constitutive and authorizing *by virtue of their difference*: one cannot be invoked without alluding to the other. Balzac's text works to replace the Tory's private love story with an objective, full-blown political narrative, but the latter requires the affective, subjective confirmation and validation of "family" pathos. In *Les Paysans* familial melodrama will emerge as the most vigorous narrative and cognitive force of the novel.

Private and Public Spheres in Crisis

Les Paysans distributes questions of public and private space, sexuality, gender relations, and domesticity along a sociogeographical axis that opposes the Montcornets' household at Les Aigues and the Tonsards' peasant family household at the cabaret the Grand-I-Vert. Having set up these opposing terms, the novel then proceeds to discredit both of them and to propose a mediation in Michaud's household, which lies geographically between the axis's two extremes.

The first positive figure of social desire is the great estate, and the body of Mme de Montcornet, with whom the château is identified. The novel positively invests in the great estate, for it not only represents a waning feudal world but, paradoxically enough, is also a locus of bourgeois domesticity. The edifice conceals a remarkably elaborate functional interior space (57–58) that is, according to Philippe Ariès, more "modern" and bourgeois than feudal and aristocratic.[8] After a fashion, the château figuratively embodies the contradictory postrevolutionary world in which the emergent bourgeoisie dominated economically (Montcornet is of modest origins) but still sought to strike a compromise with the defeated aristocracy, which continued to hold immense prestige as figures of social power and legitimacy. The heterogeneous nature of Les Aigues is the very condition of its status as a figure of social desire. As does *Les Mystères de Paris*, *Les Paysans* rewrites the most fundamental symbol of the Old Regime aristocracy in terms that elicit, authorize, and affirm a very domestic if reactionary social desire. Only here, Les Aigues, unlike Rodolphe's estate, is situated in a field of contending social forces. Like château, like chatelaine: Mme de Montcornet cuts a heterogeneous figure as well. She abstains from any involvement in managing the estate's substantial affairs. Montcornet carefully shields her from all such annoying matters and strives to keep secret the growing underground threat to the estate's very existence (178). The countess rarely ventures beyond the estate's grounds. The daughter of a ruined noble family, she is almost a caricature of the retiring *bourgeoise* of her time.

However, all is not well in the Montcornet household: the Montcornets have no heirs. Childless, the general and his wife barely constitute a nuclear household. Under assault from all sides, Montcornet, son of an artisan, is in the eyes of the local petty bourgeois and peasants a *usurper*. Tellingly, the ambitious former Napoleonic officer does not even enjoy the phallic power of legitimacy. By means of the couple's fundamental deficiency—their sterile legitimate sexuality—the novel inscribes the sad historical fate that awaits them and the cause of great landed property. Moreover, the text links the thematics of illegitimacy and sterility to an imbalance in gender relations in the household. In a circular manner the former explain the latter and vice versa. The countess is indeed powerful: she's a "fragile little woman who arranges her strings to lead this tall, fat, square-shouldered general, precisely as he himself used to lead his cuirassiers" (63/29). Not unlike her female aristocratic ancestors, she enjoys her husband's remarkable tolerance of her love affair with Blondet. The countess's power seemingly stems at once from her retirement to the household and from the fact that she is not a mother. By escaping the duties and responsibilities of motherhood, she no longer has a fixed and controlled position within the corporate hierarchy of the family household. Since she is childless, the text can give her a *carnal* lover. In accordance with familial discourse of the nineteenth century, which split erotic desire into "passion" (an infinite, aesthetic desire reserved for the social elites) and "instinct" (an attribute of the lower classes in which erotic pleasure was identified with animality),[9] Mme de Montcornet's desire enjoys the privilege of textual discretion. But then we may ask what happens to the body of upper-class woman as a figure of social desire in the narrative. Blondet's oneiric countess seemingly displaces female eroticism and maternity in the social body onto women of the lower orders. There, female desire and reproductive sexuality take strong, "distorted," animal forms. Banished from the male discourse of her lover and that of the omniscient narrator, the countess's erotic life is named in confrontation with a peasant, Nicolas Tonsard, accused of attempting to rape La Péchina, a young girl. It is named brutally and in public: "'Bah! What do you people do in your salons?' demanded Nicolas, looking at the countess and Blondet, who shuddered at his glance. 'You play, don't you? Very good, the fields are ours, we can't work all the time, so we were playing! Ask my sister and La Péchina'" (215/281).

At the other pole of the sociogeographical axis bourgeois private space and domesticity vanish altogether. Just outside the walls of the estate in alarming proximity to it stands the Grand-I-Vert, that formidable gathering place where the life of the château is known intimately to all, thanks to Les Aigues's servants who stop in for a drink. At the same time a household, a workplace, a place of leisure and popular sociality, the rural cabaret owned by the Tonsard family manifests a wanton confusion of space, activities, bodies, and private and public spheres that worried bourgeois observers (81–82). Harboring both a cottage and a cabaret, the Grand-I-Vert's architecture, as opposed to that of Les Aigues, is not only ramshackle but also multipurpose; it is no example of modern, functionally designed interiors. In marked contrast to the Montcornets' sterile conjugal sexuality, reproductive sexuality reigns in the Tonsard household, but uncontrollably and illegitimately. There reside Tonsard and his wife (the illegitimate daughter of old *père* Fourchon who lives there as well), his mother *mère* Tonsard; two illegitimate daughters, Catherine and Marie; two sons, Nicolas and Jean; and Mouche, *père* Fourchon's illegitimate grandson (in the reproductive confusion we never do learn who his parents were).

In line with the dictates of familial discourse, the text employs a social hermeneutic that reaches its climax in the familial and sexual. The Tonsards' crowded quarters naturally lead to the worst of all possible private activities: carnal incest.[10] In the following passage, the text elicits an initial sexual fascination with the two beautiful daughters—victims of a decidedly *non*–child-centered family—and then shifts to a fascination with sexualized interior space, where the familial and the sexual are collapsed into one: "These two girls, the gypsies [*bohémiennes*] of the valley, did not receive a sou from their parents, who simply fed them and provided them with horrible beds, with their grandmother, in the loft, where their brothers also slept, curled up in the hay like animals. Neither father nor mother gave a thought to the evils of such promiscuity" (90/74, translation modified).

Worse still, the cabaret is not a locus of male authority. Mme Tonsard rules over the household. She is something of a caricature of the middle-class *femme d'intérieur* who refuses to perform the traditional heavy work outside the cottage expected of peasant women: "By remaining in the house, La Tonsard had retained her fresh, fair complexion and her plumpness, whereas the women who work in the fields fade as quickly as the flowers and are old at thirty" (90/74). Escaping the lamentable destiny of all working women which bourgeois writers repeatedly deplored, Tonsard's wife, as it turns out, is an even more formidable domestic force to reckon with; an adroit application of her domestic female arts allows her to dominate her husband. A beautiful woman, she takes advantage of her liaisons with men at Les Aigues and in the region to start the cabaret, maintain its clientele, and extend her domination over Tonsard. Here, the novel establishes distinct limits to the extension of domesticity to the lower orders of society and marks well *Les Paysans*'s conservative articulation of the discourse of "family" and its imagined community. *Les Paysans* dismisses out of hand upward social mobility of the "dangerous classes" through their adoption of domesticity.

The retirement of Mme Tonsard to interior domestic space has produced unexpected results: it has disturbed household hierarchies and has unleashed the female erotic desire which it was supposed to limit in the first place.[11] The consequences are frightful for social order: interior space is not only transformed into a site of illegitimate, almost public sexuality, but also into a public sphere of its own. The sociability of the entire canton ends up being mediated by the cabaret and the bodies of the Tonsard women (90). Their "animal" sexuality stands in stark opposition to the countess's "passion" for Blondet, to her aestheticized desire. In this dense, compact space of illicit sexuality and base self-interest the novel discursively produces a familial dystopia, the "truth" of a lower-class social threat. The cabaret is a hothouse of social *ressentiment* patiently nursed among the clientele by the Tonsards against the rich (92).

From there, a close watch is kept over the château. Indeed, the countryside's old sociality affords little protection from prying eyes. The château's elaborate, functional space is at best an illusory private sphere. Here, the minutest gesture or act by the Montcornets comes under scrutiny from below and without. While their neighbors can look in, the Montcornets cannot return the gaze in order to scan, probe, and discipline the social field. They scarcely know how deep the conspiracy mounted against them runs, let alone what transpires in other, less exalted private spaces and in the surrounding forests and fields. At one point the narrating voice exclaims:

> These details should convince Parisians who have never left their quartier, of the difficulty, let us say rather the impossibility, of keeping the slightest thing secret in the valley of the Avonne, from Conches to Ville-aux-Fayes. *In the country districts there is no space*; there are, at intervals, such places as the wine shop of Grand-I-Vert and the Café de la Paix, which perform the functions of echoes, and where the most unimportant acts, performed in the utmost secrecy, reverberate by a sort of magic. (293/411–12, emphasis mine, translation modified)

In a sense, the naïveté of Tory social vision, embodied by the Montcornets and Blondet, leaves it blind before the social forces amassed to strike at Les Aigues. It falls to the penetration of the narrator, and ultimately of "realism," to lead readers into those domains of public and private space that presumably would otherwise remain as opaque for them as for the Montcornets.

The most noteworthy result of the text's peregrinations through public and private space is the novel's notoriously fragmented character; it is broken up by lengthy introductory descriptions of different households and social milieus (Les Aigues, the Grand-I-Vert, La-Ville-aux-Fayes, Couches, Solanges, etc.), digressions, and flashbacks as the narrating voice seeks to construct a detailed picture of social causality. According to Macherey, the text's disparate nature produces literary realism through the reciprocal ironizing of all social discourses and representations and empties the text of any lingering Tory pathos. What he fails to observe is that familial discourse and its underlying affective charge survive undiminished.[12]

The description of inaccessible private homes and their interrelations results in a confused, anxiety-ridden picture of a resolutely hostile environment. This discursive construct has consequences for the general reading process. As one works one's way through the text a slight feeling of paranoia settles over the novel. The more the omniscient gaze reveals, the more the social field seems opaque and menacing. In our terms, there is no escape from dystopic private or public space. Moreover, the very length of the descriptions verges on overwhelming both readers and the plot while they detail the latter's intricacies and intermeshing mechanisms.

This process achieves its most compact form in the chapter entitled "De la médiocratie" ("On the mediocracy"). Balzac devotes the entire chapter to drawing up systematically the network of genealogies and alliances that links bourgeois and peasant families conspiring against the Montcornets. Like the Grand-I-Vert, these households are not simple private spheres where domesticity and sentiment are cultivated. They, along with the cabaret, are key points in a thick web of intersecting lines of self-interest, marriage, and clienteles reminiscent of Old Regime social relations in which the cult of domesticity and the distinction between public and private space were largely absent. Together they constitute a fearful social force in face of which the Montcornets' solitary household stands helpless. Nothing escapes their claws. Constitutive of social relations in the public sphere, but largely mediated by the private sphere, this web in which "family spirit is seconded by locality spirit" (186/233, translation modified) remains invisible for the estate's inhabitants: "This formidable league which monopolized all branches of public and private service, which was sucking the blood of the department, which clung to the ruling powers as a sucking fish clings to the keel of a vessel, escaped all eyes; General Montcornet did not suspect it" (186/233).

Once more, the novel rewrites the power of Montcornet's enemies in negative familial terms. The "mediocracy" embodies the binary logic subtending familial discourse since the eighteenth century: the new bourgeois household, the foundation of civil society, was increasingly privatized and opposed both materially and ideologically to the public sphere and to collective interests. The recurrent notion was that a disinterested, moralized familial sphere would redeem the public one dominated by the struggle of competing interests. (That was to be the vocation of the *dames patronnesses* and the goal of the moralization of society.) This has clearly not happened in the Avonne valley. The alliance between bourgeois and peasants combines the worst features of Old Regime lifestyles—tyrannical sociality destructive of domesticity—and of the new order—conquering bourgeois self-interest.

Feminine Threat and Manly Resistance

As always in familial discourse, a struggle over definitions of household arrangements turns on a semiotic battle over writing female bodies. The recoding of social struggle as familial disorder produces a textual charge that is displaced onto the female characters. This process involves Mme de Montcornet and the Tonsard women, to be sure, but also those women belonging to the households of the Montcornets' bourgeois enemies. The novel focuses anxieties concerning public and private space and imminent social strife by associating these fears with powerful and sexually active women. In this way the familialist "real" constructed by the text engenders a new subjectivity in the reader. Simmering class violence is interiorized in the form of disruptive gender relations.

Female dominance is the rule in other households in league with the Tonsards against the Montcornets. All of Soulanges is a seat of female power and property. Vermichel's huge, very masculine wife—a "virago with moustaches" (99/89)—regularly gives him a beating during bouts of drunkenness. At the Soudrys', Madame, by virtue of her age and wealth, holds sway over the household (258–61), while Vermut, faced with his wife's energetic character and henpecking, suffers from a double, disastrous decline in his *puissance maritale* (270–71). Down the street, the late Mme Socquart, hostess of Café de la Paix, even outdid Mme Tonsard in her sexual adventures with her middle-class patrons and similarly built up a prosperous business (292).

The novel does produce several men, however, who resist this overturning of male power. They are representatives of the radical political *other* of Les Aigues: Rigou and old Niseron. They are complex, discursive figures. The fact that they both seem to be relics of the past (an ex-monk and a Jacobin) perhaps explains their success; true male dominance (however the novel may ultimately qualify it) belongs to outdated political and social systems. As such, they inscribe a deep social pessimism within the text's narrative. True male authority (and thus political order) is a thing of the past. Just what acceptable male authority might look like is a question repeatedly raised by *Les Paysans*'s multiple plots, but it will go unanswered.

Rigou is something of an anachronism, for the novel's purest capitalist is a former Dominican and, true to his former vocation, a libertine in the Old Regime style. Rigou's unusual patriarchal and sexual powers designate in caricatured familial terms the tyrannical force of capitalist development. The moneylender enjoys magical patriarchal authority over his wife, daughter, and servants:

> Never was prophet, who was likely to become a god, more blindly obeyed than Rigou was in his own house, in his slightest whims. The contraction of his heavy black eyebrows caused his wife, Annette, and Jean mortal anxiety; he held his three slaves by the minute multiplicity of their duties, which was like a chain about their necks. At every moment in the day, the poor creatures were confronted by some compulsory task to be performed under the master's eye. (245/331)

The legitimate, reproductive family and male authority, so markedly absent in Les Aigues and other households, triumphs in the Rigou household in a discredited, hallucinatory form, that of mythical peasant patriarchy, which bourgeois observers stigmatized for overworking its women and letting their "beauty" go for naught. Mme Rigou's confinement to the household, and the drudgery of her domestic chores, have altered her features. The birth of her only daughter, far from enhancing or bringing out her "feminine nature" (as familial ideologues were wont to say), destroyed her good looks: "The birth of her only child, Madame Soudry the younger, had decimated her teeth, made her eyelashes drop out, dimmed her eyes, withered her complexion. It seemed that God's finger had fallen heavily on the wife of the priest" (241/324). His rapacious erotic appetites are shared by peasant men such as Nicolas and Courtecuisse, but in his case sexual and monetary power are identical:

> Holding burdensome mortgages upon the estates purchased by peasants at a price beyond their means, he took for his harem the whole valley, from Soulanges to five leagues beyond Conches toward Brie, without

other expense than *postponements of foreclosure* to obtain those ephemeral treasures which devour the fortunes of so many old men. (245/332)

The other relic of the past dates from the Revolution: *père* Niseron, the young La Péchina's grandfather. He belongs to an equally mythical but different patriarchy, that of austere Republicanism (221–22). He is without property and has long refused any dealings with the money capitalist Rigou. Yet he has been bypassed by history; he is portrayed as naive, even foolish. It is revealing that he has not much of a family. All that remains is his illegitimate granddaughter La Péchina, who is constantly pursued by two local libertines, Rigou and Nicolas. While he enjoys great moral prestige, his broken family bespeaks his historical fate.

The figure of the disinterested Jacobin patriot represents one solution to the opposition between the increasingly self-interested private sphere and the bourgeois project to moralize the public sphere in favor of the general interest: he sacrificed not only his worldly wealth but his family as well—his son who died in the Revolutionary wars—to the Republic (221–22). But his answer to the dilemma is a false, utopian one; for what he did was simply to *abolish* (fatally so) one set of terms (the private and familial). In terms of familial discourse, doing away with the family and private wealth is tantamount to exiling oneself from history. However, what events keep in store for the canton is scarcely reassuring: the Rigous, those money men whose unbridled sexual appetites and tyranny over women, servants, and peasants is a token of what is constructed by the realist text as capital's fascinating but alarming totalizing power in domestic and social relations. In the subnarrative of the crisis of small peasant landholdings the ungovernable, feminine-coded behavior of the lower classes (their dissolute sociality) must ultimately give way before the new patriarchal power of money capital.

The Michaud Household

Toward the end of part I, after having shuttled readers between opposing households across the social field, the omniscient narrator will draw them into a new erotic-political reverie, now displaced onto the mediating figures of Montcornet's chief guard Michaud and his wife. This follows upon the chapter "On the mediocracy" and constitutes something of a response to the gross materialism and narrow self-interest of bourgeois and peasant households in league against the Montcornets. The newlywed couple live in one of the estate's outlying pavilions, situated at the gates to the grounds surrounding the château. As its location suggests, the Michaud household designates a conservative social space and class where domesticity might flourish at a remove from class conflict and might serve as a mediation of the social forces contending with each other. The Michauds together stand as another figure of social desire. Selfless and devoted to their masters, the Michauds' insertion in the old corporate hierarchies of masters and servants on the one hand and that of military command (Michaud is a former soldier like Montcornet and the other guards) on the other promises to resolve the multifaceted contradictions produced by the novel. For the couple's arranged marriage has miraculously spawned both passion between husband and wife *and* a new generation. Mme Michaud is pregnant. The countess and Blondet envy the young couple's domestic bliss. Their hopeful, reproductive sexuality contrasts significantly with the lovers' situation and the Montcornets' family life. As such, the Michauds figure forth in terms of familial discourse a historical future more acceptable than the Tonsards' disruptive and illegitimate sexuality and the destructive patriarchy of Rigou's family household. Tellingly, it is a utopian future based on domesticity as such and not on private property or money capital; the household is without a firm economic basis.

Yet the narrative machine dispensing familial lack right and left continues to grind away, for these figures of social desire are in jeopardy from without and within: threats have been issued against Michaud, who has exasperated the local peasants by his vigilance. Moreover, the Michauds are afflicted by an old problem that will not go away; Mme Michaud, very much her mistress's protégée, dominates the household: "Michaud, following his general's example, looked upon his young wife as a superior being, whom he must obey in military fashion, without reservation" (192–93/244). Finally, the fate of a new social class embodying domesticity is imbricated in that of another and final figure of social desire, La Péchina, a peasant adolescent girl who lives with the Michauds. In the very passage in which the novel presents readers with a tableau of middle-class family bliss, the text curiously cuts to the fascinating figure of La Péchina and the narrative of Nicolas Tonsard's attempt to rape her with the help of his sister Catherine.

The Plots and Ends of Philanthropic Desire

La Péchina is the most discursively complex figure in Balzac's novel. In the textual oppositions between various households and arrangements and different sexualities along class lines, La Péchina takes her place somewhere in between. Thus she can claim to be yet another mediating figure, if only briefly. The peasant girl rarely strays alone away from the Michaud household for fear of being pursued and raped by Nicolas. A potential Catherine Tonsard (who carries out her numerous love affairs in the surrounding woods), La Péchina has yet to be marked by male peasant desire, a destiny the text claims awaits all young peasant girls (199). She literally escapes what is taken to be her class and gender fate to the very degree that she remains close to the Michauds' residence. There, she receives the rudiments of bourgeois female upbringing. Her body is thus written with the contradictory clichés of bourgeois and lower-class femininity; she is the object of philanthropic desire and stands as its figure of social mobility. Slender and frail in appearance like a middle-class adolescent, she has the almost "masculine" physical strength of peasant women like Catherine Tonsard who work outdoors. Yet this "animal" strength the text recodes in middle-class terms as a psychological feature, as *hysterical interiority*. This is a familiar sight to the new experts in medical and social sciences with whom the narrating voice associates itself: "Slender, thin, brown as a tobacco-leaf, small of stature, she possessed an incredible amount of force, invisible to the eyes of the peasants, to whom the mysteries of nervous organizations are unknown. Nerves are not taken into account in the medical system of the country districts" (210/274).

La Péchina moves beyond some of the terms in which familial discourse has heretofore cast social struggle. No longer simply a peasant and far from being middle class, she is both of the public sphere (a child of the field and forest and the illegitimate offspring of the public servant Niseron) and the private sphere (the Michauds' household). She thus displays more overtly a sensuality that middle-class women were forbidden to have by bourgeois culture and discourse. At the same time, she resembles her middle-class counterparts inasmuch as she is also the precocious, sexualized child—a pure discursive product of familial discourse—who alarmed physicians and educators: "La Péchina, although she was nothing more than a peasant girl, presented the spectacle of frightening precocity like many natures destined to end, as they have blossomed, prematurely. . . . At thirteen years, Geneviève had attained her full growth, although she was hardly so tall as the ordinary child of her age" (210/273–74, translation modified).[13] In this sense La Péchina is the impossible synthesis of two types of class-coded, female sexuality—"impossible," because her overt sensuality marks her irrevocably as of modest origins and thus, in the discourse of *Les Paysans*, as a "failed" domestic woman-to-be. In this respect, fetishistic descriptions of her complicate her figural status still further:

> This combination of diabolical imperfections and divine beauties, harmonious despite the many discordant features, because a sort of fierce pride tended to produce unity in all its parts, this challenge of a powerful soul to a weak body as written in the eyes, made the child unforgettable. Nature had attempted to make a woman of this tiny creature, the circumstances of her conception had given her the face and body of a boy. (211/275)

The androgynous figure combines both female and male, childlike innocence and adult sensuality, or perhaps put another way, both submission to men and provocative sexual independence. She does refuse her grandfather Niseron's patriarchal protection (206); consigned by the text to the backwaters of history, Niseron will not do as a masculine aegis. Rather, her chosen protector is Michaud; better yet, the text claims it is her elevated, middle-class *passion* for him that will keep her from being seduced or raped by her pursuers (198–99). Though an energetic girl, she willingly submits to an emissary of male, bourgeois authority. She obeys him without hesitation. She is the ideal philanthropic object. That is the function of the scene of attempted rape. Nicolas's assault enacts the narrative of social philanthropy's desire, it literally constructs the struggle over defining and thus "owning" the bodies of women of the laboring classes: middle- or upper-class women and men "saving" poor women from "threatening" working-class or peasant men and their female accomplices. This is the discourse of philanthropic (male) protection. Whence the ambiguity of the narrating voice with respect to La Péchina: she is inscribed as the object of desire for *both* parties; one desire authorizes another. Thus the narrating voice displays a startling understanding of the male characters' pursuit of the young girl, from the stance of experienced bourgeois social commentators:

> Observing minds will understand that La Péchina, with passion flowing from every pore, was calculated to awaken in wicked natures desires that had been lulled to sleep by satiety; just as, at table, your mouth waters at the sight of the misshapen fruit, full of holes and covered with black spots, which gourmands know by experience, and under whose skins nature is pleased to bestow choice flavors and perfumes. (212/ 276)

It thereby evinces its own complicity in the episode's sexual violence. This is philanthropic voyeurism in its most explicit form. Here the realist narrator and familial ideologue stands together with his social enemies Nicolas and Rigou.

La Péchina, then, is another erotic-political reverie, like the Tory Blondet's, but that of liberal philanthropy: she is an imaginary social class that the novel condemns never to see the light of day. To begin with, her protector, Michaud, is no real patriarch: he owes obedience to his wife; thus in the raging social conflict between class and private interests, he must die at the hands of the peasant enemies. With Michaud gone her fate will be sealed. And strictly speaking, her destiny could not be otherwise: La Péchina remains too sensuous and she is not the product of any *legitimate* familial agency. Her destiny emplots the conservative rejection of the feasibility of liberal philanthropy's enterprise for domesticating the social through the moralization of the poor.

Familial Catastrophe and High Melodrama

The rape scene encodes once again class antagonisms as conflicts over sexuality and gender. The sexual assault is indeed against the estate's women, gender violence is class violence:[14] it *is* the peasant Nicolas, perversely helped by his almost masculine sister Catherine, who attacks La Péchina, and it is he who subjects Mme de Montcornet to crude sexual innuendo when he is caught in the act. The emplotment of these reciprocal fears of class and gender is nowhere more powerful than in the climax of the novel, the death of Michaud and his family. His murder marks the defeat of landed property and the victory of money capital: soon afterward, upon receiving renewed threats of violence, the Montcornets sell their estate. The peasants' resentment over Montcornet's arrest of some of their own for illegal gleaning in his fields strikes out at Michaud on a cold, moonlit November evening. Tonsard and others ambush Michaud on his way to fetch a doctor for his wife, who is in labor. Mme Michaud, in the very throes of childbirth, is terror-stricken by the nightmarish sight of a riderless horse:

> Then she stood still, as if horror-stricken, motionless, and voiceless. . . . Soon, too soon for the unhappy wife, the horse reached the gate, drenched with sweat, but alone; he had broken the reins in which he had doubtless become entangled. With a haggard expression, Olympe watched the servant open the gate; she saw the horse, and, without a word, ran off toward the château like a madwoman; she arrived there at last, and fell on the ground under the general's windows, crying:
> "Monsieur, *they* have murdered him!"
> It was such a terrible cry that it woke the count; he rang, roused the whole household, and the groans of Madame Michaud, who was delivered of a child as she lay on the ground, attracted the attention of the general and his servants. They raised the poor dying woman, and she expired, saying to the general:
> "*They* have murdered him!" (340–41/494–95, translation modified)

The mediating figures of the devoted father-to-be and his burgeoning family are wiped out at the very moment of reproduction. Legitimate reproductive sexuality and domesticity—so vital to social order—are defeated by the quasi animality of the peasants and the money men. The tragedy of the Michaud family restores a pathos to the text and to the demise of the great estate that perhaps the text's "realism," based on irony and contradiction, should otherwise have banished from the novel. The pathos is preeminently familial and approaches the melodramatic mode dominant in the literature of the period.[15] High melodrama completes the familial recoding of the social and economic struggle: the only full-blooded example of bourgeois domesticity must succumb in the end, and its loss confirms familialism as the novel's dominant discourse.

The triple strand of familial narrative—that of households and interiors, female power and property, and different sexual practices in opposed social milieus—permeates Balzac's high social tragedy throughout and constructs a domestic drama at the heart of the narrative of the demise of great landed property. In turn, the social tragedy is inscribed in the drama's outcome: male authority is not reestablished, General Montcornet does not rid his household of the interloper Blondet. Rather, Blondet will replace Montcornet as the countess's husband.

Bringing It All Back Home

The novel closes with a return to Blondet and Mme de Montcornet. Thirteen years after the sale of the estate, Blondet marries the now widowed but still childless forty-year-old countess. When, on their way to Auxerre during their honeymoon, the newlyweds drive by Les Aigues, they discover to Blondet's bitter astonishment that the château has been razed and the estate replaced by a society of hundreds of burgeoning peasant households:

> The district was unrecognizable. The mysterious woods, the avenues through the park, all had been levelled and cleared; the country resembled a tailor's card of samples. The peasant had taken possession of the estate like a victor and conqueror. It was already divided into more than

a thousand lots, and the population between Conches and Blangy had increased threefold. The turning over to agricultural uses of the lovely park, formerly so well-cared-for and so charming, had isolated Michaud's gate-house, which had become the villa *Il Buen Retiro* of Madame Isaure Gaubertin; it was the only building left standing, and dominated the whole landscape, or, to speak more accurately, the collection of small cultivated fields that had replaced the landscape. The structure resembled a château, the little cottages built all about it were such miserable affairs as peasants build. (347/508)

The future *does* lie with reproductive families, but they are all doubtless without male authority and heavily in debt to the new masters of the region, the capitalists Rigou and Gaubertin. This occasions one last outburst of Tory *ressentiment* which ends the novel:

"And this is progress!" cried Emile, "It is a page from Jean-Jacques's *Social Contract*! And I am harnessed to the social machine that produces this result! My God! What will become of kings in a short time! Indeed, with affairs in this state, what will become of the nations themselves fifty years hence?"

"You love me, you are by my side. To me the present is very beautiful, and I worry little concerning a future so far away as that," his wife replied.

"Long life to the present, by your side!" said the amorous Blondet, gaily, "and the deuce take the future!" (347/508–9)

The reaction that this spectacle elicits from Blondet and the countess reproduces one last time the binary oppositions constitutive of familial discourse and of Balzac's realist critique of the Tory cause. The cultural division between the private, feminine sphere and the public, masculine sphere is once again affirmed. The countess is totally uninterested in Blondet's remarks. History and politics are not her domain; sentiment, love, and feeling are. Yet something is radically amiss in this companionate marriage: she owns and controls all the wealth and dominates the household. Having met the fate reserved for those who defended the legitimist cause under the Bourgeois Monarchy, Blondet is not only politically marginalized but is also relegated to a secondary status within the household as a rich woman's dependent husband.[16] Moreover, since the death of Montcornet, the crisis of male authority within the household has deepened, for there has been a transfer of property, not to children, but into the ethereal matriarch's hands. Female dominance, the telltale sign of the bankruptcy of legitimist politics, has reemerged stronger than ever. In Blondet's case the deficient relations of the domestic sphere signify a sorry historical fate. The novel does grant Blondet something of an Oedipal victory over the older bourgeois generation dating from the Revolution and the Empire, but the text's familial logic deflates its importance: the defeated party was in any case childless, not a real father at all. Blondet cannot assume the place of the father, for there never was one. Worse, unlike Montcornet the successful Napoleonic officer, he has suffered complete defeat in the presumably masculine public sphere. For these reasons he is unworthy of a seat among patriarchs. In a sense, he has lost his pen, meant to replace the general's sword. Tory discourse is indeed dead. His private authority is no greater than the general's and his public authority substantially less. In terms of familial discourse, the novel leaves the couple with a dismal historical future; given the countess's age, they will most likely remain childless. Finally, in addition to the historical and social marginalization of legitimism, the novel also maps out for us the tenuous class position of the nineteenth-century middle-class intellectual: Blondet never really belongs to his class; propertyless, he is also without descendants.

In the course of the novel no one household arrangement, male character, or female body emerges unscathed. Mme de Montcornet (and Les Aigues by the same token) is discredited, as are Mme Michaud and La Péchina, not to mention peasant and middle-class women and their respective households. Similarly, Montcornet and Michaud are inadequate to the demands made upon them; the money men Rigou and Gaubertin and young peasants like Nicolas are too tyrannical or brutal. No man embodies acceptable masculine behavior or qualities. The text, as it shifts back and forth from one household to another, recodes the demise of landed property in terms of negative familialist features. General social turmoil and unacceptable political and economic change are matched by deficient family relations. In *Les Paysans* the crisis of "family" is identical with its functioning; its satisfactory resolution, just as that of the social crisis, is an impossible one: that signals the very measure of *Les Paysans*'s conservative social pessimism. The future holds little promise. In this respect Macherey's observations on the relationship between literary figuration and ideology in *Les Paysans* are too idealist. According to him, the movement of literary figuration throws into contradiction ideologies present in the text and demystifies them. In this view, ideologies ultimately remain exterior to the text and enter it only to be drawn and quartered and to die at the hands of literary negativity. The production of the figures and tactics of familial discourse by Balzac's narrative suggests something quite different: one discourse (familialism) may deconstruct another (Toryism's social vision) while itself remaining intact; indeed, in the case of familial discourse, far from discrediting domesticity by highlighting its binary oppositions (public/private, male/female, etc.) as insoluble contradictions, *Les Paysans* reinscribes "family" on every page as the fundamental grid of intelligibility of French social relations.

Familial lack so pervades the social body as to discredit all social classes in the text (and even the philanthropic attempt to create a new one in the case of La Péchina), leaving "family" as the disembodied object of social desire. Here, the serial novel situates "family" at odds with both an outmoded social vision and ideology (Toryism or legitimism) and emergent capitalist development in the countryside. In so doing, Balzac's text introduces a major new discursive figure in commercial print culture, the struggling peasantry, and circulates it among a wide, "democratic" readership, but only to pathologize and marginalize it, refusing it any hope of full membership in the French national community through plots of social mobility. (This latter will be the affirmative task of George Sand's rustic novels.) Indeed, rather than expanding the sense of national community *Les Paysans* contracts it: both the peasants and their middle-class masters are stigmatized for their animal appetites, disorderly household life, and narrow self-interest. However, since Balzac's novel designates them as the wave of the future, it would perhaps be more accurate to say that *Les Paysans* articulates a dissident position within what it constructs as the New France, if not to say a complete withdrawal from it.

~ CHAPTER 6

Midwiving Subjectivities and Female Knowledges: Sand's *La Petite Fadette*

> Yes, civic equality, equality in marriage, equality in the family, that is what you can, what you must demand and call for, but this should be done with a profound awareness of the sanctity of marriage, of conjugal fidelity, and of the love of family.
>
> —George Sand, "Aux membres du comité central," April 1848

Locating Women in Familial Discourse

In the eighteenth and nineteenth centuries the discursive practices of familialism both in fiction and in other forms of writing expended much effort in dismantling older concepts and practices of sociality, household life, and sexuality that were stigmatized as repressing and blocking the fruition at all levels of society of new forms of social relations, family, and subjectivity. A privileged target of familial discourse was the body itself, in particular the female body, which through extensive reinscriptions became both the symbol of the new self and society and the very ground upon which a new map of them was to be drawn. I have claimed that a new discursively based imagined community and its social body was articulated in and through print culture by a deluge of literature ranging from serial novels, children's literature, and educational manuals to philanthropic inquiries and treatises on sexual "pathologies"; this literature encoded a powerful new liberal subjectivity and the body which encloses it as "feminine," in opposition to the older social body marked by the sign of discredited patriarchy (to which the governor and the priest in *Paul et Virginie*, Rodolphe's father and Sarah of *Les Mystères de Paris*, and the tyrannical usurer Rigou of *Les Paysans* all belong).

In familial discourse, gender became *the* master code, yet it functioned in a paradoxical fashion: within the field of "feminine"-coded subjectivity, distinctions were introduced between "male" and "female," between "masculine" and "feminine" bodies, sexualities, activities, and spheres. This was the effect of the forceful interventions of writings such as Bernardin de Saint-Pierre's *Paul et Virginie*. Later, as amply demonstrated by *Les Mystères de Paris* and even by the avowedly conservative Balzacian text *Les Paysans*, respect and observance of these same distinctions became the hallmarks and legible signs of membership in the imagined community of postrevolutionary France; neglect, violation, or transgression of these norms constituted the indelible signifiers of marginality with respect to this new "community," and of abject subjective and collective existence. And indeed, by virtue of its deployment of narratives of deficient or jeopardized familial relations, familial discourse helped generate the anxiety-causing perception that no one social group or household stood at a safe remove from the threat of social marginalization through lack of "family."

Up till now the working assumption of this book has been that familial discourse enjoyed the increasing allegiance of men and women alike, especially of those who came to see, or wished to see, themselves as "middle class" or perhaps even "working class"; and that the very gender distinctions this discourse promoted didn't trouble the constructions, emplotments, and circulation of its own crucial concepts and presuppositions. I have given to understand in Part I that male and female apologists of domesticity produced fundamentally the same discourse. Yet through examinations of familialist fictions, we've observed tensions that deny such a facile consensus, or rather suggest that within the consensual parameters of "family" a new struggle was beginning to form between male and female authors, or at least between different literary genres and their perceived single-sex publics, over what constituted appropriate practices and fields of knowledge. For example, in both Sue and his critic Nettement a certain feudal, patriarchal nostalgia floats over their texts. After all, what is Rodolphe if not a middle-class dream of a reformed aristocracy which now accepts the new domesticity but to which it lends a semblance of patriarchal authority? Similarly, in his attack on Sue, Nettement rhetorically stages the struggle between the domestic household and the serial novel as a battle between *male authorities*: he addresses his remarks not to a bourgeois mother but rather to an aristocratic husband, whom he warns against the usurpation of the priest's influence as the wife's confessor by the *homme invisible* who is none other than the personification of Sue's serial novel, *Les Mystères de Paris*. In these examples I think it is fair to say that what we are witnessing is a shift by Sue and Nettement toward placing domesticity under some sort of male aegis. Of course, the irony here is that what counts as "male" and "masculine" is very much the product of familial discourse itself, which repositioned and reframed masculinity and men's activity squarely within the broad finalities of the female-dominated family.

Balzac's preface to *Les Paysans* also gestures toward a discursive struggle along gender lines when he authorizes his own novelistic practice as a quasi-scientific "study" of imminent social upheavals over against earlier forms of melodramatic fiction that he disparages for their limited subject matter, the "private dramas" destined to thrill a female readership. Clearly, Balzac is advocating a rigid distinction between two forms of knowledge, a masculine one of the political and social field and a feminine one of the private familial sphere. Here, he performs something similar to the acts of eighteenth- and nineteenth-century physicians and biologists who, according to Thomas Laqueur, introduced a "biology of incommensurability" into the discourse of sexual and gender difference.[1] As I suggested regarding *Paul et Virginie*, the trope of biological difference was a serviceable one, for it helped fix new gender differences in a semantic field that was inherently unstable because of its discursive nature and because of its fundamental premise that New Men and Women shared an underlying "feminine" liberal subjectivity and sensibility.

However, Balzac seems anxious to deny on the level of sensibility and knowledge any common ground at all between men and women and their respective spheres. His hostility toward a mode of knowledge and subjectivity identified with women and the familial sphere but promoted by earlier familial discourse as available to women and men alike signals that the old internal, discursive boundaries of domesticity, which Balzac inherited, have solidified to the point that they may be used by, say, men such as Balzac to deauthorize the "feminine" as such and thus the private sphere as merely "female." This constitutes something of a reversal; formerly, as in *Paul et Virginie*, the model family discredited the Old Regime sphere of political representation and issued an appeal for the construction of institutions ratified by the new familial values; now, the opposite appears to be the case: the masculine world of "real" politics and the *question sociale* is employed to marginalize private life and domesticity. Yet the reversal promised in the preface is not realized in the body of the novel. As we had ample opportunity to observe in the preceding chapter, Balzac's attempt to do away with the "feminine" sphere failed miserably; his own narrative strategies, far from jettisoning the authenticating figures and protocols of familial discourse, actually reinscribed them on every page. Not only did the plot turn on the distinction between the two spheres but it also privileged the discourse of "family" and gender as the means by which the social was to be read: *Les Paysans* ended up encoding the triumph of money capital over the Montcornets and their estate in familial terms; and in so doing, the novel unwittingly produced a desire for the model family and its attendant notions of subjectivity and social relations. Thus the discursive consensus of "family" is maintained even while within its parameters tensions between gendered styles of writing mount. So Balzac's dismissal of melodrama as narrow, feminine fiction of the private sphere may be understood as a gesture performed in favor of a masculine reappropriation of that sphere and the knowledges that inhere in it.[2]

La Petite Fadette, 1848, and the Gender of Writing

George Sand's *romans champêtres* or rustic novels, and *La Petite Fadette* (translated as *Fadette*) in particular, constitute a reply to these attempts at appropriation and subsumption of the space and discourse of domesticity. In fact, I think it is fair to say that Sand both reiterates the special claims of familialism over the household and the bodies of its members and imparts a new movement to the ever-expanding semiotic work of domesticity. Indeed, in these novels, the familial discipline of bodies and sexuality evolves into a virtual science of gender that is psychological and discursive in character. And in *La Petite Fadette*, gender *understood as desire* will be constructed as the privileged domain of female knowledge and then affirmed as the source of women's power in the domestic family.[3] Finally, this tale of gendered desire that recenters "family" around the domestic woman will also be one that returns the French peasantry from the discursive exile to which it had been consigned by Balzac's disenchanted legitimism; Sand's novel places the peasants in the center of a renewed imagined community through narratives of social mobility and the adoption of norms of domesticity.

La Petite Fadette was first published in serial form in *Le Crédit* from December 1, 1848, to February 28, 1849. Briefly, it is the pastoral tale of how the excessive bonding between twin boys of wealthy peasant stock, Sylvinet and Landry Barbeau, is resolved by the intervention of Fadette, a poor peasant girl who is the object of universal mockery and derision in the local village because of her broken family, tattered clothing, and tomboy ways. The outcome is as predictable as it is conventional: Fadette and Landry fall in love, and out of affection for Landry Fadette adopts the garb and manners of acceptable femininity, and in rapid order she inherits a fortune (which will constitute her dowry), wins over Landry's reluctant father, cures Sylvinet of his morbid love of his brother, and marries Landry. Her entry into the Barbeau household will displace both the jealous brother (Sylvinet will fall in love with his new sister-in-law and then depart for a career in the French revolutionary army) and the patriarchal authority of the father. Several narratives intertwine here: stories of dysfunctional families, courtship, and social advancement intersect with tales of new knowledges and rivalry between men and women over moral and psychological authority. Through these multiple narratives Sand builds an alternative political and discursive space, subsequent to the crisis of the Second Republic in the June Days, in which women constitute the dominant force. That space will be none other than that of the "family" and novel-writing.

Written and published in 1848 in the immediate aftermath of the massacre of the June Days, which dashed socialist hopes born with the February Revolution and marked the end of substantial reforms by the Republican government, Sand's third and last rustic novel stands as her conscious repudiation of the world of both electoral and revolutionary politics, in which she had played no small part. In her second preface to *La Petite Fadette*, dated December 21, 1851, shortly after Louis Napoleon's coup d'état of December 2, Sand wrote:

> It was after the terrible days of June 1848, that, troubled and grieved [*troublé et navré*] to the bottom of my soul by the storms from without, I tried to find again in solitude, if not calm, at least faith. . . .
> For men of action, who take a personal part in politics, there is in every party, under all circumstances, a fever of hope or anguish, rage, or joy, the intoxication of triumph, or the wrath of defeat. But for the poor poet as for the idle woman [*le pauvre poète comme pour la femme oisive*], who watch events without having any direct and personal interest, be the issue of the struggle what it may, there is a deep horror of the blood spilled on either side, and a kind of despair at the sight of the hatred, wrongs, threats, and calumnies which mount toward heaven like an unclean holocaust in the train of social convulsions.[4]

Sand allots herself a multiple positionality: the grammatical agreements I have underscored direct our attention to the masculine gender of her pen name; at the same time her self-designation as a poet (also of masculine gender), as opposed to the "man of action," is compared with the marginality of the woman of leisure who, horror-stricken, watches political violence from the distance of her domestic interior. The text yields another version of the classical trope of the abandonment of public affairs for the consolations of meditative interiority and artistic creation. But here the version is a complexly gendered one. Rhetorically, in this passage Sand's political involvement neatly coincides with the masculine gender of the authorial "I" (the only *je* of the preface receives masculine predicates *troublé* and *navré*); meanwhile, disengagement and writing, by means of a comparison ("the idle woman"), feminizes the otherwise masculine positionality of the author-poet. A renunciation of traditional political involvement, the shift from one activity to another entails a displacement from the public to the private, the masculine to the feminine. But, of course, the transition is never complete, for the masculine pen name that signs the preface remains unchanged. This suggests several things. Most obviously, for Sand and other women, publishing was still successfully pursued under the guise of a male persona (however "feminized") who could negotiate barriers posed to women by the reading public and by literary circles and places of assembly.[5] More interesting, Sand's preface returns to an identity played out in *Paul et Virginie* between an oppositional subjectivity, femininity, and the private sphere in the context of political paralysis or oppression. But in the move from preface to plot, instead of arguing in favor of the claims of a "feminine" liberal subjectivity available to men and women alike, Sand's text works to convert a "feminine" positionality into a female one, into a privileged locus of power and knowledge from which women may write, speak, and act. That is to say, the novel will pass the mantle of authority from the "feminine" authorial persona of the preface to the female peasant character Fadette. Still, just how feminist this novel may be is an open question. As Naomi Schor has pointed out, one must eye with suspicion the inclusion in textbooks and curricula of Sand's pastoral novels to the exclusion of her fiction published in the early 1830s—*Indiana*, *Lelia*, and *Valentine*—which overtly challenged bourgeois conventions and institutions.[6]

Clearly, the writing and publishing of *La Petite Fadette* does not amount to a complete renunciation of public influence by Sand but is rather an attempt to map out a new space of writing and politics for women in a moment when political activity has been foreclosed by political catastrophe. And as Claire Moses has pointed out, the dictatorship of the Second Empire was soon to spell the end of women's political agitation for twenty years; what would remain would be the power of the printed word alone and even that was severely restricted by repressive laws governing the press.[7] In the pages that follow, I will briefly consider current debates over Sand's feminism in the context of the Revolution of 1848; then I will explore the ways in which Sand authorizes her own voice and a female politics in relation to a new and modified discourse of "family" and gender produced by the multiple narratives that structure *La Petite Fadette*.

George Sand and Feminism

The issue of Sand's feminism has been a vexed one for contemporary critics. In the work of feminist scholars of Sand, an inevitable note of frustration makes itself heard. They are forced to concede that an unbridgeable disjunction exists between Sand's reputation on the one hand and her writings and actions on the other. Recently, Wendy Deutellbaum and Cynthia Huff have acknowledged that "however much Sand's name has come to embody the effort towards women's liberation in the mid–nineteenth century, the limits of her feminism and her socialism are nonetheless real. . . . The more one examines Sand's position during this period, the more her feminist demands seem limited to the revision of civil rights for married women, that is, divorce."[8]

Indeed, although she worked for the provisional government of 1848 in the Ministry of Information as an anonymous political columnist for the official newspaper *La République*, she violently opposed women who proposed her and Jeanne Deroin as candidates to National Assembly seats.[9] Sand minced no words when she wrote: "As for you women who want to start out by exercising political rights, allow me to say to you again that you are indulging in childish pursuits. Your house is on fire, your domestic family [*foyer domestique*] is in peril, and you want to expose yourselves to public mockery and insults when it is a matter of defending your interior and putting back on their feet the violated household gods [*vos pénates outragés*]?"¹⁰ To accept official political office amounts to forsaking the duties of hearth and home: "Women who pretend that they would have time to be senators and raise their children haven't raised them themselves.... At a given moment, woman can inspire a social and political role, but not fulfill a function that deprives her of her natural mission: love of family."¹¹

Sand's scathing remarks directed at the revolutionary feminists of the *Voix des femmes* [The voice of women] scarcely lead us to think that *La Petite Fadette* will enact a major shift in the discourses of family, sexuality, and the social body. If anything, the opposite would seem true: Sand's anger targets those women who would use their domestic responsibilities to sanction their entry into politics as citizen-actors. As we saw in Chapter 1, during the French Revolution and afterward women who attempted to win political enfranchisement as mothers and wives saw their arguments turned against them; likewise Sand in the quote above resorts to the same strategy, and goes so far as to suggest that they are poor mothers at that (their "house is on fire"). It is worth remembering that women's domestic duties and their retirement from the sphere of politics don't constitute so much a contradiction in familial discourse as one of its fundamental organizing principles.¹² In its positions the *Voix des femmes* has transformed familial discourse into something utterly unrecognizable to Sand. The discourse that Sand adheres to is one that underwrote the forceful retirement of women from political life during and after the French Revolution and promoted the idea of women "inspiring" a "social and political role" for men. Sand locates women in the home, then specifically as *mères éducatrices* and tutors of children; that is to say, as repositories—and even authors—of moral and social knowledges and as such authorized—if they were of good family—to return to the public sphere as *dames patronnesses*. Now, Sand's own position as a woman and a writer pushed the role to the breaking point as the anonymous, behind-the-scenes columnist of the revolutionary government's official bulletin. That final rupture is what her discourse precluded altogether. Similarly, Schor notes the "utter conventionality" of Sand's model of desire and fictional plots—particularly in the later novels, which have attracted much attention from psychoanalytic criticism. Thus in her study of *La Petite Fadette* Schor explores Sand's rustic novel less as an example of disruptive, female-authored writing than as a text which raises questions about the relationship between emplotments of gender and the inscription of history in novels, how "history," as she puts it, "inhabits sexual difference."[13]

Finding a Voice: Pastoral and the Traffic with "Nature"

Paul et Virginie stands as proof of how effective the pastoral genre can be as an inscription device once it has been reworked by an adroit author. In Chapter 3 I argued that *Paul et Virginie*'s use of contemporary characters and its shameless sentimentalism broke with the aristocratic decorum of traditional pastoral romance and transmuted the genre's nostalgia for a bygone lifestyle into a forward-looking, almost revolutionary discourse. Similarly, rather than mere tokens of a past ideological and formal order, Sand's rustic novels must be seen as dynamic aesthetic and discursive interventions in an age of rapidly evolving democratic print culture whose public is expanding and whose genres, no less than the discursive formations in which they operate, are in a state of continuous transformation and differentiation. This is something that critics overlook; one has even claimed that *La Petite Fadette* is not a pastoral novel because of its use of modern characters and realistic landscapes.[14]

The pastoral novel (Sand adopts the eighteenth-century term herself—*la pastorale*—in her prefaces to *François le Champi*[15] and *La Petite Fadette*) affords an opportunity for Sand to narrativize a heavy cultural traffic with "nature"; these exchanges are framed by the traditional oppositions of city/country, politics/disengagement, action/leisure, core/periphery, center/margin, etc., among which the 1851 preface to *La Petite Fadette* explicitly foregrounds the opposition male/female. Such are the semiotic tools that *Paul et Virginie* and other pastoral novels have placed at Sand's disposal, down to the privileging of the problematics of sex and gender. "Nature" will sanction at once Sand's own novelistic practice, a domain of knowl-

Midwiving Subjectivities and Female Knowledges 223

edge as specifically "female," and an implicit socialist politics, familialist to the core, which targets households, both peasant and urban, poor and middle class.

This discursive labor involves an act of ventriloquism. This quite common rhetorical gesture—passing off one's own voice as that of another—in particular contexts can set in motion a process of ratification and authentication whose stakes are very high. Ventriloquism in one form or another probably lies at the heart of all traffic with "nature" by writers and intellectuals—be they from metropolitan centers, industrialized countries, or first world postcolonial societies—who seek to find *their* voices in or to *be spoken by* rural sages, provincial "common men," people of color of the former colonies, or even by animals belonging to the primate order. Trafficking in voices of this kind involves at once reconceptualizations of "culture" and "nature" and repeated negotiations over where the boundary falls between the two, especially with respect to other social categories such as race, class, and gender.[16] The hemp hackler [*chanvreur*], the extradiegetic narrator of *François le Champi* and *La Petite Fadette*, represents such a device. In her multiple prefaces Sand takes great care to motivate the peasant narrator's function, particularly in the dialogue-form preface to *François le Champi*, published in December 1847. In turn, Sand will claim the role of mere translator of the hemp hackler's tales for a larger cultivated public—but in such a way as to move her voice to the center.

The hemp hackler who sings and recounts tales is presented, paradoxically, as *voiceless*. He is doubtless related to the idealized "scrupulous and sage peasant" about whom Sand writes: "who works and profits from his labor, who enjoys decent living [*de la vie propre*] without need, without desire, and without a way to manifest and express his inner life" (41–42). He stands in marked contrast to the famous novelist: "I try to put myself at the heart of the mystery of rustic and natural life; I who am civilized do not know how to take pleasure through instinct alone and am always tormented by the desire to explain to others and to myself my contemplation or meditation" (42). Voiceless, the peasant man of nature lives by instinct; the civilized author lives tormented by the desire to write and speak constantly. As such, Sand occupies one side of a cultural and social divide but will also have rights over bridging the two. For one thing, she can move between the two ("I try to put myself at the heart of the mystery of rustic and natural life"); more interesting, she is something of a communications specialist whose field is interiority ("contemplation," "meditation"). The position Sand creates for herself recalls that constructed often by "culture" for "woman" who, as Sherry Ortner remarked in her classic essay drawing on anthropological sources, is both marked as "nature" and yet assigned the role as mediator *between* culture and nature.[17] And sure enough, in a series of shifts, the preface posits "sentiment" *first* between nature and culture and *then* moves it over into the realm of nature alone. The bridge is established; between what she terms peasant "primitive life" and upper-class urban "artificial life," between what Sand calls "sensation" or "instinct" on the one hand and "knowledge" on the other, stands "sentiment": "the relation between knowledge and sensation is sentiment" (43). And *feeling*, which is the mediating link between nature and culture, then becomes the voice of nature itself: "Nature is beautiful: sentiment flows from every pore" (44). Thus what connects nature and society is actually something found in nature itself which it is now the vocation of the rustic novels to express. Sand concludes, "Here is art, the relation, the sentiment in a word [*Voici l'art, le rapport, le sentiment en un mot*]" (45).

Sand's art is a modest one, a simple one of relating, *translating*, yet it is founded on an interiority or sentiment that authorizes her to enact a discursive exchange by which she will claim immense cultural authority: she first lends her voice to a peasant speaker (*noblesse oblige*) and in return she can speak in her own voice a language susceptible of unifying in a single audience two extremes of French society, the rural peasantry and the cultivated urban elites. When in the preface the author's companion and interlocutor requests her to deliver her version of the hemp hackler's tale, he puts it this way:

"But tell it to me as if you had on your right a Parisian speaking modern language and on your left a peasant to whom you would not want to pronounce a sentence or a word he could not grasp. Thus you must speak clearly for the Parisian and naïvely for the peasant. One will reproach you for lacking color, the other for lacking elegance. But I will be there, too, who am seeking in what way art *without ceasing to be art for everyone* can enter into the mystery of primitive simplicity and communicate to the mind the charm widespread in nature." (53, emphasis mine)

In this act of double ventriloquism (Sand speaks through two men, both the hemp hackler and her interlocutor) the author assumes the right to occupy a sociodiscursive middle ground reserved for a resolutely "democratic" art, not unlike the position that, in prerevolutionary France, Bernardin de Saint-Pierre appropriated for himself and *la petite société* in *Paul et Virginie*.

The ingredients of Sand's discourse should be familiar to readers of this book by now: nature, sentiment, writing, and social class—the founding elements of an imagined community based on domesticity and articulated through the verbal practices of fiction. All that is missing, of course, are intradiegetical female agents and bodies and a discourse of "family." Sand's narratives supply them accordingly.

A New Trade

So far, I have discussed how the prefaces to *François le Champi* and *La Petite Fadette* carried out a discursive exchange in which writers like Sand receive a "feminine" positionality both in their distance from the male world of politics and in their intimate traffic in sentiment, nature's voice. Now, I want to show how *La Petite Fadette*'s narrative advocates a militant position within familial discourse—almost in reply to Sue, Nettement, and Balzac—that awards women nearly exclusive knowledge and control over the psychodynamics of family life and the bodies that inhabit the household. And, fundamentally, this knowledge is one of gender and gendered desire. *La Petite Fadette* transacts a second exchange whereby female folk medicine is brought into service to discredit patriarchal authority in peasant households, empower new female knowledges, and sanction household arrangements that are ultimately domestic, urban, and middle class.

The new female agents of familial discourse and women's power are Sagette, a local midwife; Fadette, a poor child of the fields abandoned by her mother, a *vivandière* or camp follower who left her family to follow revolutionary soldiers off to war (90); Fadette's grandmother, *mère* Fadet, with whom Fadette lives and who is respected and feared by the local peasantry because of her mysterious medicinal powers (66–67); and Baigneuse de Clavière, yet another peasant wisewoman. The bodies (and the desires they enclose) targeted by familial discourse are those of the twin brothers (*bessons*) Landry and Sylvinet and that of Fadette. Indeed, the transformation and regulation of the former requires that of the latter: Fadette must assume the body and manners of a conventionally respectable woman before she can intervene to cure Sylvinet of his hysterical illness by which he threatens to die if Landry marries Fadette. In this process Sylvinet will redirect his affections away from his brother to another object—a female one to boot.

As Schor aptly remarks, this drama points to the centrality of the heterosexual contract and to Fadette's role as its guarantor.[18] Hence the title of the novel. The text burdens her with negotiating the second exchange between nature and culture, in which domesticity incorporates the authority of the healing practices of peasant women. In this, Fadette, like Sand herself in the prefaces, will play the role of mediator and will speak the voice of nature, which is none other than that of domesticity and of a highly gendered interiority. It is a very complex transaction that takes place figuratively between two extremes of peasant society, between those impoverished segments, populated by strong female figures such as Sagette, Baigneuse, *mère* Fadet, and Fadette herself, and the wealthy landed peasantry whose households are run by men like *père* Barbeau, the twins' father, and *père* Caillaud. The maneuver is an intricate one, for the novel draws on female peasant traditions in order to colonize not just urban but also peasant households with the norms of femininity and domesticity promoted by France's educated elites. Here, as in the prefaces, the textual trade with nature is very much a social one. It seems that something must be discursively received, or rather extracted, from nature (female traditions of herbal medicine) and from one social class (the poor peasantry) for the benefit of culture and another social class (landed peasants who largely stand in for the propertied, even urban, classes). Yet Fadette's marriage to Landry is also one of social mobility. This story recalls what we saw in *Les Mystères de Paris*, where social betterment is promised through the adoption of the regime of domesticity and "family life." At the same time, Fadette takes her place in a social class (landed peasants) transformed by domesticity. As we will see, in a manner similar to what we saw in *Les Paysans*, both extremes of peasant society are simultaneously validated, and constructed as wanting in terms of the new norms.

Like any true nineteenth-century proletarian, Fadette (the Cricket, *le grelet*) comes from a broken family (both her parents are absent); her life at home with her grandmother and handicapped younger brother (the Grasshopper, *le sauteriot*) is notoriously devoid of warmth and affection. Passing by their house, Sylvinet remarks to Landry:

> "There are always screams and blows to be heard in that odious house. I know the Grasshopper is as horrid and fractious as he can be; and I would not give two pennies for the Cricket. Those poor children have neither father nor mother, and have to depend on an old witch [*vieille charmeuse*] who is always in some mischief or other, and who does not give them anything."
>
> "That is not the way we were brought up," answered Landry. "We never had any beating from our father or our mother, and even when they scolded us for our childish mischief, they did it so gently and quietly that the neighbors could not hear it." (82/86–87)

It would seem that the Barbeau family has already integrated the new precepts of child education that distinguish the middle classes from all others; this is the textual marker of the Barbeau family's relative wealth and social standing and by contrast designates in turn Fadette's low social origins. By the same token, the drama of Fadette and Landry's love will draw out the shortcomings of the twins' family, dominated by male authority, mired in material self-interest and the calculations of the alliance system still in force, and woefully ignorant of the subtleties of the dynamics of desire and gender in the children's inner lives. The Barbeau family into which Fadette will ultimately marry stands as a transitional form awaiting its final transformation under a female aegis. Both families and milieus are afflicted with variants of familial lack.

Legible Bodies and Female Knowledge

Sand will prepare Fadette's "conversion" to conventional womanhood in terms of peasant traditions of female knowledge (embodied by the older women), which are related to nature and its processes, most notably the health and biological reproduction of humans and animals. In turn these customs and knowledges will empower Fadette to enter the Barbeau household and place it under the tutelage of her own peculiar authority.

The novel dramatizes female expertise in the arts of healing and obstetrics. In *La Petite Fadette* Sagette and later Fadette step forward as the guardians and gatekeepers of the *legible, gendered body* and its desires.[19] As the local midwife, not only is the venerable Sagette responsible for delivering babies like any obstetrician, she must also "read" them in terms of their sex, individuate them, and render them "legible" if need be. The case of Landry and Sylvinet presents peculiar problems, for they are identical twins of the same sex. It is all the more imperative to be able to distinguish between them because the Old Regime's alliance system still operative in the narrative allotted substantial rights to the elder brother (*le droit d'aînesse*). Accordingly, Sagette inscribes a cross on Sylvinet's body:

> *Mère* Sagette, who received them in her apron when they came into the world, did not forget to make a little cross with her needle on the arm of the first born, because, as she used to say, "one can make a mistake about a bit of ribbon or necklace, and the birthright [*le droit d'aînesse*] may be lost. When the child grows stronger," she went on, "we must mark him with a sign that will never rub off"; and this they did not fail to do. (20/10)

Without the distinguishing marks, declares the hemp hackler's narrating voice, only a mother's eye would be capable of identifying the twins (22). Here, mothers and midwives are the sole brokers of bodily difference and they are assigned the task of socializing these differences, making them culturally intelligible.

The catastrophe, which Sagette attempts to forestall but in vain, is precisely that of the fusion of the two boys' identities, brought about, and fatally so, by their parents' reluctance to have them engage in separate activities independent of each other. The first preventive measure Sagette recommends is *not* to nurse them with the same milk. Now, how are we to read this advice so contrary to the prescriptions of *Paul et Virginie*? It is necessary to remember that the *petite société* was just that, a model society based on family bonds but in which nonetheless the minimal, incestuous difference and displacement were operative: Paul and Virginie were *born* of different parents. Incestuous desire, yes, biological incest, no. Exogamy, however exiguous, is respected. However, in *La Petite Fadette* both exogamy and the heterosexual contract—the biological reproduction of the household—are threatened by the drama of individuation[20] of male twins in a discursive system where difference and distinction revolve around those of sex and gender.

Gender as Master Code

That gender is the master fiction regulating the diegesis from beginning to end in Sand's tale is made quite clear by the manner in which the twin brothers bond after their parents, *père* Barbeau in particular, do not heed Sagette's advice. The boys' fusion entails their forming a *couple*, and in forming a couple the twin brothers inevitably form *two genders*. Sylvinet, the elder of the two, is "feminized": he's the crybaby and clings to his mother's skirts; while Landry retains his "masculine" identity—he's independent, more adventurous, and enjoys physical work. *Mère* Barbeau reflects on their respective characters: "My Landry is a real boy; he cares only for life and bustle, for work and variety. But this one has the heart of a girl; he is so gentle and sweet that I cannot help loving him as the apple of my eye" (38–39/35). Here we have identical bodies but two opposed, gendered subjectivities. Far from subverting the sex/gender system as totally arbitrary (as Schor argues), *La Petite Fadette*, I want to suggest, operates on the basis of its massive inscription. Bodies are to be read through the lens of gender alone. What is awry in the Barbeau family household is not so much that Sylvinet has a "feminine" character (though it is noteworthy that the problem child is coded as feminine and even hysterical by the text) but that the brothers have bonded too strongly. These bonds are necessarily given as *heterosexual* in *aim* (a "feminine" disposition attracts a "masculine" one and vice versa) if not in *object* (male or female body); desire is heterosexual (between opposite genders if not opposite sexes) or not at all. This is a sure sign of what Judith Butler calls the "heterosexual matrix" at work in the novel.[21] Their bonds have produced two gendered subjects, and in turn these subjects will in the end have two distinct bodies. What is properly subversive about the new generation's relationship as a couple is that it shares and does everything together: the Old Regime hierarchical bonds between elder and younger brothers are abolished. However, in the absence of any visible markers of difference, a new distinction is introduced which establishes a new hierarchy—an inversion of the old one and more "democratic" perhaps—based on gender.

Eventually, with the passage of time, their different subjectivities will mark their bodies with legible, physical differences and these bodily differences will be read by the older peasants in terms of the traditional masculine hierarchies but now inverted:

> The small differences between them, which had always been apparent, became intensified, and *passed from their souls into their faces* [*de leur esprit, passèrent sur leur figure*]. When they had completed their fifteenth year, Landry grew into a fine-looking fellow, while Sylvinet was still a pretty lad, more slender and less manly than his brother. They were never mistaken for each other, and though they always looked like brothers, no one at first sight thought them twins. Landry, who was called the younger, as he was born an hour after Sylvinet, seemed to strangers the elder by a year or more. This increased the love of *père* Barbeau, who, like the true peasant he was, esteemed muscle and stature before everything. (86/91, emphasis mine)

Midwiving Subjectivities and Female Knowledges   231

In this instance, to paraphrase Foucault, the soul is truly the prison of the body. And Sylvinet's soul—his *esprit*—will be the target of Fadette's intervention; for, as we saw in Chapter 2, it is the feminine hysteric—enclosed in the body of either a woman or a man—that is named by familial discourse as the problem, the disruptive force requiring discipline. Sylvinet, the dependent, feminized man, fearing that his brother plans to marry Fadette, takes to bed and refuses to get up. In this case, gender is no longer simply a biological body (if it ever was) but a question of *desire* and its discourse.

The Regulation of Desire: From Body to Words

Sand's text does not really question the discourse of gender operative here. Nor does it subvert the notion of the domestic family. Rather, as with Sue, Nettement, and Balzac (and later Zola) it's a question of where the shifting line that divides female from male authority and knowledge is to be drawn. In *La Petite Fadette* Fadette will follow in Sagette's footsteps less as a peasant marker of bodies than as a (middle-class) "midwife" and "physician" of souls; that is, in tandem with her social ascension she effects a switch from the practice of literal inscriptions to that of figurative or discursive ones. This constitutes the middle-class power she will exercise in the Barbeau family and defines her superiority over the patriarchal but ineffectual *père* Barbeau.

Sylvinet and Landry's "narcissistic" coupling is no more deconstructive of familial discourse than it is of gender as a master code. On the contrary, *La Petite Fadette* must be read as an attempt to construct a story of the vagaries of familialized desire and of bodies whose management in this text calls for the expanded and deepened role of women. In the Barbeau household the father dominates and is consumed by material and social considerations while the mother is fearful and weak; both prove helpless when faced with the psychological problems presented by Sylvinet's excessive love of his brother Landry.

After consulting several physicians who had little to offer by way of advice, the parents turn to Baigneuse, an old peasant woman who succeeded Sagette, now dead, and the declining *mère* Fadet as the leading practitioner of folk medicine. Her response lays the foundation for Fadette's role in resolving Sylvinet's destructive attachment to Landry:

> "Well," said La Baigneuse, who had great insight into all maladies of mind and body, "the day your son Sylvinet loves a woman, he will love her still more madly than he loves his brother. I tell you this beforehand. He has an excess of love in his heart, and because he has always directed it toward his twin, *he has almost forgotten his sex*; and thus he has sinned against that law of God which decrees that a man shall cherish a woman above mother or father, sister or brother." (199/239–40, translation modified, emphasis mine)

She remains confident that the voice of nature will redirect Sylvinet's incestuous desire and displace it onto the proper object of affection: "But take comfort; *it is not possible that nature should not dictate to him in this*, however behind he may be; and take care that you do not hesitate to give him in marriage the woman he loves, whether she be poor, or ugly, or disagreeable; for it is evident that he will never love more than one in his life" (200/240, translation modified, emphasis mine). Ultimately, nature's voice will be none other than Fadette's own, *as spoken back to her by Sylvinet*. She will speak, he will reply, and their discursive exchange will bring his desire into alignment with the teleologies of a heterosexual male body, thereby dissipating his hysteria. The Barbeau household will no longer be the same. Nature in the guise of female knowledge and power will make itself heard and domesticity will finally fall under female aegis. Thereupon, the novel's second trade with "nature" will be sealed.

In a sense, Sylvinet is the ideal familial subject, incestuous to the point that only companionate marriage will fulfill his desire. Yet the necessary displacement, the exiguous difference on which exogamy depends requires careful negotiation, for the familial practices that inscribe and intensify incestuous attachments are the very same practices that also forbid these desires' unmediated realization. In Sand's text the regulation of familialized desire with the "outside," the nonfamilial, requires not a male (medical) authority, still less simply the mediation of a party from without; rather it calls for a

Midwiving Subjectivities and Female Knowledges 233

familial figure of that displaced desire who, while from "without," also has entered "within" the family sphere as a domesticated woman on the one hand and as the object of Landry's love on the other: Fadette.

Her intervention replays the transition from a method based on the physical inscription of the body to one whose instruments are words. Fadette begins with the corporeal methods of a peasant healer and midwife such as Sagette and ends with the discursive ones more properly associated with a literate middle class. To repeat, this shift stands as the very measure of Fadette's upward social mobility from a familyless, impoverished existence to a comfortable life of domesticity as Landry's wife. She first lays her hands on Sylvinet's feverish body while he lies asleep; touch establishes the first bond between the two. Whereupon, Sylvinet's body, threatened with severance from his brother's body by Landry's imminent marriage with Fadette, begins to recover from its hysterical illness. This physical contact is repeated several times: "Fadette returned, and, as in the morning, remained alone with him for more than an hour, performing no other magic than gently holding his head and hands and breathing cool air around his face which was on fire" (221/264). Unbeknownst to the sleeping Sylvinet, a bond and a debt has been contracted, leaving the "soul" enclosed in his body vulnerable to Fadette's discursive manipulation. She must reach beneath the skin to the morbid desire holding Sylvinet's body prisoner: "'No,' said Fadette; 'it is not his body that is sick; I must deal with his mind; I am going to try to influence it [*c'est à son esprit que j'ai affaire; je vas essayer d'y faire entrer le mien*], but I cannot promise you success.'" (230/275).

Fadette saves Sylvinet from his mortal languor through discursive exchanges that involve a series of confessions and acts of recognition: first, that some bond of trust does exist between him and Fadette; second, that he did indeed wish to die; and third, that his hysterical illness was nothing less than psychological blackmail of his brother and family to prevent Landry's marriage from taking place. Fadette's words to Sylvinet are direct and alternate between accusation and understanding, a "good cop/bad cop" routine that draws out Sylvinet's anger and love. The switch from harsh accusation to gentle support works the intended effect; the hysterical protest takes the more acceptable route of tearful confession, which inscribes in Sylvinet's body and mind weakness, dependency, self-knowledge, lack, and the demand for help:

> Fadette sat down at his bedside, and began to talk to him in an entirely new way; she was so kind, so sweet, and so tender that Sylvinet's relief and pleasure were the greater for having believed her incensed with him. He wept much, confessed his faults, and even requested her forgiveness and friendship so prettily and winningly that it was easy for her to see his heart was better than his head. (240/285)

In this moment, Sylvinet places himself under Fadette's power. Now Fadette and Landry's marriage may proceed as planned and she may join the Barbeau family, thanks to her exceptional psychological skills.

In this fashion *La Petite Fadette* stakes claims for the expansion of women's authority in the household in the direction of mediating between the family and the world that lies outside it, one of the key moments of which is of course the successful marriage of offspring. This widened power operates on the level of gendered *desire*. Here, the ideal mediator with the public sphere is no longer the New Man, such as *Paul et Virginie*'s Paul; *Les Mystères de Paris*'s Rodolphe, Morel, or Germain; or *Les Paysans*'s Michaud but rather wives and mothers whose psychological and discursive skills direct the offspring's desires toward the proper finality upon which the continuance of the domestic family depends. From the perspective of the master code of gender, desires and the bodies they inhabit dictate the fate of households. Only women like Fadette can guarantee the element of difference and distinction in the field of incestuous desire (nurtured so carefully by the family) so that households can continue reproducing and survive.

The Productivity of "Family" and Its Failures

Fadette's intermediate status as sister-in-law places her position somewhere between that of a biological sibling or relative and that of a spouse. As such she stands for the preordained displacement of Sylvinet's desire, the minimum difference that will fix his desire forever. The fatefulness of Sylvinet's (heterosexual) displacement stems from the fatefulness of the closed circuits of familial desire, which *La Petite Fadette* carefully posits and deploys in its diegesis. Like the family itself, women must both guarantee the circuit's integrity and break it, a task so contradictory as to render it unending or impossible altogether.[22] Fadette's "sessions" with Sylvinet both succeed and fail; he drops his hysterical protest against Landry and Fadette's marriage but, as critics have noted, he falls in love with Fadette, his future sister-in-law. His desire will be displaced no further, and thus he is condemned to be displaced in turn forever outside the family, and will lead the life of a bachelor and soldier for the rest of his days: he joins the revolutionary army and never marries.

Here in Sand's novel the dynamic of familial lack takes a new course. Paradoxically, *La Petite Fadette* recounts the production of the male bachelor—who is often the object of derision and pity in familial discourse—by the family itself. Furthermore, Sylvinet's loss—his departure and his bachelorhood—seemingly results from too much "family," not too little; from too-intense familial relations, not from their absence or lack. The discursive strategy adopted by the novel is fascinating: the success of "family" risks assuring its failure. Sylvinet's story implies that "family" is weakest when it is strongest and that its own structure can lead to its collapse or at least to its partial dismantling.

Yet what the narrative sets up is not the tale of the destruction of the domestic family household which founders upon its own internal contradictions. Rather, these contradictions are very productive ones. *La Petite Fadette* is yet one more story of the increasing "fragility" and "vulnerabilty" of the model family, on a par with *Les Mystères de Paris*. Like Sue's novel, it is a tale whose telling actually affords an opportunity to broaden the number of objects that fall within the purview of familial discourse and the field of action of its (female) agents. However, here, rather than an external threat that may suborn the domestic family from without—*la question sociale*—it is an internal force that disrupts home life. Careful watch is kept not of the "dangerous classes," but of the relations of intimacy; for the more intense the familial bonds, the more fine, subtle, and insistent the supervision of each member's inner life must be. Sylvinet's untutored love for his brother ultimately inscribes lack in two ways, not only in his future (he remains single) but also in his family's past: the absence in *père* Barbeau's patriarchal household of any agent capable of overseeing the intricate psychological dynamics of household life under the new regime of domesticity. This lack authorizes a need that Fadette and women like her are destined to fill. Fadette's partial "failure" with Sylvinet does not discredit the mandate for women's greater authority in the management of family members' desires; rather, it works to call for their endless intervention. Had someone with Fadette's competence and skill only intervened when Sylvinet was a young boy! As always in familial discourse, lack is first produced and then turned to account; it serves to create new opportunities and occasions for "family" to happen.

Even those who presumably fall outside the imagined community constituted by the discourse of family are included as honorary outlaws, as it were. I have shown previous examples of this, particularly in *Les Mystères de Paris*: villains such as Le Maître d'école and Sarah, before they are dispatched from the novel's pages, tearfully pay homage to the familial norms they so often mocked throughout their fictional careers. In *La Petite Fadette* the strategy is subtler still: "family" in the form of incest marks and shapes Sylvinet's bachelor desire from earliest childhood. The bachelor, presumably the very anti-thesis of all that is attached to domesticity and marriage, turns out to be the imagined community's most loyal member. In Sand's pastoral novel nothing escapes the inscription of familial desire. Sylvinet signals the colonization of the nonfamilial domain by the familial; he is even *propelled* into the public sphere and into a life of soldiering by the dynamics of household relations and turns in a brilliant career of service to the *patrie*. In the narrative's discursive economy utility prevails; all characters and elements find their place, if not in the "family" proper at least in the service of the imagined community as the basis of which it serves: the nation.

Profit in Trading with Nature

At this juncture it will perhaps be worthwhile to draw up a balance sheet on the exchanges with "nature" that constitute *La Petite Fadette*'s fundamental discursive strategies. As writer, poet, and implicitly as woman, Sand enlists knowledge of sentiment and inner life to authorize her role as "translator" of the tales recounted in the rustic novels. This extradiegetic trade in the novel's prefaces ratifies her right to speak for "nature," whose voice is embodied in that of the hemp hackler, the extradiegetic peasant storyteller. The ventriloquist's act ultimately allows Sand to shift from her assumed marginal position as translator to that of purveyor of a novelistic discourse that will claim to speak for all and to everyone: peasant, Parisian, and "nature." And what speaks to everybody through George Sand is a tale of family and gender.

Now, intradiegetically—within the frame of *La Petite Fadette*'s narrative—a second exchange with "nature" takes place, this time disguised as transpiring *within* the setting of peasant society. The story transacts a trade closely parallel to the first one. Fadette moves from "nature" to "culture," from one social class to another; in this transition the semantic values attached to both terms and the two sectors of peasant society associated with them undergo a discursive transformation. To whose benefit? First of all, by virtue of their empowerment of Fadette, the poor peasantry's female traditions of folk knowledge are valorized by the novel and they constitute "nature's" authorization of her social ascension in marrying Landry. Now Sand's gesture must be read here as one of solidarity with folk medicine, coded as exclusively female, and the French traditions of midwifery, which was dominated by women at a time (the nineteenth century) when male professional medicine actively sought to disenfranchise female medical practice through legislation that granted monopolistic rights to practitioners in new medical fields such as obstetrics.[23] To call Fadette a "scientist" who must give up her "phallic attributes" (according to psychoanalysis's stage theory of female development) is to read anachronistically: her knowledge of folk medicine designates her *as female* in the text.[24]

However, we must bear in mind that Sand's gesture of solidarity is also one of appropriation that discredits the source as *lacking*: Fadette's grandmother, who taught her all the intimate secrets of herbal medicine, is a harsh and brutal guardian, and her own mother was a woman of loose morals. Impoverished peasant women and the class to which they belong may be closer to nature by virtue of their medicinal knowledges but they also lack true households and families, which are found among the well-to-do, such as those of *père* Barbeau and *père* Caillaud. Fadette, then, offers these latter households unusual knowledges (medicinal, veterinary, obstetrical, and eventually psychological) that can endow them with the aura of "nature," but on several conditions: first, the exchange can be realized only if these families give up their class prejudice and their patriarchal domestic arrangements, both of which are embodied in the figure of *père* Barbeau. Second, Fadette must adopt the norms of conventional femininity and this involves a change in her manner of speech; known and feared for her acerbic tongue that always struck out at those who shunned her, Fadette must "give up," not the phallic attributes of science, but rather those of the language of class and social conflict (coded as masculine and male) in favor of the speech of feeling and interiority that will constitute her true authority over her future in-laws. In a word, the second exchange involves displacing the language of class difference and patriarchy by a *transformed* "nature" which operates through the figure of the domestic woman and her mastery of the idiom of sentiment and gender. In a sense the narrative of masculine-coded and male-dominated social and political differences is resolved and superseded by a drama of gender.[25]

The second trade with "nature," then, turns out to be a profoundly social one. The story of Fadette, Sylvinet, and Landry is to everyone's benefit: Fadette offers the redemptive touch of "nature" and female knowledge (women's and families' gain), which assures proper gender and sexual destinies (here, men's gain); she promises upward mobility (poor peasants' gain), and she embodies a renewed sense of middle-class domesticity ("society's" and middle classes's gain).

This is the wager of Sand's post-1848 politics: the universal adoption of the norm of domesticity under female aegis will diminish class barriers and their language of conflict and thereby promote upward mobility between a now "civilized" impoverished class and a "naturized" propertied class whose fundamental values have less to do with wealth than with human relations based on feeling. From this perspective only "family" can restore a semblance of imagined community in the aftermath of the June insurrection, and this is accomplished through the national community's expansion outward from the urban, literate elites to the haves and have-nots alike in the cities and, more especially, in the countryside. A very liberal middle-class domesticity is the new (and not so new) broker of *la question sociale*. Sand unabashedly inscribes a political space, that of the private sphere and writing. At the center of her project stand the marginalized figures of the "feminine" writer of the prefaces and the domestic woman of the narrative. The latter figure—Fadette—marks Sand's feminist reply both to the *Voix des femmes* and to those male writers and experts in the nineteenth century who attempted to wrest household life from women's control. Fadette rewrites the "feminine" as "female." Once again, as in *Paul et Virginie*, the margins displace the center and relegate it to the periphery; there the male and masculine world of politics and war, like Sylvinet himself, stands at a distance, opposed to family dramas while bearing the indelible marks of their outcome in the form of gendered desire. Twenty years later, Zola will impart a new articulation of the imagined community and social body in his novel *La Curée* [The kill]; there, on the eve of the Franco-Prussian War, the Republican author will deploy a narrative of sexual pathology to discredit an entire social class—the Second Empire's ruling elite—and to authorize a new male science of gender and desire.

~ CHAPTER 7

Perverse Commerce: Familial Pathology and National Decline in *La Curée*

> I must say it, since I have been misunderstood and I have not been able to complete my thought: *La Curée* [The kill] is an unhealthy plant that grew on the imperial dung heap, an incest that developed on the compost pile of millions. In this new *Phèdre* I wanted to show the dreadful collapse we come to when morals are rotten and family ties no longer exist. My Renée is the Parisian woman driven wild and to crime by luxury and a life of excess; my Maxime is the product of an exhausted society, a man-woman, inert flesh that accepts the most vile deeds; my Aristide is the speculator born of the upheavals of Paris, the brazen nouveau riche who plays the stock market using whatever is at hand—women, children, honor, bricks, conscience. I have tried, with these three social monstrosities, to give an idea of the dreadful quagmire in which France was sinking.
>
> —Zola, letter to Louis Ulbach, November 6, 1871

> The normal is then at once the extension and the exhibition of the norm. It increases the rule at the same time that it points it out. It asks for everything outside, beside and against it that still escapes it. A norm draws its meaning, function, and value from the fact of the existence, outside of itself, of what does not meet the requirement it serves. The normal is not a static or peaceful, but a dynamic and polemical concept.
>
> —Georges Canguilhem, *The Normal and the Pathological*

The Sexualization of the Social

Emile Zola's *La Curée* (The kill, as in foxhunting, but also The scramble, as in spoils), published in 1872, marks yet another moment in the novelistic production of familial discourse in France. This is true not so much because the novel embodies a different literary genre—naturalist fiction—but because Zola's text introduces a shift in the discourse of family that capitalizes on the sexualization of social categories already begun in earlier literature—both fictional and medical—and generalizes it on a massive scale in a sweeping indictment of the Second Empire. As with *Paul et Virginie, Les Mystères de Paris, La Petite Fadette,* and *Les Paysans,* a political project in the traditional sense of politics—identifiable ideologies and parties such as Bernardin de Saint-Pierre's reformist Republicanism, Sue's protosocialism, Balzac's legitimism, Sand's socialist-Republicanism, and now Zola's middle-class Republicanism—draws its main features and lineaments from a discourse of family. The imminent collapse of Napoleon III's regime is signified in *La Curée* by means of the unparalleled *systematic* transgression of those boundaries promoted by the apologists of domesticity: public and private space, class sexualities, gender differences, and family hierarchies. Indeed, the familial figures of social disorder and revolution that define the urban and rural laboring classes in *Les Mystères de Paris* and *Les Paysans* respectively are now applied by *La Curée* to the Second Empire's new social elite: riotous sexuality and, more especially, the greatest of familial sins—carnal incest. This development in familial discourse does not represent a reversal (even though the new bourgeoisie is now targeted the way the lower orders were in Sue's and Balzac's texts); rather, it must be seen as a *generalization* of the work of familial figuration of social decadence to *all* sectors and classes of society. Zola's later novels were to do just that with the author's customary thoroughness. Yet the earlier social valence of decadence and disorder is not lost, for most of Zola's examples of sexual and mental dissolution among the upper classes trace their origins either to the Old Regime aristocracy or, most often, back to the laboring classes. The latter is the very measure of Zola's condemnation of Second Empire *arrivisme*. He is very explicit about this; in the 1872 preface to *La Fortune des Rougon* in which he announces his plan of the *Rougon-Macquart*, Zola declares, concerning the family members: "Historically, they take their start in the people, they radiate throught all of contemporary society, they rise to all situations by that essentially modern impulse which the lower classes on the march through the social body receive; thus they recount the Second Empire with the help of individual dramas, from the ambush of the coup d'état to the betrayal in Sedan."[1]

Briefly, *La Curée* recounts the astonishing success of Aristide Rougon, a real estate mogul and financial speculator of obscure origins who rises to the highest echelons of Second Empire society. Upon his arrival in Paris he changes his name to Saccard and by virtue of his employment at the Hôtel de Ville, he gains access to Haussmann's reurbanization plans and discreetly buys up properties slated for purchase by the state. His career begins when his first wife Angèle (who gave him two children, Maxime and Clothilde) falls ill and is dispatched to her grave by the attentive ministrations of his sister Sidonie, a wily businesswoman; she has made preliminary arrangements for her brother's second marriage to eighteen-year-old Renée, the daughter of a venerable Parisian bourgeois family, who is made pregnant by a rape (but whose miscarriage Sidonie confidently predicts). In return for saving Renée's honor, Saccard receives a large sum of money together with Renée's dowry in the form of prize real estate. With this capital he initiates his speculative ventures. In short order the couple commence leading separate lives and little by little Renée and Maxime, destined to be engaged to the aristocratic Louise de Mareuil, become lovers. When Saccard discovers their incestuous affair he coolly seizes the opportunity to despoil Renée of her real estate and to precipitate Maxime's marriage, thus leaving Renée to die propertyless and loverless.

The focus on Renée's incestuous relationship with her stepson Maxime underscores the level of abstraction that desire *in its detailed and particularized representation* has reached in Zola's novel. Desire is featured as purely *psychological*, "expressive" of an already acquired interiority, albeit a hysterical and sick one attributed by Zola to a social elite he stigmatizes. One could claim that Zola merely revives the rhetoric of early familial discourse which before, during, and after the French Revolution discredited Old Regime sexual and alliance practices, especially those associated with the aristocracy. Readers may recall the terms in which Marie Antoinette, Madame Roland, and Olympe de Gouges were sentenced to the guillotine: the first was accused of seducing one of her sons, the second of being a *mère dénaturée*, and the third of forgetting her "sex." These figures of perverse mothers and forgetful women certainly return, ghostlike, in the figure of Renée. Yet by the time we reach Zola the main impetus of familial discourse lies in tracking down, sorting out, and labeling the manifold murmurs of a diseased social body, the very filaments and subtle wanderings of hysterical desire. Whence the interest and power of those new medical categories of sexual behavior. Since in Zola *all* behavior is assigned a sexual etiology and a gender—what Jean Borie has termed "les fatalités du corps [the destiny or avatars of the body]"[2]—these categories tend to assume a power of emplotment unheard of before. The recoding of class in terms of medically defined sexuality—of which La Péchina in *Les Paysans* is the most striking example—continues apace in *La Curée*. Finally, I want to suggest that it is precisely these minute manifestations of desire that *La Curée* trains the reader in detecting, ferreting out, and interpreting. The dispersion by the novel of Renée's and Maxime's desires across bodies, words, and material objects is a lesson in social hermeneutics and readership that *La Curée* transmits indelibly to readers. And as we shall see, the narrating voice, halfway through the text, will bludgeon dull readerly minds, in case the point escaped them, into alert attention.

Perverse Commerce

The sexualization of social categories and of subjectivity takes place in the context of the gross violation of the private familial sphere by the commercial public one. Critics have been quick to point out this disruption of family life, even citing the letter by Zola that prefaces this chapter.³ And, as if to confirm our thesis that familial discourse produces its normative concepts and categories by virtue of their transgression or absence, Borie even claims that in Zola the public/private opposition appears forcefully in the tradition of the French novel for the first time.⁴ Yet there is something curious, once again, about a tradition of interpretation that reproduces what an author openly claimed to be doing all along. Again, in a sense, there is nothing to be "interpreted" about Zola, the familial hermeneutic is there in full view, to be accepted and applied by readers and academics to books and their environment. What is missing, then, in these appreciations of Zola is the continuing awareness of the *constructed* nature of Zola's texts, that they serve less as a recording instrument of the social and political "truth" of the Second Empire than as a powerful inscription device that crafts and disseminates that "truth" through the social body by means of particular rhetorical and narrative strategies. What I am driving at is that the "scandal" of *La Curée*—the disruption of family life by Second Empire decadence—is part and parcel of familial discourse and shouldn't constitute our standpoint from which to read the text; or rather, this story is the truth-effect of a textual production whose mechanisms and workings it is our task to analyze. Moreover, it is worth recalling that the categories of the public and private were produced *simultaneously*, long before the publication of *La Curée*, as mutually authorizing concepts with which to think collective and individual relations. As I have stated before, one cannot think or mentally entertain one category without reference to the other. We must also remember that since the inception of familial discourse— since *Paul et Virginie*—the space of the "family" has always already been "invaded" and "dominated" by the public domain. In *La Curée* the weakness of family life becomes the "truth" of public corruption and, conversely, the corrupt power of commerce and politics stands as the "truth" of the debased household.

Now I have suggested that what constitutes the novelty of Zola's text is the organization of both the narrative and social economies in terms of the categories of "perverse" desire and its ugliest consequence will be the massive homophobia pervading the novel. "Perversion" is how the invasion of the family household by the public sphere is plotted; it is the symptom of the reduction of household relations to commercial and monetary ones governed by self-interest and financial speculation. Sexual pathology in the general form of hysteria affects all major characters: from Zola's "social monsters"—Aristide, the monomaniacal man of ambition; Renée, the bored, nervous woman of leisure; and Maxime, the effeminate, sensual youth—to the sickly Angèle, sexless Sidonie, and consumptive Louise. The figure of La Péchina, which *Les Paysans* introduced almost as an afterthought, is now the body that *La Curée* invests completely. Transposed to the world of Paris's financial elite, Péchina's "perversities" and hysteria are now worked out in terms of Renée's body: as in the novels examined in preceding chapters, a female body becomes the laboratory of familialism's semiotic work. Yet in *La Curée*, Renée's body—its signifying function—is not the only body at stake. Renée's femininity and her female desire are embodied in Maxime's desiring body. And to the degree that his gender and sexuality are problematic, so are Renée's. The deterritorialization of desire and identity—their drift from normative boundaries and teleologies—matches the flow of exchange value in Saccard's real-estate speculations.

In this fashion the drama of "perversion" and the conversion of familial bonds into commercial ones mutually signify each other; the drama of the Second Empire is one of the flattening of all hierarchies and differences (sexual, gender, familial, and social) into what Marx called the relations of general equivalence imposed by exchange value as embedded in the commodity form,[5] to which Zola adds the twist of sexual "pathology." This is what Charles Bernheimer has termed the naturalist narrative of the fear of *indistinction* stemming from writers' profound disgust for and loathing of the female body.[6]

However, rather than positing a primordial fear of female sexuality underwriting naturalist writers' dread of the prospect of losing gender and social distinctions, in my view it will be more helpful to show how *La Curée* stands less as the expression of some prior psychology than as the active construction and inscription of social desire through a narrative of generalized hysteria and, as it turns out, of transsexuality and latent homosexual desire. *La Curée* creates something new: the logic of familial lack is so extreme here that no one major character or agent within the narrative frame even remotely embodies normative family relations; in fact, the father—Aristide—will even make money off Renée and Maxime's incest. In a sense, *what is lacking is lack itself*, an intradiegetic perception of the transgression of the norm. But what is the "norm"? As I will make clear, it is *the family as Law*, or better still, familial desire as the Law of the Father. And where is this Law to be found? Ultimately in Zola's patriarchal science of desire, whose disciplinary agent is the narration itself. Zola's hermeneutic of desire both *is* the Law (insofar as, by virtue of being a "science," it is coded in the nineteenth century as patriarchal and male) and *produces* the Law (to the degree that it constructs and disseminates the desire of the Law).

In this sense does Zola join in the struggle between men and women writers over the aegis—male or female—under which the domestic household shall be run. After a fashion, *La Curée* can be understood as a male response to the kind of special claims that Sand advanced in *La Petite Fadette* for female authority over the inner lives of family members. *La Curée* unfolds a tale of incest, hysteria, and "perverse" desire and in so doing produces the desire for the Law, or rather (which is the same thing) the inscription of the Law of the Father at the heart of social desire. Finally, this subsumption of familial desire under the Law of the Father by Zola's novel will afford us an opportunity to witness that paradoxical moment in the nineteenth century when, according to Foucault, a regime of norms that operated through the play of positive inducements established itself in the form of the older regime of law based on negative prohibitions.[7]

Social Monsters: Science, Art, and Cultural Intelligibility

Much of the rhetoric of Zola's letter to Ulbach reappears in the preface to the first edition. There, the author literally hawks his literary wares to a public already alerted by the scandal surrounding the suspension in November 1871 of the book's serial publication by *La Cloche*, a Parisian daily. "In the natural and social history of a family during the Second Empire, *La Curée* is the note of gold and flesh. The artist in me refused to diminish [*faire de l'ombre sur*] the glamor of this life of excess that illuminated the entire reign with the suspect light of a place of ill repute."[8] Family, gold, and sex—the standard themes of bourgeois fiction—are the very obligatory subjects of nineteenth-century artistic representation and authorize Zola's own project in a recognizable way. What is new and strange, or so Zola seems to claim, is how they come together in the form of sociosexual pathology:

> I wanted to show the premature exhaustion of a race which has lived too quickly and ends in the man-woman of rotten societies, the furious speculation of a epoch embodied in an unscrupulous temperament, the nervous breakdown of a woman whose circle of luxury and shame increases tenfold native appetites. And with these three social monstrosities I tried to write a work of art and science which was at the same time one of the strangest pages of our morals. (311)

The thematics of social teratology give the full measure of Zola's attack on the Second Empire and his attempt to mark it off as a space and a time outside of the imagined community of middle-class Republican France he and other writers were busily preparing on the eve of the Franco-Prussian War. Foucault reminds us that in the nineteenth century a politics of self and other encapsulates a change in regimes and turns on normative sexual-familial practices that are present tacitly and negatively through forms of "deviance":

> The legitimate couple, with its regular sexuality, had a right to more discretion. It tended to function as a norm, one that was stricter, perhaps, but quieter. On the other hand, what came under scrutiny was the sexuality of children, madmen and women, and criminals; the sensuality of those who did not like the opposite sex; reveries, obsessions, petty manias, or great transports of rage. It was time for all these figures, scarcely noticed in the past, to step forward and speak, to make the difficult confession of what they were.[9]

This game of the norm played out upon the social body also determines what counts as interesting and readable narratives and in turn these stories of deviancy construct what passes for "normal."

Zola's evocation of "perverse" social monsters is doubly advantageous for him, for it at once expels a whole political class and the new bourgeoisie of the Second Empire from the body politic, and it authorizes Zola's own project as art and *as science*. Monsters are not simply threatening; they are also enigmatic and even at times unrecognizable, they require decipherment and investigation. As purveyor of social monsters, Zola establishes his credentials as the guardian of their cultural intelligibility through his writing, an intelligibility that is primarily one of gender and sex.[10] This play of authorization that ratifies an author's voice should be familiar to readers of the book by now: in the preceding chapter I analyzed George Sand's appeal to "nature" to sanction her narratives; for "nature" Zola has substituted his social freaks. Thus, if monsters necessitate art and science to render them comprehensible to a large, uninformed public, then perhaps the reverse will also be true for Zola's novels: his narrative authority (as art and science) hangs on the presence of strange psyches and bodies. In fact, it would be fair to say that they *mutually produce one another*. The risk—but perhaps a very productive one at that—is that Zola may end up making himself *and* his scientific novels, replete with social-sexual monstrosities, scandalously unintelligible to the reading public. In the conclusion to his preface Zola admits that *La Curée*'s sexualization and medicalization of social and political history contributed in part to the suspension of its publication in serial form in the fall of 1871: "If I believe it is necessary to explain *La Curée*, a true depiction of the collapse of a society, it is because the literary and scientific aspect of it seemed to be so little understood in the newspaper where I tried to publish the novel that it was necessary to suspend publication halfway through the venture" (311). Zola's social science courts misunderstanding but also occasions new prefaces, letters, publicity—in short, more writing.

What Zola is offering, then, is not simply sex and finance scandals but also—which was "misunderstood"—new literary and scientific knowledge of the social. Reading *La Curée* promises to transmit those new secrets *and* their knowledge, but clearly untutored readers must be forewarned. This is a precaution that Zola rhetorically turns to his advantage: advance notice not only protects Zola from any further attacks with the shield of science and literary obligations to truth but also has the effect of placing readers under the firm paternal tutelage of the author and his scientific narrative. Thus my tactic of approaching *La Curée* as the patient (and not so patient) training of readers in a new social hermeneutics of desire and in new forms of narrative authority. We have come a long way from *Paul et Virginie* where the Old Man's authority was mediated by domesticity itself; here, it is the novel's very narrative structure that embodies authority, but it is based less on "family" than on the omniscient science of its pathologies.

Writing and Reading the Social Body

In *La Curée* readerly knowledge of the social lies in scanning the various bodies that circulate in the novel's pages. Thus readers decode or interpret what is already there in the narrative. However, if we keep in mind the notion of the simultaneous production of the Second Empire as monstrous and Zola as scientist, then perhaps it is more accurate to say that the act of readerly "discovery" in fact involves the textual encoding and emplotment of the social body on the one hand and readers as its decoders or hermeneuticists on the other.[11] *La Curée* entails a production that is threefold: perverse bodies, Zola as pathologist, and readers as detectives of deviant desire.

Now, there are more monsters in Zola's text than he initially lets on in his preface. In the line-up must also be included Sidonie and Louise. They are part and parcel of the construction of a system of deviance in which everyone is assigned a gender and a sexuality by the narrative. The attempt to identify characters in terms of a sexualized interiority involves readerly activity, elicited or directed by the novel itself, that matches the feverish preoccupations of legal medicine at that time. According to Foucault, "The years from around 1860 to 1870 were precisely one of those periods when investigations of sexual identity were carried out with the most intensity, in an attempt not only to establish the true sex of hermaphrodites but also to identify, classify, and characterize the different types of perversions. In short these investigations dealt with the problems of sexual anomalies in the individual and the race."[12] One must have a sex, or more precisely a sex, a gender, and a sexuality—even if "perverted" or "sexless"—in order to accede to individual and narrative existence.

Transgression and the Norm

Sidonie, Saccard's sister, and Louise, Maxime's fiancée-to-be, offer ample opportunity for observing how *La Curée*'s freak show targets, marks, and otherwise regulates bodies through a semiotic description—in short, how Zola's sex/gender system operates. Both Sidonie and Louise usurp male roles, an action that transsexualizes them, the most dramatic sign of social decadence and familial catastrophe. Their textual presentation has the effect of deeply polarizing gender identities in terms of rigid oppositions.

The depiction of Saccard's sister, who engineered the death of Angèle and Saccard's subsequent marriage to Renée, is enlightening. As a businesswoman of sorts, she violates the sexual boundaries between public and private domains. She too, like her brother Saccard, is an agent of the wild dealings of the Second Empire, but not with impunity. Let's follow Sidonie's textual portrait, one brush stroke at a time. The first mention of Sidonie alludes to some sort of infraction of the cultural narrative of womanhood; she leads a life outside the confines of marriage and life at home: "Aristide had a sister in Paris. Sidonie Rougon had married at Plassans an attorney's clerk, and together they had set up business in the Rue Saint-Honoré as dealers in fruit from the South of France. When her brother came across her, the husband had vanished, and the business had long ago disappeared." Moreover, "she never spoke of her husband, nor of her childhood, her family, her personal concerns" (356/58). As it turns out, her present business is ostensibly selling junk but actually is one of arranging shady deals and overseeing a *maison de passe* for male and female clients in the apartment below. Once her various occupations are established, the narrating voice delivers a harsh, unremitting physical portrait of her: "Madame Sidonie was thirty-five; but she dressed herself with so little care, and had so little of the woman in her manner, that one would have thought her much older. As a matter of fact she had no age. She wore an everlasting black dress, frayed at the edges, rumpled and discolored by use, recalling an attorney's gown worn out by wear and tear of the bar" (354–55/56, translation modified). An entrepreneur in her own right, Sidonie dons the black color of men's public clothing; she literally "forgets her sex" and almost passes as a man in the street:

> The woman in her withered away [*La femme se mourait en elle*]; she became a mere man of business [*un agent d'affaires*], a commission agent hitting the Parisian pavement at all hours, carrying in her fabulous basket the most equivocal articles, selling everything, dreaming of billions, and appearing in court, on behalf of a favorite client, over a contested matter of ten francs. Short, lean, and sallow, clad in the thin black dress that looked as though it had been cut out of a lawyer's gown, she had shrivelled out of recognition, and to see her creeping along the houses, one would have taken her for an errand-boy dressed up as a girl [*un saut-ruisseau déguisé en fille*]. (356/58, translation modified)

However, a man she is not but rather a boy, a gofer [*saut-ruisseau*], and disguised as a girl at that.

Sidonie forgets her sex, but of course it is the text that forgets it for her, in a curious reversal whereby she becomes a male imitating a female—or better still, an imitation of an imitation, a "woman" at a double ontological remove from her "natural," sexed body. It's worthwhile examining more closely the textual operations in the order in which they are deployed in these rather amazing passages. The novel progresses from Sidonie's various occupations, to her clothing, then to her body and her sex and back again in an interlocking logic of mutual association. Instead of following the cultural rules of derivation of what Gayle Rubin has termed the "sex/gender system," whereby one's desires, sexuality, demeanor, and activities proceed from one's biological, sexed body,[13] Sidonie's transgression of normative female behavior has upset and reversed cultural expectations: her biological sex *is* determined by her occupations and activities in public.

Far from following the dictates of her sexed body, Sidonie, in pursuing her multiple careers, has shorn herself of all outward signs of femininity, and the text carefully enforces her nonfeminine appearance through its own interpretations. Nowhere, for example, is her black dress associated with, say, widowhood but is always carefully compared to a lawyer's garb; in fact, it's as if her tattered clothing had shrunk and shriveled her body to the point of rendering it culturally unintelligible in terms of "femaleness": the somatic signifiers—the hips, breasts, and hair usually served up to nineteenth-century readers—are simply not there. In a sense, Sidonie's transvestism has literally transsexualized her, or seemingly so: a boy disguised as a girl.

The twofold, simultaneous textual construction (encoding) and interpretation (decoding) of Sidonie's transgressive behavior both problematizes gender (one can *easily* cross over) and fixes the sex/gender system into a polarized dyad of male/female (distinct but narrowly defined psychologies, activities, and roles). Her semiotic description does suggest that gender and sexual identities are a complex affair but avails itself of the most reductive dualism to suggest that complexity: a boy disguised as a girl. This is the fundamental tension in the text: the need and desire to designate a transgressive "outside" to the sex/gender system of familial discourse (in order to inscribe the norm), but an "outside" that nonetheless does not stand altogether "beyond" the horizon of normalizing discourse. The way in which the novel concludes its case against Saccard's sister is revealing: "This extraordinary hermaphrodism of the woman grown sexless [*être neutre*], man of business and procuress in one" (356/59). The symmetrical syntax of this sentence repeats and mimics the polarized gender opposition into which Sidonie is inserted by virtue of her unconventional activities and demeanor. The figure of androgyny is a conservative trope, a controlling rhetorical device that returns Sidonie to a simple male/female, masculine/feminine opposition in which the truth of sex and gender remains unproblematically and symmetrically male or female. That is to say, it remains comfortably ensconced in the borders of the "heterosexual matrix."[14]

Now, it is very interesting that, in terms of her appearance, the text compares Sidonie to a boy rather than to a man. Clearly, the text refuses her the status and prestige of an adult male, if only to maintain a sense of fundamental gender hierarchies. She may act as a man but she is only a boy. At the same time, Sidonie's change of sex entails a relative desexualization of her body. The "forgetting" of her "sex," the loss of her femininity, translates into the forgetting of her body to such a degree that, although she may be a mediator in the sexual commerce of bodies, her own is never bought and sold: "There was only one thing that she never sold and that was her person; not that she had any scruples, but because the idea of such a bargain [*marché*] could not possibly occur to her" (356/58). It is as if she is literally unaware of her body and indifferent to the heterosexual matrix's policing gaze. The fact that she does not prostitute herself may be a smart business practice but it is also a tease thrown at readers. *They* cannot forget her oversight, and the question arises, does she indeed have a body? does her body desire? does she escape the imperatives of compulsory heterosexuality?[15] The novel cleverly leaves readers to their own interpretive devices to ferret out and discover on their own in a maze of allusion and association Sidonie's latent (and that's the tease) lesbianism. Alert readers can piece the evidence, culled from later pages, together: she loves women by virtue of the pleasure they afford men, doubtless because both men and women are clients of her *maison de passe* (357–58); she has affection for priests in much the same way she admires women, for both groups wear skirts (359); finally, we later learn that in arranging her brother's second marriage with Renée she half-hoped to "marry" Renée at the same time, if only in hopes of recruiting her as a future customer. Ultimately, it's on the level of desire that the question of one's identity is resolved: Sidonie transacts business and desires women "like a man."

Her neglect and indifference, then, ultimately authorize the novel's own policing of her actions and of her body, sex, and gender: she should and does have a sex but since it does not derive from her body, her body as such does not exist otherwise than in the form of a pathetic absence of feminine charms, at best a boy's imitation of a girl. Having been denied her own "femininity," Sidonie is ready to play the part in Saccard's marriage that will transform the household into a public space of speculation and carnal incest. She will commit the ultimate transgression of nineteenth-century womanhood: the murder of a mother (Saccard's first wife) and the abortion of Renée's fetus.

The Hunchbacked Aristocrat

Another female figure of sociosexual pathology will complete my analysis of the polemics of sex/gender in *La Curée*. Hardly a modern businessman, Louise de Mareuil, destined for marriage to Maxime, stands as a throwback to an early moment in familial discourse, then peopled with scandalous aristocratic women, but here notions of biological degeneracy have updated the representation: "That poor Louise, as she was called, a child of seventeen, puny, a little humpbacked, wearing with a sickly grace a white foulard dress with red spots" (326/18). Loving to crack coarse jokes with men (332) and very forward with Maxime, Louise, by virtue of her aggressive behavior, takes after her mother, who led until her death a life of riotous scandal and debauchery for which the daughter has paid dearly:

> Her mother during her lifetime had also been a tall, strong woman; but stories were told about her which explained the child's stuntedness, her manners like a bohemian millionaire's, her vicious and charming ugliness. . . . Borne in these diseased flanks, Louise had issued from them with impoverished blood, deformed limbs, her brain threatened, and her memory already filled with filthy life. (407–8/128, translation modified)

Never did Louise come to know the peace and discipline of orderly domesticity: "She occasionally fancied she had a confused recollection of a former existence; she saw unfolded before her, in a vague outline, bizarre scenes, men and women kissing, a whole fleshly drama in which her childish curiosity found amusement. It was her mother that spoke within her" (408/128, translation modified). She "lacks" those loving childhood memories that are the preconditions of a familial sensibility to which moralists and educators could then appeal. Readers will recall that even Sue's archvillain Le Maître d'école (the Schoolmaster) remained vulnerable to the tug of family and domesticity. Not so Louise. Her childhood was irreparably compromised by her libertine mother who passed on to her daughter a "sick" interiority. Her body is inscribed with her mother's speech, that of a "mad nymphomaniac" whom retrospectively the Baron de Mareuil realized he should have had locked up in an insane asylum long before her death. The excesses of the mother's unregulated desire are legible in the deformities, consumption, and hysteria that contort Louise's body: "Deformed, ugly, and adorable, she was doomed to die young; consumption [*une maladie de la poitrine*] was stealthily undermining her, giving her a nervous gaiety and a tender grace. Sick little girls quickly grow old, and become women before their time. She was naïvely sensual, she seemed to have been born when she was fifteen, in full puberty" (407/127). Her oversexed, adolescent body classes her in the same category as Sidonie Rougon: a boy disguised as a girl: "And in fact, in her frock of white foulard with red spots, with her high-cut bodice, her flat breast, and her ugly, cunning little street boy's head, she resembled a boy dressed up as a girl [*un garçon déguisé en fille*]"(341/38–39, translation modified).

In *La Curée* the codes of gender and sex are the ultimate signifiers of political and financial corruption. It is not by chance that the marriage which seals Renée's fate and virtually closes the novel is between the most ambiguously gendered characters, Louise and Maxime, the "degenerate" offspring, respectively, of the landed nobility and the new elite of high finance that bears the curse of its impure, low origins.

Renée, Maxime, and the Policing of Desire

Saccard's new household marks the beginning of his rise in fortune. Bearing the appropriate signs of a perverse "family," it is faithful to Balzac's melodramatic dictum that behind every great family fortune lies a perfectly executed crime, while perhaps adding the spice of sexual "perversion."[16] Saccard's new marriage is rendered possible by the murder of one woman and the rape of another. This founding violence serves as the indictment of a male homosocial economy out of control that threatens the domestic family either with the imposition of male prerogatives of the oldest kind (rape) or the dictates of the new world of financial speculation (murder and arranged marriage for real estate and cash).[17] This does not mean that Zola's text dispenses with homosocial relations altogether. Quite the contrary. The textual examples we have seen of homophobia should assure us on that score. Rather, the novel's tale of the dissolution of family life points to the need to control and territorialize male homosociality (and the public sphere) through the mediation of domesticity, and conversely to regulate the household by means of a new (male) domestic science of desire.

In his definition of "monomania" published in Pankoucke's *Dictionnaire des sciences médicales* (1819) Pinel's most illustrious student Esquirol associated the mental disorder more with "male" temperaments than with those of women. He wrote:

> The causes that predispose one to monomania and produce it are the same as those of madness [*la folie*] in general. However, passionate and nervo-sanguine temperaments [*les tempéraments sanguins et nervoso-sanguins*], strong and robust individuals endowed with a fiery, vivid, and wild imagination; well-tempered, meditative minds, which seem susceptible to only one string of exclusive ideas and affections and which give themselves over to meditation and prolonged research on special objects, particularly on metaphysical or ascetic ones; and individuals dominated by pride [*amour-propre*], vanity, arrogance, and ambition, who indulge themselves in excessive ideas and hopes and extravagant pretensions, are predisposed more than others to monomania. But it is worth noting that almost always individuals who have fallen into monomania were struck by some reversal of fortune, stripped of their hopes before being ill. Thus a man presently happy, powerful, and rich who becomes insane [*aliéné*] will not be monomaniacal at all; *whereas an ambitious, arrogant man, or one in love who falls on hard times or has lost the object of his love will be excited* [*exalté*] *by monomania.*[18]

Frustrated ambition, like unrequited love, can drive men crazy.

Here is Zola's portrait of Aristide upon his arrival in Paris shortly after Louis Napoleon's coup d'état. It opens chapter 2:

Aristide Rougon swooped down upon Paris on the morrow of December 2, like a carrion bird that scents the field of battle from afar. . . . . He himself, still young, had compromised himself like a fool, without fame or profit, and could consider himself fortunate to have emerged safe and sound from the scrimmage. He came running, furious at having taken a false step, cursing the provinces, talking of Paris with the ravenous hunger of a wolf, swearing "that he would never be such a fool again"; and the bitter smile which accompanied these words seemed to take a terrible significance on his lips. (346/44, translation modified)

Saccard easily qualifies as a candidate for clinical monomania but Zola characteristically complicates things by *sexualizing* his social monster's illness: Saccard embodies an erotics of social ambition. Libidinally, love and ambition have become interchangeable but asymmetrically so; the master trope will be sexual desire.

Aristide's obsessive drive toward wealth is consistently and repeatedly sexualized early on. His first excited walks through the quarters of Paris are characterized as "a true taking of possession" [*une vraie prise de possession*] (346/44, translation modified). Later, over Sunday dinner at Montmartre, his avid glance glides away from Angèle, his first wife, to Paris below: "At dessert he called for a bottle of Burgundy. He smiled into space, he was unusually gallant. And his looks always redescended amorously to that living, seething ocean, from which issued the deep voice of the crowd" (369/76). Saccard's desire breaks away from the confines of family life to deploy itself over the prostrate body of the French capital, penetrating and cutting it to pieces:

> Night was falling. His dry, nervous hand kept cutting through space. Angèle shivered slightly before this living knife, those iron fingers mercilessly slicing up the boundless mass of dusky roofs. . . . The smallness of his hand, hovering pitilessly over a gigantic prey, ended by becoming disquieting; and as, without effort, it tore asunder the entrails of the enormous city, it seemed to assume a strange reflex of steel in the blue of the twilight. (370/78–79)

Rape and murder, which will found Saccard's second family, are also the fate that awaits pre-Haussmann Paris. Aristide is slated to be the Jack the Ripper of the Parisian cityscape, Le Chourineur writ large in the lettering of the new financial bourgeoisie.

It is under Saccard's dubious paternal aegis that Renée and Maxime, Saccard's son, play out the novel's politics of gender and the desiring social body. Like Saccard, they represent the irruption of outside forces: Renée has been literally branded a "public" woman by having been raped and thereby losing her honor, and they have both been raised and educated outside the home in those institutions notorious for their "unhealthy" influence in the eighteenth and nineteenth centuries: the convent and the boarding school. These hotbeds of unregulated space and bodies were seen as promoting same-sex sociability and precocious sexuality inimical to family life and compulsory reproductive heterosexuality. These lawless, unrestrained sociosexual relations are what is meant by Zola's recurrent phrase *camaraderie* ("boon companionship") (322, 447, 455, 534), a phrase that the nameless narrator will eventually apply to the Saccard household itself. Finally, the two characters have evolved in a world of dead mothers and absent fathers. Questionable *camaraderie* and lack of family will flourish together in the new household as Saccard's success grows:

> The street invaded the apartment [*La rue monta dans l'appartement*] with its rumbling of carriages, its jostling of strangers, its license of language. The father, the stepmother, and the stepson acted, talked, and made themselves at home as though each of them had found himself leading a bachelor life alone [*vivant en garçon*]. *Three boon companions* [*trois camarades*], three students sharing the same furnished rooms, could not have made use of that room with less reserve for the installation of their vices, their loves, their noisy, adolescent gaiety. They accepted one another with a hand-shake, never seeming to suspect the reasons that united them under one roof, treating each other cavalierly, joyously, and thus assuming each the most entire independence. *The family idea was replaced by a sort of partnership* [*L'idée de famille était remplacée chez eux par celle d'une sorte de commandite*] whose profits are divided in equal shares; each one drew his part of pleasure to himself, and it was tacitly agreed that each should dispose of that part as best seemed to him. They went so far as to take their enjoyment in each other's presence, displaying it, describing it, without awakening any feeling but a little envy and curiosity. (400–401/119–20, emphasis mine, translation modified)

No one in the household, no one person, embodies any principle—

either paternal or maternal—of familial order. The lack of tutelage and discipline is a radical one and will be met only by an extradiegetical agency, the narrating voice.

Territories of Gender and Desire

Transgression of gender and sex reach their greatest pitch in Renée and Maxime's incestuous love affair. In the novel's opening chapters readers are led by the narrating voice through an apprenticeship of decoding "perverse" bodies and desires. Readerly investigations begin on the very first page. Appropriately enough, the question of sex, gender, and desire is articulated literally "outside" in the course of a conversation between a bored Renée and her mocking stepson Maxime as they return home on an autumn afternoon after a carriage promenade in the Bois de Boulogne amid the whirl of elegant carriages, liveries, and notables of Parisian society. Brian Nelson has summed up cogently the Goldmannian/Lukácsian commentary on Zola's brilliant impressionistic tableau:

> One aspect of Zola's stylistic impressionism is the fact that his descriptions are shaped and limited by the subjective point of view of the observer. Rather than being introduced into the novel by a systematic Balzacian exposition or an omniscient global description of milieu, the reader is given the fragmentation and immediacy of an outsider's view. . . . We are offered the haphazard visual and sensuous impressions of the character as they develop, without the interpretation usually supplied by an omniscient author; *or rather, the impression itself precedes identification and explanation.* Effects of immediacy mean that the character and the reader are into direct confrontation with things rather than being distanced from them. And because of the weight Zola places on description, the natural order of things is reversed: objects and things become the real protagonists of his novels and the human element is only incidentally mentioned.[19]

In *La Curée*'s profusion of artificial objects and fragmented sensation, I would argue that subjectivity is not so much overwhelmed as *foregrounded* in its isolation and dispersion across manifold objects and bodies which elicit and articulate subjects' desire. In this fashion the novel's hypersubjectivism can be seen as a discursive tactic that posits the need for some sort of interpretive frame; that is to say, it calls up the intervention of Zola's objective science of subjectivity. What unifies and interprets the novel's atomized universe is a science that designates and inscribes subjects in terms of their "sex," a new practice of knowledge under the tutelage of Zola and his narration. This knowledge joins together a double perception of perversity on the one hand and "artificial" relations mediated by man-made landscapes and decorated female bodies on the other. Indeed, the two mutually imply each other, as critics have noted: the landscape that flows past Renée's and Maxime's indifferent gaze is a theatrical staging of nature, from the artificial lake to the manicured gardens; meanwhile, during this excursion, readers learn that Laure d'Aurigny, Saccard's former mistress, has dyed her hair yet another color, doubtless to please a new lover; and that Saccard has bought back from Laure jewels he had given her and now plans to adorn Renée's body with them.[20] (Still later we learn that Saccard himself, in order to further his ambition, dropped his paternal surname Rougon for his present one.) Yet there is no need for critics to make this textual logic their own. A powerful critique of Second Empire corruption in terms of "false" desire, circulating objects, and alienated, interchangeable individuals actually turns out to be predicated on—or better still, to *produce* as its unexamined assumption—a homology between "normal" gender, sex, and sexuality on the one hand and the authentic body and "nature" on the other. Once again, the Second Empire is inscribed as profoundly "deviant": a disruption of the transmission of the patronymic from one generation to another (as in Rougon/Saccard's case) goes hand in hand with the violation of the natural features and "destiny" of the female body.

A careful consideration of the textual work by which characters' subjective sensations enlist readers as detectives of perverse desire is in order. Constructing a logic of association, the text in the first pages moves from Renée's semiconsciousness to a picture of the artificial lake back to Renée, whom a jolt wakens in time for her to catch sight of two friends whose friendship hints of a lesbian liaison:

> Renée had thrown back her head and with half-closed eyes glancing listlessly at the two sides of the avenue, seeing nothing. . . . On the left,

> at the foot of the narrow grass-plots that run down intersected by flower-beds and shrubs, the lake slept, clear as crystal. . . . This scrap of nature, that seemed like a newly-painted piece of scenery, lay bathed in a faint shadow, in a pale blue vapor which succeeded in lending the background an exquisite charm, an air of adorable artificiality. . . . But there came a jolt in the even trot of the line of carriages. And, raising her head, she nodded to two ladies lolling languidly, amorously, side by side [*couchées côte à côte, avec une langueur amoureuse*]. . . . Renée, a schoolfellow of the two inseparables, as people nicknamed them with a knowing air, called them by their first names, Adeline and Suzanne. (316/4–5)

Readers' hermeneutic work begins in earnest a half-page later when the conversation broaches the question of the "secret" of Renée's profound boredom. Explaining her indifference toward Saccard's sexual escapades, she declares simply, "You see, I am bored" (317/5). The entire textual operation turns on Renée's *desire*, a desire that is named by a masculine voice as hysterical in origin: "'You know, you're not very amusing,' said Maxime, calmly. 'It's your nerves, undoubtedly.'" Renée even acquiesces to Maxime's interpretation: "'Yes, it's my nerves,' she replied dryly" (317/6, translation modified). The exchange that follows has a familiar ring to it: "'What is it that you want? What on earth do you dream of?' [inquires Maxime.] She shrugged her shoulders to imply that she did not know" (318/7). Maxime's question anticipates by 50 years Freud's famous question, "What does woman want?"[21] Finally, she lets drop "I want something different" (318/8), and then gives her answer a Baudelairian twist: "As I said, one ought to have something different; you understand, I can't guess what; but something else that would happen to nobody but one's self, that would not be met with every day, that would give a rare unknown enjoyment" [*une jouissance rare, inconnue*] (320/10). In the end she is incapable of articulating her own desire:

> Then, with a ray of hope, there came to her, with shivers of longing, the idea of that "something different" which her mind could not strain itself to fix upon. There, her dream wandered. Constantly the word that she strove to find escaped into the falling night, became lost in the continuous rolling of the carriages. The soft vibration of the carriage was an

impediment the more that prevented her from formulating her desire. (321/11)

Hysterical desire is presented here as precisely that which cannot make up its own mind, name itself, and consciously designate its object of investment. Renée's desire is unknown, unnameable, without place or law, but a name, a place, and a law will be produced by the novel: carnal incest understood as transgressing and therefore desiring the Law of the Father. Neither Renée nor Maxime can name her desire but the narrative machine will do that for them. This will involve readers in rather pleasurable detective work. For the alert reader and critic, the trajectory of her wayward desire will land on her interlocutor Maxime. Freud would have been pleased:

> And an immense temptation rose from the empty space, from the copses asleep in the shadow on either side of the avenue, from the noise of the wheels and from the gentle oscillation that filled her with a delicious torpor. A thousand tremulous emotions passed over her flesh; dreams unrealized, nameless delights, confused longings, all the monstrous voluptuousness that a drive home from the Bois under a paling sky can infuse into a woman's worn heart. . . . She put out her foot, as she stretched herself in her feeling of well-being, and with her ankle lightly touched Maxime's warm leg; he took no notice of this contact. A jolt aroused her from her lethargy. She raised her head and with her grey eyes looked strangely at the young man, who sat lounging in an attitude of sheer elegance. (321–22/11-12)

This passage can be read two ways. The first reading would confirm the dynamics of Freudian transference whereby the object of desire is both displaced and named by a cathexis on the analyst/interlocutor. What the "original" object and aim of desire might have been is perhaps less important than the fact that the mode of displacement and transference inscribes desire under what Lacanian psychoanalysis calls the Phallus as signifier and the Law of the Father. This is what Freud ardently wished to demonstrate in the narrative of the "failed" analysis of Dora who refused to play Freud's discursive game.[22] In this first reading, Renée's first jolt (which draws her attention to the two women) designates the departure of her desire from heterosexual, familialized desire, and the second returns it to the fold, albeit in the deviant form of incest (she fixes her gaze upon Maxime). A second reading, which I think is far more fruitful, is to study the passage as precisely a moment in the scientific and literary genesis of this type of discursive practice, which attempts to encode women's desires—if only negatively as "hysterical"—within the heterosexual matrix by means of a narrative of displaced desire. Presumably, Maxime embodies her desire, or the possible *knowledge* of her desire that she "lacks." In a sense, the text presents Maxime as having what she does not possess. Yet this is to anticipate too much, for the textual production of the Law as the truth of Renée's desire actually involves a lengthy and extraordinary narrative play on the very nature of the displacement of Renée's desire. Is this a relation of radical difference—as we suggested above—between the two lesbians and Maxime or perhaps, more scandalously, one of equivalence? Zola's answer will be that it is both. Maxime is both a woman and a man. The story of Renée and Maxime's affair entails two contrary but complementary movements: first the deterritorialization of Renée's incestuous desire as homosexual and without law and then its final reinscription under heterosexuality and the Law of the Father.

Renée's Desire, Maxime's Body

As interlocutor, object of transference, and putative sign of the Law, Maxime is poorly equipped to restore Renée's desire to the comforting bounds of even simple familial pathology. Denouncing the scandalous conditions of sexual license that prevail in women's boarding schools, Zola, in a newspaper article, repeats the commonplace that women's sexual tutelage must be left to their husbands by virtue of absolute differences in gender. Sexual knowledge is the strict preserve of men:

> Our morals make of a man a combatant who must know everything; it is up to him to make his own virtue, dignity, and an upright and happy life; he is the protector, the experienced creature; he can make his way through every sin [*toutes les souillures*] and be only the stronger for it. But the young girl is not at all raised for the struggles of life. She must

be placed ignorant into the hands of her husband, receive from him all she knows [*toute éducation*], and not to leave behind her any memories of the flesh and the heart.²³

Clearly, Renée does not fit the bill; not only has she been in a convent but she came to marry Saccard only because she had been raped and made pregnant. Moreover, from this perspective, what further destabilizes her desire is that Saccard scarcely qualifies as a husband, for he is absorbed by his financial dealings and his mistresses. Analogously, Maxime as the object of her incestuous desire hardly qualifies as a "man." The heterosexual male tutelage of Renée's desire, lacking in the father, is woefully absent in the son, although for different reasons.

No doubt about it, Maxime is the *homme-femme* announced by Zola in the preface. Degenerate biology and the boarding school have conspired to undo his virility. He, like Louise, was a sexually precocious child:

> Maxime was already terribly knowing for his thirteen years. His was one of those frail, precocious natures in which the senses assert themselves early. He had vices before he knew the meaning of desire. . . . He took great pains over his hands, which were long and slender . . . he owned a little looking-glass which he drew from his pocket during school-time and placed between the leaves of his book, looking at himself in it for hours. . . . His school-fellows hung round his blouse as round a petticoat, and he buckled his belt so tightly that he had the slim waist and undulating hips of a grown woman. . . . Fortunately, age was about to improve him. But the sign of his boyish debauchery [*ses abandons d'enfant*], this effeminization of his whole being, that time he thought himself a girl, was destined to remain in him, and to strike a lasting blow at his virility. (384–85/99–100, translation modified)

He was a *fin de race*, unworthy of the gender of either parent:

> Maxime meantime had grown. He was now a pretty, slender young man, who had retained the rosy cheeks and blue eyes of childhood. His curly hair had completed that "girl look" that so enchanted the ladies. He resembled poor Angèle with her soft expression and blond paleness. But he was not even the equal of that indolent, hopeless woman. The race of the Rougons became refined in him, grew delicate and vicious. Born

of too young a mother, constituting a strange, jumbled, and, so to speak, scattered mixture of his father's furious appetites and his mother's self-abandonment and lethargy, he was a defective offspring in whom the parental shortcomings were fulfilled and aggravated. (400/118, translation modified)

Worst of all, he has betrayed his manhood by renouncing his destiny as a productive male and has contented himself with the spendthrift consumer habits of women of leisure: "This family lived too fast; it was dying out already in the person of this frail creature, whose sex must have remained in suspense [*chez laquelle le sexe avait dû hésiter*]; he represented, not greedy eagerness for gain and enjoyment like Saccard, but a weak nature [*une lâcheté*] devouring ready-made fortunes, a strange hermaphrodite making its entrance at the right moment in a society that was growing rotten" (400/118, translation modified). Certainly, in terms of the pathologies constructed and circulated in medical literature and clinical practice, it makes sense that "perverts" should attract one another. In the logic of equivalence I sketched out in Chapter 2, following Jean Borie, hysterical women, homosexuals, androgynes, masturbators, and sexually precocious children are metonymically associated with one another and can even serve as substitutions for each other. In effect, Renée's transgression turns out to be a double one: incest with her stepson who is not even a properly gendered man. No wonder that once she falls in love with Maxime she thinks she has fallen ill (413). Repeatedly, Maxime is referred to as a "girl manqué" (450), as having "the temperament of a girl" (489), as being a "blond girl" (506). If hysteria is a "feminine" temperament that is not only unsettled, fickle, and unstable but also hesitates as to its own sex and gender, then Renée and Maxime's liaison is an abyss of sexual ambiguity that will precipitate Renée's madness. Maxime's sexual ambivalence will compound Renée's own hysterical confusion vertiginously.

La Curée develops the lawlessness of their desire in every possible way through multiple figures of the "other" of normative family relations in the late nineteenth century which suborn the Saccard household: colonized "nature," the street, and homosexuality. The measure of Renée's drifting desire is found in its spatial figuration in the scene that closes chapter 1. During a reception in her townhouse after the promenade in the Bois de Boulogne Renée follows Maxime and Louise into the exotic hothouse off the ballroom:

> In her were aroused the senses of a woman who desires, the caprices of a woman who is satiated. And above her head, the great black marble sphinx laughed its mystic laugh, as if it had read the longing, formulated at last, that galvanized that dead heart, the fugitive longing, the "something different" vainly sought for by Renée in the rock of her carriage, in the fine ashes of the falling night, and now, suddenly revealed to her beneath the dazzling light of this blazing garden by the sight of Maxime and Louise, laughing and playing, their hands interlocked. (345/43, translation modified)

Nothing is more artificial and foreign to the domestic household and French civilization than the sensuous flowers and plants imported from the colonies that stimulate Renée's lust:

> This time she was permeated with a keen and definite desire.
> Unbridled love and voluptuous appetite haunted this stifling nave in which seethed the ardent sap of the tropics. Renée was wrapt in the puissant bridals of the earth which gave birth to those dark growths, those colossal stems; and the acrid birth-throes of this sea of fire, of this forest expansion, of this mass of vegetation all burning with the entrails that nourished it, surrounded her with perturbing effluvia full of intoxication. (344/42)

Colonial "nature" marks her body with illicit, "primitive" desire in the form of poisonous leaves whose corrupt "milk" enters Renée's veins: "The shrub that half concealed her was a malignant plant [*une plante maudite*], a Madagascar tanghin-tree with bored boxlike leaves with whitish stems, whose smallest veins distilled a venomous fluid. . . . Renée, her mind wandering, her mouth parched and stung, took between her lips a sprig of the tanghin-tree which came to the level of her teeth, and closed them on one of its bitter leaves" (345/43). Although the plant is from the neighboring island of Madagascar, we are a long way from bucolic Mauritius and *Paul et Virginie*. Renée and the hothouse function here as *mères dénaturées*.

Renée and Maxime seal their liaison in another "foreign" space, that of a restaurant dining room overlooking a busy boulevard. There, the confusion of the street invades the restaurant in the form of incestuous and homosexual desire. The consummation of their mutual attraction is heralded for readers, now schooled in the symptoms of "deviance," by Renée's wish to dress up in drag and accompany Maxime to cafés off-limits to women of polite society. Rather than an example of neglect of appearances, as in Sidonie's case, Renée's cross-dressing is a choice fully aware of the boundaries between public and private spaces policed by gender differences: "we are having a debauch tonight. . . . I'm a man, see?" (415/138). Enveloped by the sensuous warmth of the café's private dining room whose mirrors are covered with the names of Maxime's other lovers, the mutual seduction reaches its term, climaxing, literally, with the rumble of the street: "In the profound silence of the room, where the gas seemed to flare higher, she felt the ground tremble and heard the clatter of the Batignoles omnibus turning the corner of the boulevard. And it was all over" (426/154).

One transgression seemingly contains another. The secret outrage of their carnal incest is that it also constituted a violation of the heterosexual matrix; Maxime was caught off guard, for he thought he was playing with a "boy" (!):

> He was angry at the adventure. He laid the blame on the black satin domino. Whoever saw a woman rig herself out like that! You couldn't even see her neck. He had taken her for a boy and romped with her, and it was not his fault that the game had become serious. He certainly would not have touched her with the tip of his fingers, if she had shown only a tiny bit of her shoulders. He would have remembered that she was his father's wife. (428/156–57)

In fact their later trysts in the transgressive space of the hothouse confirm that Renée clearly desires the "woman" in Maxime as much as he the "man" in Renée:

> They passed a night of mad love. Renée was the man, the passionate, active will. Maxime submitted. Smooth-limbed, slim and graceful as a Roman stripling, fair-haired and pretty, stricken in his virility since

childhood, this epicene being [*être neutre*] became a great girl in Renée's inquisitive arms. He seemed born and bred for a perversion of sensual pleasure. Renée enjoyed her domination, and she bent under her passion this creature with the still indeterminate sex [*dont le sexe hésitait toujours*]. . . . This pretty little fellow, whose frail figure was revealed by his clothes, this abortive girl [*fille manquée*], who strolled along the boulevards his hair parted in the middle, with little bursts of laughter and bored smiles, became in Renée's hands one of those debauching influences of the decadence which in certain periods among rotten nations exhaust a body [*une chair*] and unhinge a brain.

And it was in the hot-house especially that Renée played the man. The ardent night they spent there was followed by many others. (449–50/185)

The two different moments of Renée's erotic reverie—the "jolts" that focused her gaze first on a lesbian couple and then on Maxime—turn out to be identical in content and aim. This is the scandalous measure of Renée's wandering, hysterical desire. Desiring Maxime is not a return to the heterosexual fold but its definitive abandonment, and this will entail her descent into madness. Her incipient illness will later frighten Maxime who will associate her mental instability with the disorder of the street: "Maxime himself began to be frightened of this head in which madness was shooting up, and in which he thought he could hear, at night, on the pillow, all the din of a city in rut with pleasure"(467/209, translation modified). As the spatial metaphors suggest, the term of Renée's transgression of gender and sexual codes, the term of her hysteria, is the death of interiority itself, which succumbs to the dissolution of the social and corporeal boundaries of identity. The street now dances in Renée's head.

Readerly Pleasures and Discipline

Now, the two lovers' incestuous passion should afford considerable pleasure to those readers whose eye for suggestive detail and metonymic association allowed them to anticipate the lovers' affair as the "truth" of the Second Empire household. To those who were caught unaware of the impending crime and remain unconvinced by the turn of the plot Zola offers the following retrospective reading of the narrative:

They had drifted towards incest since the day when Maxime, in his threadbare schoolboy tunic, had hung on Renée's neck, creasing his French guard's coat. From that time forward there had been a long and constant perversion between them. The strange education the young woman gave the child; the familiarities that made boon companions [*des camarades*] of them; later on, the laughing audacity of their confidences; all this dangerous promiscuity had ended by linking them together by a singular bond, in which the delights of friendship came near to carnal indulgence. *They had long since given themselves to one another*; the animal act was but the acute crisis of this unconscious malady of passion. (445/179–80, my emphasis)

Such a passage constitutes both a demonstration in hermeneutics and a lesson in familial discipline. The latter in fact requires the former. A simple act of carnal incest, were it discovered, would have necessitated a single corresponding sanction and punishment. But *La Curée* proposes a different regime, one in which the conjunction of knowledge and power alters the very temporality and ontology of the "crime." Renée and Maxime's incest is not a discreet, easily verifiable *act* but rather a transgressive *condition of desire* to be deciphered. Thus the novel introduces a temporal depth and extension to their incest that parallels that of the reading process itself. In turn readers' progress through *La Curée* spatializes desire by displaying it on and beneath the surface of every bodily utterance, whether verbal or gestural. If readers missed the signs and symptoms of Renée and Maxime's approaching affair, for the remainder of the novel they surely will no longer idly consume images of female boredom and sexual ambiguity.

Incest and the Absence of the "Law"

Carnal incest constitutes the sign and symptom of domesticity without law in the form of desire run wild. Yet Zola's daring portrait of extreme familial disorder also affords him the opportunity to bind the lack of family to the Law of the Father, to produce order—or at least the desire for such a new order—out of anarchy. This is the movement of reterritorializing or fixing desire. And this order cannot be defined in terms of discreet acts but stands as the fundamental condition of a gendered and sexualized subjectivity that is the law of desire.

The discursive machine, even as it marks Renée's and Maxime's bodies as hysterical, transsexual, and homosexual, constructs their lovemaking in such a way as to establish the imperatives of gender difference and heterosexual desire, presumably assured by the incommensurable biology of their bodies, even as the lovers transgress them: "female" and "male," they play symmetrically inverted but opposite "masculine" and "feminine" roles that leave intact the presuppositions of the heterosexual matrix; Renée is the "man" by virtue of her active desire, Maxime plays the "woman" by giving in to her. In the cited passage, desire is still being read within the frame of compulsory heterosexuality in which only opposites (dialectical "others") may attract.[24] This identifies Renée's desire as desire of "male" desire, desire of the Law of the Father.

More important, the novel plays with readers' anxieties and need to know by allowing incest to happen, as it were, by chance, not as a transgressive act, but almost as a random occurrence within the state of *absolute* lawlessness that reigns in Saccard's household. Maxime was the closest body at hand, so to speak, capable of distracting Renée from her crushing boredom. As for Maxime, she was a "comrade," a boy whom he happened to be playing with at the moment in the restaurant. At most, Renée was "the first married woman he had had. He did not reflect that the husband was his father" (446/181–82). Here, desire is intradiegetically formulated, if only briefly, as unrelated to lack or negativity and thus to a law. Only later, and *retrospectively*, does *La Curée* begin the second movement of reinscribing Renée's desire as a *transgression* in her own mind and body. Like Zola's enlightened reader, she too rereads the earlier episodes, and only then does she frame her desire in terms of transgression and incest. At first, we get the novel's interpretation of the beginnings of her desire:

> It was during that autumn drive in the twilight, when the Bois was falling asleep, that the vague idea of incest came to her like a titillation that sent an unknown thrill over her skin; and in the evening, in the semi-intoxication of the dinner, lashed by jealousy, this idea became

more defined, rose up ardently before her, amid the flames of the conservatory, as she stood before Maxime and Louise. At that moment she craved for sin [*le mal*], the sin that no one commits, the sin that was to fill her empty existence and bring her at last to that hell of which she was still afraid, as in the days when she was a little girl. Then, the next day, through a strange feeling of remorse and lassitude, her craving had left her. It seemed to her that she had already sinned, that it was not so pleasant as she had fancied, and that it would really be too disgusting [*sale*]. (447/182)

The text has her adopt its retrospective reading as her own:

> But after this stupid fall, she returned to her dream of nameless pleasure, and then took Maxime back to her arms, curious about him, curious as to the delights of a passion which she regarded as a crime. *Her volition accepted incest, demanded it, resolved to taste it to the end, even to remorse, should that ever come.* She loved with the transports of a woman of fashion, with the restless prejudices of a woman of the middle class, with all the struggles, joys, and disgusts of a woman drowning herself in disdain. (447/182, emphasis mine)

She is now fully committed to the bourgeois battle of first resisting desire and then transgressing the norm, a struggle that she will soon transform into a badge of honor:

> Incest lent her a fire that glowed in the depths of her eyes and warmed her laughter. Her eye-glass looked supremely insolent at the tip of her nose, and she glanced at the older women, at the dear friends pluming themselves upon the enormity of some vice or other, with the air of a boastful adolescent boy, with a fixed smile that said: "I have my crime." (456/194–95, translation modified)

Progressively, then, *La Curée* has Renée articulate her desire with respect to the incest taboo. Though an unlikely heterosexual object choice for incest, effeminate Maxime was nonetheless an easy one, for he was hardly a "man" or a "true" son; he was someone she could dominate. Saccard was another matter, however. Hence her profound malaise when, after years of neglect, Saccard wished to renew conjugal relations with her: "He smiled good-naturedly. Renée remained in a state of cruel anguish. She felt that she would lose the little equilibrium left her, if she gave herself to her husband. Her last pride was that she was married to the father but was the wife of the son alone" (461/200). *He* embodied the incest taboo and its power—or so she thought. For at the very moment poor Renée has assumed the rebellious positionality of a depraved, incestuous stepmother the incest taboo proves to be nonexistent, or rather is displaced by another law, that of the marketplace in the form of unbridled male appetites.

One of Zola's most provocative strokes in his unremitting satire of the Second Empire is to show that, in a fully decadent period, even incest can be turned to account. This occurs appropriately enough in the famous episode of a transvestite ball held at the Saccards' luxurious townhouse for the purpose of announcing—unbeknownst to Renée—Maxime's engagement to Louise: the transgression of gender codes (the ball) and the final subsumption of the Saccard household under the demands of Aristide's speculative adventures are one and the same event.

That very evening, Saccard discovers his wife and son's affair and to the astonishment of the guilty parties, instead of exploding in Oedipal anger, Saccard calmly decides to take the deed to the Parisian property that constituted Renée's dowry and that was meant for her children. He needed it sorely to carry out yet another real estate speculation. At the end of the confrontation Renée stands speechless as father and son march off together, arm in arm, to rejoin the party and announce Maxime's engagement to Louise: "What! They had gone off quietly, amicably! The two men had not smashed one another! . . . Her crime, the kisses on the great gray-and-pink bed, the wild nights in the hot-house, all the accursed love that had consumed her for months came to this mean, vulgar ending. Her husband knew all, and did not even beat her" (519/280).

Renée's shocked realization that her crime of incest transgressed no law is what precipitates the final phase of her descent into hysterical madness begun with the *homme-femme* Maxime: "She had come to that, to be a big doll from whose chest there issues a mere squeak of sound" (521/282). Then: "She saw herself dead.

Every feature told her that the breaking down of her brain was nearly accomplished. Maxime, the last perversion of her senses, had finished his work, had exhausted her flesh, unhinged her intellect. No joys remained for her to taste, no hope of reawakening" (523/286).

In a sense, Zola presents Renée as desiring the Law of the Father, if only by virtue of transgressing it, but the Law was doubly absent: in Maxime who "is not" a (heterosexual) man and in Saccard, his father, who traded the negative sanctions of the Law for a real-estate title. Thus Renée loses her only intelligible identity, which the novel inscribed as a purely negative one: pregnant fiancée, sterile wife, and incestuous stepmother. Stripped of the law of her desire and the last of her family property, Renée is dispatched to oblivion less than a year later by an attack of meningitis. The combined forces of the market and its implacable homosocial relations between men (here, between father and son) have overturned the incest taboo, not by transgressing it but by simply recuperating it in flows of capital and speculation. In one stroke the novel both posits the domestic family and the Law of the Father as identical by means of a narrative of incestuous love and has them swept away by those very men destined to instantiate the Law within the household. The play of familial lack has reached a radical stage here: the incest taboo both inscribes desire as complicitous with a patriarchal law (Renée's drama of transgression) and subsumes all family relations under the latter's rule, while the law itself turns out to be devoid of agents of inscription and channels of transmission. Thus, in a sense, *La Curée* produces the *lack of a lack*, the lack, on the intradiegetic level, of a "transgression" and its scandal. The displacement of the Law of the Father by market forces as the rule of family relations, and of desire, constitutes the privileged figuration of the invasion of the domestic household by commercial imperatives and encodes the extent to which the Second Empire's bourgeoisie has betrayed middle-class traditions, family life, and, not least, the nation. The narrative of incest is a powerful one insofar as it strives to bind desire—if only negatively—to the comforting parameters of Oedipal relations, and keep it within "the endogomous rules of the bourgeoisie."[25] The crime and scandal of incest is better than no crime and no law at all.

The Law exists only in the narrative of its absence and intradiegetically in Renée's feeble consciousness. This process of reinscription of the domestic family under the sign of the Phallus (the Great Signifier) reaches its term in the final pages before Renée dies. The text will not allow the hysterical body of the unstable, incestuous stepmother to depart without first fully investing it with the signifiers of the Law for the pleasure of decipherment by the now well-trained readers. Unlike in the novel's opening scene, here Renée finally names her desire and in so doing speaks the Law. The method remains identical; it is based on the play of the gaze: her anxious eyes fix upon three paternal objects: first Saccard, then Napoleon III, and finally her venerable father. Between those objects of desire, in the displacement of her gaze, the text writes the "truth" of her hysteria. During a final promenade in the Bois de Boulogne she comes upon Saccard and Maxime discussing business, and at that very instant the Emperor appears:

> He occupied alone the back seat of a landau. Dressed in black with his frock-coat buttoned up to his chin, he wore, a little on one side, a very tall hat, whose silk glistened. . . .
> Renée thought the Emperor aged. His mouth opened more feebly under his thick waxed moustache. His eyelids fell more heavily to the point of half covering his lifeless eyes, the yellow grayness of which was yet more bleared. And his nose retained its look of a dry fish-bone set in the vagueness of his face. (540/307)

The sight of the aging Napoleon III—the failing patriarch of a discredited regime—precipitates a visit by Renée to the townhouse of her childhood where her old father still lives: "She remained for a moment with wide-open eyes, full of this vision, which reminded her of another moment in her life. . . . She sought about, her hands folded on her breast, as though burnt with an internal fire; and it was with a sudden hope of relief, of healing coolness, that she leaned forward and said to the coachman: 'To the Hotel Béraud!'" (541/307–8).

Critics have remarked that Renée's belated return to "family" and her social origins marks Renée's homage to honest middle-class values, but they overlook the fact that the episode also rewrites the recent past of the domestic family in terms of a mythical patriarchy. Zola's history of the Second Empire translates into a story of misguided choices of paternal objects (hence Renée's sense of betrayal) whose effect is to subsume the domestic household, previously coded and constructed by familial discourse as the domain of female authority, under paternal rule and to designate the Law of the Father as the fundamental condition of desire. As a consequence, the nostalgia for a mythical bourgeois patriarchy closes the novel on a compelling note of *loss* that actually erases the bourgeoisie's own recent history and discursive investments. In this fashion *La Curée* adopts for its own purposes the tactics of earlier familial discourse that elicited readers' desire for new, gendered household relations and arrangements by deploying a narrative and rhetoric of lack and pathology. *La Curée* advances this process further in two ways: first by constructing "deviant" sexuality as pathological forms under the sign of the Law—Renée's deepest desire, even transgressively expressed, is finally determined by the Name of the Father; second, this same construction induces a perception of family lack that is narrowed to the absence of paternal authority. The various productive illnesses of the model family are now subsumed under one master signifier.

However, the signifier of the Father and the Law that marks Renée's body as the latter's fundamental desire in the final pages of *La Curée* does not constitute a reinscription of an unproblematic patriarchy. This is so on several accounts. Clearly Zola's science and his disciplinary narrative mechanisms are deployed in the name of domesticity disrupted by the crushing homosociality of the male world of commerce in which everything is traded for profit, including women's bodies, family heirlooms, and sexual normativity.[26] Thus Zola differentiates between forms of male dominance and abhors social and material economies that dispense altogether with the mediation of women's bodies and "family." That is precisely the heart of his indictment of the Second Empire. Second, the fictional strategies Zola deploys in order to elicit readerly investments and participation in the Law belong to a *normative* regime, and not one based on a juridical, prohibitive form of power. This is the modality of Zola's science. Zola proposes a new knowledge of the social in terms of the family as defined by its members' incipient sexual deviancies. His is a male science of the private sphere, a territory and knowledge previously encoded as specifically feminine even when authors were male: for a time liberal subjectivity was constructed as "feminine" and "female," and opposed to the discredited practices and authority of the old patriarchy, which dominated the world outside of the family and stood for vestigial conservative social forces of the Old Regime. Zola's positionality is akin to that of physicians, who, according to Jacques Donzelot, allied themselves with lower- and middle-class housewives in a strategy to inculcate new norms of personal hygiene and household organization.[27] But there was a difference: Donzelot claims that these tactical alliances operated to weaken husbands' and fathers' traditional authority, whereas Zola's tactic actually consists in a call for a restoration of male authority based on the inscription of desire as Law—but a Law that is bound to a new science in the name of a new social and political national culture, that of middle-class Republicanism and its imagined community.

The tale of Zola's three "social monstrosities" expands the apparatus of "sexuality" in order to produce the "family" as Law. This operation actually lends a language to practices whose entry into discourse can unpredictably elicit readerly voyeuristic fascinations and pleasures, and thereby can sediment in bodies, and give discursive space to, practices that may escape inscription by the law of familial desire. This is the risk and the power of the putting into discourse of sex, sexuality, gender, and desire. The more fine and minute the policing of deviance and transgression is, the greater the opportunities to expand the scope and reach of normalizing discourse (the parameters of "family" and the heterosexual matrix); but also the more those fundamental discursive identities are put into play and *thus* contestation, the greater the risk that the norms may simply be replaced or consigned to irrelevance. The production of the Law in the late nineteenth century is, like "family," just that: a production, a *re*coding and not merely an expression. It is even less simply the drama of a prohibition, that is to say, it remains vulnerable to counterproductions and positive counterinvestments.*

* That is precisely what happened in Zola's case during his lifetime. A homosexual man wrote a lengthy confessional letter to Zola expressing his admiration for his depiction of upper-class life and his gratitude for Zola's portraits of sexual marginals, which he read with an enthusiasm tinged with guilt. Zola never dared publish the letter, which he calls a "Roman d'un inverti" (Novel by an invert), but allowed Dr. Laupts to include it as a medical document in his *Tares et poisons: perversion et perversités sexuelles*, with a preface by the novelist. See Zola, Preface.

~ CHAPTER 8

Straight Is the Gait: Modernism as Celibate Writing in Gide's *La Porte étroite*

> I take a woman other than my sister in order to constitute the differentiated base of a new triangle whose inverted vertex will be my child—which is called surmounting Oedipus, but reproducing it as well, transmitting it rather than dying all alone, incestuous, homosexual, and a zombie.
>
> —Deleuze and Guattari, *Anti-Oedipus*

UNDERLYING THE ANALYSIS in Part II of the fictional production and inscription of familial discourse in terms of tales of familial lack and loss is the following question: Just where do narrative figurations of endangered or deficient family household life cease producing desire for the normative family and its gendered bodies and, on the contrary, begin constructing other desires, bodies and practices that have little to do with "family" or "lack" at all? This is a complex problem played out on the intricate textual surfaces of André Gide's modernist novel *La Porte étroite* [Strait is the gate]. Moreover, like much modernist fiction, Gide's *récit* pushes to the extreme the interplay between writing, embodiment, subjectivity, and familial lack that has characterized every novel I have examined in the preceding chapters. Indeed, I want to argue that this dynamic constitutes the very subject of the novel.

Published in 1909, *La Porte étroite* was Gide's first commercial success. It warrants our attention on several accounts. First of all, the narrative of the failed courtship of two first cousins, Jerome and Alissa, has as its setting bourgeois family life in a stage of dissolution. Moreover, as if to testify to the scope and power of familial ideologies in France at the turn of the century, the extended upper-middle-class family of Jerome's mother literally fills up the text's discursive horizon, outside of which no class or character other than the family friend Miss Ashburton exists. Moreover, Jerome and Alissa's marriage would at best signify a very restricted case of exogamy and suggests, once again, that "family" designates the only possible parameter of desire. On the one hand, this implies that this is a juncture in which "family" at once knows no "outside" and would perhaps be utterly powerless to deal with social or sexual alterity. On the other, Jerome and Alissa's failed engagement signals nothing less than the implosion of atrophied familial relations, which then collapse in upon themselves, rupturing the heterosexual contract; something *internal* to "family" has disrupted the circuits of desire by which family households reproduce themselves and maintain their boundaries while colonizing and controlling their social and sexual others.

With Gide's novel we find ourselves a long way from *Paul et Virginie*, where "family" was narrativized in a constitutive moment of retreat from the absolutist political sphere, a rhetorical tactic that elicited the desire to transform Old Regime social and political relations standing in the way of the fruition of "family" life; we also are at some distance from *La Petite Fadette*, a novel that enacted the enforcement of the heterosexual contract and promised social mobility through the adoption of domesticity's norms. And we are beyond *La Curée*, where dysfunctional family life—a most extreme case of familial lack—produced the Law of the Father as the law of "family" and social desire and promised new knowledges through omniscient, objective narration under the aegis of "male" science. In *La Porte étroite*, dysfunctional family life seems to produce nothing except the baffling subjectivity of Jerome, the first-person narrator, who scarcely appears to desire at all.

In Gide's novel the crisis of the bourgeois family household that underwrites so much realist and naturalist fiction reaches a hyperbolic, caricatured state within a single family. The stereotypes of crisis are common ones: dead or weak fathers abound (Jerome's father—indeed, the entire paternal side of the family is absent, Uncle Bucolin, and Pastor Vautier); orphans or abandoned children proliferate (Lucile Bucolin, Jerome, and, in a sense, Alissa); widows and spinsters cross and recross the novel's pages (Aunt Plantier, Jerome's mother, and Miss Ashburton); mothers and daughters fall victim to fits of hysteria (Lucile, Alissa, and Juliette); and only one of Jerome's generation manages to marry, and marries unhappily at that (Juliette); while the novel, in its growing obsession with the subjectivity of unmarried Alissa, slowly and relentlessly suppresses all female characters but one (Juliette).

In addition, *La Porte étroite* will prove helpful in tracing a new turn in fiction's production of familial discourse, for out of the cramped confines of the overwrought family drama there emerges an aesthetic problematic: Jerome's tale is a fragmented narrative that eschews the traditional orderings and certainties of the novel. For example, the opening page warns us not to expect a book but rather scraps of the exhausted narrator's past, a story whose beginning lies in the death of Jerome's father:

> Other people might have made a book out of it; but the story I am going to tell is one that took all my strength to live and over which I wore out all my virtue. So I shall set down my recollections quite simply, and if in places they are ragged I shall have recourse to no invention and neither patch them nor connect them; any effort I might take to dress them up would take away from the last pleasure I hope to get in telling them.
>
> I was not twelve years old when I lost my father. As there was nothing to keep my mother at Le Havre, where my father had a practice as a doctor, she decided to go to Paris, where she thought I should be better able to finish my education.[1]

The "lack" of the putative organizing paternal principle has seemingly had two concomitant effects: the radical destabilizing both of the narrator's self and of the novel. The novel, with its Oedipal infrastructures, certainly seems to elicit a straightforward psychoanalytic interpretation and, just as surely, this interpretation is one

Zola's novels and countless others like them have taught contemporary readers to apply to texts, to themselves, and to others.[2] Yet this cultural assumption about masculine authority in the family household and its consequences for psychic and textual order must be read in tandem with other narratives in *La Porte étroite*: the successive stories about Aunt Lucile and her daughter Alissa and the incorporation of Alissa's diary into the novel's fictional structure. The narrative of the genesis of the male modernist writer is decisively mediated by stories about women and by "feminine" writing. As always in familial discourse, the juncture of bodies and desires is articulated through the "female" and the "feminine" but in *La Porte étroite* it also directly intersects with questions of writing and discursive relations. The communication situation (who is authorized to speak or not, what constitute valid languages and knowledges, etc.), so often naturalized by the omniscient third-person narrative of realist and naturalist fiction, is foregrounded here by tentative, highly subjective narratives and knowledges. At one point in the narrative Jerome exclaims, "How should I, by a simple narrative [*récit*], make clear at once what I myself understood at first so ill?" (103/566, translation modified). As in the opening pages, the text mobilizes readers' desire to know, but unlike in *La Curée*, where the hypersubjectivity of each character's registering of sensation and thought was countered and contained by the omniscient narration's science of desire, readers of Gide's modernist novel are largely left to their own hermeneutic devices and are placed in a position identical to that of Jerome, who tries to make sense out of both Alissa's behavior and writings and his own. Readers are enlisted in the task of writing and deciphering bodies and the desires they enclose—just as I am doing here—but this task, rather than simply furthering old knowledges and desires or even producing new ones, will reach the dead end of reinstating the desire for "family," but furnishes no character who belongs *or even fully desires* (in contrast to Balzac's *Les Paysans*) to belong to "family." By the novel's end, no one successfully occupies the positionalities of father or mother, either in the present or proleptically in the future.

Modernism and "Celibate" Writers

La Porte étroite weaves together stories of broken bourgeois family life, failed desire, and new forms of writing. These are the very stuff of modernist literature. One of the most fruitful views of modernism is that which traces its rise in the interstices of realist and naturalist fiction. From this perspective, modernism contested the latter's slow fall into the realm of mass or popular literature, which was characterized by reified plots and simplified characters. These developments, which were part and parcel of late nineteenth-century capitalism's reorganization of daily life and cultural production, were contemporary with counterstrategies by authors who sought to preserve their writing from what they perceived to be the onslaught of middle-class and popular commercial culture and its degraded objects and languages.[3] While many critics have enumerated the aesthetic consequences of modernism's critical and negative stance—the collapse of traditional narrative and hermeneutics in favor of a more narrow investment in private languages, personal style, and sheer sentence-making—few have commented on this process's relationship to discourse on "families."

It is perhaps easy to see how a modernist French author's antibourgeois position was one with a broadly antifamilial stance and a rejection of realism's old referential project of social and psychological representation. According to Edward Said, with the rise of modernism there ensued "a general loss of faith in the ability of novelistic representation directly to reflect anything other than the author's dilemmas."[4] This involved on the part of many male authors a rejection of the classical novel's model for fiction writing, which was one of paternity, reproduction, and succession. These natural, biological metaphors for the practice of novel writing proved unsuitable to writers who saw their work as sterile artifice and contrivance par excellence or, as Sartre put it, as *anti-physis*.[5] The jettisoning of the familial analogy (to use Said's term),[6] however, meant more than the simple abandonment of an outdated thematics of artistic self-reflexivity by writers faced with an increasingly commodified world; rather, as Jean Borie would certainly insist, it involved an entire discursive formation of which the old model of novelistic practice was an essential component.[7] Said and Borie remind us that modernist fiction's revolt against the realist novel and familial discourse found its discursive colors in the banner of "celibate" (*célibataire* in French; or in the pejorative English form, "bachelor" or "spinster") writers and their novels. This peculiarly familialist thematization of modernist writing (as that of unmarried men and women) underscores how difficult it must have been for novelists to distance themselves from official discourse. The space of their rebellion had already been mapped out in advance on familial terrain: for in the minds of politicians, jurists, philosophers, and public health officers the figure of the marginal writer and that of the bachelor merged in such a way that the two were virtually indistinguishable and were attributed the same sociomedical pathology, particularly by the champions of natalism or population growth. This figural convergence resulted in the discursive identification of social or cultural marginality with familial marginality.[8] Inevitably, one response to this was to ironize one's position with respect to family, marriage, and the dominant discourses. It therefore should not be surprising to find that divided, fissured *récits* of broken, scattered families are the staple of modernist or "celibate" fiction.

La Porte étroite may be read as the tale of the genesis of the modernist text and its author. Like other novels that are productive of familial discourse, the story of the moment of familial dissolution by which Jerome comes to write his fragmented, retrospective narrative enacts struggles over different forms and styles of writing and over cultural narratives that have long told the tale of heterosexual desire. I will show that the two framing shocks of Jerome's narrative—his eroticized encounters with Aunt Lucile, and the death of her daughter Alissa and his reception of his cousin's diary—amount to reformulated clichéd presentations of female desire, the mother's and the daughter's. They are the two poles of the novel's trajectory, which traverses Jerome and constitutes him as a complexly gendered writing subject. This structure will be the vehicle for the deployment of an intricate fictional strategy by Gide, whereby he constructs a presentation of familialism's other, the celibate writer whose possible homosexuality—his familial otherness—is approached asymptotically and negatively by the text. Gide does this by placing Jerome in specular relationships to what are ultimately paranoiac figurations of other familial outcasts—spinsters, emancipated women, and the colonized—and through the absence in the young writer of any genital heterosexuality. Similarly, the novel's own fitful generic identity is strikingly complicated by the texts it transcribes, Alissa's letters and diary. The dead woman's correspondence and journal, included in Jerome's text, fragment Jerome's otherwise rather simple first-person narrative.

Furthermore, Jerome's narration authorizes itself not only through these bodies and writings but also in opposition to religious discourse and dominant middle-class popular fiction (the novel frustrates readerly expectations and pleasures formed by nineteenth-century fiction) and their inscription of the heterosexual contract.

In what follows, however, I will steer clear of modernism's own mythical narrative of its "triumph" over repressive cultural forms and practices. For the incitement of readers to use their interpretive skills in some sense marks a deep continuity with earlier fictional and discursive practices. The search for alternative narratives, bodies, and desires in the *detail* of fragmented texts must also stand as an expansion of the apparatus of textual surveillance and discipline; only now, what Gide's discourse of repression promises is a freedom of interiority that "escapes" the seamless unitary narratives of desire inscribed by middle-class print culture in the intimate and private spaces of sentences, metaphors, and semiotic minutiae. This will fit all too well later in the twentieth century with academic departments' teaching students the pleasures of tracing an infinitely expansive, *sexualized* interiority through the endless practice of rereading modernist texts. Nonetheless, this scarcely constitutes Gidean fiction as a "failure"; I simply want to point out that Gide's novel joins battle with familial discourse and he does it where familial discourse operates most openly yet most subtly and effectively, on the level of semiotic and bodily detail. That, too, is where the flows of power are, and they run through and through modernist writing.

The Geography of Modernist Desire: Colonialism and the Family

The novel's title introduces a key set of spatial metaphors for what is essentially (domestic) feminine territory: from the bedrooms, salons, and garden of the eighteenth-century provincial bourgeois house at Fongueusemare belonging to the maternal uncle Bucolin to Alissa's body and her *journal intime*. Outside of these lies Paris, to be sure, largely the world of masculine ambition (where Jerome and Abel both study and pursue their careers), but also the French colonial empire whence comes Lucile Bucolin, the female character whose example and actions cast such a long but indeterminate shadow in Jerome's narrative.

With respect to the question of space, it is noteworthy that in *La Porte étroite* many characters feel out of place—because of the whence and whither of their desire—not least Jerome's Aunt Lucile. She has an unusual narrative existence; for though seemingly a major cause of the failure of Jerome and Alissa's courtship, once she has left husband and family the novel consigns her to total novelistic oblivion, an oblivion that critics have faithfully respected. An orphaned white Creole from Martinique, Lucile Bucolin had been brought up in France by Pastor Vautier and his wife, who, once they realized that the Good Word was completely lost on the precociously mature Lucile, allowed her to marry Bucolin at the age of 16, in hopes that she would settle down, but to no effect. An orphan cut free from the imperatives of the traditional limits assigned to women in the family, she is seemingly infected by those untamed forces, social and sexual, that familial discourse projected onto "Nature" and the colonized lands, and that were colonialism's post-hoc justification of its entire enterprise in the nineteenth century. The character of the "charming child" had begun to develop "oddly" and she had embarrassed her stepparents "terribly," leaving poor Pastor Vautier "quite defenceless" (498/8).

Indeed, she is a disturbing replica of the Creole lady, the Baudelairian avatar of what Christopher Miller terms "Africanist discourse." Here is her portrait:

Lucile Bucolin was very beautiful. I have kept a little portrait of her in which I can see her as she then was, looking so young that she might have been taken for the elder sister of her daughters, sitting sideways in an attitude habitual to her, her head leaning on her left hand, her little finger curved rather affectedly toward her lip. A large-meshed net confines the masses of her woolly hair [*cheveux crêpelés*], which fall half-uncoiled upon her neck. In the opening of her bodice a locket of Italian mosaic hangs from a loosely tied black velvet neck ribbon. . . .

Lucile Bucolin took very little share in our life; she did not come downstairs from her room till after the midday meal was over, and then immediately stretched herself on the sofa or in a hammock and remained there till evening, when she would rise, no less languid than before. She used sometimes to raise a handkerchief to her forehead as if wiping away some imaginary moisture, though her skin was a perfection of smooth purity. This handkerchief filled me with wonder because of its fineness and its scent, which seemed more like the perfume of a fruit than of a flower; sometimes she would draw from her waist a minute mirror with a sliding silver lid, which hung with various other objects from her watch-chain; she would look at herself, wet her finger at her lips, and then moisten the corner of her eyes. (498–99/7–9, translation modified)

In the nineteenth century, French usage of the word "Creole" was applied to both the colonized population (indigenous or slave) and the white colonizers, but ambiguously: for what at first was a *geographical* distinction—the inhabitants of a colony—became a racial one; that is writers from Baudelaire to Gobineau ascribed to colonizers attributes commonly associated by Africanist discourse with the colonized populations of color: in this case Aunt Lucile's "woolly hair" (*cheveux crêpelés*), fragile grace, languorous posing, and unreflective or unseeing gaze betraying little or no subjectivity.[9] It suffices to open *Le Petit Robert* to *crêpelé, ée* in order to grasp the extent of the literary and discursive inscription of Lucile's portrait. "*crêpelé*: frisé à très petites ondulations (cheveux). Cf. crépu. 'Tes cheveux crespelés (sic), ta peau de mulâtresse.' (Baudelaire)." Lucile Bucolin carries what was perceived to be the corruption of colonial experience (here in the undisciplined form of carnal female desire) back to metropolitan France to the inner reaches of the Bucolin household. No longer the precondition of formulating an alternative model of household life, as in *Paul et Virginie*, the colonies are the fulcrum and breeding ground of its enemies.

The Creole Lucile scandalously subverts the sphere designated by contemporary discourse as the realm of domesticity and legitimate family life. This is the source of Jerome's horror when, on his way to Alissa's room, he catches sight of his aunt in her quarters stretched out on a chaise longue, surrounded by her lover and two of her children, Robert and Juliette. She constitutes, as it were, the "dark" secret of the family household, what lies behind every closed door of nineteenth-century fiction, something that by virtue of its concealment demands to be revealed.

> The door past which I had to go was open, and a flood of light came from the room and fell on the landing; afraid of being seen, I hesitated a moment and drew back into the dark. This is what I beheld, to my unspeakable amazement: my aunt was lying on a sofa in the middle of the room; the curtains were drawn, and it was illuminated by the cheerful light of two candelabras full of candles; Robert and Juliette were at her feet, and behind her was a strange young man in a lieutenant's uniform. The presence of the two children seems to me today monstrous; at that time in my innocence I thought it was reassuring rather than otherwise. (503/14)

The perversion of the family portrait is the occasion for mocking the name of the father and marital *impuissance*:

> They were laughing and looking at the stranger, who was saying in a piping voice: "Bucolin! Bucolin! . . . If I had a pet lamb I should certainly call it Bucolin."
> My aunt herself burst out laughing. I saw her hold out a cigarette for the young man to light, smoke a few whiffs of it, and then let it fall to the floor. He rushed forward to pick it up, made as if he had caught his feet in the scarf, tripped, and fell on his knees before my aunt. Thanks to this ridiculous performance, I was able to slip by without being noticed. (503/14)

This woman so out of place in the middle-class family is a figure left over from the repository of stock characters belonging to realist authors, that of the hysterical *femme d'intérieur* confined to the household.[10] The modernist novel reworks the traditional discursive construct, taking it beyond the bounds of realist cliché and transforming it into a newer, more contemporary figure, that of the emancipated woman (which the cigarette serves to signify), a latter-day follower of George Sand. Lucile is a force to be reckoned with, for her fits of hysteria—her "attacks" (500–501/10–11)—are not the euphemistic recoding of repressed feminine desire; she uses them to create opportunities for secretly receiving her lovers' visits. Her "perversion" of domestic space deals a blow to the middle classes' "cult of the family, the irrefutable alibi of its imperialism."[11]

Jerome's narrative performs two operations here. It both transforms the realist character and mobilizes colonial and familial paranoia in order to construct the carnal expression of female heterosexuality as threatening. It is noteworthy that in the novel's figuration of Lucile, there are also overtones of eugenicist discourse that had traced the transmission of "weak" or "degenerate" traits from one generation to another among indigenous colonized peoples, the metropolitan "dangerous classes," and the best of bourgeois families.[12] A familial outsider who will eventually abandon her own husband and children to run off with her lover, Lucile passes on to her children her own malaise and her presumably congenital "weaknesses": both daughters, Alissa and Juliette, are prone to bouts of hysteria; Alissa will die single; and her son will remain a bachelor. It may be true that Alissa dies of a severe dose of Calvinist doctrine, but among the causes of her death (left vague by the text) must be counted anorexia nervosa. As for Juliette, her most violent fit of hysteria strikes her appropriately enough upon the announcement of her engagement with Tessière, and leaves her unconscious (539–40/63–64). Notwithstanding later assurances she makes to Jerome that marriage and motherhood have "cured" (*guérie*) her (552/82), the book closes with Juliette, mother of six children, weeping and swooning before Jerome (598/148).

The figure of Aunt Lucile conveniently reinscribes "family" as norm by virtue of her multiple transgressions. Jerome's shocked reaction to her adulterous behavior brazenly carried out in full view of her children designates him as the defender of the sanctity of home life. Yet her scandalous conduct and her playful sexual teasing of

Jerome point to other possibilities that may lie in store for him, and that "family" may serve to defer or deny. In this respect, it's significant that while the narrator has at best a sketchy memory of Alissa's face and body (501/12), he has kept in his possession a miniature portrait of his "evil" aunt, the only pictorial icon in an overly writerly novel. It suggests that, here, lack of "family" intradiegetically elicits as much a fascination with its other as it does the desire to reinstate the discipline and finalities of domesticity. That Lucile's alterity inscribes Jerome's own (his possible homosexuality) is suggested in the "family portrait." First of all, the exchange of a cigarette between Lucile and her lover implies an alterity that has as much to do with the permutability of gender characteristics—a woman becoming a "man" (and conversely in that play of mirrors called voyeurism, a man becoming a "woman")—as with female sexuality. Second, her refusal and transgression of gender positionalities marks her as hysterical by definition; and in the discourse of the day, that carried associations of homosexuality which could only resonate with the fact of her colonial/racial otherness. Finally, the *mise en scène* of gender permutability in the context of mocking the absent father's name moves toward the construction of the late nineteenth-century homosexual type, something of a subset of the "bachelor": the effeminate, sickly, male intellectual, thought to be the result of lack of male authority in the domestic sphere.

Now, the fate of Jerome's desire, the nature of his subjectivity, lies not only with the bodies of Aunt Lucile and her daughter Alissa but also with literary texts. With, behind, or within a female body is written discourse. Repeatedly the novel portrays the languorous Creole aunt as holding a *closed book*:

> She used often to hold a book, but it was almost always shut; a tortoiseshell bookmarker was stuck between the pages. If you came near she did not turn from the contemplation of her dreams to look at you. Often from careless or tired hand, from the back of the sofa, or from a fold of her dress, her handkerchief would drop to the ground, or her book, or a flower, it might be, or the bookmarker. One day when I picked up her book—this childish memory I am telling you—I blushed to see that it was a book of poetry. (498/9)

Ineluctably, Jerome's brush with his seductive aunt links his sexual and literary destinies: his other fateful encounter, in which she provocatively caresses him, transpires while he is looking for a *book*; instead of a text he comes across a desiring woman. His shock is such that he rushes to remove the taint of physical contact: "I rushed away to the other end of the kitchen-garden, and there I dipped my handkerchief into a little tank, put it to my forehead—washed, scrubbed my cheeks, my neck, every part of me that woman had touched" (500/10, translation modified). Here, Jerome meets with a *semiotic object of desire*: a body scripted by realist conventions of female adultery that inspires fascinated horror, but this body also *rewritten* into something new, the emancipated woman of modernist writing whose desires perhaps lie outside of the boundaries of "family" in another discourse altogether.

Homosexuals together with emancipated women were the *bêtes noires* of familial discourse and signified in the literature of the day the irreversible decline of French civilization and empire; in short they were "calamitous emblems of a civilization on the verge of disappearing."[13] The figural face-off between *flasque* (Gide's term) Jerome and his Creole aunt is, first, a mute allegory of alternate sexualities and gender constructions and, second, a natalist, end-of-the-empire narrative, the product of the pessimism of disenchanted Republicanism and liberalism in France. The universalizing impulse of bourgeois culture, whose horizon was both the family and metropolitan France, is circumscribed by sexual and geographical otherness, and this radical difference will constitute one of the privileged preoccupations of modernist fiction, and will be used less to reproduce "family" than to tell the story of bodies and desires that do not concern "family" at all. Tellingly, the fullest exploration of homosexuality in Gide's work is repeatedly relegated to places outside maternal, familial Normandy: to Paris and the Mediterranean basin.

Cultural Narratives and the Dead Ends of Desire

The episode in which Jerome surprises his aunt surrounded by her lover and two of her children throws Jerome in the arms of both his cousin Alissa and religious discourse. This can be understood as his attempt to shore up familial hierarchies and structures fast collapsing around him. Finally reaching Alissa's room, behind a second door Jerome discovers a different spectacle of a woman, that of Alissa grieving over her mother's outrageous behavior:

> I found myself outside of Alissa's door. For a moment I waited. Bursts of laughter and voices came up from the floor below; perhaps they drowned out the sound of my knock, for I heard no answer. I pushed the door, and it opened silently. The room was so dark that I did not at once distinguish Alissa; she was on her knees by the bedside, through the window behind her came the last glimmer of daylight. She turned as I came near: "Oh Jerome, why have you come back?"
> I bent to kiss her; her face was bathed in tears . . .
> My whole life was decided by that moment; even to this day I cannot recall it without a pang of anguish. Doubtless I understood very imperfectly the cause of Alissa's wretchedness, but I felt intensely that it was far too strong for her little quivering soul, for her fragile body, shaken with sobs.
> I remained standing beside her, while she remained on her knees. I could express nothing of the unfamiliar transport of my breast, but pressed her head against my heart and pressed my lips to her forehead while my whole soul came flooding through them. Drunk with love, with pity, with an indistinguishable mixture of enthusiasm, self-sacrifice, and virtue, I appealed to God with all my strength—I offered myself up to Him, unable to conceive that existence could have any other object than to shelter at last this child from fear, evil, from life. I knelt down at last, my whole being full of prayer. I gathered her to me; vaguely I heard her say: "Jerome! They didn't see you, did they? Oh! go away quickly. They mustn't see you." Then, lower still: "Jerome, don't tell anyone. Poor papa doesn't know about it . . ." (503–4/14–15)

This passage mobilizes major cultural narratives that frame and inscribe Jerome's desire, that of Christian religious devotion and a second one, closely related to the first: that of bourgeois courtly love. Both narrativize and elicit desire through a rhetoric of mutual sacrifice and deferral which will be played out by Jerome and Alissa, particularly in their extensive correspondence. However, the junction between these structuring tales of desire and Jerome's and Alissa's bodies is problematized, for as critics have frequently remarked, these discourses end up frustrating the aims assigned heterosexual desire.[14] Instead of furthering desire toward its goal, these cultural narratives actually block its realization. At the heart of both cultural plots operates a dynamic of family hierarchies and positionalities that in Jerome's and Alissa's case will defer their engagement and marriage once and for all. As their relation evolves, Jerome's protective paternalism will be more than matched by his cousin's tender maternalism. Unlike in *Paul et Virginie*, *Les Mystères de Paris*, *La Petite Fadette*, and *La Curée*, "family" is no longer given in *La Porte étroite* as the positive condition of the realization of heterosexual desire but rather as the cause of its undoing. In this modernist text, dominant cultural narratives of desire collapse completely.

This is made clear by the transformation that Christian discourse undergoes in Jerome and Alissa's hands. Doubtless, Pastor Vautier has been no more successful in transmitting the Gospel to Jerome and Alissa than to his adoptive daughter Lucile. But then again, Alissa is Lucile's daughter and Jerome his aunt's unwitting protégé. Shortly after Aunt Lucile's flight with her lover, Vautier delivers a sermon whose structuring theological and sexual metaphor—the strait gate [*la porte étroite*]—exhorts the young listeners to practice moral discipline and follow the dictates of heterosexual marriage. In their case, however, the words of Saint Luke will be turned against the finalities of marriage in favor of an ascetic discourse of abstinence.

Another such example is that of the amethyst cross that belonged to Jerome's mother. Jerome gives it to Alissa as a private token of his affection for her. To be worn on her person, the jewelry appropriately inscribes her body with his desire, in which narratives of religious sacrifice and "family" meet and join. Now, during an extended visit by Jerome to Alissa at the Bucolin residence during Easter vacation, the couple agrees that should Alissa wish Jerome to depart all she need do is not wear the cross, and Jerome will leave without a word of protest or even a farewell. And indeed this is what transpires the very day Jerome plans to broach again the subject of their engagement. Kevin Newmark has astutely observed that in this episode the cross is torn from the semiotic context in which it enjoyed a signifying function (the promise of the Cross and the Word, that of Easter) and now operates arbitrarily and negatively to designate—and significantly so—the deferral of the young couple's physical union.[15] In other words, the narrative of sacrifice (the crucifixion) does not lead to the fulfillment of desire (the resurrection). It is as if privatized, modernist language turned against the family in favor of the "sterile" individual; for inasmuch as the "family" and its attendant discourses are constitutive of the real—both the domestic and the public spheres—it seems that any individual reworking of public discourse disrupts the chain of familial signification whose circulating signifiers are both discourses and bodies. The nonreproduction of bourgeois discourse and the family are emplotted inseparably by the modernist text.

Heterosexuality, Commodified Literature, and Bourgeois Delights

There remains one other form of cultural inscription of desire with which Gide's novel does semiotic battle, and this one the text discredits and rejects outright: that afforded by commercial middle-class literature, one of whose authors is Abel Vautier, Jerome's classmate and friend. He tries to intervene in order to cut short Jerome and Alissa's sterile game of written deferral and to get the business of reproduction underway. His methods are as direct and straightforward as his heterosexuality:

> During the last year he had acquired some experience of women, and in consequence, put on rather a conceited and patronizing manner, which, however, did not offend me. He teased me for not having finally clinched the matter, as he expressed it, giving forth as an axiom that a woman should never be given time to go back on herself. I let him talk, but thought to myself that his excellent arguments were not applicable either to her or to me, and simply showed that he did not understand us. (522/40)

For an experienced young man like him, dilly-dallying, so to speak, with women will not do: "If you begin arguing with a woman you're lost" (522/41). He advises Jerome not to answer Alissa's second letter in writing but rather to make a surprise visit to her in order to win her hand. Interestingly, Abel's tactic will fail and Jerome is mocked by Alissa for being so "romantic" (*romanesque*; 527/47). Indeed, there is something both literary and superannuated about Abel's ideas—they smack of the bygone era of the mythical heroes of early realism. Moreover, Abel has got the plot all wrong, for he is in love with Juliette and in his virile assurance of sweeping Juliette off her feet he does not realize that Alissa's sister is in love with Jerome. His peculiar, masculine behavior is based on not only past literary practices but contemporary ones as well, namely, those of commodified fiction that perpetuates realist conventions in vulgarized form. Not surprisingly, his own best-selling book *Privautés* (Wantonness) later draws Alissa's disdain for its "folly," "indecency," and "incurable futility" (551/80), and *Le Nouvel Abailard* [The new Abelard], a play destined for a Boulevard theater, elicits her pity (551/81).

After this literary episode, Abel drops out of the picture, never to be seen again, much like Lucile who literally vanishes from both her family and the novel. Here, the novel performs on the level of diegesis what Jerome and Alissa do with cultural narratives of desire: it solicits and suspends the traditional expectations and finalities and frustrates readerly desire. The novel teases bourgeois readers by offering them tantalizingly realist figures and their conventional heterosexual plots for investment and gratification, only to withdraw them abruptly, thereby deferring realist narrative pleasure, and deferring it, not till the end of the novel, but forever. Gide's novel sketches out commonplace narrative trajectories that never reach completion: the narrative of female adultery, the outcome of which is often the birth of illegitimate children followed by the humiliation, repentance, and punishment (usually by death) of the guilty woman, and the triangles of unrequited love in which all the parties are separated in unhappy marriages. Here, the fate of the interested parties remains obscure (does Lucile fall outside of the bourgeoisie and become a *courtisane?* does Abel ever marry?) or improbable (once Juliette is married off, Jerome and Alissa still do not become engaged). Rather, the novel produces for the reader's consumption the frustrating, repetitious narrative of missed opportunities, reticent desire, and Alissa's painful religious asceticism. The latter is transmitted by Jerome primarily through her letters and private diary. Alissa and her story emerge as both realism's and popular literature's negation, modernist high literature defined as nonpleasure.

Bodies and Books: The Daughter's Text

As the family crisis grew, it was Jerome who first initiated the game of parental solicitude with Alissa (to which she would later reply); through his paternalism he constructed Alissa as the object of his sexual desire—and to that extent she looks like her mother, Aunt Lucile—but also of his will to know:

> That Alissa Bucolin was pretty, I was incapable yet of perceiving; I was drawn and held to her by a charm other than mere beauty. *No doubt she was very much like her mother*; but the expression of her eyes was so different that it was not till later that I became aware of this likeness. I cannot describe faces; the features and even the color of the eyes escape me; I can only recall the expression of her smile—a smile that was already almost sad—and the line of her eyebrows, which were so extraordinarily far from her eyes, raised above them in great circles. I have never seen any like them anywhere ... but I have though! there is a Florentine statuette of the time of Dante; and I like to fancy that Beatrice as a child had eyebrows wide-arched like hers. They gave her look, her whole being, an expression of enquiry at once anxious and trusting—yes, of passionate enquiry. She was all question and expectation. You will hear how this questioning took possession of me, became my life. (501/12, my emphasis, translation modified)

Jerome transforms the plastic sensuality of Alissa's body into a cipher; her moral authority lies in hidden meanings and ineffable psychological states whose depths remain to be fathomed. As their correspondence evolves, Jerome's attempts to interpret Alissa's questioning look will begin in earnest and shift to reading and interpreting the traces of her scripted self—her letters and messages. His inquiry, however, is doomed to failure, for as most critics agree, his relationship with Alissa is largely a circular, specular one with Alissa repeating back to him the same rhetoric of deferral and denial he first used with her and underscoring her reasons with passages drawn from literary works he had her read.[16] Jerome's hermeneutic efforts will lead him nowhere, or rather will lead from her body and mind to so many texts; this in turn will return readers back to the question of his equally baffling subjectivity, its discursive inscription, and the production of his fragmented narrative.

The female mediation of Jerome's writerly subjectivity, then, switches from that of the mother to that of the daughter, passing from the mother's body to the daughter's text. If Lucile is something of an "inverted" (so to speak) mirror of Jerome's sexual otherness, Alissa is a confirming reflection of his modernist hyperintellectuality; both place him on the margins of the bourgeois family and its discourses: the writer as cerebral bachelor/spinster.

La Porte étroite deploys the written female body of familialism as the occasion and mode of authorization of Jerome's own discourse. His tale of himself as nascent modernist writer is predicated on Alissa's letters and diary. If the "truth" of Jerome's sexuality and subjectivity is enclosed in Alissa, it is so in the form of a thoroughly semioticized female desire and body. Presumably, her desiring body in all its reticence and indirectness designates Jerome's own ambiguous position with respect to the multiple cultural narratives that discipline and guide desires in terms of the finalities of domesticity and compulsory heterosexuality; but what are her desires and her body but her letters and diary that fill up the pages of Jerome's text? Indeed, as the novel progresses, Alissa substitutes her writing for her body (she literally withers away from anorexia nervosa as ink flows from her pen), while her letters gradually supplant Jerome's own first-person narrative, a process that will reach its grim conclusion in her death and the subsequent transmission of her diary to her cousin and its inclusion in his book. This is the second of two shocks that frame Jerome's narrative (the first being his encounters with Aunt Lucile). Moreover, rather than "expressing" her "secret" self, her words write her body and her desires with words and texts not entirely her own, for they are replete with quotations drawn from the classics of the French canon and from religious literature. Alissa is constructed as colonized by dominant discourses. Indeed, her very bedroom, that space of presumably female desire and feminine interiority, is crammed with literary and devotional books.[17] The locus of the "feminine" turns out to be the space of written discourse and an entire print culture. As such, Alissa prefigures the modernist literary fate that awaits Jerome. It is in this sense that her writerly existence is a mimicry of her cousin's. To extend Said's remarks, quoted earlier, on the thematics of sterility, we can say that Alissa designates a literary impasse, the paralyzing pressure of sedimented past literary and discursive practices that were constitutive of modernism's peculiar historical situation. Alissa offers the spectacle of modernism's dilemma: the impotence of those who had tried to "make new" when faced with an unrelieved cultural closure.

So what *La Porte étroite* plays out is the drama of (failed) heterosexual desire as a discursive construct. In the end, what Jerome desires, and desires to know, is a "dysfunctional" semiotic object whose "truth" is his own. And just what "secrets" of Alissa are revealed by her diary are thus ambiguous at best. The reception of Alissa's diary takes on the trappings of an illumination that is seemingly predicated on the silencing of Jerome: "The sealed packet [*le pli cacheté*] that the lawyer sent me contained Alissa's journal. I here transcribe a considerable number of pages. I transcribe them without commentary. You will imagine well enough the reflections I made as I read, and the commotion of my heart, of which I could give only a too imperfect idea" (580/122).

Jerome hands over the hermeneutic project structuring his narrative to readers in the very gesture of replacing his voice with Alissa's own. We, too, must now make Jerome's desire, and desire to know, our own and join in the labor of deciphering the written inscriptions of the dead woman's inner life.

The generic form itself seems to promise much with respect to the dead woman's subjectivity. Béatrice Didier reminds us that diaries have always offered a generic "refuge of peace and interiority" and that along with letter-writing, private diaries have historically represented one of the few literary avenues open to women excluded from power.[18] Yet Alissa's gesture has other strong literary resonances, which complicate matters. They go back to Rousseau's *Julie, ou la Nouvelle Héloïse* [Julia, or the new Eloisa] down to Balzac's *Le Lys dans la vallée* [The lily in the valley], and look forward to Proust's *Albertine disparue* [The sweet cheat gone].[19] An unanswerable utterance from beyond the grave in all its performative facticity, Alissa's journal turns out to be just one more discursive trope that scripts her desire, as does the familial figure of hysteria (anorexia nervosa) that sends her to her grave. As Naomi Schor puts it, death is seemingly both the literary precondition and the consequence of the scriptural venting of female desire.[20]

Jerome's authority as a male writer turns on Alissa's as a female author. And literally so—for as the narration unfolds, the narrator's effort is increasingly spent quoting and recopying fragments of Alissa's correspondence. The slow superimposition of Alissa's writing on Jerome's signifies his relegation to a dependent position with respect to her written discourse, such that with the incorporation of sections of her diary at the end, Jerome is reduced to writerly silence. His discourse is dependent on one which he has no choice but to repeat and which is authored by a woman. Her words fragment and replace his own. Now insofar as *her* words are not entirely hers either but embody discredited cultural narratives of desire, her authority is no greater than the culture that has written her and thus Jerome. Or rather, the dead woman enjoys authoritative power over her cousin to the very degree that her diary writes him and his text with the story of her desires deferred and disrupted by her adoption of the very discourses that are meant to emplot it.

Indeed, that is how Alissa's diary can be read. There is a poor fit between her body and religious discourse. Her diary becomes the very tool of religious askesis, the disciplining of her body and desire through writing and reading:

> I have stopped reading the *Interior Consolation*. The old-fashioned language greatly charmed me, but it was distracting, and the almost pagan joy it gives me is far removed from the edification that I set myself to get from it. (588–89/134)

In Alissa's case this will eventually involve "repressing" her desires and purging her library of all books that remind her of Jerome:

> I have been obliged to banish from my bookshelves ...
> I fly from him in one book only to find him in another. I hear his voice reading me even those pages which I discover without him. I care only for what interests him, and my mind has taken the form of his to such an extent that I can distinguish one from the other no better than I did at the time when I took pleasure in feeling they were one. (588/133–34)

Spiritual training entails the disciplining of writing itself:

> Long interruption of this journal, which I had scarcely begun; birth of little Lise [Juliette's daughter]; long hours of watching beside Juliette; I take no pleasure in writing anything here that I can write to Jerome. *I should like to keep myself from the intolerable fault which is common to so many women—that of writing too much.* Let me consider this notebook as a means of perfection. (583/126, emphasis mine)

Finally comes the page where her desire of Jerome "speaks" most directly, of course after all hope for their engagement has vanished:

> All is over. Alas! he has slipped out of my arms like a shadow. He was here! I feel him still. I call him. My hands, my lips seek him in vain in the night ... (592/140)

Reading Alissa's diary produces another figure of desire, that of some other kind of "body" that lies perhaps "beyond" those "repressive" discourses that otherwise inscribe it. Just what that "body" might be remains unclear. The putting into discourse of Jerome's writerly self—the production of his first-person narrative—is predicated on two written female bodies; there is a displacement from one stereotype of female hysteria, the "nymphomaniac" Creole woman, to another, the "repressed," pious spinster. The narrative shifts from the ("unnatural" mother's) body to the (daughter's) book, from explosive (colonized) "nature" to atrophied (bourgeois) culture. The mirroring power of the two clichés inscribes women's bodies with the same familial discourse of desire. For Alissa ultimately continues the mother's story in a precise but inverted way: she finishes the narrative of the "fallen" adulterous mother and wife who, her penance done, dies in a hospital ward or an unfurnished garret. To the very extent that the mother mocked the paternal name and the imperatives of patriarchy, the daughter attempts to respect and adhere to them, however imperfectly. Insofar as these figures of familial pathology produce the body of the domestic mother as norm and figure of desire, they also name Jerome, his body, and his desire, as "deviant"; for the irony is that Jerome is beyond the pale of any "true" heterosexual response to either of these women. Thus the guilt that suffuses his narration: his reception of Alissa's diary "reveals" not only Alissa's unspoken desire but also his failure to fulfill the duties and obligations incumbent upon a heterosexual man. Her diary stands in accusation against him from beyond the grave: Alissa may have spoken her desire "too late" but as a "real" man, it was up to him to make a gesture, to act on his desire and close the heterosexual contract:

> What can I paint here save the occasion of the wretchedness that from that moment overwhelmed me wholly? For if I have no forgiveness in my heart today for my failure to recognize love that was still throbbing beneath the surface of false appearances; and so, no longer finding my friend, I accused her . . . (566/103, translation modified)

Jerome didn't "measure up." Outside of any genital heterosexuality yet still a "man," he exercises his prerogative to make his grief public and publish the dead woman's edited words, to let her utterances supersede his own in an act of self-accusation and penance. Here, guilt—the most interior form of lack—reconstitutes the liberal subject and normative sexuality through the figure of the *flasque* heterosexual man. (This probably goes a long way in explaining the unexpected commercial success of *La Porte étroite*.)

Still, the domestic woman (and conversely, the domestic man) no longer stands as the unqualified figure of desire produced by the diegesis; for the text carefully, almost ruthlessly eliminates all the women except Juliette: first Aunt Lucile, then Jerome's mother and Miss Ashburton, and finally Alissa. If Borie is correct in claiming that female characters are the privileged mediators of the "real" in "celibate" literature, the departure of women from the text and the fragmentation of Alissa's textual body surely proclaim modernism's radical questioning of the bourgeois body and the discursive real.[21]

La Porte étroite, then, would be the semiotic struggle to write the body differently, the inscription of the very desire to name and construct a body that lies beyond the boundaries of the discursive system of gender and sex and its literary and cultural narratives. Insofar as the latter are constituted upon the female body perhaps Alissa's death amounts to killing the "angel of the house," which for Virginia Woolf was the precondition of the aesthetic and gender ideals that discursively imprisoned women and men alike in the nineteenth century.[22]

What the body might look like is only implicitly stated. Neither productive nor reproductive, it is textually related to the figure of the hysterical (homosexual) man or woman. Jerome's writing is constituted by that of a woman and *her* utterances are shot through with the discourse of male-authored texts. In this sense their bodies, speech, and writing are ambiguously gendered. Moreover, Alissa has radically withdrawn from the circulation of women and Jerome at the very most stands on the periphery of "family" and its narratives of desire. This is the manner in which, moreover, the concluding scene of the novel must be read: protected by the social barriers of Juliette's marriage and motherhood, Jerome can safely be the object of her hysterical tears.[23] He both pays homage to the norm of "family" and stands in silent exile from its discourse.

In this modernist text the deterritorialization of the male writer is conflicted and uncertain. In other male modernist narratives, the task of scripting new bodies and desires will continue; there, the "free" bachelor will renew the picaro tradition of male friendships and adventures while wandering through Europe and on to the colonies. There, he will play out the unending crisis of bourgeois subjectivity and the isolated individual as he toys with new collective identities and ideologies.

Epilogue:
A History of the Present

Familial Discourse and Liberal, "Democratic" Culture

In the course of this book I have attempted to trace a genealogy of dominant French discourses on "family" up to the beginning of our century. I have focused especially on how familial discourse was part and parcel of a burgeoning commercial and learned print culture that sought to redraw social space, regulate bodies, and otherwise discipline multiple collective and individual practices in terms of a new master idiom of sexuality, gender, and family households. This language laid the foundation for relations between self and other in France primarily for social groups that came to see themselves as "middle class" in the frame of a larger, national imagined community.

These semiotic practices took place in local sites of print culture, from physicians' treatises on masturbation, hysteria, and sexual "deviance" to manuals of domesticity, social inquests, political commentary, and prose fiction. In their very dispersion these discourses produced an impersonal strategy consisting not of static representations and ideas but rather of direct articulations of spaces, bodies, and desires less mimetic than performative in character. To paraphrase Michel Foucault's pronouncement on "power," familial discourses constituted actions upon other discursive and non-discursive actions that destabilized and reworked identities in a field of fluid differences.

This is why I see the inscription of "lack of family" as a crucial feature of these discourses. For through the deployment of narratives and figures of abnormal, deficient, and illicit sexual and familial practices, not only does familialism produce norms and render them invisible but it also sets in motion a dynamics of social desire and flows of power that leave all identities, distinctions, and relations in flux. No one family household, profession, social class, gender identity, or political arrangement stands free of the dangers of pathological deviance or lapses issuing from within or descending from without. Nothing is settled once and for all: the frontier between the normal and the pathological remains shifting and porous, such that "lack" may erupt anytime, anywhere. "Family" and the social and gender identities that turn on it are always already in jeopardy and thus always desired as an absence.

Like "family" itself, "lack" (of being, the Phallus, proper hygiene, heterosexuality, femininity, family, what have you), then, is not the fundamental condition of desire and subjectivity (as Lacanians would have it) but rather a more banal yet powerful discursive *mechanism* and *tactic* for constructing and articulating specific bodies and spaces with particular desires in ways that both meet up with and help constitute the paradoxical nature of social relations in capitalist, "democratic" France: as I stated in the chapter on Sue's *Les Mystères de Paris*, within so-called liberal societies the desire for social mobility and equality is matched only by the dread of social disorder and the longing for stable hierarchies. In such a culture social identities must be at once elastic and open, yet reliably fixed and restrictive.

Discontinuous Narratives

The changing articulations of familial discourse have led to the discontinuous structure that organizes this book, especially Part II. Generally speaking, I follow familialism as it first targets Old Regime practices, in particular those of the aristocracy and their willful Third Estate imitators. The attacks on male primogeniture; arranged marriages; the forced celibacy of clergy, apprentices, soldiers, and servants; libertinage; mercenary wet-nursing; and so forth discredited the noble body of alluring surfaces, display, power, and pleasure and the social and gender relations for which it served as relay and support. Simultaneously, the discursive blitz also produced a new, highly gendered body, the private casing of the liberal (eventually middle-class) subject whose universal qualities of sentiment, interiority, and familial desire were presumably available to one and all, provided that one adopted the imperatives and practices of domesticity. That was the promise and attraction of Virginie once the Old Regime structures had been swept away; indeed, simply to weep over her fate constituted the first step on the royal road to a new social identity and a new society.

The next major articulation puts familialism's liberal body in contact with social threats from below—the bodies of the urban working poor, the disenfranchised peasantry of the countryside, and the newly colonized. The narrativization of these "monstrous proximities" is the fictional task of Sue's *Les Mystères de Paris*, Sand's *La Petite Fadette*, and Balzac's *Les Paysans*, as well as the semiotic labor of philanthropic treatises, social inquiries, and public hygiene investigations. Familialism's social extension in the nineteenth century scripts bodies of "others" and the spaces they inhabit with dystopic features that reformulate domesticity's normative body (its gender, sexuality, class, and race) as increasingly fragile and even compromised by the "outside." The power of familial norms to inscribe ever-widening groups of people is coextensive with these very same norms' perceived weakness and vulnerability: imperial expansion entails proliferating "dangers" which in turn authorize yet more policing, investigating, and disciplining of transgressive practices "at home," across town, and abroad.

The final shift in familial discourse constitutes something of a return to a now-etiolated bourgeoisie rife with hysterical mothers and daughters, sickly sons, unmarriageable cousins, sexual "perverts," emancipated women, and maniacal or impotent fathers. The petty details of gesture, speech, and clothing constitute the semiotic battleground on which the fates of bodies and desires—and thus that of whole family households and social classes—are determined and worked out. Through their hermeneutics of such minutiae, the writings of the new psychiatry on the one hand, and naturalist and modernist fiction on the other induce the construction of the site of "family" primarily as the psychic space of *gendered desire*.

Familial Discourse Since 1910

Insofar as *Families in Jeopardy* works as a history of the present, it asks the question to what extent familial discourse has been superseded, if it has been at all, since Gide's time. My answer will be a simple one: from 1910 to 1970 (until the advent of full-blown women's and gay liberation movements in the wake of decolonization, the civil rights movement, and student revolts) discourses of "family" have undergone *far fewer* shifts and realignments than they did between 1750 and 1910. In the twentieth century what has remained fairly constant until very recently in France (and indeed in Europe and the United States) has been familialism's set of narratives, characters, figures, and pathologies and the "celibate" cultural practices opposed to it. To the degree that "celibate" texts employ tactics like Gide's, which dramatize sexual and familial relations as deficient, lacking, or endangered, they have run the risk of being received in the conventional manner by the dominant public—namely, as calling for the establishment of normative domestic arrangements and for reinstating the age-old imperative for individuals or private and public authorities to intervene to "restore" things. And certainly literary modernism, with the help of psychoanalytic criticism, has been read as family drama and the vexed *bildungsroman* of the writing subject's sexualized interiority in the context of compulsory heterosexuality.

However, between 1910 and 1970, familial discourse ceased to be the special province of the French novel. Clearly, prose fiction never was the exclusive site of production of "family"; this book has argued that familial discourse was produced in many places across the social formation but that novels were a peculiarly effective technology of subjectivity that reached a wide, newly literate public and inscribed new subject positions as well as social geographies. During this century, the successive narratives and norms promulgated by legal and medical experts, social commentators, and novelists have passed into the daily practices of households and of public institutions commonly associated with the welfare state. Obvious examples of this in France are the legislation of 1920 following the slaughter of World War I, which banned abortion and the sale of contraceptives; the creation in the 1930s of the endless play of welfare and school counseling and assistance practices in conjunction with a watered-down form of psychoanalysis that at once suffuses family households with the incitements and expectations of traditional domesticity, weakens parental authority and household structures, targets and individuates members ("problem" children, juvenile delinquents, "domineering" housewives, etc.), and, in the case of "deviance" or noncompliance on the part of parents or children, threatens to put family households in receivership;[1] and state subsidies for child support [*les allocations familiales*] first introduced by the fascist Vichy regime in 1940 in order to encourage mothers to stay out of the work force, remain at home, and bear more children for the *patrie*.

Still, it would be misleading to focus exclusively on the interaction of family households and state agencies as the privileged sites of familial discourse in our day, for that would simply reinscribe the old narrative of state interference in the life of the home (the "fall" into the social) and thus the desire to view them as separate. On the contrary, genealogical analysis has shown us two things: first, that "family" has always been constituted by the "outside," even at the very moment when familial ideologues and social theorists have deemed it an autonomous sphere of free interiority; and, second, that "family" and its households have never existed in and for themselves but have always been a method for individuating and governing bodies. Moreover, as Michèle Barrett and Mary McIntosh remind us, even as daily practices depart from the regulative "family," familialism seems omnipresent: from the division of labor and job segregation in the workplace to insurance policies, advertisements, and travel brochures to films, TV soap operas, newscasts, mail-order catalogs, school curricula, and so on.[2] It is within this broad cultural and social matrix that familial discourse thrives, especially since feminism and gay liberation threatened to alter radically the articulation of bodies, gender, and sexuality in the 1970s.

Clearly, much has shifted over the last twenty years, provoking an outcry on the right (and even among some progressives) both in France and in the United States. In the 1970s and 1980s French demographers, journalists, and politicians like Pierre Chaunu, Jean Legrand, Georges Suffert, Michel Debré, and Albert Sauvy decried the decline in overall birthrates and the increase in illegitimate births, teenage pregnancies, and divorce, and resuscitated the old natalist rhetoric of national decadence and consequent economic catastrophe. They attributed France's current ills to the general permissiveness of consumer society, the social movements of the 1960s and 1970s (feminism in particular) and to laws legalizing the sale of contraceptives (1967) and abortion (1974).[3] Their words have fallen mostly on deaf ears and skeptics have pointed out that the Federal Republic of Germany, whose new economic ascendancy over Europe has been an endless subject of lament, had even lower birthrates.[4] Yet, at the same time, norms of "family" and domesticity have proved to be extremely resilient, but flexible. In the French context, couples or single parents raising children out of wedlock have become acceptable, parents increasingly show a general tolerance for active teenage sexuality, and in greater numbers, adult children reside with their lovers in their parents' homes while they wait out economic hard times.[5] To be sure, such a revolution in "family" attitudes has not extended to gay couples either in the private sphere or in terms of public policy. By the same token, on these shores, an unprecedented number of family households are single-parent, or include not only stepchildren and stepparents issuing from divorces but also surrogate parents;[6] and the discourse of domesticity enjoys a powerful appeal to gay men and lesbian women who wish to script their lives in terms of its norms, promises, and the satisfactions of parenting.[7]

Are we witnessing yet another shift in familial discourse of the same magnitude as when in the nineteenth century serial novels and social philanthropy extended the promises of domesticity and its imagined community to the urban laboring classes and the poor peasantry? Do the new household arrangements in France and the United States announce a postmodern normative "family" and new forms of governance that no longer insist on marriage or even heterosexuality but rather on the couple, qualities of intimacy, and attentive child care in a "middle-class" setting? Or, on the contrary, is the discourse of "lack" (deviance, pathology, deficiency, and loss) simply no longer productive, so that it is now succumbing to a rival discourse of "diversity" (which the new president, Bill Clinton, appears to support)? This is an open question, which certainly worries cultural conservatives who wish at once to preserve the older regulative family household (often reconstructed along the lines of a mythical patriarchy) and to control what it means to belong to the "nation" and its imagined community of citizens.

Thus, as of this writing, the cultural politics of bodies, sexuality, gender, and "family" has reached unprecedented intensity in the United States. Conservatives and the religious right, with the help of some liberals, are expending considerable energy to reimpose normative household and bodily practices that owe their origin to familial discourse of the nineteenth century. *Roe vs. Wade* may well be irreparably weakened by the time of this study's publication. During the 1992 presidential campaign, candidate H. Ross Perot served notice to the nation that he would refuse to appoint homosexuals and adulterers to sensitive cabinet posts.* And new obscenity

* It is worth noting that Republican political strategist Kevin Phillips, author of his party's highly successful strategy of emphasizing divisive "moral" issues in their campaigns since 1968, pointed out that Perot's remarks may have cost him votes in the June 1992 California primary. Phillips did not elaborate, but I think it is safe to say that Perot's comments offended not only conservative gays, who may have wanted to vote for him (Log Cabin Republicans), but, more importantly, heterosexual voters. It seems that Perot departed from the very effective familial rhetoric of the religious right that has stigmatized primarily gay sexuality, carefully dissociating it from the sin of adultery. Clearly, the "othering" of adulterers along with gays in a state with one of the highest divorce

laws and antipornography legislation targeting visual culture in general and the art world in particular have dropped the tactic of defining "obscenity" in terms of explicitness—which failed miserably in court battles over printed matter—and have now sought to redefine as obscene specific sexual acts (sadomasochism, sodomy, etc.) and representations that presumably encourage homosexuality.[8] Even yuppies, mythically known for their 1980s fast lifestyles disdainful of conventional domesticity, are being induced to return to "family": on the ideological level, witness the numerous films on adultery (*Fatal Attraction*) and mercenary child care (the evil nannies and child abusers in *The Babysitter* and *The Hand That Rocks the Cradle*) and, on the level of daily practices, the McMartin day-care scandal in Los Angeles.[9] The moral panic that ensued in California during and after the McMartin trial, which constructed day-care personnel as professional child molesters, has had the unexpected effect of reversing the diciplining gaze: day-care centers and their employees are now under orders from the State of California to report to the police any signs of child abuse *in their charges' homes*. Thus from first being the objects of suspicion these government-licensed private organizations, which have stood as unworthy surrogates of parental care, have been transformed into familial agents of the state, with the result that the same professional classes who accused day-care personnel of child abuse now find themselves the objects of unwanted scrutiny, denunciation, and criminal investigation.

Familial Discourse, "Multiculturalism," and National Community

Most powerfully, familial discourse has returned in force during the so-called multicultural 1980s and 1990s in major struggles over definitions of national community and identity in the context of government budget cuts and recurring economic recessions, on the

---

rates in the country strikes too close to "home"; see Kevin Phillips, "G.O.P. Crackup," *New York Times*, June 4, 1992, A19. Thanks to Steve Shaviro for bringing this to my attention.

one hand, and, on the other, of a new space of world communications in which, according to Etienne Balibar, a French political theorist,

> all populations are somehow immediately "visible" to, and in contact with, one another. . . . they interpenetrate more and more within the same space of communications, representations, and life. Exclusion takes the form of *internal exclusion at the world level*: precisely the configuration which, since the beginnings of the modern era, has fueled not only xenophobia or fear of foreigners, but also racism and hatred of *neighbors* who are near and different at the same time.[10]

In these heated debates nonnormative sexual practices have often been made to intersect with race and geography. Thus, as is well known to many readers of this book, with the onset of the AIDS pandemic scientists, physicians, and commentators in the media in France and the United States constructed the HIV virus as a "gay cancer" or "gay disease" whose origins could presumably be traced back to Africa. For Simon Watney, a British cultural critic and AIDS activist, this age-old configuration of "nonnatural" sexuality with nonwhite peoples can only be understood today in the framework of "the changing organization of sexual and racial boundaries in the West." He wrote in 1988:

> This new politics aspires to realign national/popular identities, replacing the vulnerable barriers of class identities, which can no longer be easily policed, with strongly pathologized distinctions between "normality" and "perversion." As Europe draws together in the likeness of a federation and the Soviet Union is increasingly accepted as a legitimate nation-state, Africa has been effectively demonized in post-colonial discourse of perpetual catastrophe and *unnatural* disasters. This undifferentiated apocalyptic Africa has proved an ideal site in which to find and "see" a disease.[11]

Thus, until very recently, in the United States scientific reports and popular media accounts of the AIDS pandemic have reinscribed an imagined national community divided between a supposedly safe "general population" (read heterosexual, white, and suburban) that truly belongs to the nation and the expendable persons with AIDS and IV drug users (read gay, Black, Latino, and urban) who scarcely merit allocation of national resources to ensure their survival.[12] Similarly, the "War on Drugs" in the United States has been engraved in the public imagination in terms of "promiscuous" Black and Latino mothers by contemporary visual and print narratives. Finally, there has been a revival of scapegoating Black family households for the poverty of African-Americans (first begun in 1965 by the publication of the Labor Department study, "The Negro Family: The Case for National Action," directed by the then Harvard sociologist Daniel Patrick Moynihan) that started with Bill Moyer's televised documentary entitled "The Vanishing Black Family—Crisis in Black America" (broadcast January 26, 1986); this culminated in Vice-President Dan Quayle's attack on the (white) TV star Candice Bergen's sympathetic portrayal of a single mother's pregnancy. In the spirit of philanthropic thinking dating from the 1830s, Quayle blamed such household and sexual practices among the Black community for the Los Angeles rebellion of May 1992 that followed the acquittal of police officers involved in the Rodney King beating.*

That the rearticulation of familial discourse with (post)colonial discourse works primarily to reconfigure the "nation" is most notoriously demonstrated in France by Jean-Marie Le Pen and his National Front party, who have appropriated demographers' rhetoric of national decline in terms of very successful xenophobic law-and-order appeals to the white electorate. They blame high unemployment, drugs, and crime on North African immigrant workers and

---

* Quayle's remarks meshed perfectly with the overwhelming tendency of the media to report the Los Angeles rebellion as "Black," whereas anyone with eyes could detect in the biased images served up to viewers and readers that the revolt was Latino, even white and Asian-American, as well as Black. Almost two months later, it was then revealed that over half of those arrested by the LAPD were Latino, while 36 percent were African-American and 11 percent "white" (no mention if this figure includes Asian-Americans). See "Fifty-One Percent of Arrested Hispanic," *San Diego Union*, June 20, 1992, A3. All of which suggests that class as well as race was an important factor in the rebellion. On Moynihan's report and on scapegoating Black family households consult "Scapegoating the Black Family," *Nation*, July 24–31, 1989 (Special Issue); and for a summary of Quayle's comments see "Quayle Deplores Eroding Values; Cites TV Show," *Los Angeles Times*, May 20, 1992 (San Diego County Ed.), A1.

their French-born children [*les Beurs*] who are also accused of burdening the welfare and school systems and—nothing less—of carrying the HIV virus.* Moreover, Le Pen and his followers have even revived anti-Semitic rhetoric in an attempt to link AIDS, gays, and Jews: they have coined a term for people with AIDS [*SIDA*], "*les sidaïques*," which directly echoes the old French adjective *judaïque* long favored by the political discourse of French fascists in the 1930s and 1940s.[13]

Familial Discourse and the New Technosciences

Lastly, the site of production—or perhaps dismantling—of familial discourse is to be found more and more in the new medical and biological sciences and technologies, if only because they have undergone unprecedented expansion in the last ten years. Generally, genetics has contributed to the publicizing of concepts of gender and sexual difference of the most conventional kind, particularly as they are reformulated by sociobiologists.[14] Likewise, neurobiology has entered the limelight of late. Simon LeVay, a gay researcher at the Salk Institute, affiliated with the University of California, San Diego, where I teach and work, announced to the press in August 1991 his discovery that the hypothalamus gland in the brains of presumably gay men (nineteen of whose bodies were conveniently made available to his laboratory thanks to the AIDS pandemic) is half the size of that of presumably heterosexual men and approximate in size to that of presumably heterosexual women (LeVay omitted to study the brains of lesbians). Happy to report his findings to the nation, LeVay claimed that homosexuality resulted not from moral lapses or psychological disorder but from physiological determinants, thereby safely removing sexual orientation from the realm of moralizing

---

* The ugliest formulation of this idea was the slogan "Socialisme *I*mmigration *D*rogue et *A*ffairisme" that appeared on political posters. A court decreed in 1991 that the National Front pull them down and withdraw them from circulation, and fined the party 1,000 francs for each infraction. Its decision was later overturned on appeal. See "Le Front national condamné pour usage abusif du mot 'sida,'" *Le Monde*, Jan. 28, 1991, p. 20.

debate. Of course, what LeVay has done is to replicate the strategy of familial discourse that assigns "lack" to nonnormative behaviors, thus not only pathologizing but essentializing them as well. Here, he has replaced psychological deficiency or deviance with a physiological one (the hypothalamus gland substituting itself for the older but equally measurable penis and clitoris) as if that constituted a resolution to the debate over sexual orientation. LeVay overlooks the fact that biological and psychological explanations have never been mutually exclusive in the discourse of "family," but oftentimes have reciprocally authorized each other in the framework of "sin," biology here being the definitive mark of moral "depravity."[15]

More ambiguously, the new reproductive technologies, while destabilizing conventional meanings of motherhood and shifting the focus onto the fetus, have been subsumed by an older ideology of domesticity, gender, and even class, as the fate of working-class surrogate mother Mary Beth Whitehead of the Baby M case amply demonstrates.[16] Still, "motherhood" and "family" are denaturalized every day through the new technosciences, and it is by no means clear that any recognizable familial discourse will survive. And while the perinatal technologies of fetal monitoring not only have contributed to transforming the fetus into a "person" but also have occasioned intense surveillance of women's bodies (as potential "containers" of fetuses) in the workplace (exclusion of women but not men from jobs that are deemed hazardous), in restaurants (harassment of pregnant women who consume alcohol, tobacco, or caffeine), and in their homes (diet, substance abuse), it is not certain that other technologies will not provide avenues for circumventing disciplinary measures.[17] In France one such example is the RU-486 "abortion pill" developed by Roussel-Uclaf S.A., which, after first deciding not to market the pill in response to pressure from conservatives and the Catholic Church, was ordered to distribute the pill by the government which also promised to reimburse women for their prescriptions.[18]

The future of familial discourse in France and the United States is not simply a question of whether "representations" continue to circulate or repressive measures continue to be enacted; what is also at issue is whether "family" can persist in producing bodies through concrete practices of positive inducements relayed by a master language of sexuality, gender, home, and work that, through tales of lack and loss, accounts for all that matters in individual and collective life.

Reference Matter

Notes

Complete authors' names, titles, and publication data for sources cited in short form in the notes are given in the Works Cited, pp. 335–49.

Introduction

1. Pinel, p. 141. Quoted by Michel Foucault, *Histoire de la folie à l'âge classique*, pp. 513–14; emphasis and translation mine.
2. See Latour, *Science in Action*.
3. See B. Anderson. The normative family can also be seen as a product of those social processes that "invent" traditions; see Hobsbawn and Ranger.
4. I borrow the word from Gilles Deleuze and Félix Guattari; see their *Anti-Oedipus*, particularly chapter 3, "Psychanalysm and Familialism: the Holy Family," pp. 51–137.
5. Laclau and Mouffe, p. 96.
6. Ibid., pp. 95–96, 111–12.
7. The figure drops to 5 percent of U.S. households if one adds the condition—belonging to a still older ideal—that the present marriage is the first and only one for either partner; see L. Anderson. Thanks to Mark Salfi for the reference.
8. Armstrong, p. 251.
9. See Hartouni, pp. 27–56.
10. Deleuze and Guattari, pp. 72–73. In fact, it would not at all be misplaced to accuse psychoanalytic theory of a base realism of its own insofar as the Law of the Father and the Phallus as master signifier constitute bedrock, unvarying truths of selfhood of the last instance.
11. Foucault, *An Introduction*, pp. 80–91, 144–45.
12. See Guizot and Du Camp.
13. Habermas, *The Structural Transformation of the Public Sphere: An*

Inquiry into a Category of Bourgeois Society; Donzelot, *The Policing of Families*; Lasch, *Haven in a Heartless World*; and Sennett, *The Fall of Public Man: On the Social Psychology of Capitalism*.

14. See Rapp, Ross, and Bridenthal, p. 177; Barrett, p. 186.
15. On Lasch and Donzelot see Engel and also Barrett and McIntosh, pp. 95–105, 110–24; on Habermas consult Landes, pp. 18–50.
16. Donzelot, *Policing*, p. 92.
17. See comments by Barrett and McIntosh, p. 103.
18. Habermas, p. 28.
19. Ibid., pp. 175–80.
20. Ibid., pp. 175–76.
21. Ibid., pp. 25, 27, 28, 51, 104, 176, and so on.
22. Ibid., pp. 50–51, my emphasis.
23. Ibid., p. 51.
24. As in the following sentence: "To the degree to which commodity exchange burst out of the confines of the household economy, the sphere of the conjugal family became differentiated from the sphere of social reproduction" (ibid., p. 28).
25. See Landes, pp. 18–50.
26. See, for example, Macherey; and Deleuze and Guattari.
27. See Nicholson, pp. 16–30.
28. Such a field is science studies where, according to Donna Haraway, scholars and scientists are increasingly comfortable with the idea of scientific practices as "war"; see Haraway, *Simians*, pp. 183–201.
29. Bersani; Prendergast; Frappier-Mazur; Felman; Jameson, *Political Unconscious*; Tanner; Brooks, *Reading for the Plot*; Schor; Terdiman; Stallybrass and White; Hertz; Beizer, *Family Plots*; Bernheimer; Mozet; Apter, *Feminizing the Fetish*.
30. Scott, p. 94.
31. Armstrong, p. 10.
32. See, in particular, Bloch et al.
33. For an example of such an approach to novels as performative rhetoric see D. A. Miller.

Chapter 1

1. Hunt, *Politics, Culture, and Class*; Landes; Okin; and Outram.
2. On this matter see Armstrong, pp. 59–95.
3. On the concept of "sex/gender system" as that form whereby cultural constructions of gender are naturalized through biological sexual difference, see Rubin's classic essay "The Traffic in Women: Notes on the 'Political Economy' of Sex."
4. Foucault, *An Introduction*; Donzelot, *Policing*; Deleuze and Guattari; Corbin, *Les Filles de Noce*; and Aron and Kempf.

5. B. Anderson.
6. Moheau, p. 197.
7. Rousseau, p. 258.
8. Foucault, *An Introduction*, p. 68; Donzelot, *Policing*, pp. 16–17; Joseph, Fritsch, and Battegay, pp. 56–57; Knibielher and Fouquet, p. 135.
9. B. Anderson, p. 74. On the new print culture in France (new production techniques, distribution systems, reading publics, etc.) see Landes, pp. 50–61; *Histoire de l'édition française*, 2: 545–57, 606–21 and 3: 24–45, 57–67, 103–21, 261–67; *Histoire générale de la presse française* 2: 13–28.
10. Flandrin, *Families*, pp. 170–72; Dianne Alstad, "The Ideology of the Family in Eighteenth-Century France," pp. 69–73, 96–114, 238–47.
11. de Cervol, pp. 27–28.   12. Messance, p. 27
13. See also Moheau, pp. 68–69.   14. Ibid.
15. "Célibat," *Encyclopédie*; Flandrin, *Families*, p. 240.
16. Moheau, p. 252.
17. Quoted by Knibielher and Fouquet, p. 145.
18. Moheau, pp. 258–59.
19. Donzelot, *Policing*, pp. 13–15.
20. Knibielher and Fouquet, pp. 144–45.
21. Ibid., pp. 70–78, 135–55. See also Ehrenreich and English, p. 30.
22. Verdier-Heurtin, p. 27; cited by Badinter, p. 193.
23. Laqueur, p. 24.
24. Quoted by Knibielher and Fouquet, p. 152.
25. Donzelot, *Policing*, pp. 23–25.
26. See Armstrong, pp. 61–75.
27. Agulhon, pp. 7–53; Knibielher and Fouquet, p. 156; Hunt, *Politics, Culture, and Class*, pp. 58–67; Landes, pp. 158–68.
28. Robespierre, pp. 376–77.   29. Saint-Just, p. 165.
30. Flandrin, *Families*, p. 117.   31. Foucault, *Discipline*, pp. 113–14.
32. Balzac, *Mémoires*, pp. 242–43.
33. du Voisin, p. 75. Quoted by Darrow, p. 55.
34. Cited in Demel, p. 105.
35. Indeed, Joan Scott has shown that in the protosociological studies of the day *femmes-isolées* designated both independent women workers and prostitutes. See pp. 142–43. All of chapter 7, entitled "'L'ouvrière! Mot impie, sordide . . .': Women Workers in the Discourse of French Political Economy, 1840–1860" (pp. 139–63) is essential reading on this topic.
36. Landes, p. 147, and for her remarks on revolutionary feminist discourse see pp. 126–27, 167–68.
37. "Aux Républicaines," as cited by Duhet, pp. 205–6.
38. Duhet, p. 206.
39. Armengaud, 3: 175.
40. Quoted by Albistur, pp. 140–48.

41. Necker de Sassure, 1: 1–2, emphasis mine.
42. Ibid., 3: 33.
43. Darrow, pp. 41–43.
44. Ibid., p. 42.
45. Pope.
46. Mme. Pariset, p. 6.
47. Lajolais, p. 23.
48. Ibid., p. 99.
49. Madame de Flesselles, p. 25.
50. Aimé-Martin, 2: 470.
51. See note 9 to this chapter. Supplementing and extending the discursive work of lengthy treatises on child education and home economics, there arose in the course of the nineteenth century numerous women's magazines, a voluminous children's literature written by women (a major author was Zulma Carraud, one of Balzac's closest friends), as well as the "domestic novel," of which the best-known authors were Joséphine de Gaulle (1806–86, the grandmother of Charles de Gaulle), Mathilde Bourdon (1817–88), and Julia Bécour (1840–1917). In the latter narratives, large, extended households were appropriately rare and female rule was undivided: fathers were almost always absent. See Knibielher and Fouquet, pp. 179–81. For the domestic novel see Smith, chapter 8, "The Domestic Myth," pp. 187–213.

52. Necker de Sassure, 1: 6, my emphasis; she reiterates the same point later in the third volume (3: 5–6).

53. As determined from the catalogue of the Bibliothèque Nationale, Paris; see also Fox-Genovese and Genovese, pp. 304–5. Chapter 11 in its entirety, "The Ideological Bases of Domestic Economy: The Representation of Women and the Family in the Age of Expansion," (pp. 299–336) is of greatest interest.

54. This section owes much to Nancy Armstrong's work on domestic budgets in British conduct manuals; see pp. 81–88.

55. Le Bègue de Prasle and the Abbé Lalauze, I: xvii–xviii.
56. Le Bègue de Prasle and Lalauze, 1, part II: xiv–xv; my emphasis.
57. Le Bèque de Prasle and Lalauze, 1: xxv.
58. See, for example, Necker de Sassure, 2: 480–81.
59. Pope, pp. 369–71; Knibielher and Fouquet, pp. 195–96; and Hellerstein, p. 383.
60. *Bibliothèque des propriétaires*, pp. 178–79.
61. Mesdames Pariset and Celnart, p. 5.
62. Lajolais, p. 37.
63. Quoted by Ronsin, p. 25.
64. Lajolais, p. 99.
65. Gacon-Dufour, p. 188.
66. Ibid., pp. 212–13.
67. Hellerstein, p. 383.
68. Ariès, pp. 450–530.
69. Smith, pp. 45, 55, 65–71, 78, 79.
70. Ibid., pp. 79–80.
71. Necker de Sassure, 2: 347–48.
72. McBride, pp. 26–30; Joseph et al., pp. 109–10, 121, 295–97; Hellerstein.

73. Stallybrass and White, p. 20.
74. Joseph et al., p. 281.
75. See Gallop, "Keys to Dora," pp. 200–220.
76. Bernardin de Saint-Pierre, *Voyage à l'île de France*, p. 114.
77. Tissot, pp. 119–20. As quoted in Aron and Kempf, p. 62.
78. Flandrin, *Families*, pp. 194–96.
79. M. Lallemand, 1: 630. My attention was first brought to this passage by Aron and Kempf, p. 206; on the Orientalist connotations of masturbation, see Aron and Kempf, pp. 194–95.
80. M. Lallemand, 1: 409.
81. Lanteri-Laura, p. 16.
82. Féré, *L'instinct sexuel*, pp. 322–23, my emphasis. Of course, the most famous exposition of this thesis is by R. von Krafft-Ebing, pp. 286, 389.
83. H. Lauvergne, pp. 288–89; quoted by Aron and Kempf, pp. 87–88.
84. Zola, "Preface," p. 4.
85. Aron and Kempf, p. 57.
86. J. Chevalier, pp. 219–20, 227.
87. Krafft-Ebing, pp. 282–84, my emphasis.
88. J. Chevalier, pp. 486–87.
89. Laupts, p. 168; and Krafft-Ebing, pp. 285–86.
90. Butler, p. 12.
91. Abelove.
92. See Rubin and Butler.
93. Knibielher, pp. 838–43.
94. Veith, p. 178.
95. Briquet, pp. 35, 36.
96. Ibid., p. vii.
97. Ibid., pp. 49, 50.
98. Beizer, *Ventriloquized Bodies*; Briquet, pp. 48–51.
99. On the notion of discursivity, in particular "social" discursivity as a shifting process of suturing identities in their porousness and openness to the outside, see Laclau and Mouffe, pp. 86, 108–9, 111, 170–71.
100. Krohn, pp. 188–89.
101. Didi-Hubermann; Charles Bernheimer, Preface.

Chapter 2

1. Sewell, pp. 36–37; Thompson, pp. 56–97.
2. de Gérando, *De la bienfaisance publique*, 4: 536.
3. Quoted by Castel, pp. 120–21.
4. Castel, p. 120; see also Doerner.
5. Tilly, p. 88. L. Chevalier's title mimics those of two important treatises of the July Monarchy with no traceable irony: Buret, *De la misère des classes laborieuses en Angleterre et en France* [On the poverty of laboring classes in England and France] (1841) and Frégier, *Des classes dangereuses de la population des grandes villes, et des moyens de les rendre meilleures* [On

the dangerous classes of the population of great cities and the ways of improving them] (1840).

6. Tilly, p. 104.
7. Corbin, *The Foul and the Fragrant*, pp. 53–56, 155–56.
8. See Furet; and Scott, pp. 1–11, 113–38.
9. "Prospectus," 1: Part I: v. On the biological model see Foucault, *An Introduction*, and Rabinow.
10. "Prospectus," pp. vi–vii.
11. Ibid., p. vii.
12. See Coleman; and Latour, *The Pasteurization of France*.
13. See Delaporte. 14. Shapiro, pp. xiii–xiv.
15. de Lajolais, pp. 96, 97. 16. See Benjamin.
17. Corbin, *Les Filles*; Bernheimer, *Figures of Ill-Repute*.
18. See Habermas; Donzelot, *Policing* and *L'Invention du social*; see also my remarks in the Introduction.
19. See Donzelot, *Policing*, pp. 42–48, 58–63, 93; Joseph et al., pp. 83–97; Vigarello, pp. 192–201.
20. Joseph et al., pp. 31–32, 51, 56, 101.
21. de Gérando, *De la bienfaisance publique*, 3: 337.
22. Ibid., 3: 354. 23. Ibid., 3: 379.
24. See B. Anderson. 25. Prost, pp. 92–93.
26. Guizot, pp. 139–41.
27. Du Camp, *Paris: ses organes*, 4: 71.
28. Villeneuve-Bargemont, *Economie politique chrétienne* (1834), 3: 158–59. Quoted by Joseph et al., p. 257.
29. Quoted by Armengaud, 3: 175.
30. Scott, p. 136.
31. Villermé, p. 74.
32. On ethnographic practices and writing see James Clifford's essay "On Ethnographic Authority."
33. de Gérando, *The Observation of Savage Peoples*.
34. de Gérando, *De la bienfaisance publique*, 4: 244.
35. Ibid., 1: x–xi.
36. On the concept of "virtual witnessing" as a tool for producing truth for and eliciting consent by absent observers, see Shapin and Schaffer, p. 60.
37. de Gérando, *De la bienfaisance publique*, 1: xi.
38. Ibid.
39. For recent views of the aesthetics of melodrama which emphasize its conservative and stabilizing effects, see Brooks, *The Melodramatic Imagination*, and Prendergast.
40. Parent-Duchâtelet, *De la prostitution dans la ville de Paris* (originally

published Paris: Baillière, 1836), 2: 495, 513. This passage is quoted by Corbin, *Les Filles*, pp. 15, 30.

41. Esquiros, p. 69; quoted by Corbin, *Les Filles*, p. 21.
42. Parent-Duchâtelet, *De la prostitution*, pp. 97–99, 105–6, 193; Corbin, *Les Filles*, pp. 22–23.
43. Corbin, Introduction, pp. 13–15, 38–41.
44. See Stallybrass and White, pp. 125–48. In this regard see the title of Maxime Du Camp's famous book on Paris, *Paris: ses organes, ses fonctions, sa vie de la seconde moitié du XIXe siècle*.
45. Gobineau, 1: 143.
46. Du Camp, 6: 387.
47. Borie, *Mythologies*, p. 170.
48. Le Bon, p. 19; quoted by Borie, *Mythologies*, pp. 182–83.
49. Morel, pp. 353, 461; quoted by Borie, *Mythologies*, p. 116.
50. Féré, *La Famille névropathique*, p. 36.
51. Moreau de Tours, p. 305; quoted by Borie, *Mythologies*, pp. 90–91.
52. Krafft-Ebing, p. 375.
53. Du Camp, *Paris*, 6: 362. 54. Ibid., 3: 381.
55. Ibid., 3: 359, 380. 56. Ibid., 3: 356.
57. Corbin, *Les Filles*, pp. 182, 186, 259, 296–97.
58. Ronsin, p. 126 n. 12.
59. Corbin, *Les Filles*, pp. 387–89.
60. Huysmans, p. 137.
61. Corbin, *Les Filles*, pp. 391–94.
62. (Paris: 1889), p. 164; as quoted by Corbin, *Les Filles*, p. 43, n. 102.
63. On "distinction" see Jean-Paul Sartre, *L'Idiot de la famille*, 3: 245–48, 283–89, 304.
64. Sartre, *Qu'est ce que*, p. 213.
65. Donzelot, *Policing*, p. 42.
66. Shapiro, pp. 132–33.
67. Scott, pp. 93–112; see also McMillan.
68. Aimé-Martin, 1: 48.
69. Necker de Sassure, 3: 38–39.
70. Paul Rabinow drew my attention to this text in his *French Modern*, pp. 21–23.
71. Evans-Pritchard, Preface, p. x.
72. de Gérando, *The Observation*, pp. 63–64, emphasis mine.
73. Buret, *Question d'Afrique*, p. 2.
74. Ibid., p. 18. 75. Ibid., p. 19.
76. Montagnier. 77. Said, public lecture.
78. Corbin, *Les Filles*, p. 142; see Lombroso and also Ferrero, *La femme criminelle et la prostituée* (1896).

79. Louyer-Villermay.
80. *Grand Dictionnaire*, s.v. "pédérastie."
81. Tardieu, p. 205.
82. J. Chevalier, pp. 128–31.
83. Lallemand, 1: 646; quoted by Aron and Kempf, *Le Pénis*, pp. 194–95.
84. Ibid., 3: 475.
85. Latour, *The Pasteurization of France*, pp. 111–45.
86. Poskin, p. v. 87. Ibid., p. vi.
88. Canguilhem, p. 239. 89. Said, *Orientalism*, pp. 181–92.
90. Flaubert, 11: 49; Terdiman quotes part of this passage in *Discourse/Counter-Discourse*, p. 243.
91. See Terdiman, pp. 256–57. On the concept of "bachelor" or celibate literature, which I borrow from Edward Said and Jean Borie, see Chapter 8, on Gide's *La Porte étroite*.

Chapter 3

1. Trahard, pp. xxvi–xxxii.
2. Only Fenelon's didactic romance *Télémaque*, first published in 1699 for the edification of the Duke of Burgundy, went through more editions (576). See Goulemot, "L'Histoire littéraire en question," p. 205.
3. For the provocative thesis that in Europe and North America the modern, liberal subject was first and foremost a (middle-class) female, see Armstrong, pp. 77–95.
4. The term is Benedict Anderson's and has already enjoyed a rich career among scholars of nationalism and national cultures; see B. Anderson.
5. For extended remarks on this matter by historians of the French Revolution see Landes, pp. 104–5, 172; and Hunt, "The Unstable Boundaries of the French Revolution."
6. Laclau and Mouffe, pp. 86, 108–9, 111, 170–71. In a similar vein Landes considers the new discursivity of the social in terms of a long process of "textualization of life" that accelerated in the late eighteenth century; Landes, pp. 11, 50–52, 173, 288–89.
7. See Showalter.
8. Racault, "Proposition d'une relecture de *Paul et Virginie*," p. 14.
9. Trahard, p. xxvi n. 1.
10. Prost, pp. 92–93.
11. Goulemot, p. 209.
12. Quoted by Racault, "Balzac et Bernardin de Saint-Pierre," p. 203.
13. Bernardin de Saint-Pierre, *Discours*, 1: 456.
14. Ibid., 1: 470.
15. Racault, "Pastorale et roman," pp. 179–80.

16. Fabre, pp. 167–99.
17. Panofsky, pp. 301–13.
18. See Caplan, esp. pp. 20–25.
19. Trahard, p. xxvii.
20. See D. A. Miller, p. 148.
21. For summary of the structures and functions of the alliance system that predominated among Old Regime nobility, see Donzelot, *Policing*, pp. 23–26; Armstorng, pp. 61–75. For an interpretation of *Paul et Virginie* in the narrow terms of Freudian family romance, see Hunt, *The Family Romance*, pp. 29–31.
22. Alain, pp. 326, 336.
23. Bernardin de Saint-Pierre, *Paul et Virginie*, p. 84; *Paul and Virginia*, p. 42, translation modified. Subsequent references to the novel will appear in the text: the first number refers to the French original and the second to the English translation.
24. See Donzelot and Smith.
25. Borie, *Le Célibataire*, p. 144.
26. Carter, p. 60.
27. Deleuze and Guattari, p. 270.
28. For the reproduction of familial desire through structures of parenting and the gender division of labor, see Chodorow.
29. For a thorough investigation of the new discursive valences attached to the female body in terms of reproductive biology and gender, see Laqueur.
30. Quoted by Racault, "Virginie entre la nature et la vertu," p. 389.
31. Flandrin, *Families*, pp. 15–18.
32. See Landes, pp. 134–35, 158–59, 205–6; and Caplan.
33. Borie, *Le Célibataire*, 64–66.
34. Landes, pp. 131–34.
35. See Outram, pp. 48–51, 86, 125–27, 158.
36. Also, we must remember that in medical literature at this time female orgasm was no longer considered a necessary precondition for conception. See Knibielher and Fouquet, p. 152; and Laqueur, p. 1.
37. Williams, p. 65.
38. Cited by Landes, p. 186.
39. Mylne, pp. 245–62.
40. D. A. Miller, p. 25.
41. Smith, pp. 65–71.

Chapter 4

1. Laclau and Mouffe, p. 96.
2. Ibid., pp. 95–96, 112.
3. For accounts of *Les Mystères*'s fabulous success see Orecchioni, pp. 157–66; and Bory, pp. 243–56.
4. Bory, pp. 272–86; see also Thiesse.
5. B. Anderson, pp. 34–35.
6. Ibid., pp. 39–40.
7. Marx and Engels, pp. 192–208.
8. Eco, pp. 137–40; Brooks, *Reading for the Plot*, pp. 146–66.

9. Eco, p. 141.
10. See, for example, Jochen Schulte-Sasse's critical review of Michael Denning's *Mechanic Accents: Dime Novels and Working-Class Culture in America* (London: Verso, 1987); he faults the book's use of Volosinov's notion of "accented speech."
11. McMillan, p. 14.
12. Throughout his text Nettement employs indiscriminately the terms *feuilleton-roman* and *roman-feuilleton* when speaking of serial novels.
13. Nettement, 2: 445.
14. Ibid., 2: 446–47.
15. Ibid., 1: 263.
16. Quoted by Olivier-Martin, p. 45.
17. Bory, p. 262.
18. Sue, *Les Mystères*, 1: 15; *The Mysteries*, p. 3, translation modified. It should be noted that this translation is imperfect, for many passages have either been excised or embroidered upon. Subsequent references to Sue's novel will be given in the text, citing the French edition first and then (for quoted passages only) the English translation.
19. D. A. Miller, p. 77.
20. Nettement, 1: 327.
21. Ibid., 2: 453–54.
22. See L. Chevalier, pp. 58–73.
23. See Buisine, pp. 29–30.
24. See Corbin, *Les Filles*.
25. Prendergast, pp. 62–63.
26. Marx and Engels, pp. 198–208.
27. Prendergast, pp. 175–76.
28. Eco, p. 137.

Chapter 5

1. See Sainte-Beuve, 2: 445–71; the essay, "De la littérature industrielle" (On industrial literature), was first published in 1839. Balzac's *roman-feuilleton* was *La Vieille fille* [The spinster], published in Emile de Girardin's *La Presse* in 1836; see Guise.
2. Balzac, *Les Paysans*, 9: 49; *The Peasants*, pp. 3–4. Subsequent references to *Les Paysans* will be given in the text, citing the French edition first and then (for quoted passages only) the English translation.
3. The word is Fredric Jameson's; see Jameson, *Political Unconscious*, p. 169.
4. L. Chevalier, "Preface," pp. 23–25; for Pierre Macherey's comments on the novel's realism, see Macherey, pp. 319–20. For a recent constructionist and feminist critique of nineteenth-century French statistics, see Scott, pp. 113–38.
5. Jameson, *Political Unconscious*, pp. 151–52. The entire third chapter, "Realism and Desire: Balzac and the Problem of the Subject" (pp. 151–84), is of greatest interest. Georg Lukács's major statement on realism is of course his *Studies in European Realism*.
6. See Macherey, pp. 259–60.
7. On the connections between nineteenth-century melodrama and the

familial consult Brooks, *The Melodramatic Imagination*, pp. 31–35, 42–44, 86–87; and Prendergast, pp. 68–82, 135–44, 175–79.

8. Ariès, pp. 450–53.

9. Borie, *Le Célibataire*, pp. 64–66.

10. On familial discourse's overdetermination of social inquests of the period see Joseph et al., pp. 275–77.

11. On the prospect of female eroticism's resurgence in the midst of "dead time" in domestic life, see Pope, p. 373.

12. Macherey, 269–72, 278–86.

13. The most complete treatment of discourse on the (male) sexualized child is to be found in Aron and Kempf.

14. Peter Fitting is correct to point out that the social conflict takes the form of threats against the château's women. What he fails to remark is that the text also codes the social menace as *feminine* in origin. See Fitting, p. 189.

15. See note 7 to this chapter.

16. Lukács, p. 39.

Chapter 6

1. Laqueur, p. 24.

2. See Smith on domestic novels of the 1860s, where there is the opposite deauthorization of men and the public sphere; Smith, pp. 187–213.

3. See Armstrong.

4. Sand, *La Petite Fadette*, pp. 15–16, emphasis mine; *Fadette*, pp. 5–6. Subsequent references to the novel will be given in the text, citing the French edition first and then (for quoted passages only) the English translation.

5. See also the case of Daniel Stern (Marie d'Agoult), astutely analyzed by Mary Rice.

6. Schor, "Idealism in the Novel."

7. Moses, p. 149. On the repression of the press and publishing under the Second Empire, see Guiral; Casselle.

8. Deutellbaum and Huff, pp. 262, 263.

9. Jordan, pp. 253–56.

10. Sand, "Aux membres," 8: 407, my translation.

11. Cited by Deutellbaum and Huff, p. 263.

12. Thus I disagree with Margaret Cohen, who favors an understanding of domesticity as inherently contradictory. On the contrary, I hold that familial discourse becomes contradictory only when an older familial discourse is opposed by a newer one that has reformulated traditional notions such as, say, the sphere of politics. Thus, for Cohen, Sand's refusal to question women's place in the home remains "to be explained." I came

across her essay after the bulk of the present chapter had been written. See Cohen, p. 38 n. 15.

13. Schor, "Reading Double," pp. 255–56, 266–67.
14. Cohen, p. 27.
15. Sand, *François le Champi*, pp. 48–50 (subsequent references to the novel will appear in the text). Therein, Sand actually debates the interest of reviving pastoral fiction in the wake of recent novelistic practices.
16. A particularly gruesome send-up of the power relations that underlie cultural ventriloquism is Paul Bowles's short story "A Distant Episode," in which an American professor's presumption of understanding, translating, and being accepted by Morroccan society is ferociously repaid when he is waylaid by local thieves who cut out *his tongue*; for a critique of the practices of Western ethnography see Clifford; on "nature" and primates in the discourses of modern science see Haraway, *Primate Visions*.
17. Ortner, pp. 67–87, esp. pp. 83–87.
18. Schor, "Reading Double," p. 266.
19. The term "legible body" I have borrowed from the work of Allucquère Rosanne Stone on cyborgs, cyberspace, and subjectivity in contemporary computer technologies and the phone sex industry; see her "Will the Real Body Please Stand Up?"
20. Schor has astutely analyzed this dynamic from the perspective of feminist psychoanalysis; Schor, "Reading Double," pp. 257–61.
21. Butler, pp. 35–78.
22. This will become the double bind underlying Lacanian psychoanalysis's formulations of the duties of early child care by mothers with respect to the child's entry into the symbolic.
23. See Fouquet and Kniebiehler, pp. 144–45.
24. Such is Schor's interpretation; see "Reading Double," pp. 254–55.
25. Indeed, Cohen reads the conflict between Sylvinet and Landry as an allegory of the alliance between working and middle classes that degenerated into civil war in June 1848.

Chapter 7

1. Zola, *La Fortune*, 2: 19.
2. Borie, *Zola*, pp. 13–40.
3. Ibid., p. 144; Nelson, p. 67.
4. Borie, *Zola*, p. 128.
5. Marx. For an application of Marxist analysis of commodification to *La Curée* (although it does not question the narrative of the "invasion" of the private sphere by commodity relations) see Bell, pp. 57–95.
6. Bernheimer, *Figures of Ill-Repute*, p. 208. See also Schor, *Breaking the Chain*, pp. 30–31, on sexual indifferentiation in Zola; and Hertz, pp. 161–93.
7. Foucault, *An Introduction*, pp. 144–45.

8. Zola, *La Curée*, 2: 311. The English translation, *The Kill*, omits the Preface. All subsequent references to *La Curée* will be given in the text, citing the French edition first and then (for quoted passages only) the English translation.

9. Foucault, *An Introduction*, pp. 38–39.

10. I borrow the notion of cultural intelligibility from Butler, pp. xi–xii.

11. See Woolgar for an elegant formulation concerning the unacknowledged constructionist impulse of scientific investigations and discoveries.

12. Foucault, Introduction to *Herculine Barbin*, pp. xi–xii.

13. Rubin.

14. Butler, p. 12.

15. See Adrienne Rich's essay of the same title; and Monique Wittig's related essays: "The Straight Mind," "One Is Not Born a Woman," and "The Mark of Gender."

16. Vautrin's sententious pronouncement reads: "The secret of great fortunes without apparent cause is a crime that has been forgotten because it was properly executed" (Balzac, *Le Père Goriot*, pp. 145–46).

17. On the social and discursive economies of male homosociality see Sedgwick, *Between Men*.

18. Esquirol, "Monomanie," emphasis mine; I have modernized the spelling.

19. Nelson, p. 85, emphasis mine.

20. See Bell, pp. 68–70.

21. Sigmund Freud, "Femininity."

22. See Bernheimer and Kahane, *In Dora's Case*.

23. Zola, "Au couvent," p. 221.

24. See Butler's very interesting remarks on Freud's heterosexist conceptualization of his theory of primary bisexuality; Butler, p. 61.

25. Stallybrass and White, p. 159.

26. See Sedgwick, *Between Men*.

27. Donzelot, *Policing*.

Chapter 8

1. Gide, *La Porte étroite*, p. 498; *Strait Is the Gate*, p. 3, translation modified. Subsequent references to the novel will appear in the text, citing the French first and then the English translation.

2. For a Lacanian feminist reading of the novel, consult Apter, pp. 124–34.

3. Jameson, *Fables of Aggression*, pp. 6–9.

4. Said, *Beginnings*, pp. 136–37.

5. This is related to the concept of "distinction" that regulated nineteenth-century bourgeois practices; see Sartre, *L'Idiot*, 3: 245–48, 283–89, 304.

6. Said, *Beginnings*, pp. 162–63.
7. Borie, *Le Célibataire*.
8. Ibid., pp. 9, 19, 68–70; see also his *Le Tyran timide*, p. 17.
9. C. Miller, pp. 93–107. 10. Hellerstien, p. 383.
11. Borie, *Le Célibataire*, p. 144. 12. Borie, *Mythologies*, pp. 15–17.
13. Ibid., p. 159. 14. See Knecht.
15. Newmark, pp. 1102–4. 16. Ibid., pp. 1100–1101.
17. Sonnenfeld, pp. 177–78.
18. Didier, *Le Journal intime*, pp. 91, 40–41, 106–7; "Pour une sociologie," pp. 256–57.
19. Kadish, pp. 67–83.
20. Schor, *Breaking the Chain*, pp. 19–20.
21. Borie, *Le Tyran*, p. 15.
22. As quoted by Gilbert and Gubar, p. 17.
23. In this regard, our analysis is consonant with Gide's decision to excise a long passage from the beginning of chapter 8 that recounts Jerome's life of debauchery after Alissa's death. A stereotypical episode of male grief would have diminished the unsettling quality of Jerome's sexuality.

Epilogue

1. See Donzelot, *Policing*, pp. 96–234, and Rose, pp. 121–209.
2. Barrett and McIntosh, pp. 28–34.
3. The rhetoric of their book titles is revealing: *Le Refus de la vie: analyse historique du présent* [The refusal of life: a historical analysis of the present] (1975), *Un Futur sans avenir: histoire et population* [A future without a future: history and population] (1979), and *Histoire et décadence* [History and decadence] (1981) by Chaunu; *La Peste blanche* [The white plague] (1976) by Chaunu and Suffert; and *Les Berceaux vides de Marianne: l'avenir de la population française* [Marianne's empty cradles: the future of the French population] (1981) by Biraben and Dupâquier.
4. It is interesting to note that the French antiabortion movement ("Laissez-les vivre") has been rather ineffective, and the 1974 law remains on the books in its original form. This may have to do partly with the fact that abortion was legalized, not by the courts, but by a conservative-dominated National Assembly, which passed the legislation in 1974 and reaffirmed its decision in 1979. In this way did the struggle for abortion rights actively involve political parties on the national level in the liberalization process.
5. See "Famille, je vous aime," *Le Nouvel Observateur*, June 15, 1981.
6. See Stacey.
7. See Salfi. He is conducting research on the intersection between familial discourse, the media (both mainstream and alternative), and gay and lesbian households; his research was prompted by an article titled, "Baby Would

Make Three in Gays' Unfinished Family," *San Diego Union*, May 16, 1990, C1.

8. See Vance.

9. The whole ordeal lasted seven years, five of which the principally accused, Raymond Buckey, spent in jail without bond. The affair ended in deadlocked juries twice and prosecution dropped the case in July 1990. For a history of the case and its fallout see "Trial May Be Over—But McMartin Will Never End," *Los Angeles Times*, July 29, 1990, A1.

10. Balibar, p. 14. Balibar makes the provocative thesis that the construction of the New Europe is sustained by an ideal image that is racist to the core (p. 6) and reminds readers that "until the middle of the twentieth century, the principal meaning of ['Europeans'] referred to groups of colonizers in each of the colonized regions elsewhere in the world" (p. 7).

11. Watney, "Missionary Positions," p. 97.

12. See both Grover and Treichler. In France, cultural analysis of the same order has been hard to come by. It seems that to "risk group" [*groupe à risque*] (gays, drug users, and hemophiliacs) there exists no corresponding opposite term such as "general population"; see Herzlich and Pierret.

13. The French equivalent to "people with AIDS" (PWAs) is *les sidéens*.

14. See Lewontin, Rose, and Kamin.

15. See Angier; LeVay.   16. See Doane and Hodges.

17. See Hartouni; Terry.   18. Greenhouse.

Works Cited

Abelove, Henry. "Some Speculations on the History of Sexual Intercourse During the Long Eighteenth Century in England." *Genders* 6 (1989): 125–30.

Agulhon, Maurice. *Marianne au combat*. Paris: Flammarion, 1979.

Aimé-Martin, Louis. *De l'éducation des mères de famille ou de la civilisation du genre humain par les femmes*. 2 vols. Paris: Charles Gosselin, 1834.

Alain. "Les Sentiments familiaux. Essai de sociologie de la famille." In *Les Passions et la sagesse*. Ed. Georges Bénézé. Paris: Gallimard, Pleiade edition, 1960 [1927].

Albistur, Maïté. *Histoire du féminisme français du Moyen Age à nos jours*. Paris: Editions des Femmes, 1977.

Alstad, Dianne. "The Ideology of the Family in Eighteenth-Century France." Ph.D. diss., Yale University, 1971.

Anderson, Benedict. *Imagined Communities: Reflections on the Origin and Spread of Nationalism*. London: Verso, 1983.

Anderson, Lauren. "Property of Same-Sex Couples: Toward a New Definition of Family." *Journal of Family Law* 26, no. 2 (Mar. 1987): 357–72.

Angier, Natalie. "Zone of Brain Linked to Men's Sexual Orientation." *New York Times*, August 30, 1991, A1.

Apter, Emily. *André Gide and the Codes of Homotextuality*. Saratoga, Calif.: ANMA Libri, 1987.

———. *Feminizing the Fetish: Psychoanalysis and Narrative Obsession in Turn-of-the-Century France*. Ithaca: Cornell University Press, 1991.

Ariès, Philippe. *L'Enfant et la vie familiale sous l'ancien régime*. Paris: Plon, 1960.

Armengaud, André. "Le Rôle de la démographie." In vol. 3 of *Histoire économique et sociale de la France*. Ed. Fernand Braudel and Ernest Labrousse. Paris: Presses Universitaires de France, 1976.

Armstrong, Nancy. *Desire and Domestic Fiction: A Political History of the Novel.* New York: Oxford University Press, 1987.

Aron, Jean-Paul, and Roger Kempf. *Le Pénis ou la démoralisation de l'Occident.* Paris: Grasset, 1978.

Badinter, Elisabeth. *L'Amour en plus. Histoire de l'amour maternel (XVIIe–XXe siècle).* Paris: Flammarion, 1980.

Balibar, Etienne. "*Es Gibt Keinen Staat in Europa*: Racism and Politics in Europe Today." *New Left Review,* 186 (March–April 1991): 5–19.

Balzac, Honoré de. *Mémoires de deux jeunes mariées.* In vol. 1 of *Oeuvres complètes.* Ed. Pierre-Georges Castex. Paris: Gallimard, 1976.

———. *Les Paysans.* In vol. 9 of *Oeuvres complètes.* Ed. Pierre-Georges Castex. Paris: Gallimard, 1976.

———. *The Peasants.* Trans. George B. Ives. Philadelphia: George Barrie, 1899.

———. *Le Père Goriot.* In vol. 3 of *Oeuvres complètes.* Ed. Pierre-Georges Castex. Paris: Gallimard, 1976.

Barker, Francis. *The Tremulous Private Body: Essays on Subjection.* London: Methuen, 1984.

Barrett, Michèle. *Women's Oppression Today.* London: Verso, 1980.

Barrett, Michèle, and Mary McIntosh. *The Anti-Social Family.* London: Verso, 1982.

Beizer, Janet. *Family Plots.* New Haven: Yale University Press, 1988.

———. *Ventriloquized Bodies: Writing the Text of Hysteria in France.* Ithaca: Cornell University Press, forthcoming.

Bell, David F. *Models of Power: Politics and Economics in Zola's "Rougon-Macquart."* Lincoln: University of Nebraska Press, 1988.

Benjamin, Walter. *Charles Baudelaire: A Lyric Poet in the Age of High Capitalism.* Trans. Harry Zohn. London: New Left Books, 1973.

Bernardin de Saint-Pierre, Jacques-Henri. *Discours sur l'éducation des femmes.* In vol. 3 of *Oeuvres.* Ed. Louis Aimé-Martin. Paris: n.p., 1836 [1818].

———. *Paul and Virginia.* Trans. John Donovan. London: Penguin, 1989.

———. *Paul et Virginie.* Paris: Garnier-Flammarion, 1967 [1788].

———. *Voyage à l'île de France. Un officier du roi à l'île Maurice 1768–1770.* Paris: La Découverte, 1983 [1773].

Bernheimer, Charles. *Figures of Ill-Repute: Representing Prostitution in Nineteenth-Century France.* Cambridge, Mass.: Harvard University Press, 1989.

———. Preface to *In Dora's Case: Freud-Hysteria-Feminism.* Ed. Charles Bernheimer and Claire Kahane. New York: Columbia University Press, 1985.

Bersani, Leo. *Baudelaire and Freud.* Berkeley: University of California Press, 1977.

Bibliothèque des propriétaires ou Journal d'Economie rurale et domestique. Par une Société de Savants et de Proprietaires. No. 5 (Thermidor an IX [July 1803]).

Biraben, J.-N., and J. Dupâquier. *Les Berceaux vides de Marianne: l'avenir de la population française.* Paris: Le Seuil, 1981.

Bloch, E., et al. *Aesthetics and Politics.* London: New Left Books, 1977.

Borie, Jean. *Le Célibataire français.* Paris: Le Sagittaire, 1976.

———. *Mythologies de l'hérédité au XIXe siècle.* Paris: Galilée, 1981.

———. *Le Tyran timide. Le naturalisme de la femme au XIXe siècle.* Paris: Klincksieck, 1973.

———. *Zola et les mythes, ou, de la nausée au salut.* Paris: Seuil, 1971.

Bory, Jean-Louis. *Eugène Sue.* Paris: Hachette, 1960.

Bowles, Paul. "A Distant Episode." In *A Distant Episode: The Selected Stories.* New York: Ecco, 1988.

Briquet, Dr. P. *Traité clinique et thérapeutique de l'hystérie.* Paris: Baillière, 1859.

Brooks, Peter. *The Melodramatic Imagination.* New Haven: Yale University Press, 1976.

———. *Reading for the Plot.* New York: Atheneum, 1984.

Buisine, Alain. "Peuple et famille." *Littérature* 26 (1977): 24–31.

Buret, Eugène. *De la misère des classes laborieuses en Angleterre et en France.* 2 vols. Paris: Jules Renouard, 1841.

———. *Question d'Afrique. Double conquête de l'Algérie par la guerre et la colonisation, suivi d'un Examen critique du gouvernement, de l'administration et de la situation coloniale.* Paris: Ledoyer, 1842.

Butler, Judith. *Gender Trouble: Feminism and the Subversion of Identity.* London and New York: Routledge, 1990.

Canguilhem, Georges. *The Normal and the Pathological.* Trans. Carolyn R. Fawcett with Robert S. Cohen. New York: Zone, 1989.

Caplan, Jay. *Framed Narratives: Diderot's Genealogy of the Beholder.* Minneapolis: University of Minnesota Press, 1985.

Carter, Angela. *The Sadeian Woman and the Ideology of Pornography.* New York: Harper Colophon, 1978.

Casselle, Pierre. "Le Régime législatif." In vol. 3 of *Histoire de l'édition française.* Ed. Henri-Jean Martin and Roger Chartier. Paris: Promodis, 1985.

Castel, Robert. *L'Ordre psychiatrique. L'âge d'or de l'aliénisme.* Paris: Minuit, 1976.

"Célibat." In *Encyclopédie ou dictionnaire raisonné des sciences, des arts et des métiers.* 1779.

de Cervol. *Mémoire sur la population.* Reprint. Paris: Editions d'Histoire Sociale, 1973 [1768].

Chaunu, Pierre. *Un Futur sans avenir: histoire et population.* Paris: Calmann-Lévy, 1979.

———. *Histoire et décadence.* Paris: Librairie Académique Perrin, 1981.

———. *Le Refus de la vie: analyse historique du présent.* Paris: Calmann-Lévy, 1975.

Chaunu, Pierre, and Georges Suffert. *La Peste blanche.* Paris: Gallimard, 1976.

Chevalier, Dr. Julien. *L'Inversion sexuelle: une maladie de la personalité.* Paris: Masson, 1893.

Chevalier, Louis. *Classes laborieuses et classes dangereuses à Paris pendant la première moitié du XIXe siècle.* Paris: Plon, 1958.

———. Preface, *Les Paysans* by Honoré de Balzac. Paris: Gallimard, Folio, 1975.

Chodorow, Nancy. *The Reproduction of Mothering: Psychoanalysis and the Sociology of Gender.* Berkeley: University of California Press, 1978.

Clifford, James. "On Ethnographic Authority." In *The Predicament of Culture: Twentieth-Century Ethnography, Literature, and Art.* Cambridge, Mass.: Harvard University Press, 1988.

Cohen, Margaret. "A Woman's Place: *La Petite Fadette v. La Voix des femmes.*" *L'Esprit créateur* 29, no. 2 (Summer 1989): 26–38.

Coleman, William. *Death Is a Social Disease: Public Health and Political Economy in Early Industrial France.* Madison: University of Wisconsin Press, 1982.

Corbin, Alain. *Les Filles de noce. Misère sexuelle et prostitution aux XIXe et XXe siècles.* Paris: Aubier, 1978.

———. *The Foul and the Fragrant: Odor and the French Social Imagination.* Trans. Miriam L. Kochan, Roy Porter, and Christopher Prendergast. Cambridge, Mass.: Harvard University Press, 1986.

———. Introduction to *De la prostitution dans la ville de Paris, considérée sous le rapport de l'hygiène publique et de l'administration*, by Alexandre Parent-Duchâtelet. Ed. Alain Corbin. Paris: Seuil, 1981.

Darrow, Margaret H. "French Noblewomen and the New Domesticity, 1750–1850." *Feminist Studies* 5, no. 1 (1979): 41–65.

Delaporte, François. *Disease and Civilization: The Cholera in Paris, 1832.* Trans. Arthur Goldhammer. Cambridge, Mass.: MIT Press, 1986.

Deleuze, Gilles and Félix Guattari. *Anti-Oedipus: Capitalism and Schizophrenia.* Trans. Robert Hurley, Mark Seem, and Helen R. Lane. Minneapolis: University of Minnesota Press, 1983.

Demel, Raymond. *Une Image de la famille et de la société sous la Restauration (1815–1830).* Paris: Editions Ouvrières, 1965.

Denning, Michael. *Mechanic Accents: Dime Novels and Working-Class Culture in America.* London: Verso, 1987.

Deutellbaum, Wendy, and Cynthia Huff. "Class, Gender, and Family System: The Case of George Sand." In *The (M)other Tongue. Essays in Feminist Psychoanalytic Interpretation*. Ed. Shirley Nelson Garner, Claire Kahane, and Madelon Springnether. Ithaca: Cornell University Press, 1985.

Didi-Hubermann, Georges. *Invention de l'hystérie: Charcot et l'iconographie photographique de la Salpêtrière*. Paris: Macula, 1982.

Didier, Béatrice. *Le Journal intime*. Paris: Presses Universitaires de France, 1976.

———. "Pour une sociologie du journal intime." In *Le Journal intime et ses formes littéraires. Actes du Colloque de septembre 1975*. Ed. V. Del Litto. Geneva: Droz, 1978.

Doane, Janice, and Devon Hodges. "Risky Business: Familial Ideology and the Case of Baby M." *differences* 1, no. 1 (Winter 1989): 67–82.

Doerner, Klaus. *Madmen and the Bourgeoisie: A Social History of the Insane*. Trans. Joachim Neugroschel and Jean Steinberg. Oxford: Basil Blackwell, 1981.

Donzelot, Jacques. *L'Invention du social. Essai sur le déclin des passions politiques*. Paris: Fayard, 1984.

———. *The Policing of Families*. Trans. Robert Hurley. New York: Vintage, 1979.

Du Camp, Maxime. *Paris: ses organes, ses fonctions, sa vie de la seconde moitié du XIXe siècle*, 5th ed. 6 vols. Paris: Hachette, 1875.

Duhet, Paule-Marie. *Les Femmes et la Révolution 1789–1794*. Paris: Julliard, 1971.

Eco, Umberto. *The Role of the Reader*. Bloomington: Indiana University Press, 1979.

Ehrenreich, Barbara and Deirdre English. *For Her Own Good: 150 Years of Experts' Advice to Women*. Garden City: Anchor-Doubleday, 1978.

Encyclopédie ou dictionnaire raisonné des sciences, des arts et des métiers, 1779 ed.

Engel, Stefanie. "Femininity as Tragedy." *Socialist Review* 53 (Sept.–Oct. 1980): 77–104.

Esquirol, Jean-Etienne-Dominique. "Monomanie." In *Dictionnaire des sciences médicales*. Paris: Panckoucke, 1819.

Evans-Pritchard, E. E. Preface to *The Observation of Savage Peoples*, by Jean-Marie Gérando. Trans. F. T. C. Moore. London: Routledge, 1969.

Fabre, Jean. *Lumiéres et romantisme. Energie et nostalgie de Rousseau à Mickiewicz*. Paris: Klincksieck, 1963.

Felman, Shoshanna. *La Folie ou la chose littéraire*. Paris: Seuil, 1978.

Féré, Dr. Charles. *La Famille névropathique. Théorie tératologique de l'hérédité et de la prédisposition morbides et de la dégénérescence*. 2nd ed. Paris: Alcan, 1898.

———. *L'Instinct sexuel. Evolution et dissolution.* Paris: Alcan, 1899.

Fitting, Peter. "Effet esthétique, effet idéologique: lectures de Balzac (*Les Paysans*)." In *Le Roman de Balzac.* Ed. Roland Le Huenen and Paul Perron. Montreal: Didier, 1980.

Flandrin, Jean-Louis. *Families in Former Times: Kinship, Household and Sexuality.* Trans. Richard Southern. Cambridge, Eng.: Cambridge University Press, 1979.

Flaubert, Gustave. *Oeuvres complètes.* Vol. 11. Paris: Club de l'Honnête Homme, 1972.

Madame de Flesselles. *La Jeune mère institutrice.* Limoges: Babou frères, 1876 [1830].

Foucault, Michel. *Discipline and Punish: The Birth of the Prison.* Trans. Alan Sheridan. New York: Vintage, 1979.

———. *Histoire de la folie à l'âge classique.* 2nd ed. Paris: Gallimard, 1972 [1961].

———. Introduction to *Herculine Barbin, Being the Recently Discovered Memoires of a Nineteenth-Century Hermaphrodite.* Trans. Richard McDougal. New York: Colophon, 1980.

———. *An Introduction.* Vol. 1 of *The History of Sexuality.* Trans. Alan Sheridan. New York: Vintage, 1978.

———. *La Volonté de savoir.* Vol. 1 of *Histoire de la sexualité.* Paris: Gallimard, 1976.

Fox-Genovese, Elizabeth, and Eugene D. Genovese. *Fruits of Merchant Capital.* Oxford: Oxford University Press, 1983.

Frappier-Mazur, Lucienne. *L'Expression métaphorique dans la "Comedie humaine": domaine social et psychologique.* Paris: Klincksieck, 1976.

Frégier, H.-A. *Des classes dangereuses de la population des grandes villes, et des moyens de les rendre meilleures.* 2 vols. Paris: Baillière, 1840.

Freud, Sigmund. "Femininity." In vol. 22 of *The Standard Edition of the Complete Psychological Works of Sigmund Freud.* Ed. James Strachey. London: Hogarth, 1964.

Furet, François. *Interpreting the French Revolution.* Trans. Elborg Forster. Cambridge, Mass.: Cambridge University Press, and Paris: La Maison des Sciences de l'Homme, 1981.

Gacon-Dufour. *Manuel complet de la maîtresse de maison et de la parfaite ménagère, ou Guide pratique pour la gestion d'une maison à la ville et à la campagne, maintenant les moyens d'y maintenir le bon ordre et d'y établir l'abondance,* 2nd edition. Ed. Mme Celnart. Paris: Manuels Roret, 1828.

Gallop, Jane. "Keys to Dora." In *In Dora's Case. Freud-Hysteria-Feminism.* Ed. Charles Bernheimer and Claire Kahane. New York: Columbia University Press, 1985.

Gérando, Joseph-Marie de. *De la bienfaisance publique*. 6 vols. Paris: J. Renouard, 1839.
———. *The Observation of Savage Peoples*. Trans. F. T. C. Moore. London: Routledge, 1969.
Gide, André. *La Porte étroite*. In *Romans, récits et soties*. Ed. Maurice Nadeau. Paris: Gallimard, Pleiade edition, 1951.
———. *Strait Is the Gate*. Trans. Dorothy Bussy. New York: Vintage, 1952.
Gilbert, Sandra M., and Susan Gubar. *The Madwoman in the Attic: The Woman Writer and the Nineteenth-Century Literary Imagination*. New Haven: Yale University Press, 1979.
Gilman, Sander. *Difference and Pathology: Stereotypes of Sexuality, Race, and Madness*. Ithaca: Cornell University Press, 1985.
Gobineau, Joseph-Arthur. *Essai sur l'inégalité des races humaines*. In *Oeuvres*. Ed. Jean Gaulemin and Jean Bousel. Paris: Gallimard, Pléiade edition, 1923.
Goldstein, Jan. *Console and Classify: The French Psychiatric Profession in the Nineteenth Century*. Cambridge, Eng.: Cambridge University Press, 1987.
Goulemot, Jean-Marie. "L'Histoire littéraire en question: l'exemple de *Paul et Virginie*." In *Etudes sur Paul et Virginie et l'oeuvre de Bernardin de Saint-Pierre*. Ed. Jean-Michel Racault. Paris: Didier-Erudition, 1986.
Grand dictionnaire universel du XIXe siècle. Ed. Pierre Larousse. Paris, 1866.
Greenhouse, Steven. "A New Pill, a Fierce Battle: Politics and Profits." *New York Times Magazine*, Feb. 12, 1989, p. 22.
Grover, Jan Zita. "AIDS: Keywords." In *AIDS: Cultural Analysis/Cultural Activism*. Ed. Douglas Crimp. Cambridge, Mass.: MIT Press, 1989.
Guiral, Pierre. "La Presse de 1848 à 1871." In vol. 2 of *Histoire générale de la presse française*. Ed. Claude Bellanger, Jacques Godeshot, Pierre Guiral and Ferrand Terrou. Paris: Presses Universitaires de France, 1969.
Guise, René. "Balzac et le roman feuilleton." *Année balzacienne* (1984): 283–338.
Guizot, François. *De la démocratie*. Paris: V. Masson, 1849.
Habermas, Jürgen. *The Structural Transformation of the Public Sphere: An Inquiry into a Category of Bourgeois Society*. Trans. Thomas Burger and Frederick Lawrence. Cambridge, Mass.: MIT Press, 1989.
Haraway, Donna J. *Primate Visions: Gender, Race, and Nature in the World of Modern Science*. New York and London: Routledge, 1989.
———. *Simians, Cyborgs, and Women: The Reinvention of Nature*. New York: Routledge, 1991.
Hartouni, Valerie, "Containing Women: Reproductive Discourse in the 1980s." In *Technoculture*. Ed. Constance Penley and Andrew Ross. Minneapolis: University of Minnesota Press, 1991.

Hellerstein, Erna Olafson. "French Women and the Orderly Household." In *Proceedings of the Annual Meeting of the Western Society for French History.* No. 3 (1975), 378–89.

Hertz, Neil. *The End of the Line.* Ithaca: Cornell University Press, 1987.

Herzlich, Claudine, and Janine Pierret. "Une Maladie dans l'espace public: le SIDA dans six quotidiens français." *Annales. E. S.* 43, no. 5 (Sept.–Oct. 1988): 1109–34.

Histoire de l'édition française. 3 vols. Ed. Henri-Jean Martin and Roger Chartier in collaboration with Jean-Pierre Vivet. Paris: Promodis, 1983–85.

Histoire générale de la presse française. 3 vols. Ed. Claude Belanger, Jacques Godechot, Pierre Guiral, and Fernand Terrou. Paris: Presses Universitaires de France, 1969–72.

Hobsbawn, Eric and Terrence Ranger, ed. *The Invention of Tradition.* Cambridge, Eng.: Cambridge University Press, 1983.

Hunt, Lynn. *The Family Romance of the French Revolution.* Berkeley: University of California Press, 1992.

———. *Politics, Culture, and Class in the French Revolution.* Berkeley: University of California Press, 1984.

———. "The Unstable Boundaries of the French Revolution." In *From the Fires of Revolution to the Great War.* Ed. Michelle Perrot. [Vol. 4 of *A History of Private Life.* Ed. Philippe Ariès and Georges Duby.] Trans. Arthur Goldhammer. Cambridge, Mass.: Harvard University Press, 1990.

Huysmans, J. K. *A rebours.* Paris: Garnier-Flammarion, 1978 [1884].

Jameson, Fredric. *Fables of Aggression: Wyndham Lewis, the Modernist as Fascist.* Berkeley: University of California Press, 1979.

———. *The Political Unconscious: Narrative as a Socially Symbolic Act.* Ithaca: Cornell University Press, 1981.

Jordan, Ruth. *George Sand: A Biography.* London: Constable, 1976.

Joseph, Isaac, Philippe Fritsch, and Alain Battegay. *Disciplines à domicile: l'édification de la famille.* Fontenay-sous-Bois: Recherches, 1977.

Kadish, Doris Y. "Alissa dans la vallée: Intertextual Echoes of Balzac in Two Novels by Gide." *French Forum* 10, no. 1 (1985): 67–83.

Knecht, Loring D. "A New Reading of Gide's *La Porte étroite*." *PMLA* 82 (1967): 640–48.

Knibielher, Yvonne. "Les Médecins et la nature 'féminine' au temps du Code Civil," *Annales. E. S. C.* 31, no. 4: 838–43.

Knibielher, Yvonne, and Catherine Fouquet. *Histoires des mères du moyen âge jusqu'à nos jours.* Paris: Montalba, 1977.

Krafft-Ebing, R. von. *Psychopathia Sexualis: With Especial Reference to the Antipathic Sexual Instinct. A Medico-Forensic Study.* Trans. F. J. Rebman. London: Heinemann, 1928.

Krohn, Alan. *Hysteria: The Elusive Neurosis.* New York: International Universities Press, 1978.
Laclau, Ernesto, and Chantal Mouffe. *Hegemony and Socialist Strategy.* London: Verso, 1985.
Lajolais, Natalie de. *Education pratique des femmes. Manuel à l'usage des mères de famille et des institutrices.* Paris: Didier, 1841.
Lallemand, M. *Des pertes séminales involontaires,* 2nd ed. 3 vols. Paris: Bechet jeune, 1838.
Landes, Joan B. *Women and the Public Sphere in the Age of the French Revolution.* Ithaca: Cornell University Press, 1988.
Lanteri-Laura, Georges. *Lecture des perversions: histoire de leur appropriation médicale.* Paris: Masson, 1979.
Laqueur, Thomas. "Orgasm, Generation, and the Politics of Reproductive Biology." *Representations* 14 (1986): 1–41.
Lasch, Christopher. *Haven in a Heartless World.* New York: Harper Colophon, 1977.
Laslett, Peter. *The World We Have Lost.* New York: Scribner's, 1971.
Latour, Bruno. *The Pasteurization of France.* Trans. Alan Sheridan and John Law. Cambridge, Mass.: Harvard University Press, 1988.
———. *Nous n'avons jamais été modernes.* Paris: La Découverte, 1991.
———. *Science in Action.* Cambridge, Mass.: Harvard University Press, 1987.
Dr. Laupts. *Tares et poisons: Perversion et perversité sexuelles.* Paris: G. Carré, 1896.
Le Bègue de Prasle, Achille, and the Abbé C. F. A. Lalauze. *L'Economie rurale et civile, ou moyens les plus économiques d'administrer et de faire valoir ses biens de campagne et de ville.* 6 vols. n.p.: n.p. 1789.
Le Bon, Gustave. *Psychologie des foules.* Paris: Presses Universitaires de France, 1983.
LeVay, Simon. "A Difference in Hypothalamic Structure Between Heterosexual and Homosexual Men." *Science,* Aug. 30, 1991: 1034–37.
Lewontin, R. C., Steve Rose, and Leon J. Kamin. *Not in Our Genes: Biology, Ideology, and Human Nature.* New York: Pantheon, 1984.
Louyer-Villermay. "Nymphomanie." *Dictionnaire des sciences médicales.* Paris: Pankoucke, 1819.
Lukács, Georg. *Studies in European Realism.* New York: Grosset and Dunlap, 1964.
McBride, Theresa. *The Domestic Revolution: The Modernization of Household Service in England and France 1820–1920.* London: Croom Helm, 1976.
Macherey, Pierre. *Towards a Theory of Literary Production.* Trans. Geoffrey Wall. London: Routledge and Kegan Paul, 1978.

McMillan, James F. *Housewife or Harlot: The Place of Women in French Society 1870–1940*. New York: St. Martin's Press, 1981.
Mantion, Jean Rémy. "Figures du repos. Idylles et peinture de paysage." *Critique* 467 (1986): 355–71.
Marx, Karl. *Capital: A Critique of Political Economy*. 3 vols. Trans. Ben Fowkes. New York: Vintage, 1978.
Marx, Karl, and Frederick Engels. *The Holy Family, or Critique of Critical Criticism*. Moscow: Progress, 1975.
Messance. *Nouvelles recherches sur la population de la France avec quelques remarques sur divers objets d'administration*. Reprint. Paris: Editions d'Histoire Sociale, 1973 [1788].
Miller, Christopher L. *Blank Darkness: Africanist Discourse in French*. Chicago: University of Chicago Press, 1985.
Miller, D. A. *The Novel and the Police*. Berkeley: University of California Press, 1988.
Moheau. *Recherches et considérations sur la population*. Reprint. Paris: Geuthner, 1912 [1778].
Montagnier, Pierre. *La Conquête de l'Algérie, 1830–1871*. Paris: Pygmalion, 1986.
Moreau de Tours, J. *La psychologie morbide dans ses rapports avec la philosophie de l'histoire, ou de l'influence des névropathies sur le dynamisme intellectuel*. Paris, 1859.
Moses, Claire Goldberg. *French Feminism in the Nineteenth Century*. Albany: SUNY Press, 1984.
Mozet, Nicole. *Balzac au pluriel*. Paris: Presses Universitaires de France, 1990.
Mylne, Vivienne. *The Eighteenth-Century French Novel: Techniques of Illusion*. Manchester: University of Manchester Press, 1965.
Necker de Sassure, Albertine. *L'Education progressive ou étude du cours de la vie*. 3 vols. Lausanne: George Rouiller, 1834.
Nelson, Brian. *Zola and the Bourgeoisie*. London: Macmillan, 1983.
Nettement, Alfred. *Etudes critiques sur le feuilleton roman*. 2 vols. Paris: Perrodil, 1845–46.
Newmark, Kevin. "Love's Cross in *La Porte étroite*." *MLN* 99, no. 5 (1984): 1094–115.
Nicholson, Linda. "Feminism and Marx: Integrating Kinship with the Economic." In *Feminism as Critique*. Ed. Seyla Benhabib and Drucilla Cornell. Minneapolis: University of Minnesota Press, 1987.
Olivier-Martin, Yves. *Histoire du roman populaire en France de 1840 à 1980*. Paris: Albin Michel, 1980.
Orecchioni, Pierre. "Eugène Sue: mesure d'un succès," *Europe* 643–44 (1982): 157–66.
Ortner, Sherry B. "Is Female to Male as Nature Is to Culture?" In *Women,*

Culture, and Society. Ed. Michèle Zimbalist Rosaldo and Louise Lamphere. Stanford: Stanford University Press, 1974.

Outram, Dorinda. *The Body and the French Revolution: Sex, Class, and Political Culture.* New Haven: Yale University Press, 1989.

Panofsky, Erwin. *Meaning in the Visual Arts.* New York: Doubleday Anchor, 1955.

Parent-Duchâtelet, Alexandre. *De la prostitution dans la ville de Paris, considérée sous le rapport de l'hygiène publique et de l'administration.* Ed. Alain Corbin. Paris: Seuil, 1981 [1836].

Mme Pariset. *Nouveau manuel complet de la maîtresse de maison, ou Lettres sur l'économie domestique.* Paris: Manuels Roret, 1852.

Mesdames Pariset and Celnart. *Nouveau manuel complet de la maîtresse de maison contenant l'organisation de la Maison, Entretien des Vêtements et du Linge, l'Eclairage et le Chauffage, L'Alimentation, Hygiène et Puériculture.* Paris: Manuels Roret, 1913 [1852].

Pinel, Philippe. *Traité médico-philosophique sur l'aliénation mentale.* Paris, 1801.

Pope, Barbara Corrado. "Maternal Education in France, 1815–1848." In *Proceedings of the Annual Meeting of the Western Society for French History.* No. 3 (1975), 368–77.

Poskin, Alphonse. *Afrique Equitoriale. Climatologie, nosologie, hygiène.* Brussels: Société belge de librairie, 1897.

Prendergast, Christopher. *Balzac: Fiction and Melodrama.* London: Edward Arnold, 1978.

"Prospectus." In *Annales d'hygiène publique et de médecine légale.* Vol. 1. Paris: Gabon, 1829.

Prost, Antoine. *Histoire de l'enseignement en France 1800–1967.* Paris: Armand Colin, 1968.

Rabinow, Paul. *French Modern: Norms and Forms of the Social Environment.* Cambridge, Mass.: MIT Press, 1989.

Racault, Jean-Michel. "Balzac et Bernardin de Saint-Pierre et l'héritage des lumières." *Année Balzacienne*, New Series 8 (1987): 201–26.

———. "Pastorale et roman dans *Paul et Virginie*." In *Etudes sur Paul et Virginie et l'œuvre de Bernardin de Saint-Pierre.* Ed. Jean-Michel Racault. Paris: Didier-Erudition, 1986.

———. "Proposition d'une relecture de *Paul et Virginie*." In *Etudes sur Paul et Virginie et l'œuvre de Bernardin de Saint-Pierre.* Ed. Jean-Michel Racault. Paris: Didier-Erudition, 1986.

———. "Virginie entre la nature et la vertu. Cohésion narrative et contradictions idéologiques dans *Paul et Virginie*." *Dix-huitième siècle* 18 (1986): 389–404.

Rapp, Rayna, Ellen Ross, and Renate Bridenthal. "Examining Family History." *Feminist Studies* 5, no. 1 (1979): 174–200.

Rice, Mary. "Masculine/Feminine: Daniel Stern's *Histoire de la Révolution de 1848.*" *L'Esprit créateur* 29, no. 3 (Fall 1989): 84–91.
Rich, Adrienne. "Compulsory Heterosexuality and Lesbian Experience." London: Onlywomen Press, 1981.
Robespierre, Maximillien. *Discours et rapports.* Ed. Charles Vellay. Paris: Charpentier and Fasquelle, 1908.
Ronsin, Francis. *La grève des ventres. Propagande néo-malthusienne et baisse de la natalité en France, 19e–20e siècles.* Paris: Aubier-Montaigne, 1980.
Rose, Nikolas. *Governing the Soul: The Shaping of the Private Self.* London: Routledge, 1990.
Ross, Kristin. *The Emergence of Social Space: Rimbaud and the Paris Commune.* Minneapolis: University of Minnesota Press, 1988.
Rousseau, Jean-Jacques. *Emile ou l'éducation.* In vol. 4 of *Oeuvres complètes.* Ed. Bernard Gagnebin and Marcel Raymond. Paris: Gallimard, 1969.
Rubin, Gayle. "The Traffic in Women: Notes on the 'Political Economy' of Sex." In *Toward an Anthropology of Women.* Ed. Rayna R. Reiter. New York: Monthly Review Press, 1975.
Said, Edward W. *Beginnings: Intention and Method.* Baltimore: Johns Hopkins University Press, 1975.
———. *Orientalism.* New York: Vintage, 1978.
———. Public lecture. Department of Literature, University of California, San Diego. January 1990.
Saint-Just, Louis de. "Sur les factions de l'étranger" (Mar. 13, 1794). In *Discours et rapports.* Ed. Albert Soboul. Paris: Editions Sociales, 1977.
Sainte-Beuve, Charles-Augustin. "De la littérature industrielle." In *Portraits contemporains.* Vol. 2. Paris: Calmann-Lévy, 1876.
Salfi, Mark. "Lesbian and Gay Parents: Challenging Exclusive Definitions of Family?" Seminar paper. Department of Literature, University of California, San Diego, 1991.
Sand, George. "Aux membres du comité central." Unpublished ms., mid-April 1848. In vol. 8 of *Correspondance de George Sand.* Ed. Georges Lubin. Paris: Garnier, 1971.
———. *Fadette.* Boston: Little, Brown, 1893.
———. *François le Champi.* Paris: Gallimard, Folio edition, 1976.
———. *La Petite Fadette.* Paris: Livre de Poche, 1984.
Sartre, Jean-Paul. *L'Idiot de la famille.* 3 vols. Paris: Gallimard, 1971–72.
———. *Qu'est ce que la littérature?* Paris: Gallimard, Idées, 1948.
Schor, Naomi. *Breaking the Chain.* New York: Columbia University Press, 1985.
———. "Idealism in the Novel: Recanonizing Sand." *Yale French Studies* 73 (1986): 56–73.

———. "Reading Double: Sand's Difference." In *The Poetics of Difference*, ed. Carolyn G. Heilbrum and Nancy K. Miller. Ithaca: Cornell University Press, 1985.

Schulte-Sasse, Jochen. "Can the Disempowered Read Mass-Produced Narratives in Their Own Voice?" *Cultural Critique* (Fall 1988): 171–99.

Scott, Joan Wallach. *Gender and the Politics of History*. (New York: Columbia University Press, 1991.

Sedgwick, Eve Kosofsky. *Between Men: English Literature and Male Homosocial Desire*. New York: Columbia University Press, 1985.

———. *The Epistemology of the Closet*. Berkeley: University of California Press, 1990.

Sennett, Richard. *The Fall of Public Man: On the Social Psychology of Capitalism*. New York: Vintage, 1978.

Sewell, William H., Jr. *Work and Revolution in France: The Language of Labor from the Old Regime to 1848*. Cambridge, Eng.: Cambridge University Press, 1980.

Shapin, Steven, and Simon Schaffer. *Leviathan and the Air-Pump: Hobbes, Boyle and the Experimental Life*. Princeton: Princeton University Press, 1985.

Shapiro, Ann-Louise. *Housing the Poor of Paris, 1850–1902*. Madison: University of Wisconsin Press, 1985.

Showalter, English. "*Un coeur simple* as an Ironic Reply to Bernardin de Saint-Pierre." *French Review* 50, no. 1 (1966): 47–55.

Smith, Bonnie. *Ladies of the Leisure Class: The Bourgeoises of Northern France in the Nineteenth Century*. Princeton: Princeton University Press, 1981.

Sonnenfeld, Albert. "On Readers and Reading in *La Porte étroite* and *L'Immoraliste*." *Romanic Review* 67 (1976): 172–88.

Stacey, Judith. *Brave New Families: Stories of Domestic Upheaval in Late Twentieth Century America*. New York: Basic Books, 1990.

Stallybrass, Peter, and Allon White. *The Politics and Poetics of Transgression*. Ithaca: Cornell University Press, 1986.

Stone, Allucquère Rosanne. "Will the Real Body Please Stand Up? Boundary Stories About Virtual Cultures." In *Cyberspace: First Steps*. Ed. Michael Benedikt. Cambridge, Mass.: MIT Press, 1991.

Sue, Eugène. *Les Mystères de Paris*. 4 vols. Paris: Editions Hallier, 1977 [1843].

———. *The Mysteries of Paris*. London: George Routledge, n.d.

Tanner, Tony. *Adultery and the Novel: Contract and Transgression*. Baltimore: Johns Hopkins University Press.

Tardieu, Ambroise. *Etude médico-légale sur l'attentat aux moeurs*. 6th ed. Paris: Baillière, 1873.

Terdiman, Richard. *Discourse/Counterdiscourse: The Theory and Practice of Symbolic Resistance in Nineteenth-Century France.* Ithaca: Cornell University Press, 1985.
Terry, Jennifer. "The Body Invaded: Medical Surveillance of Women as Reproducers." *Socialist Review* 19, no. 3 (July–Sept. 1989): 13–43.
Thiesse, Anne-Marie. "Écrivain/publics: les mystères de la communication littéraire." *Europe* 643–44 (1982): 36–46.
Thompson, E. P. "Time, Work-Discipline, and Industrial Capitalism." *Past and Present* 38 (1967): 56–97.
Tilly, Charles. "The Chaos of the Living City." In *An Urban World.* Ed. Charles Tilly. Boston: Little, Brown, 1974.
Trahard, Pierre. Introduction to *Paul et Virginie* by Bernardin de Saint-Pierre. Paris: Garnier, 1958.
Treichler, Paula A. "AIDS, Homophobia, and Biomedical Discourse: An Epidemic of Signification." In *AIDS: Cultural Analysis/Cultural Activism.* Ed. Douglas Crimp. Cambridge, Mass.: MIT Press, 1989.
Vance, Carole S. "Misunderstanding Obscenity." *Art In America* 78, no. 5 (May 1990): 49–53.
Veith, Ilza. *Hysteria: The History of the Disease.* Chicago: University of Chicago Press, 1963.
Vigarello, Georges. *Concepts of Cleanliness: Changing Attitudes in France since the Middle Ages.* Trans. Jean Birrell. Cambridge, Eng.: Cambridge University Press, and Paris: La Maison des Sciences de l'Homme, 1988.
Villermé, Dr. Louis René. *Tableau de l'état physique et moral des ouvriers employés dans les manufactures de coton, de laine et de soie.* Ed. Yves Tyl. Paris: Union générale d'éditions, 1971 [1840].
Watney, Simon. "Missionary Positions: AIDS, Africa, and Race." *differences* 1, no. 1 (Winter 1989): 83–100.
———. *Policing Desire.* Minneapolis: University of Minnesota Press, 1989.
Williams, Linda. *Hard Core: Power, Pleasure, and the Frenzy of the Visible.* Berkeley: University of California Press, 1989.
Williams, Raymond. *The Country and the City.* New York: Oxford University Press, 1973.
Wittig, Monique. "The Mark of Gender." *Feminist Issues* 5, no. 2 (Fall 1985): 3–12.
———. "One Is Not Born a Woman." *Feminist Issues* 1, no. 2 (Winter 1981): 47–53.
———. "The Straight Mind." *Feminist Issues* 1, no. 1 (Summer 1980): 103–111.
Woolgar, Steven. *Science: The Very Idea.* London: Tavistock, 1988.
Zola, Emile. "Au Couvent" (Feb. 2, 1870). In *L'Atelier de Zola. Textes et journaux 1865–1870.* Ed. Martin Kanes. Geneva: Droz, 1963.

———. *La Curée*. In vol. 2 of *Oeuvres complètes*. Ed. Henri Mitterand. Paris: Cercle du Livre Précieux, 1970.

———. *La Fortune des Rougon*. In vol. 2 of *Oeuvres complètes*. Ed. Henri Mitterand. Paris: Cercle du Livre Précieux, 1970.

———. *The Kill*. Trans. A. Teixeira De Mattos. New York: Farrar Strauss and Young, 1954 [1895].

———. Preface to *Tares et poisons: Perversion et perversité sexuelles* by Dr. Laupts. Paris: G. Carré, 1896.

Index

In this index "f" after a number indicates a separate reference on the next page, and "ff" indicates separate references on the next two pages. A continuous discussion over two or more pages is indicated by a span of numbers. *Passim* is used for a cluster of references in close but not consecutive sequence.

Abelove, Henry, 59
Abortion: legalization of, 308, 332n4; "Abortion pill," 314
Adorno, Theodor, 18
AIDS pandemic, 4, 311–12, 313
Aimé-Martin, Louis, 45, 89, 104f
Alain (Emile-Auguste Chartier), 113
Alliance system, 132, 166, 199, 243. *See also* Old Regime; Patriarchy
Alterity, 279, 289
Althusserian theory, 6, 13f
Anderson, Benedict, 3, 28, 139–40
Architecture, 49–50, 72
Ariès, Philippe, 194
Aristocracy: women among, 32–36, 80, 166, 194–95; familialism among, 41–43, 46; threat from peasant society and, 186–87, 196–200; decadence and, 241–42, 246–49. *See also* Body: aristocratic; Old Regime; Patriarchy; Second Empire, corruption of; Social relations
Armstrong, Nancy, 4, 16, 125n

Baby M case, 314
Bachelor, 54, 236. *See also* Celibacy
Balibar, Etienne, 311, 333n10
Balzac, Honoré de, 38, 103, 106, 231; *Splendeurs et misères des courtisanes*, 56; *La Comédie humaine*, 102, 193; politics of, 186–87, 241; *Le Lys dans la vallée*, 298
—*Les Paysans*, 17, 186–212, 214; as realist novel, 188–90; lack in, 190, 211
Barker, Francis, 101
Barrett, Michèle, 9, 307

351

Bécour, Julia, 322n51
Beizer, Janet, 60, 320n29
Bernardin de Saint-Pierre, Jacques-Henri, 45, 103, 144, 241; *Discours sur l'éducation des femmes*, 106–8
—*Paul et Virginie*, 17f, 35, 101–36, 147, 159f, 214, 222, 225; contemporary reception of, 101–4; imagined community and, 103, 108, 145f; as best-seller, 104–6; lack in, 110–12; incest in, 117–20, 129, 230. *See also Petite société*
Bernheimer, Charles, 245, 320n29
Best-seller novel, 104–6, 140, 293–95
Binary oppositions, 16, 191, 209, 211, 250, 252
Biology: familial discourse and, 32, 313–15; gender discourse and, 58, 59–61, 124–25, 250–54; hereditary disorders and, 82–83, 288; Pasteurian, 94
"Biology of incommensurability," 61, 124–25, 215
Blacks, 114n, 312. *See also* Racism
Body: and sensation, 18, 111–12; household arrangements and, 24–25; interiority and, 24–25, 60–61, 109–11, 128–30, 161–62, 174–76, 204–7, 231–34, 295–97; male fighting, 31f; aristocratic, 32–36, 39, 127; city as, 80; sentimental, 109–12, 133–35; desexualization of, 253–54; modernist writing of, 299–301; liberal, 305; "legible," 330n19. *See also* Discipline; Female body; Interiority; Social body
Body fluids, 34, 118, 123, 131. *See also* Wet nursing

Bonald, Louis de, 39
Borie, Jean, 2, 81, 83–84, 117, 243f, 265, 282–83, 300
Bourdon, Mathilde, 322n51
Bowles, Paul, 330n16
Briquet, P., 59–61
Brooks, Peter, 140, 181
Buckley, Raymond, 333n9
Buret, Eugène, 90
Butler, Judith, 58, 230

Camus, Albert, 104
Canguilhem, Georges, 95, 240
Capitalism, *see* Liberal societies
Caplan, Jay, 111, 126
Carraud, Zulma, 322n51
Carter, Angela, 118
Catholic charities, 72
Celibacy: condemnation of, 30f; forced, 38, 305; familial lack and, 134–35; modernist writing and, 282–84, 296, 300
Celnart, Mme, 46, 48
de Cervol, 29
Charity, 50, 72, 74–75. *See also* Philanthropy
Chateaubriand, François René de, 102
Chaunu, Pierre, 308
Chevalier, Julien, 57–58, 93
Chevalier, Louis, 67, 184, 188
Children: education of, 43, 48, 72, 120, 221, 227; supervision of, 47–49, 55; masturbating, 54–55; child-centered "family" and, 113, 117, 120; day care and, 310
Children's literature, 322n51
City: construction of pathologies in, 65–69; domestic discipline and, 69–76; reorganization of public space and, 70–71; as

body, 80; writings on colonies and, 89–97; sexual desire and, 257–58. See also Laboring classes; Social crisis; Urban pathologies
Civilization, decline of, 80–85, 97. See also Decadence
Class, see Social class
Clifford, James, 324n32, 330n16
Clinton, Bill (U.S. president), 309
Cohen, Margaret, 329n12
Colonialism: familial discourse and, 63–65, 81–82, 88–97, 285–90, 312–13; writings on city and colonies and, 89–97; desire and, 266–67
Commodification, narrative of, 245–46, 330n5
Community of tears, 101–3, 112
Companionate marriage, 29, 36, 108; *Paul et Virginie* and, 108, 120; *Les Mystères de Paris* and, 147, 168f; *La Petite Fadette* and, 232
Comte, Auguste, 113, 132–33
Conjugal family household, 26, 36
Contemporary culture, 4–5, 303–4, 307–15
Contraception, 30, 308
Conversion narratives, 165–79
Corbin, Alain, 67, 78, 86
Courtly love, middle-class, 291–92
Criminality, 148–49, 154f, 162–65, 174–77. See also Lumpenproletariat
Cult of the family, 117
Cultural categories: genealogy of, 15–16; sexualization of, 243–44
Cultural-sexual exploration, 95–97
Cultural theory, 8–13

Dame patronnesse, 72, 152f, 179–80, 199, 221
"Dangerous classes": threat from, 56; domestication of, 69–80; familial destitution and, 158–61, 184; criminalized, 162–65; discursive role of, 184–85, 235–36. See also Colonialism; Laboring classes; Peasants; Urban pathologies
Darrow, Margaret, 42–43
Day-care centers, 310
Debré, Michel, 308
Decadence, 4, 241–49 *passim*, 255, 260, 272, 275, 308
Déclassement, 162–65, 183
De Gaulle, Joséphine, 322n51
Degeneration, 80–88
De Gérando, Joseph, 66, 72–73, 76–77, 90, 137
Deleuze, Gilles, 6, 23, 119, 278
Democratic culture, 303–4
Demography, 4, 25–33 *passim*, 48–49, 86, 188, 308
Deroin, Jeanne, 220
Des Essartz, Jean Charles, 33
Desire: lack as "condition" of, 5–7, 9–10, 110–11, 269–76, 304; policing of, 53–55, 231–34, 255–59; gender discourse and, 58–59, 217; familialized, 118–20, 231–36, 246, 279; social, 194, 203; as psychological, 242–43, 260–63; "perverse," 243–46, 249–50, 263–68; science of, in *La Curée*, 246, 248–49, 259–63, 275–76; ambition as, 256–58; sexualized, 257; literary texts and, 289–90; cultural narratives of, 291–94, 298. See also Heterosexual discourse; Identi-

ties, instability of; Incest; Psychoanalytic theory; Sexuality
Deutellbaum, Wendy, 220
Deviance, see Norms; Pathology
Dialectics, 10–13
Dictionnaire des sciences médicales, 35–36, 92, 256
Diderot, Denis, 111
Didier, Béatrice, 297
Discipline: in childrearing, 47–48; domestic pathology and, 52–53; urban pathology and, 69–76; in *Les Mystères de Paris*, 174–79; in *La Curée*, 268–69. See also Norms
Discourse: and discursivity, 3–4, 60–62, 71, 140–42, 182–84; as strategy, 7, 303; as material force, 13–17; performative aspects of, 14–15, 18, 183–84, 303–4; power of gender and, 61–62; social theory and, 66–69; transformation of social practices and, 102–3; politics of, 133–36, 138; of diversity, 309. See also Familial discourse; Gender discourse; Heterosexual discourse
Distinction, ideology of, 87–88, 331n5
Divorce: legalization of, 29
Domesticity: discourse of, 26; female authority and, 33–36, 43–52, 124, 138, 200–202, 218, 225–28, 234; peasant society and, 37, 197, 203–4, 208; aristocratic appropriation of, 41–43; transformations of, 46–47, 63–65, 70–72, 81–82, 84–85, 89–90, 138–40, 144–46, 303–15; and Taylorism, 52; as political authority, 106–8; boundaries of, 152f, 216, 241–42; male authority and, 215–16, 234; without law, 269–77; as contradictory, 329n12. See also Familial discourse; "Family"; Household; Manuals of domesticity
Domestic "monsters," 52–55. See also Homosexuality; Hysteria; Masturbation
"Domestic novel," 322n51
Donzelot, Jacques, 8, 10, 34, 71, 276
Du Camp, Maxime, 8, 74, 81, 85–86, 95
Dupont de Nemours, Pierre-Samuel, 102

Eco, Umberto, 140, 141–42, 181
Education of children, 43, 48, 72, 120, 221, 227
Elias, Norbert, 129
Enlightenment culture, 27–29, 30–36
Esquirol, Jean-Etienne-Dominique, 256
Esquiros, Alphonse, 79
Ethnography, 90–91
Etiemble (critic), 122–23
Evans-Pritchard, E. E., 90
Exoticism, 95–97, 108f

Familial discourse, 23–29; in contemporary culture, 4–5, 303–4, 310–13; contemporary France and U.S. and, 4–5, 306–15; reproductive technologies and, 4, 313–15; rhetoric of lack and, 5–8, 109–10, 304; psychoanalysis and, 5–6, 110–11, 118–19, 246; in social theory, 8–13, 71; in Habermas's dialectic, 10–13; social discourses within, 27; at-

Index 355

tacks on Old Regime practices, 29, 30–36, 304–6; social threats and, 33–34, 55–59, 63–65, 305; French Revolution and, 36–41; postrevolutionary France and, 41–47, 97–98; gendered desire and, 58–59, 229–30, 305–6; colonial discourse and, 63–65, 81–82, 91–97, 312–13; transformations of, 63–65, 71–72, 81–85, 89–90, 138–40, 144–46, 153–54, 303–15; social relations and, 69–72, 147–48, 161–62; social extension of, 71, 235–36, 305; semiotic codes vs. discursive structure and, 141–42; realist novel and, 189, 190–93; location of women in, 213–16; as discontinuous, 304–6; twentieth century shifts in, 306–10
Familialism, as "discursive structure," 3–4. See also Familial discourse
"Family": inscription into social body, 7–8, 17–18, 103, 109–17; and its "outside," 8, 10–13, 71; discursive nature of, 8, 112–14; as always endangered, 8, 278, 304; as term, 9; as absent, 9–10, 109–12, 134–35, 147, 158–61, 304; broken, 35, 53, 74, 162–65, 202, 227; public domain and, 71, 244, 307–8; child-centered, 113, 117, 120; outcasts from, 236, 284; as Law, 276–77; the state and, 307–8; postmodern, 309
"Family household," as term, 9
Feeling, 60, 167, 224. See also Interiority
Female body: aristocratic, 24, 127; politics of gender and, 33–36, 39; as target of familial discourse, 121–26, 127–33, 213, 245, 301; in *Paul et Virginie*, 121–26, 127–33; laboring classes and, 206; male world of commerce and, 275–76; as the "real," 300
Female modesty, 121–33 *passim*. See also Innocence
Female sexuality: class-coded, 32–36 *passim*, 39, 42, 53, 64, 75, 79–80, 85, 87, 151, 160–62, 182, 188, 194–96, 202–7, 241, 205; rewriting of, 87–88; in *Paul et Virginie*, 111–30 *passim*; passion vs. animality and, 188, 195, 197; as threatening, 194–96, 288; *La Porte étroite* and, 283, 290, 296–97, 298–301. See also Desire; Female body; Heterosexual discourse; Homosexuality
Feminism, 6, 9, 308; Sand and, 219, 220–22
Femme d'intérieur, 287–88
Féré, Charles, 56, 83
Fitting, Peter, 329n14
Flaubert, Gustave, 95–97, 104
Flesselles, Mme de, 44–45
Fluids, theory of, *see* Body fluids
Folk medicine, 225–28, 232
Foucault, Michel, 7, 29, 110, 142, 149, 231, 247, 249–50, 303
Fournier, Alain, 87
Frégier, H.-A., 184
French Revolution, 36–41, 221
Freud, Sigmund, 6n, 262
Fritsch, Philippe, 52–53
Furet, François, 68

Gacon-Dufour (writer), 45–46, 48f
Gender discourse: identity and, 25, 53, 58, 60–61, 229, 249–50; politics of gender and, 33–36, 229; and social body, 53; desire and, 58–59, 119–20, 217, 229–30, 250–54, 263–64, 270–72, 289–95 *passim*, 299, 305–6; hysteria and, 59–62; power of, 61–62; division of labor and, 119; in *La Petite Fadette*, 229–31. See also Desire; Heterosexual discourse; Identities, instability of
Genealogy: of cultural categories, 15–16; interaction of "family" and state and, 307–8
Gide, André, 306; *La Porte étroite*, 17, 278–302; lack in, 280–81; female sexuality and, 283, 290, 296–97, 298–301
Girard, H., 66
Girardin, Emile de, 186
Gobineau, Joseph-Arthur de, 80–81
Goethe, Johann Wolfgang von, 101
Gouges, Olympe de, 40, 243
Guattari, Félix, 6, 23, 119, 278
Guizot, François, 8, 63, 73–74, 105, 186

Habermas, Jürgen, 8, 10–13, 71
Haraway, Donna, 330n16
Hegel, G. W. F., 113
Hellerstein, Erna Olafson, 49
Hereditary biology, 82–84
Heterosexual discourse: and compulsory heterosexuality, 53, 58–59, 253, 270–76, 293–95, 305, 309; homosexual threat and, 58–59; hysteria and, 59–62; *La*

Petite Fadette and, 230, 232; *La Curée* and, 250–52, 267–68, 269–77; failed desire and, 293–95, 297, 300
Homo clausus, 129
Homosexuality: French law and, 55–56; construction of threat from, 55–59; masturbation and, 56–57; colonialism and, 92–93; *La Curée* and, 253, 256, 258, 263–68; in Gide's fiction, 290; gay liberation movement and, 308; national community and, 311–12; neurobiology and, 313–14. See also Heterosexual discourse
Housecleaning, 49
Household: interiority of, 11–13, 307; reorganization of, 24–30, 43–52; public "invasion" of, 29, 72, 244–45, 273; female authority and, 33–36, 43–44, 45–52, 124, 138, 200–202, 225–28, 234; authority of men in, 191, 193. See also Conjugal family household; Domesticity; "Family"
Huff, Cynthia, 220
Hunt, Lynn, 320n29
Huysmans, J. K., 86–87
Hygiene, *see* Personal hygiene; Public health
Hysteria, 59–62, 232f; *La Curée* and, 245, 262–68 *passim*, 274; *La Porte étroite* and, 287–88, 298

Identities, instability of, 3–4, 61, 65, 137–41, 148, 161, 183–85, 250–54, 304
Ideology, as representation, 13, 103
Illegitimacy, 196

Imagined community, 17, 25, 81, 187–88, 211–12, 236, 247, 276, 303, 309; reorganization of city and, 70, 139–40; colonies and, 89–90; dynamics of, 98, 145–46, 186–90, 211–12, 236, 304; *Paul et Virginie* and, 103, 108, 145f; *Les Mystères de Paris* and, 139–40, 169, 184; honorary outlaws and, 236
Incarceration practices, 69, 175–76
Incest: carnal, 76, 196, 241; *Paul et Virginie* and, 117–20, 123, 129, 230; *La Petite Fadette* and, 230, 232, 234; *La Curée* and, 241, 259–63, 265, 267, 268–77
Innocence, 170–71. *See also* Female modesty
Inscription: of "family" in social body, 7–8; as term, 14
Interiority: household and, 11–13, 307; body and, 24–25, 42; women and, 42, 44, 88, 268; guilt as, 114n, 177, 300; female modesty and, 128–29; dialectic of, in *Les Mystères de Paris*, 165–66, 169–74; blinding and, 174–76; punishment and, 174–77; link between nature and culture and, 224; desire as psychological and, 242–43; sick, 254–55; sexualized, 284. *See also* Feeling; Hysteria; Sentimentality; Subjectivity, liberal

Jameson, Fredric, 18, 189

Kitsch, *see* Tears
Knowledge: power and, 1, 7, 60–69, 76–77, 94, 246–49, 269; experts', 2, 60–69, 76–77, 248; cultural, 118, 246–49, 260;

pleasure and, 118–19, 262, 268–69; female, 215–16, 225–29, 231–32, 237–39; in public and private spheres, 216; male, 246–49, 276, 279; sexual, as male domain, 263–64
Krafft-Ebing, R. von, 58f, 84–85

Laboring classes: as threat, 63f; moralization of, 72–76, 88; state authority over, 75; incest as truth of, 76, 196; hereditary biology and, 82–83; print culture and, 139–40, 143–45; familial lack and, 158–61, 184. *See also* "Dangerous classes"
Lack: as discursive mechanism, 5–8, 109–12, 304; as "condition" of desire, 5–7, 9–10, 110–11; aristocratic excess as, 31; domestic pathology and, 52f; in *Paul et Virginie*, 110–12; urban pathology and, 158–62; in *Les Mystères de Paris*, 158–65, 170–71, 179–85; in *Les Paysans*, 190, 211; in *La Petite Fadette*, 227–28, 235–36; as productive, 234–37, 276–77, 278; lack of, 246, 273; in *La Porte étroite*, 280–81; guilt as, 300; discourse of, and contemporary culture, 309, 313–14
Laclau, Ernesto, 3–4, 137–38, 141f
Lacombe, Claire, 40
Lajolais, Natalie de, 44, 49, 70–71
Lalauze, Abbé C. F. A., 46–47
Lallemand, M., 54–55, 93–94, 95
Lamartine, Alphonse de, 137
Landes, Joan, 13, 126
Laqueur, Thomas, 35, 61n, 124–25, 215

Larousse, Pierre Athanase, 23, 92–93
Lasch, Christopher, 8
Latour, Bruno, 319n2
Laupts, Dr., 57f, 277n
Lauvergne, 56f
Law: regime of norms and, 7–8, 246, 273, 275–77; production of, 7, 246, 277; homosexuality and, 55–56; prostitution and, 78
Law of the Father, 246, 262–63, 269–77, 319n10; as production, 276–77
Le Bègue de Prasle, Achille, 46–47
Le Bon, Gustave, 82
Legrand, Jean, 308
Le Noir, Dr., 86
Léon, Pauline, 40
Le Pen, Jean-Marie, 4, 312–13
Le Pileur, Dr. Louis, 86
LeVay, Simon, 313–14
Liberal societies, 7, 97, 133–34, 138, 182–85, 246, 282, 303–4
Libertinage, 26, 31, 305
Literacy, 72–73
Literary reception theory, 141–42
Literature: middle-class identity and, 27–30; on maternity, 34–35; advent of popular novel and, 104–6; bachelor or celibate, 278–301; commodified, 283–95; children's, 322n51. *See also* Best-seller novel; Manuals of domesticity; Modernism; Pastoral narrative; Realist novel; Serial novel
Lombroso, Cesare, 92
Louis XVI (king of France), 38, 107
Louis-Napoleon (Napoleon III; emperor of France), 218
Louis-Philippe (king of France), 108
Louyer-Villermay, Jean-Baptiste, 92
Lukàcs, Georg, 18, 189f
Lumpenproletariat, 162–65, 182ff

Macherey, Pierre, 18, 188, 198, 211
McIntosh, Mary, 307
McMartin day-care scandal, 310, 333n9
Male primogeniture, 32, 38, 43, 305
Manuals of domesticity, 24, 34–35, 43–50; laboring classes and, 72–73
Marie Antoinette, 107, 243
Marriage: sentimentality and, 28–29; arranged, 305. *See also* Companionate marriage
Marx, Karl, 18, 140, 170, 245
Marxist criticism, 13, 18. *See also* Althusserian theory
Masturbation: condemnation of, 31; children and, 54–55; homosexuality and, 56–57; colonialism and, 93
Medical science: exclusion of women from, 34; homosexual threat and, 55–59; hysteria and, 59–62; female knowledge and, 228–29. *See also* Folk medicine
Melodrama, rhetoric of, 77–80, 179, 207–8; as destabilizing, 161–62, 181
Men: male authority and, 9, 191, 193, 200–202, 209–10; aristocratic, 43; bachelor, 54, 236; hysteria and, 60f, 230–34; "New Man" and, 113–14, 124–25. *See also* Celibacy

Mental disorders, 1–2, 110, 256.
  See also Hysteria
Mère dénaturée, 33–34, 166, 243
Messance, M., 30–31
Michelet, Jules, 81
Middle class: print culture and, 3,
  27–28; family discourse and, 25,
  28, 135–36; domestic role of
  women and, 50; laboring classes
  and, 70, 144–45; invention of,
  in *Paul et Virginie*, 115–17; *Les
  Mystères de Paris* and, 182–85;
  social desire and, 184–85
Milk, flow of, 117–18. See also
  Body fluids; Wet nursing
Miller, Christopher, 285
Miller, D. A., 112, 134, 149
Modernism, 282–84
Modernization theory, 66–67
Moheau (demographer), 26, 31ff
"Monomania," 256f
"Monsters": domestic, 52–55; social, 63–98. See also Threats
"Monstrous proximities," 148–54,
  161–62, 181. See also Threats
Moreau de Tours, J., 84
Morel, B. A., 82–83
Moses, Claire, 220
Motherhood, see Children; Domesticity; Wet nursing; Women
Mouffe, Chantal, 3–4, 137–38,
  141f
Moyers, Bill, 312
Moynihan, Daniel Patrick, 312
Multiculturalism, 310–13
Mylne, Vivienne, 134

Napoleon Bonaparte (Napoleon I;
  emperor of France), 34, 102f,
  111–12
Napoleon III (Louis-Napoleon;
  emperor of France), 218

Narrative, cultural 2, 4–5
Narrator: in *Paul et Virginie*, 133–
  35; in *La Petite Fadette*, 222–25
Natalism, see Demography
Nation, see Imagined community
National community, see Imagined
  community
National Front party (France),
  312–13
Naturalist fiction, 241. See also
  Zola, Emile: *La Curée*
Nature, 222–27, 237–39. See also
  Pastoral narrative
Necker de Saussure, Albertine, 41–
  42, 45, 51, 89
Nelson, Brian, 259
Nettement, Alfred, 143–44, 150,
  151–52, 215, 231
Newmark, Kevin, 292
Newspapers, 139–40, 144–45.
  See also Serial novel
Norms: as powerful yet unstable, 7,
  59, 61, 65, 71, 276–77, 304–5,
  308; constructed through pathology, 7–8, 304; family model
  and, 23–24, 64–65; social extension of, 71, 305; feudal, 169,
  190–93; transgression and,
  241–42, 246, 250–54; in *La
  Curée*, 246f; in twentieth-century France, 307f; contemporary
  return to "family" and, 309–10
Nostalgia, 9–10, 109, 111
Novel, 1–2, 12, 17–19, 98, 104,
  134, 139–40, 305–7. See also
  Best-seller novel; Literature;
  Modernism; Pastoral narrative;
  Realist novel; Serial novel

Old Regime: colonization of aristocracies of, 24; attacks by family discourse on, 29, 30–36,

304–6; social order and, 65–66; Bernardin's politics and, 106–8; *Paul et Virginie* and, 113–14, 115–16, 121–26, 168; *Les Mystères de Paris* and, 168–69; alliance practices of, 199, 243. *See also* Aristocracy; Nostalgia; Patriarchy
Onanisme: use of term, 54. *See also* Masturbation
Orphan, 159–60
Ortner, Sherry, 224
Outram, Dorinda, 129

Pankoucke, 92, 256
Parent-Duchâtelet, Alexandre, 63, 78–79, 80, 150
Paris Commune, 80–81, 85, 91
Pariset, Mme, 46, 48
Pastoral narrative, 103, 108–9. *See also* Bernardin de Saint-Pierre, Jacques-Henri: *Paul et Virginie*; Sand, George: *La Petite Fadette*
Pathology, norms as constructed through, 7–8, 23–24, 52–53, 61, 65, 71, 247, 304. *See also* "Monsters"; Urban pathologies
Patriarchy: revolutionary metaphors and, 38–39; domestic management and, 46–47; colonialism and, 97; *Paul et Virginie* and, 112f, 126; slave labor and, 131–32; mythical, 200–203; in peasant society, 201–2; Law of the Father and, 246, 262–63, 269–77. *See also* Aristocracy; Nostalgia; Old Regime
Peasants: domesticity and, 37, 197, 203–4; philanthropy and, 186–87, 204–7; social threat from, 186–87, 196–200. *See also* Balzac, Honoré de: *Les Paysans*; Sand, George: *La Petite Fadette*
Perot, H. Ross, 309
Personal hygiene, 49
Petite société: as model "family," 115; incest and, 117–20; as feminized, 124–26; economic reproduction of, 131–33
Phallus, as master signifier, 6, 262, 274, 319n10
Philanthropy: women and, 50, 72, 152–53, 179–80, 204–7; urban domestication and, 72, 76–77; colonial, 91; peasants and, 186–87; desire and, 204–7
Phillips, Kevin, 309n
Pinel, Philippe, 1–2, 5, 110, 120, 163f, 256
Policing, 29, 81; of desire, 53–55, 255–59; urban pathologies and, 152–53, 173, 177. *See also* Discipline; Social control
Politics: cultural categories and, 15–16; participation of women in, 38, 39–41, 219–20; domestic authority and, 106–8, 238–39; female modesty and, 131–33; of powerlessness, 133–36; of discourse, 138. *See also* Public sphere
Population, *see* Demography
Poskin, Dr. Alphonse, 94–95
Power: dynamics of, 1, 7, 51, 61, 65, 72, 246–49; male, 9, 191, 193, 200–202, 209–10; of women in household, 33–36, 43–44, 45–52, 124, 138, 200–202, 225–28, 234; powerlessness and, 51, 65n, 133–36, 177; phallic, 194; patriarchy and, 275–76. *See also* Knowledge

Prendergast, Christopher, 18
Print culture: familial discourse and, 3–5, 213–14, 303–4; middle class and, 3, 27–28; reorganization of household and, 27–30; stability of, 45–46; social pathology and, 76–77, 248; transformations of, 139, 186–87; laboring classes and, 139–40, 143–45; ideological struggle within, 187. *See also* Imagined community; Liberal societies; Literature; Manuals of domesticity; Serial novel
Private sphere: construction of public sphere and, 10–13; public "invasion" of, 29, 72, 244–45; women's involvement in public sphere and, 43, 50–52; mode of knowledge in, 216. *See also* Domesticity; "Family"; Household; Public-private distinction
Production: as term, 13–14; of "family" as ideal, 24; of the Law of the Father, 276–77
Prostitution, 70, 78–80, 85–87; colonized peoples and, 92; *Les Mystères de Paris* and, 151–52, 155, 160–61
Proust, Marcel, 298
Psychiatric cure, 1–2, 110
Psychoanalytic theory: Freudian, 5, 14, 110–11, 118–19, 261f; ideology of lack in, 5–6, 304; Lacanian, 5–6, 14, 246, 262, 330n22; and cultural studies, 5–7; Law of the Father and, 246, 262, 269, 319n10
Public health: urban pathologies and, 65–69, 75, 79, 158; colonies and, 91, 94–95, 288
Public-private distinction: gender and, 38, 250–51; urban reorganization and, 70–71; female modesty and, 128–29; *Les Paysans* and, 193–200, 209; in *La Curée*, 243–45; production of, 244. *See also* Private sphere; Public sphere
Public sphere: assumed existence of private sphere and, 10–13; domestic role of women and, 43, 50–52; female modesty and, 131; realist novel and, 192–93. *See also* Politics

Quayle, Dan, 312
Question sociale (social crisis), *see* Social crisis; Urban pathologies
Queyrat, Frédéric, 87

Rabinow, Paul, 325n70
Racism, 53–54, 311–12, 333n10. *See also* Blacks; Colonialism
Rapp, Rayna, 9
Reader: training in social knowledge and, 15, 248–50, 253, 259, 260–63, 268–69; transformation of, 102–3; imagined community and, 108, 142; inscription of lack in, 110–12; Freudian gaze of, 118–19; "monstrous proximities" and, 148–54, 161–62, 181; social voyeurism and, 149–50; knowledge of, 181; of modernist text, 284, 294, 296f
Reading: as social hermeneutics, 19, 243, 262, 284, 297; as family affair, 145, 151–53; effects of, 111–12, 143–44, 151–53, 161, 181, 269, 284
Realism, 282f, 287–88, 294f

Realist novel, 188–93, 279–80, 294. See also Balzac, Honoré de: Les Paysans
Religious discourse, 290–93
Resistance, 142, 277, 284, 308
Revolution of 1848, 217–20, 238–39
Richardson, Samuel, 131, 144
Robespierre, Maximillien, 37, 40f, 103
Roe vs. Wade, 309
Roland, Madame, 40–41, 243
Roman-feuilleton (serial novel), see Serial novel
Rousseau, Jean-Jacques, 26–27, 102, 298
Rubin, Gayle, 251
Rustic novel, see Pastoral narrative

"Safer sex," 4
Said, Edward, 92, 282f, 297
Sainte-Beuve, Charles-Augustin, 102, 186
Saint-Just, Louis de, 37
Sand, George, 102, 211, 288; gender of writing and, 217–20; politics of, 218f, 238–39, 241; feminism and, 219, 220–22; François le Champi, 222–25; nature and, 222–27, 237–39, 248
—La Petite Fadette, 17, 213–39; plot of, 217; nature and, 222–27, 237–39; lack in, 227–28, 235–36
Sartre, Jean-Paul, 87–88, 282
Sauvy, Albert, 308
Say, Jean-Baptiste, 49
Schor, Naomi, 219, 226, 298
Science: relationship of novel with, 1–2; familial discourse and, 81–82; of desire, in La Curée, 246, 248–49, 259–63, 275–76. See also Biology; Medical science
Scott, Joan, 15–16, 68, 321n35
Second Empire, corruption of, 241–49 passim, 255, 260, 272, 275
Semiotic codes vs. discursive structure, 141–42
Sennett, Richard, 8
Sensibilité, 129
Sentimentality: marriage and, 28–29; utilitarianism and, 36; democratic aesthetics of, 102–3, 104, 109; popularity of Paul et Virginie and, 102–3, 104; gender distinctions and, 126; dialectic of, 165–68, 172. See also Interiority
Sentimental novels: vs. masterworks, 18
Serial novel (roman-feuilleton), 138, 140, 143–45. See also Balzac, Honoré de; Les Paysans; Sand, George: La Petite Fadette; Sue, Eugène: Les Mystères de Paris
Servants, 30, 53–54, 81, 131–32, 195–96
Sewer imagery, 155–56
Sexuality: nonreproductive, 31, 57, 195; feeling vs. pleasure and, 35–36; policing of, 53–55; familialized, 53–62, 87, 117–20, 129–30; nonnormative practices, 64, 311–12; illegitimacy and, 196. See also Desire; Female sexuality; Heterosexual discourse; Homosexuality; Masturbation
Shapin, Steve, 324n36
Shaviro, Steve, 310n
Slave labor, 131–32
Smith, Bonnie, 50–51
Snow, C. P., 2

Social, the, 3–4, 8, 10, 71–72, 104; discursivity of, 137, 142, 148
Social body: inscription of "family" in, 7–8, 17–18, 109–17; perception of lack and, 52–53; diseased, 155, 243, 247; feminine coded subjectivity and, 213–14; "perverse" desire and, 243–46, 249–50. See also Body; Female body
Social class, discourse and, 3–4, 27–28, 103, 137–40, 148, 161–62, 183, 304. See also Aristocracy; Laboring classes; Liberal societies; Middle class; Social relations
Social control, 65–69, 150–51. See also Policing
Social crisis (*question sociale*), 64; discursive construction of, 65–69; perception of, 69–70; familial lack and, 158–61; peasants and, 186–87, 191; domestic authority and, 238–39
Sociality, 32, 35–37, 42–44, 50, 73, 115–17, 176, 195–96, 258
Social mobility, 161–62, 171–73, 174, 181, 227, 233f, 239
Social "monsters," 63–98, 145–48, 246–49. See also Transsexuality
Social relations: familial discourse and, 69–72, 147–48; familial destitution and, 158–61; social mobility and, 161–62, 171–73, 174; *déclassement* and, 162–65; in *Les Mystères de Paris*, 182–85; peasant society and, 199. See also Aristocracy; Laboring classes; Middle class; Peasant society

Social theory, 8–13, 66–69
Spatial metaphors, 285, 287f
Stallybrass, Peter, 52, 80
State agencies, 307
Stone, Allucquère Rosanne, 330n19
Strategy: as term, 14
Strategy of governance, 7–8
Subjectivity, liberal, 103, 133–34, 176–79, 276; gender difference and, 24–25, 33, 35, 61, 124–26, 215, 276; *Paul et Virginie* and, 117, 124–26; feminine coding of, 213–14
Sue, Eugène, 186, 231; politics of, 241
—*Les Mystères de Paris*, 15, 17, 71, 136, 137–85, 214f; plot of, 146–47; "monstrous proximities" and, 148–54; paranoid landscapes in, 154–58; familial lack in "dangerous classes" in, 158–61; social mobility and, 161–62, 227; *déclassement* and, 162–65; conversion narratives in, 165–79; *Paul et Virginie* and, 168f; *Les Paysans* and, 188
Suffert, Georges, 308
Surface, metaphor of, 14
Surrogate motherhood, 314
Syphilis, 86–87

Tardieu, Ambroise, 56, 93
Tears: production of, in readers, 101–3, 112; social bonding and, 101–3, 112, 114, 127; perception of lack and, 110–12
Terdiman, Richard, 95
Terminology, 13–17
Threats, 33–34, 55–59, 63–98; domestic "monsters" and, 52–55; construction of urban pa-

thologies and, 63–69; social extension of familialism and, 71, 235–36, 305. *See also* Homosexuality; Incest; Laboring classes; "Monstrous proximities"; Peasants; Prostitution; Social "monsters"; Urban pathologies
Thrift, concept of, 46–47
Tilly, Charles, 67, 78
Tissot, Dr. Samuel Auguste David, 54
Transgression, 5, 77–78, 149–50, 152; norms and, 241, 246, 250–52, 265–68, 288; the law and, 246, 262, 260–76. *See also* Lack; Law; Norms
Transsexuality, 246, 250–54
Truth, 6–7, 18, 244; as secret or depth, 13–14, 18, 75–76, 248, 296–97; hermeneutics and, 14, 18–19; pain as purveyor of, 114n; gender and, 187–88. *See also* Knowledge
Tuke, Samuel, 110, 164

United States: familialism in, 4, 307–15
Urban pathologies: threats to "family" and, 63–65; construction of, 65–69, 150–51; decline of civilization and, 80–85; colonial discourse and, 89–97; Sue's paranoid landscapes and, 154–58; *déclassement* and, 162–65

Ventriloquism, cultural, 223–25, 237
Verdier-Heurtin, 35
Vichy regime, 307
Villeneuve-Bargemont, Alban, 74

Villermé, Dr. Louis René, 75–76
Voisin, Abbé du, 39
Voltaire, 102
Voyeurism, 149–50, 206

"War on Drugs," 312
Watney, Simon, 311
Welfare policies, 10, 71–73
Western culture: decline of, 80–85, 97; corruption of colonies by, 95–97
Wet nursing, 33, 53, 305
White, Allon, 52, 80
Whitehead, Mary Beth, 314
Williams, Linda, 6n
Williams, Raymond, 18, 131, 133
Women: unmarried, 30, 38, 280, 305; aristocratic, 32–36, 80, 166, 194–95; power of, 33–36, 43–44, 45–52, 124, 138, 200–202, 225–28; participation in politics, 38, 39–41; rewriting of aristocratic body by, 41–47; interiority and, 42, 44, 88; of leisure, 44–45; emancipation of, as threat, 57–58, 290; gendering of political reform and, 106–8
Woolf, Virginia, 301
Writing: gender of, 217–20; social monsters and, 246–50; celibate, 282–84, 296, 304; modernism and, 282–84

Xenophobia, 312–13

Zola, Emile, 57f, 231
—*La Curée*, 17, 240–77; plot of, 242; perverse desire and, 243–46; monsters in discursive strategy of, 246–50; polemics of sex/gender in, 250–55

Library of Congress Cataloging-in-Publication Data

Reid, Roddey, 1952–
Families in jeopardy : regulating the social body in France, 1750–1910 / Roddey Reid.
    p. cm.
Includes bibliographical references and index.
ISBN 0-8047-2224-2 :
1. French fiction—19th century—History and criticism. 2. French fiction—18th century—History and criticism. 3. Domestic fiction, French—History and criticism. 4. Literature and society—France—History. 5. Problem families in literature. 6. Social problems in literature. 7. Sex role in literature. 8. Family in literature.
I. Title.
PQ653.R45   1993
843.0098'355—dc20
                               93-16664
                               CIP

⊗ This book is printed on acid-free paper.
It has been typeset in 10/13 Sabon by Terry Robinson & Co.

EUCH
1/99
3950